DATE DUE

03

Directory,

Edition.

Cabell's Directory Of Publishing Opportunities In Accounting

EIGHTH EDITION 2001-02

David W. E. Cabell, Editor
McNeese State University
Lake Charles, Louisiana

Deborah L. English, Editor
Brooke S. Abernethy, Assistant Editor

To order additional copies
visit our web site
www.cabells.com

or contact us at

CABELL PUBLISHING CO.
Box 5428, Beaumont, Texas 77726-5428
(409) 898-0575
Fax (409) 866-9554

$89.95 U.S. for addresses in United States

Price includes shipping and handling for U.S.
Add $50 for surface mail to countries outside U.S.
Add $100 for air mail to countries outside U.S.

ISBN # 0-911753-13-3

Although every reasonable effort has been made to ensure the accuracy of the information contained in this directory, the author cautions the reader that there may be mistakes in the information provided. Thus, the reader is responsible for his or her actions resulting from the use of this information.

TABLE OF CONTENTS

ii

Preface

The objective of ***Cabell's Directory of Publishing Opportunities in Accounting*** is to help you publish your ideas.

The ***Directory*** contains the editor's name(s), address(es), phone and fax number(s), and e-mail and web address(es) for 130 journals.

To help you in selecting those journals that are most likely to publish your manuscripts the **Index** classifies the journals into twenty-two different topic areas. In addition, the Index provides information on the journal's type of review process, number of external reviewers and acceptance rate.

To further assist you in organizing and preparing your manuscripts, the *Directory* includes extensive information on the style and format of most journals. If a journal has its own set of manuscript guidelines, a copy of these guidelines is published in the *Directory*. Also, each entry indicates the use of a standard set of publication guidelines by a journal. For example, some journals use the *Chicago Manual of Style* or the *Publication Manual of the American Psychological Association.*

Furthermore, the *Directory* describes the type of review process used by the editor(s) of a journal, type of review, number of reviewers, acceptance rate, time required for review availability of reviewers comments, fees charged to review or publish the manuscript, copies required and manuscript topics. Information on the journal's circulation, readership and subscription prices are also provided.

Although this *Directory* focuses on journals in the specialized area of **Accounting**, other directories focus on **Economics and Finance**, **Management**, and **Marketing**. The division of business journals into these four directories more appropriately meets the researcher's need for publishing in his area of specialization.

The decision to place journals in their respective directory is based on the manuscript topics selected by the editor as well as the journals' guidelines for authors. If you wish to find the most current information on the *Directory*, visit **www.cabells.com**. Please contact us for the login registration procedure.

Also, the *Directory* includes a section titled "**What is a Refereed Article?**" which tends to emphasize the value of a blind review process and use of external reviewers. However, this section cautions individuals using these criteria to also consider a journal's reputation for quality. Additionally, it indicates that differences in acceptance rates may be the result o different methods used to calculate these percentages and the number of people associated with a particular area of specialization.

How To Use the Directory

TABLE OF CONTENTS
Table of Contents provides 130 journals to help your locate a publication.

INDEX
Index classifies the journals according to twenty-three (23) different manuscript topics. It also includes information on the type of review, number of external reviewers, acceptance rate and page number of each journal.

ADDRESS FOR SUBMISSION
Address for Submission provides: the Editor's Name(s), Mailing Address(es), Telephone and Fax numbers(s), and E-mail and Web address(es).

PUBLICATION GUIDELINES
Manuscript Length refers to the length of the manuscript in terms of the number of double-spaced typescript pages.

Copies Required indicates the number of manuscript copies you should submit to the editor.

Computer Submission indicates whether the journal prefers hardcopy (paper) or electronic submissions such as disk, e-mail attachment, or a combination of methods.

Format refers to the type of word processing programs or computer programs the journal requires for reviewing the manuscript. Some examples of these programs are Microsoft Word, Word Perfect, or ASCII.

Fees to Review refers to whether the journal charges a fee to review the manuscript. Knowing this item permits the author to send the required funds with the manuscript.

Manuscript Style refers to the overall style guide the journal uses for text, references within the text and the bibliography. This is usually either the *Chicago Manual of Style* or the *Publication Manual of the American Psychological Association (APA)*.

REVIEW INFORMATION
Type of Review specifies blind, editorial, or optional review methods. A blind review indicates the reviewer(s) does not know who wrote the manuscript. An editorial review indicates the reviewer knows who wrote the manuscript. The term "optional" indicates the author may choose either one of these types of review.

No. of External Reviewers and *No. of In House Reviewers*
These two items refer to the number of reviewers who review the manuscript prior to making a decision regarding the publication of the manuscript. Although the editor attempted to determine whether the reviewers were on the staff of the journal or were outside reviewers, many of the respondents had trouble distinguishing between internal and external reviewers. Thus it may be more accurate to add these two categories and determine the total number of reviewers.

Acceptance Rate refers to the number of manuscripts accepted for publication relative to the number of manuscripts submitted within the last year. The method of calculating acceptance rates varies among journals.

Time to Review indicates the amount of time that passes between the submission of a manuscript and notification to the author regarding the results of the review process.

Reviewer's Comments indicates whether the author can obtain a copy of the reviewer's comments. In some cases, the author needs to request that the editor send these remarks.

Invited Articles indicates the percentage of articles for which the editor requests an individual to write specifically for publication in the journal. The percentage is the number of invited articles relative to the total number of articles that appeared in a journal within the past year.

Fees to Publish refers to whether the journal charges a fee to publish the manuscript Knowing this item assists the author in his decision to place the manuscript into the review process.

CIRCULATION DATA
Reader indicates the predominant type of reader the publication seeks to attract. These are divided into a group designated as practitioners and professionals, or another group referred to as researchers and academics in the accounting discipline.

Frequency of Issue indicates the number of times a journal will be published in a year.

Copies per Issue indicates the number of copies the journal distributes per issue.

Sponsor/Publisher indicates the journal's affiliation with a professional association educational institution, governmental agency, and/or publishing company.

Subscribe Price indicates the cost to order a year's subscription unless otherwise indicated.

MANUSCRIPT TOPICS
Manuscript Topics indicates those subjects the journal emphasizes.

MANUSCRIPT GUIDELINES/COMMENTS
Manuscript Guidelines/Comments provides information on the journal's objectives, style and format for references and footnotes that the editor expects the author to follow in preparing his manuscript for submission.

How the Directory Helps You Publish

Although individuals must communicate their ideas in writing, the *Directory* helps the author determine which journal will most likely accept the manuscript. In making this decision, it is important to compare the characteristics of your manuscript and the needs of each journal. The following table provides a framework for making this comparison.

Information Provided by the Directory for Each Journal	**Manuscript Characteristics**
Topic(s) of Articles Manuscript Guidelines	Theme
Acceptance Rate Percentage of Invited Articles	Significance of Theme
Type of Reader	Methodology and Style
Circulation Review Process	Prestige
Number of Reviewers Availability of Reviewers Comments Time Required for Reviewer	Results of Review

This framework will help the author determine a small number of journals that will be interested in publishing the manuscript. The *Directory* can assist the author in determining these journals, yet a set of unwritten and written laws prevent simultaneous submission of a manuscript to more than one journal. However, a manuscript can be sent to another journal in the event of a rejection by any one publication.

Furthermore, copyright laws and editorial policy of a given publication often require the author to choose only one journal. Consequently, some journals will require the author to sign a statement indicating the manuscript is not presently under review by another publication.

Publication of the manuscript in the proceedings of a professional association does not prevent the author from sending it to a journal, however there usually are some restrictions attached. Most professional associations require that the author acknowledge the presentation of the manuscript at the associate meeting.

Since the author is limited to submission of a manuscript to only one journal and the review process for each journal requires a long period of time, a "query" letter may help the author determine the journal most likely to publish the manuscript.

The query letter contains the following information:
- Topic, major idea or conclusion of the manuscript
- The subject sample, research setting conceptual framework, methodology type of organization or location
- The reasons why the author thinks the journal's readers would be interested in your proposed article
- Asks the editor to make comments or suggestions on the usefulness of this type of article to the journal

While the query letter is helpful in selecting a journal that will be likely to publish the manuscript, the author could use the *Directory* and the framework presented to develop a set of journals which would be likely to publish the manuscript. With this number of possible journals, it makes the sending of a query letter more feasible and tends to achieve the objective of finding the journal most likely to publish the manuscript.

Relating the Theme of the Manuscript to the Topics of Articles Published by Each Journal

To begin the process of choosing the journals to receive the "query" letter and, at some future time, the manuscript, the author needs to examine the similarity between the theme of the manuscript and the editor's needs. The *Directory* describes these needs by listing the topics each publication considers important and the manuscript guidelines. To find those journals that publish manuscripts in any particular area, refer to the topic index.

In attempting to classify the theme, the author should limit his choice to a single discipline. With the increasing specialization in the academic world, it is unlikely that reviewers, editors, or readers will understand an article that requires knowledge of two different disciplines. If these groups do not understand a manuscript, the journal will reject it.

If a manuscript emphasizes an interdisciplinary approach, it is important to decide who will be reading the article. The approach should be to explain the theoretical concepts of one discipline to the specialist in another discipline. The author should not attempt to resolve theoretical issues present in his discipline and explain their implications for specialists in another discipline.

Although the discipline classifications indicate the number of journals interested in your manuscript topic, the manuscript guidelines help the author determine the journals that will most likely have the greatest interest in the manuscript. The manuscript guidelines provide a detailed statement of the criteria for judging manuscripts, the editorial objectives, the readership and the journal's content and approach. This information makes it possible to determine more precisely the congruence between the manuscript and the type of articles the journal publishes. **The *Directory* contains the manuscript guidelines for a large number of journals.**

The Relationship Between the Journal's Acceptance Rate and Significance of the Theme of the Manuscript

In addition to determining the similarity between the topic of the manuscript and the topic of articles published by the journal, an examination of the significance of the theme to the discipline is also an important criterion in selecting a journal. The journals with the lowest acceptance rate will tend to publish those manuscripts that make the most significant contributions to the advancement of the discipline. Since these journals receive a large number of manuscripts, the editors distinguish those manuscripts likely to make a significant contribution to the reader's knowledge.

Defining newness or the contribution of any one study to the understanding of a discipline is difficult. However, it is possible to gain some insights into this definition by asking the following questions:

1. Is the author stating the existence of a variable, trend or problem, not previously recognized by the literature?

2. Is the author testing the interactions of a different set of variables or events?

3. Is the author presenting a new technique to cope with a problem or test an idea not previously presented in the literature?

4. Is the author using a subject sample with different characteristics than previously presented in the literature?

If the manuscript does not satisfy one of the first two categories, it is unlikely that a journal with a low acceptance rate will accept it for publication. Thus, the author should send the manuscript to those journals where the acceptance rate is higher.

Although the *Directory* provides the acceptance rates of manuscripts for many different journals, it is important to examine the data on percentage of invited articles for each journal. A high acceptance rate may result because the editor has asked leaders in the discipline to write articles on a particular subject. These invited articles are usually accepted. Since the author of an unsolicited manuscript competes with the leaders in the discipline, the manuscript will have to make a significant contribution to receive the editor's approval.

The Relationship of the Manuscript's Style and Methodology to the Journal's Readership

Another factor in selecting the journal to receive the manuscript is the journal's readership. The readers of each journal include either, practitioners and professionals, academics and researchers in accounting, or a combination of these groups.

Since the most important goal for an author is to publish the manuscript, the author should consider the prestige of the journal only after the manuscript has a relatively high probability of being published by more than one journal. This probability is determined by the responses the author received to his query letter and the similarity between the finished manuscript and the needs of the journal.

The method of determining the prestige of a journal varies depending on its readership and the goals of the author. If the readership is primarily administrators or practicing professionals and the goal of the author is to improve the author's image and that of the institution, the journal's circulation would probably be the best indicator of prestige.

In contrast, the author whose goal is to become known among the author's colleagues might consider the type of review process the journal uses as well as its circulation. With a few exceptions, the most prestigious journals with academic readership use a refereed review process.

The Possible Results of the Review Process and the Selection of a Journal to Receive the Manuscript

Despite the fact that a journal with lower prestige would most likely publish the article, the author might be willing to take a chance on a journal with a greater amount of prestige. Since this will decrease the chances of manuscript acceptance, the author should also consider the consequences of rejection. The consequences include the knowledge the author will gain from having his manuscript rejected.

To determine the amount of knowledge the author is likely to gain requires consideration of the number of reviewers the journal uses in the review process, the availability of the reviewer's comments and the time required for the review process. If the journal makes the reviewer's comments available to the author, this provides a great learning opportunity. Also, the more people that review the manuscript, the greater the author's knowledge will be concerning how to improve the present manuscript. Hopefully, the author will transfer the knowledge gained from writing this manuscript to future manuscripts.

Should the review process take a small amount of time relative to a long period of time, the author is provided with a greater opportunity to use this knowledge to revise the manuscript. To assist the author in determining those journals that provide a suitable learning opportunity, each journal in the *Directory* includes information on the number of reviewers, availability of reviewer's comments to the author and time required for review.

Sending the Manuscript

Before sending the manuscript to an editor, the author should write a cover letter, make sure the manuscript is correctly typed, the format conforms to the journal's guidelines and the necessary copies have been included. **The author should always keep a copy of the manuscript.**

The cover letter that is sent with the manuscript makes it easy for the editor to select reviewers and monitor the manuscript while it is in the review process. This letter should include the title of the manuscript, the author name(s), mailing address(es) phone and fax number(s) and e-mail addresses. In addition, this letter should provide a brief description of the manuscript theme, its applicability and significance to the journal's readership. Finally it should request a copy of the reviewer's comments regardless of whether the manuscript is accepted or rejected.

Receipt of the Reviewer's Comments

The reviewers may still reject the article although the author may have followed this procedure and taken every precaution to avoid rejection. When this occurs, the author's attitude should be focused on making those changes that would make the manuscript more understandable to the next editor, and/or reviewer. These changes may include providing additional information and/or presenting the topic in a more concise manner. Also, the author needs to determine whether some error occurred in selecting the journal to receive the manuscript. Regardless of the source of the errors, the author needs to make those changes that will improve the manuscript's chances of being accepted by the next journal to receive it.

Unless the journal specifically requests the author to revise the manuscript for publication, the author should not send the manuscript to the journal that first rejected it. In rejecting the manuscript, the reviewers implied that it could not be revised to meet their standards for publication. Thus, sending it back to them would not improve the likelihood that the manuscript will be accepted.

If your manuscript is accepted, go out and celebrate but write another one very quickly. When you find you're doing something right, keep doing it so you won't forget.

"What is a Refereed Article?"

With some exceptions a refereed article is one that is blind reviewed and has two external reviewers. The blind review requirement and the use of external reviewers are consistent with the research criteria of objectivity and of knowledge.

The use of a blind review process means that the author of the manuscript is not made known to the reviewer. With the large number of reviewers and journals, it is also likely that the name of the reviewers for a particular manuscript is not made known to the author. Thus, creating a double blind review process. Since the author and reviewers are frequently unknown, the manuscript is judged on its merits rather than on the reputation of the author and/or the author's influence on the reviewers.

The use of two (2) reviewers permits specialists familiar with research similar to that presented in the paper to judge whether the paper makes a contribution to the advancement of knowledge. When two reviewers are used it provides a broader perspective for evaluating the research. This perspective is further widened by the discussion between the editor and reviewers in seeking to reconcile these perspectives.

In contrast to these criteria, some journals that have attained a reputation for quality do not use either a blind review process or external reviewers. The most notable is *Harvard Business Review* that uses an editorial review process. Its reputation for quality results from its readership whose continual subscription attests to its quality.

In addition to these criteria, some researchers include the journal's acceptance rate in their definition of a refereed journal. However, the method of calculating acceptance rates varies among journals. Some journals use all manuscripts received as a base for computing this rate. Other journals allow the editor to choose which papers are sent to reviewers and calculate the acceptance rate on those that are reviewed that is less than the total manuscripts received. Also, many editors do not maintain accurate records on this data and provide only a rough estimate.

Furthermore, the number of people associated with a particular area of specialization influences the acceptance rate. If only a few people can write papers in an area, it tends to increase the journal's acceptance rate.

Although the type of review process and use of external reviewers is one possible definition of a refereed article, it is not the only criteria. Judging the usefulness of a journal to the advancement of knowledge requires the reader to be familiar with many journals in their specialization and make their own evaluation.

Abacus

ADDRESS FOR SUBMISSION:

Graeme W. Dean, Editor
Abacus
University of Sydney
Dept. of Accounting
Sydney, 2006
N.S.W. Australia
Phone: 61-02-9351-3107
Fax: 61-02-9351-6638
E-Mail: graeme@abacus.econ.usyd.edu.au
Web:
Address May Change: 12/25/01

PUBLICATION GUIDELINES:

Manuscript Length: 16-20
Copies Required: Three
Computer Submission: Yes
Format: N/A
Fees to Review: 40.00 US$

Manuscript Style:
See Manuscript Guidelines

CIRCULATION DATA:

Reader: Academics
Frequency of Issue: 3 Times/Year
Copies per Issue: 1,001 - 2,000
Sponsor/Publisher: Accounting Foundation,
  Univ. of Sydney /Blackwell
Subscribe Price: 107.00 US$

REVIEW INFORMATION:

Type of Review: Blind Review
No. of External Reviewers: 2
No. of In House Reviewers: 1
Acceptance Rate: 11-20%
Time to Review: 4 - 6 Months
Reviewers Comments: Yes
Invited Articles: 0-5%
Fees to Publish: 0.00 US$

MANUSCRIPT TOPICS:

Accounting History; Accounting Information Systems; Accounting Theory & Practice; Auditing; Capital Budgeting; Cost Accounting; Government & Non Profit Accounting; Tax Accounting

MANUSCRIPT GUIDELINES/COMMENTS:

1. *Abacus* has as its objective the publication of explanatory constructive and critical articles on all aspects of accounting and on those phases of the theory and administration of organizations and of economic behavior generally which are related to accounting and finance.

Manuscripts should be sent to the Editor and will be considered for publication only if accompanied by a submission fee of $40.00 U.S. The submission fee is waived if the author or a co-author is a personal subscriber to the journal. The general layout and style should follow the most recent Style Guide which is printed in the Journal from time to time.

2. Submit three copies of manuscript.

3. Use opaque quarto paper (207 mm x 260 mm) or A4 (210 mm x 297 mm); double space text; leave adequate (30 mm) margins on both sides.

4. Place name of author in BLOCK capitals above the title of the article. Give author's present position at the foot of the first page.

5. Use footnotes sparingly. Place them at the end of the manuscript, double-spaced with an extra line between entries. Number footnotes consecutively throughout the text; use superior numbering without point, thus: "...money".3 Cite books and articles in the text thus:...(Jones,1962, p. 21).
For page reference numbers use p. 21, pp. 423-32, pp. 406-571, but pp.11-13, pp.115-19.

6. List books and articles cited in alphabetical order at the end of the manuscript. When listing books and articles use the following forms respectively:

Jones, A., Depreciation of Assets, Publisher & Co.,1962.
Morrissey, Leonard, 'Intangible Costs' in Morton Backer (ed.), Modern Accounting Theory, Prentice Hall,1966.
Revsine, L. and J. Weygandt, 'Accounting for Inflation: The Controversy', Journal of Accountancy, October 1974.
Smith, B., 'An Aspect of Depreciation', The Journal of Accounting, August 1965.

Do not use brackets; use short titles for publishers unless it is essential to tracing.

7. Underline what is to be printed in italics. Use BLOCK capitals only for what is to be printed in capitals. Use italics and BLOCK capitals sparingly. Use the smallest number of styles for section headings; preferably side headings, in italics.

8. For quotations within the text use only single quotation marks, and double marks for quotes within quotes. Where quotations exceed four lines insert quoted material three spaces, but do not use quotation marks.

9. Do not use a point in standard abbreviations such as CPA, SEC, but use points in U.K., U.S.A., and similar abbreviations. Date style e.g., 19 February 1966.

10. Use double dashes (--) to indicate dashes in the text, single dashes (-) for hyphens.

11. Use 'z' for such words as capitalize; 's' for the smaller number of words such as advise, analyse, comprise, enterprise (see *Oxford English Dictionary*).

12. Use the simplest possible form for mathematical symbols.

13. Keep tables to a minimum but do not try to convey too much information, at the cost of simplicity, in any one table.

Academy of Accounting and Financial Studies Journal

ADDRESS FOR SUBMISSION:

Current Editor's Name / Check Web Page
Academy of Accounting and Financial
   Studies Journal
Submission Address / Check Web Page
Address other Questions to:
   Jim or JoAnn Carland at #'s below
USA
Phone: 828-293-9151
Fax: 828-293-9407
E-Mail: carland@wcu.edu
Web: www.alliedacademies.org
Address May Change:

PUBLICATION GUIDELINES:

Manuscript Length: 16-20
Copies Required: Four
Computer Submission: Yes
   Format: WordPerfect 6.1
Fees to Review: 0.00 US$

Manuscript Style:
   American Psychological Association

CIRCULATION DATA:

Reader: Academics
Frequency of Issue: 3 Times/Year
Copies per Issue: Less than 1,000
Sponsor/Publisher: Allied Academies
Subscribe Price: 50.00 US$

REVIEW INFORMATION:

Type of Review: Blind Review
No. of External Reviewers: 2
No. of In House Reviewers: 2
Acceptance Rate: 11-20%
Time to Review: 4 - 6 Months
Reviewers Comments: Yes
Invited Articles: 0-5%
Fees to Publish: 50.00 US$ Membership

MANUSCRIPT TOPICS:
Accounting Education; Accounting Information Systems; Accounting Theory & Practice;
Auditing; Cost Accounting; Fiscal Policy; Government & Non Profit Accounting;
International Finance; Tax Accounting

MANUSCRIPT GUIDELINES/COMMENTS:

COMMENTS. All authors of published manuscripts must be members of The Academy.
Membership fee is $50.00.

EDITORIAL POLICY GUIDELINES FOR THEORETICAL
AND EMPIRICAL MANUSCRIPTS

The Allied Academies affiliates which handle theoretical and empirical manuscripts include
the Academy of Entrepreneurship, the Academy of Accounting and Financial Studies, the
Academy of Marketing Studies, the Academy of Strategic and Organizational Leadership, the
Academy of Managerial Communications, the Academy of Educational Leadership, the
Academy of Information and Management Sciences, and, the Academy for Studies in

Business Law. These editorial guidelines reflect the Academies' policy with regard to reviewing theoretical and empirical manuscripts for publication and presentation in each of these affiliates. The primary criterion upon which manuscripts are judged is whether the research advances the discipline. The specific guidelines followed by referees show the areas of evaluation to which each manuscript is subjected. Key points include currency, interest, and relevancy.

Theoretical manuscripts are particularly vulnerable to problems in literature review. In order for theoretical research to advance a discipline, it must address the literature which exists in the discipline to support conclusions or models which extend knowledge and understanding. Consequently, referees for theoretical manuscripts pay particular attention to completeness of literature review and appropriateness of conclusions drawn from that review.

Empirical manuscripts are particularly vulnerable to methodological problems. In order to advance the literature, empirical manuscripts must employ appropriate and effective sampling and statistical analysis techniques. However, empirical papers must also incorporate thorough literature reviews in order to advance the literature. Referees will pay close attention to the conclusions which are drawn from statistical analyses and their consistency with the literature.

We ask referees to be as specific as possible in indicating what must be done to make a manuscript acceptable for journal publication. This embodies a primary objective of the Academy: to assist authors in the research process.

Our Editorial Policy is one which is supportive, rather than critical. We encourage all authors who are not successful in a first attempt to rewrite the manuscript in accordance with the suggestions of the referees. We will be pleased to referee future versions and rewrites of manuscripts and work with authors in achieving their research goals.

EDITORIAL POLICY GUIDELINES FOR EDUCATIONAL AND PEDAGOGIC MANUSCRIPTS

The Allied Academies affiliates which handle educational and pedagogic manuscripts include the Academy of Entrepreneurship, the Academy of Accounting and Financial Studies, the Academy of Marketing Studies, the Academy of Strategic and Organizational Leadership, the Academy of Managerial Communications, the Academy of Educational Leadership, the Academy of Information and Management Sciences, and, the Academy for Studies in Business Law. These editorial guidelines reflect the Academies' policy with regard to reviewing educational and pedagogic manuscripts for publication and presentation in each of these affiliates.

The primary criterion upon which manuscripts are judged is whether the research advances the teaching profession. The specific guidelines followed by referees show the areas of evaluation to which each manuscript is subjected. Key points include currency, interest, relevancy and usefulness to educators.

In order for educational or pedagogic manuscripts to be useful to educators, they must address appropriate literature to support conclusions, teaching methodologies or pedagogies.

Consequently, referees pay particular attention to completeness of literature review and appropriateness of conclusions drawn from that review. Pedagogies or teaching methodologies must be well described with sound foundations in order to be useful to educators. Referees will pay particular attention to such issues in judging manuscripts.

In every case, educational or pedagogic manuscripts must embody well developed and well documented ideas in order to be useful to educators. Referees will pay close attention to the ideas presented in the manuscript and how well they are presented and supported.

We ask referees to be as specific as possible in indicating what must be done to make a manuscript acceptable for journal publication. This embodies a primary objective of the Academy: to assist authors in the research process.

Our Editorial Policy is one which is supportive, rather than critical. We encourage all authors who are not successful in a first attempt to rewrite the manuscript in accordance with the suggestions of the referees. We will be pleased to referee future versions and rewrites of manuscripts and work with authors in achieving their research goals.

Accountancy

ADDRESS FOR SUBMISSION:

Brian Singleton-Green, Editor
Accountancy
Institute of Chartered Accountants
40 Bernard Street
London, WC1N 1LD
England
Phone: 44-0171-833-3291
Fax: 44-0171-833-2085
E-Mail: postmaster@theabg.demon.co.uk
Web: http://www.accountancymag.co.uk
Address May Change:

CIRCULATION DATA:

Reader: Business Persons
Frequency of Issue: Monthly
Copies per Issue: More than 25,000
Sponsor/Publisher: Institute of Chartered
    Accountants in England & Wales/ABC
    Press
Subscribe Price: 44.00 Pounds
    63.00 Pounds Overseas
    94.50 US$ in US

PUBLICATION GUIDELINES:

Manuscript Length: 2000 Words
Copies Required: One
Computer Submission: No
Format: N/A
Fees to Review: 0.00 US$

Manuscript Style:
    See Manuscript Guidelines

REVIEW INFORMATION:

Type of Review: Editorial Review
No. of External Reviewers: 0
No. of In House Reviewers: 2
Acceptance Rate: 11-20%
Time to Review: 1 Month or Less
Reviewers Comments: No
Invited Articles: 50% +
Fees to Publish: 0.00 US$

MANUSCRIPT TOPICS:
Accounting Information Systems; Accounting Theory & Practice; Auditing; Business
Education; Business Law & Public Responsibility; Capital Budgeting; Cost Accounting;
Econometrics; Economics; Finance & Investments; General Business; International Business;
Management; Portfolio & Security Analysis; Small Business Entrepreneurship; Strategic
Management Policy; Tax Accounting

MANUSCRIPT GUIDELINES/COMMENTS:

Most feature articles published in *Accountancy* are commissioned, and commissioning usually
takes place some months before the planned publication date. Those wishing to write feature
articles should first submit a written synopsis to the features editor, who may then commission
the article. Unsolicited manuscripts will be considered but are unlikely to be accepted.

Where topics are of immediate news interest, contact should be made by telephone to the
news editor.

Accounting and Business (Certified Accountant)

ADDRESS FOR SUBMISSION:

John Prosser, Editor
Accounting and Business (Certified
  Accountant)
10 Lincoln's Inn Fields
London, WC2A 3RP
UK
Phone: 44 207-396-5966
Fax: 44 207-396 5958
E-Mail: john.prosser@acca.org.uk
Web: www.acca.org.uk
Address May Change:

CIRCULATION DATA:

Reader: Business Persons
Frequency of Issue: 10 Times/ Year
Copies per Issue: 85,000
Sponsor/Publisher: Association of
  Chartered Certified Accountants
Subscribe Price: 85.00 Pounds Non-
  members

PUBLICATION GUIDELINES:

Manuscript Length: 6-10
Copies Required: One
Computer Submission: Yes
Format: MS Word e-mail
Fees to Review: 0.00 US$

Manuscript Style:
  American Psychological Association

REVIEW INFORMATION:

Type of Review: Blind Review
No. of External Reviewers: No Reply
No. of In House Reviewers: No Reply
Acceptance Rate: 21-30%
Time to Review: 1 Month or Less
Reviewers Comments: No
Invited Articles: 60-70%
Fees to Publish: 0.00 US$

MANUSCRIPT TOPICS:
Accounting Information Systems; Accounting Theory & Practice; Auditing; Cost Accounting;
International Economics & Trade; International Finance; Small Business Entrepreneurship;
Social and Environmental Accounting

MANUSCRIPT GUIDELINES/COMMENTS:

Accounting and Business Research

ADDRESS FOR SUBMISSION:

Professor K.V. Peasnell, Editor
Accounting and Business Research
University of Lancaster
Management School
Lancaster, LA1 4YX
UK
Phone: 44 0 1524 593977
Fax: 44 0 1524 594334
E-Mail: k.peasnell@lancaster.ac.uk
Web: www.accountancymag.co.uk
Address May Change:

PUBLICATION GUIDELINES:

Manuscript Length: No Reply
Copies Required: Three
Computer Submission: No
Format: N/A
Fees to Review: 45.00 US$

Manuscript Style:
    See Manuscript Guidelines

CIRCULATION DATA:

Reader: Academics
Frequency of Issue: Quarterly
Copies per Issue: 1,001 - 2,000
Sponsor/Publisher: Institute of Chartered
    Accountants in England and Wales
Subscribe Price: 39.00 Pounds
    9.00 Pounds Institution

REVIEW INFORMATION:

Type of Review: Blind Review
No. of External Reviewers: 2
No. of In House Reviewers: 0
Acceptance Rate: 11-20%
Time to Review: 2 - 3 Months
Reviewers Comments: Yes
Invited Articles: 0-5%
Fees to Publish: 0.00 US$

MANUSCRIPT TOPICS:
Accounting Information Systems; Accounting Theory & Practice; Auditing; Capital
Budgeting; Cost Accounting; Government & Non Profit Accounting; Portfolio & Security
Analysis; Tax Accounting

MANUSCRIPT GUIDELINES/COMMENTS:

General
Papers should be in English and consist of original unpublished work not currently being
considered for publication elsewhere. They should be typed and double-spaced. **Four** copies
should be submitted, together with a submission fee of £18 for subscribers or £36 for
non-subscribers. In order to ensure an anonymous review, authors should not identify
themselves, directly or indirectly. Experience has shown that papers that have already
benefited from critical comment from colleagues at seminars or at conferences have a much
better chance of acceptance. Where the research takes the form of field surveys or
experiments, **four** copies of the instrument should be submitted. Where the paper shares data
with another paper, **four** copies of the other paper must also be provided.

Presentation

A cover page should show the title of the paper, the author's name, title and affiliation, and any acknowledgements. The title of the paper, but not the author's name, should appear on the first page of the text. An abstract of 150-250 words should be provided on a separate page immediately preceding the text. Section headings should be numbered using Arabic numerals.

Tables and figures

Each table and figure should bear an Arabic number and a title and should be referred to in the text. Sources should be clearly stated. Sufficient details should be provided in the heading and body of each table and figure to reduce to a minimum the need for cross-referencing by readers to other parts of the manuscript. Tables and figures should appear at the end of the paper, with its most appropriate placing noted in the paper itself. Diagrams and charts should be submitted in camera-ready form.

Footnotes

Footnotes should be used only in order to avoid interrupting the continuity of the text, and should not be used to excess. They should be numbered consecutively throughout the manuscript with superscript Arabic numerals. They should not be used in book reviews.

References

References should be listed at the end of the paper and referred to in the text as, for example, (Zeff, 1980: 24). Wherever appropriate, the reference should include a page or chapter number in the journal or book in question. Only works cited in the paper should be included in the list. Citations to institutional works should if possible employ acronyms or short titles. If an author's name is mentioned in the text it need not be repeated in the citation, e.g. 'Tippett and Whittington (1995: 209) state...'

In the list of references, titles of journals should omit an initial 'The' but should not otherwise be abbreviated. The entries should be arranged in alphabetical order by surname of the first author. Multiple works by the same author should be listed in chronological order of publication. Some examples are:

Accounting Standards Steering Committee (1975). *The Corporate Report.* London: ASC.

Tippett, M. and Whittington, G. (1995). 'An empirical evaluation of an induced theory of financial ratios'. *Accounting and Business Research,* 25 (Summer): 208-218.

Watts, R. L. and Zimmerman, J. L. (1986). *Positive Accounting Theory.* Englewood Cliffs, NJ: Prentice-Hall.

Style and spelling

Abbreviations of institutional names should be written as, for example, FASB and not F.A.S.B: those of Latin terms should contain stops (thus i.e. not ie). Words such as 'realise' should be spelled with an 's' not a 'z'. Single quotations marks should be used, not double.

Mathematical notation

Mathematical notation should be used only where it adds rigour and precision, and should be properly explained in the text. Equations should be numbered in parentheses, flush with the right-hand margin.

Accounting Auditing & Accountability Journal

ADDRESS FOR SUBMISSION:

Lee D. Parker, Joint Editor
Accounting Auditing & Accountability
  Journal
University of Adelaide
School of Commerce
North Terrace
Adelaide, SA 5000,
Australia
Phone: 61-8 8303 4236
Fax: 61-8 8303 4368
E-Mail: aaaj@commerce.adelaide.edu.au
Web: www.mcb.co.uk
Address May Change:

PUBLICATION GUIDELINES:

Manuscript Length: 30 or More
Copies Required: Four
Computer Submission: No
Format: See Manuscript Guidelines
Fees to Review: 0.00 US$

Manuscript Style:
  See Manuscript Guidelines

CIRCULATION DATA:

Reader: Academics
Frequency of Issue: 5 Times/Year
Copies per Issue: Less than 1,000
Sponsor/Publisher: MCB University Press
  Limited-UK
Subscribe Price: 187.95 US$ Individual
  1139.00 US$ Institutional
  69.00 US$ Individual Electronic

REVIEW INFORMATION:

Type of Review: Blind Review
No. of External Reviewers: 2
No. of In House Reviewers: 1
Acceptance Rate: 25%
Time to Review: 2 - 3 Months
Reviewers Comments: Yes
Invited Articles: 0-5%
Fees to Publish: 0.00 US$

MANUSCRIPT TOPICS:

Accounting Communications; Accounting Ethics; Accounting Theory & Practice; Auditing;
Cost Accounting; Government & Non Profit Accounting; Planning & Control; Social and
Environmental Accounting

MANUSCRIPT GUIDELINES/COMMENTS:

About The Journal

Articles submitted to *Accounting, Auditing & Accountability* should be original contributions
and should not be under consideration for any other publication at the same time. Author's
submitting articles for publication warrant that the work is not an infringement of any existing
copyright and will indemnify the publisher against any breach of such warranty. For ease of
dissemination and to ensure proper policing of use, papers and contributions become the legal
copyright of the publisher unless otherwise agreed. Submissions should be sent to the Editor.

Editorial Objectives
The journal *Accounting, Auditing & Accountability* is dedicated to the advancement of accounting knowledge and provides a forum for the publication of high quality manuscripts concerning the interaction between accounting/auditing and their socio-economic and political environments. It therefore encourages critical analysis of policy and practice in these areas. Analysis could explore policy alternatives and provide new perspectives for the accounting discipline.

The problems of concern are international (in varying degree) and may have differing cultural, social and institutional structures. Analysis can be international, national or organization specific. It can be from a single, multi- or inter-disciplinary perspective.

Editorial Criteria
Major criteria used to evaluate papers are:
1. Subject matter: must be of importance to the accounting discipline.
2. Research question: must fall within the journal's scope.
3. Research: well designed and executed.
4. Presentation: well written and conforming to the journal's style.

The Reviewing Process
Each paper submitted is subject to the following review procedures:
1. It is reviewed by the editor for general suitability for this publication.
2. If it is judged suitable two reviewers are selected and a double blind review process takes place.
3. Based on the recommendations of the reviewers, the editors then decide whether the particular article should be accepted as it is, revised or rejected.

Manuscript Requirements
Linkage to the literature is essential in papers submitted for publication. To enable authors to carry out a comprehensive literature search, free access, via the Internet, to Anbar Management Intelligence is available for a trial period of 30 days. Anbar Management Intelligence provides on-line access to more than 420 of the world's leading management journals, has an archive going back to 1989 and is updated monthly.
Please go to http://222.anbar.co.uk/anbar.htm for access.
There are also a number of specific requirements with regard to article features and formats which authors should note carefully:
Three copies of the manuscript should be submitted in double line spacing with wide margins. All authors should be shown and author's details must be printed on a separate sheet and the author should not be identified anywhere else in the article.

1. Word length
Articles should be between 4,000 and 7,000 words in length.

2. Methodology
In papers reporting upon surveys and case studies, methodology should be clearly described under a separate heading. Particularly for survey-based articles full details should be given,

i.e. type and size of sample, data instruments used including, for mailed surveys, the final percentage response and the treatment of bias.

3. Title
A title, ideally, of not more than eight words in length should be provided.

4. Autobiographical note
A brief autobiographical note should be supplied including full name, appointment, name of organization and e-mail address.

5. Word processing
Please submit to the Editor three copies of the manuscript in double line spacing with wide margins.

6. Headings and sub-headings
These should be short and to-the-point, appearing approximately every 750 words. Headings should be typed in capitals and underlined; sub-headings should be typed in upper and lower case and underlined. Headings should not be numbered.

7. References
References to other publications should be in Harvard style. That is, shown within the text as the first author's name followed by a comma and year of publication all in round brackets, e g. (Fox, 1994). They should contain full bibliographical details and journal titles should not be abbreviated. For multiple citations in the same year use a, b, c immediately following the year of publication.

At the end of the article a reference list in alphabetical order as follows:

(a) For books:
   surname, initials, (year), title, publisher, place of publication, e.g. Casson, M. (1979), *Alternatives to the Multinational Enterprise*, Macmillan, London.
(b) For chapter in edited in book:
   surname, initials, year, title, editor's surname, initials, title, publisher, place, pages,
   e.g.Bessley, M. and Wilson, P. (1984), "Public policy and small firms in Britain", in
   Levicki, C. (Ed.), Small Business Theory and Policy, Croom Helm, London, pp. 111-26.
(c) For articles:
   surname, initials, year, title, journal, volume, number, pages, e.g. Fox, S. (1994),
   "Empowerment as a catalyst for change: an example from the food industry", Supply
   Chain Management, Vol. 2 No. 3, pp. 29-33.

If there is more than one author list surnames followed by initials. All authors should be shown. Electronic sources should include the URL of the electronic site at which they may be found. Notes/Endnotes should be used only if absolutely necessary. They should be identified in the text by consecutive numbers enclosed in square brackets and listed at the end of the article.

8. Figures, charts, diagrams
Use of figures, charts and diagrams should be kept to a minimum and information conveyed in such a manner should instead be described in text form. Essential figures, charts and diagrams should be referred to as figures and numbered consecutively using Arabic numerals. Each figure should have a brief title and labeled axes. Diagrams should be kept as simple as possible and avoid unnecessary capitalization and shading In the text, the position of the figure should be shown by typing on a separate line the words "take in Figure 1".

9. Tables
Use of tables should be kept to a minimum. Where essential, these should be typed on a separate sheet of paper and numbered consecutively and independently of any figures included in the article. Each table should have a number in roman numerals, a brief title, and vertical and horizontal headings. In the text, the position of the table should be shown by typing on a separate line the words "take in Table IV". Tables should not repeat data available elsewhere in the paper.

10. Photos, illustrations
Half-tone illustrations should be restricted in number to the minimum necessary. Good glossy bromide prints should accompany the manuscripts but not be attached to manuscript pages. Illustrations unsuitable for reproduction, e.g. computer-screen capture, will not be used. Any computer programs should be supplied as clear and sharp print outs on plain paper. They will be reproduced photographically to avoid errors. Their position should be shown in the text by typing on a separate line the words "take in Plate 2."

11. Emphasis
Words to be emphasized should be limited in number and italicized. Capital letters should be used only at the start of sentences or in the case of proper names.

12. Abstracts
Authors must supply an abstract of 100-150 words when submitting an article. It should be an abbreviated, accurate representation of the content of the article. Major results, conclusions and/or recommendations should be given, followed by supporting details of method, scope or purpose. It should contain sufficient information to enable readers to decide whether they should obtain and read the entire article.

13. Keywords
Up to six keywords should be included which encapsulate the principal subjects covered by the article. Minor facets of an article should not be keyworded. These keywords will be used by readers to select the material they wish to read and should therefore be truly representative of the article's main content.

14. Final submission of the article
Once accepted by the Editor for publication, the final version of the article should be submitted in manuscript accompanied by a 3.5" **disk** of the same version of the article marked with: disk format; author name(s); title of article; journal title; file name. The manuscript will be considered to be the definitive version of the article and the author should ensure that it is complete, grammatically correct and without spelling or typographical errors.

In preparing the disk, please use one of the following formats: Word, Word Perfect, Rich text format, or TeX/LateX. Figures which are provided electronically must be in tif, gif, or pic file extensions. All figures and graphics must also be supplied as good quality originals.

15. Journal Article Record Form
Each article should be accompanied by a completed and signed **Journal Article Record Form**. This form is available from the Editor or can be downloaded from MCB's World Wide Web Literati Club on http://www.mcb.co.uk/literati/nethome.htm

16. Copyright
Authors submitting articles for publication warrant that the work is not an infringement of any existing copyright and will indemnify the publisher against any breach of such warranty. For ease of dissemination and to ensure proper policing of use, papers and contributions become the legal copyright of the publisher unless otherwise agreed.

If you require technical assistance in respect of submitting an article please consult the relevant section of MCB's World Wide Web Literati Club on http://www.mcb.co.uk/literati/nethome.htm or contact Mike Massey at MCB, e-mail: mmassey@mcb.co.uk

Accounting, Auditing & Accountability is published by MCB University Press, 60/62 Toller Lane, Bradford, West Yorkshire BD8 9BY, UK. Tel: +44 1274 777700, Fax: +44 1274 785200 or 785201.

Accounting Business and Financial History

ADDRESS FOR SUBMISSION:

John Richard Edwards, Editor
Accounting Business and Financial History
Cardiff Business School
Business History Research Unit
Colum Drive
Cardiff, CF1 3EU
UK
Phone: 0 1222 876658
Fax: 0 1222 874419
E-Mail: edwardsjr@cardiff.ac.uk
Web:
Address May Change:

PUBLICATION GUIDELINES:

Manuscript Length: 8,000-12,000 words
Copies Required: Three
Computer Submission: No
Format: N/A
Fees to Review: 0.00 US$

Manuscript Style:
See Manuscript Guidelines

CIRCULATION DATA:

Reader: Academics
Frequency of Issue: 3 Times/ Year
Copies per Issue: Less than 1,000
Sponsor/Publisher: Routledge Journals
Subscribe Price: 90.00 US$ Individual
250.00 US$ Institution

REVIEW INFORMATION:

Type of Review: Blind Review
No. of External Reviewers: 2
No. of In House Reviewers: 1
Acceptance Rate: 40%
Time to Review: 2 - 3 Months
Reviewers Comments: Yes
Invited Articles: 10%
Fees to Publish: 0.00 US$

MANUSCRIPT TOPICS:
Accounting, Business & Financial History; Economic History

MANUSCRIPT GUIDELINES/COMMENTS:

1. Authors should submit three complete copies of their text, tables and figures, with any original illustrations, to: John Richard Edwards, Business History Research Unit, Cardiff Business School, Colum Drive, Cardiff CFI 3EU.

2. The submission should include a cover page showing the author's name, the department where the work was done, an address for correspondence, if different, and any acknowledgements.

3. Submissions should be in English, typed in double spacing with wide margins, on one side only of the paper, preferably of A4 size. The title, but not the author's name should appear on the first page of the manuscript.

16

4. Articles should normally be as concise as possible and preceded by an abstract of not more than 100 words and a list of up to 6 keywords for on-line searching purposes.

5. Within the manuscript there may be up to three levels of heading.

6. Tables and figures should not be inserted in the pages of the manuscript but should be on separate sheets. They should be numbered consecutively in Arabic numerals with a descriptive caption. The desired position in the text for each table and figure should be indicated in the margin of the manuscript.

7. Use the Harvard system of referencing which gives the name of the author and the date of publication as a key to the full bibliographical details which are set out in the list of references. When the author's name is mentioned in the text, the date is inserted in parentheses immediately after the name, as in 'Aldcroft (1964)'. When a less direct reference is made to one or more authors, both name and date are bracketed, with the references separated by a semi-colon, as in 'several authors have noted this trend (Rimmer, 1960; Pollard, 1965; Mckendrick, 1970)'. Where appropriate, page numbers should also be provided (Robert, 1980: 56). When the reference is to a work of dual or multiple authorship, use 'Harvey and Press (1988)' or 'Yamey et al. (1963)' respectively. If an author has two references published in the same year, add lower case letters after the date to distinguish them, as in 'Johnson (1984a, 1984b)'. Always use the minimum number of figures in page numbers dates etc, e.g. 22-4, 105-6 (but 112-13 for 'teen numbers) and 1968-9.

8. Direct quotations of 40 words or more should start on a separate line and be indented.

9. Footnotes should be used only where necessary to avoid interrupting the continuity of the text. They should be numbered consecutively using superscript arabic numerals. They should appear at the end of the main text, immediately before the list of references.

10. Submissions should include a reference list, in alphabetical order, at the end of the article The content and format should conform to the following examples.
Kennedy, William P. (1987) *Industrial Structure: Capital Markets and the Origins of British Economic Decline*, Cambridge: Cambridge University Press.
Chapman, S.D. (1985) 'British-based investment groups before 1914', *The Economic History Review*, 38: 230-51.
Hunt, B.C. (1936) *The Development of the Business Corporation in England* 1800 1867, Cambridge, Mass.: Harvard University Press. Reprinted (1969) New York: Russell & Russell.
Davenport-Hines, R.P.T. and Geoffrey Jones (eds) (1989) *British Business in Asia since 1860*, Cambridge: Cambridge University Press.

11. For any other matters of presentation not covered by the above notes, please refer to the usual custom and practice as indicated by the last few issues of the Journal.

12. On acceptance for publication, authors will be requested to provide a copy of their paper in exact accordance with the conventions listed in the preceding notes. If the final version of the paper is not submitted in accordance with these conventions then publication may be delayed by the need to return manuscripts to authors for necessary revisions. Authors should

note that, following acceptance for publication, they will be required to provide not only a hard copy of the final version, but also a copy on a virus-free diskette, preferably in MS-Word 6 format, if at all possible. Authors will also be required to complete a Publishing Agreement form assigning copyright to the Publisher.

13. Page proofs will be sent for correction to a first-named author, unless otherwise requested. The difficulty and expense involved in making amendments at the page proof stage make it essential for authors to prepare their typescripts carefully; any alteration to the original text is strongly discouraged.

Accounting Education: An International Journal

ADDRESS FOR SUBMISSION:

Richard M. S. Wilson, Editor
Accounting Education: An International
    Journal
Loughborough University Business School
Ashby Road
Loughborough
Leicestershire, LE11 3TU
UK
Phone: 44 1509 223139
Fax: 44 1509 223961
E-Mail: r.m.wilson@lboro.ac.uk
Web:
Address May Change:

PUBLICATION GUIDELINES:

Manuscript Length: 21-25
Copies Required: Four
Computer Submission: Yes
Format: N/A
Fees to Review: 0.00 US$

Manuscript Style:
    See Manuscript Guidelines

CIRCULATION DATA:

Reader: Academics
Frequency of Issue: Quarterly
Copies per Issue: Less than 1,000
Sponsor/Publisher: Routledge Journals
Subscribe Price: 55.00 Pounds Individual
    425.00 Pounds Institutional

REVIEW INFORMATION:

Type of Review: Blind Review
No. of External Reviewers: 3
No. of In House Reviewers: 2
Acceptance Rate: 21-30%
Time to Review: 2 - 3 Months
Reviewers Comments: Yes
Invited Articles: 0-5%
Fees to Publish: 0.00 US$

MANUSCRIPT TOPICS:
Accounting Education; Pedagogic Innovations

MANUSCRIPT GUIDELINES/COMMENTS:

In USA: Donna L. Street, Associate Editor
    Center for Research in Accounting Education
    James Madison University
    MSC 0203
    VA 22807, USA
    Tel: +1 540-568-3089
    Fax: +1-540-568-3017

Accounting Education has the following major aims:
(i) to enhance the educational base of accounting practice by providing a forum for identifying, exploring and assessing issues relating to the academic and professional preparation of future accounting practitioners;

(ii) to promote excellence in accounting education and training by acting as a catalyst to facilitate improvements via such means as curriculum development, innovative learning methods, and new teaching materials;

(iii) to stimulate research in accounting education and training and to disseminate the results of enquiries into the effectiveness of alternative teaching methods, etc.;

(iv) to provide a means of highlighting the contribution IT has to make to developing better accounting education and training both in respect of relevant content and effective delivery;

(v) to build links among those who teach, train and employ accounting/finance students and to offer a platform for the exchange of views reflecting the priorities to be attached by different parties to issues in accounting education and training;

(vi) to stimulate and develop the European and international dimensions of accounting education and training;

(vii) to assist in integrating the various elements in the overall process of accounting education and training into a coherent whole.

Notes for Contributors
Accounting Education is a quarterly international journal devoted to publishing research-based papers and other information on key aspects of accounting education and training of relevance to practitioners, academics, trainers, students and professional bodies.

It is a forum for the exchange of ideas, experiences, opinions and research results relating to (a) the preparation of students/trainees for careers in public accounting, managerial accounting, financial management, corporate accounting, controllership, treasury management, financial analysis, internal auditing, and accounting in government and other non-commercial organizations; and (b) the continuing professional education of practitioners.

The coverage includes aspects of accounting education and training policy, curriculum issues, computing matters, and accounting research as it impinges on educational or training issues.

The journal seeks to make available innovative teaching resource material that can be used by readers in their own institutions. As a necessary corollary to this, the journal seeks to publish papers dealing with the effectiveness of accounting education or training.

In addition to publishing original papers the journal also includes exemplars and reviews relating to what we teach, how we teach it, and how effective our endeavors are in providing an adequate educational and training base for accounting practice.

Submission of Papers
Manuscripts should be submitted (four copies) with original figures to the Editor, Professor Richard M. S. Wilson.

The Editor will be pleased to deal with enquiries from potential authors about papers they may be considering writing or submitting to *Accounting Education*. However, comments will not be given on drafts that have not been formally submitted.

All submissions will be subject to refereeing by experts in the field. There is no submission fee and no page charges.

If a paper appears to be generally suitable and in line with the aims of the Journal it will be passed on by the Editor to an Associate Editor with arrangements being made for at least two appropriate referees to comment on the paper via a double-blind review.

The Editor will reach a decision on publishability after taking into account the reports from referees and Associate Editors. Authors will be provided with referees' reports and publishing decisions within as short a period as possible.

In certain circumstances (e.g. when papers are submitted directly to the Associate Editors in Australia, Hong Kong or the USA) a variation on the above procedure may be employed.

Copies of questionnaires and other research instruments should be included with manuscripts to facilitate editorial review. As a result of space limitations these may not be published.

Evaluative Criteria
The principal criteria by which submissions to *Accounting Education* will be assessed are: relevance, novelty, usefulness, readability, house style, clarity, conciseness, linkages to existing literature, substance, rigour, validity, readability, ethical aspects and quality relative to the aims of the Journal.

MANUSCRIPT PREPARATION

Format And Style
Manuscripts should be in English and be typed (double-spaced) with a generous margin (at least 2.5 cm) at each edge of each page on one side of international A4 bond paper.

The first page (title page) should contain the title of the paper, authors' names and institutional affiliations. The address, telephone number, fax number, telex number and E-mail code (if available) of the author to whom decisions, proofs and offprints should be sent should also be given.

Authors should enclose a brief biographical outline with their submissions.

Abstract
The second page should include the paper's title and an abstract (up to 150 words). The abstract should be an accurate representation of the paper's contents. Major results, conclusions, and/or recommendations should be given with brief details of methods, etc. There should be no indication (other than on the title page) of the identity of the author(s) or the author's (or authors') affiliations.

Keywords
Up to six keywords or descriptors that clearly describe the subject matter of the paper should be provided. These keywords will facilitate indexing as well as help in describing the subject matter for prospective readers.

References
Citations in the text should follow the Harvard scheme (i.e. name(s) of authors(s) followed by the year of publication and page numbers where relevant, all in parenthesis). Where a source has more than two authors cite the first author's name and et al. For multiple citations in the same year use a, b, and c immediately following the year of publication.

The reference section should only contain references cited in the text. These should be arranged in alphabetical order by surname of the first author (then chronologically). Each reference should contain full bibliographic details; journal titles should not be abbreviated. The following style is expected:

Gray, R.H. and Helliar, C. (eds) (1992) The British Accounting Review Research Register. London: Academic Press 5th ed..

Novin, A.M., Pearson, M.A. and Senge, S.V. (1990) Improving the curriculum for aspiring management accountants: the practitioner's point of view. Journal of Accounting Education 6 (2) Fall, 207-24.

Walsh, A.J. (1988) The making Of the chartered accountant. In D. Rowe (ed.) The Irish Chartered Accountant, pp.155-73. Dublin: Gill and Macmillan.

Figures And Tables
All figures and tables should be given titles, numbered consecutively in Arabic numerals, and referred to within the text. Labeling should be clear and of sufficient size to be legible after any necessary reduction. Lettering on line figures should usually be prepared with a 2:1 reduction in mind.

Permission to reproduce illustrations from other published work must be obtained by the author before submitting an article and any acknowledgement should be included in the figure captions.

Tables should be titled, numbered consecutively and independently of any figures, and referred to within the text.

Acknowledgements
Should appear at the end of the paper before the list of references.

Footnotes
Should be kept to a minimum and appear at the end of the paper on a separate page.

Mathematical Notation
Mathematics should only be used if this contributes significantly to the clarity and economy of presentation, or is essential to the argument of a paper. Whenever possible authors should put mathematics in an appendix. The conclusions of articles using mathematics should be summarized in a form that is intelligible to non-mathematical readers of the Journal.

Proofs And Offprints
The designated author will receive proofs which should be corrected and returned within three days. Alterations to the proofs which were not in the original manuscript are not permitted. Such revisions may be charged for as they are expensive and time consuming.

Offprints can be ordered via the form that will accompany the proofs. The designated author will receive a copy of the issue containing the paper.

Copyright Matters
Manuscripts will only be considered for *Accounting Education* if they are unpublished and not being submitted for publication elsewhere. If previously published tables, illustrations or text exceeding 200 words are to be included then the copyright holder's written permission should be obtained, and included with the submission. A clear statement should appear in the text if any material has been published elsewhere in a preliminary form.

Authors submitting articles with a view to publication warrant that the work is not an infringement of any existing copyright and agree to indemnify the publisher against any breach of such warranty.

Upon acceptance of a paper by *Accounting Education* the author(s) will be asked to transfer copyright, via a supplied form, to the publisher: Routledge, 11 New Fetter Lane, London, EC4P 4EE, UK.

Accounting Educator's Journal

ADDRESS FOR SUBMISSION:

Jeffrey L. Harkins, Editor
Accounting Educator's Journal
University of Idaho
Department of Accounting
Moscow, ID 83844-3169
USA
Phone: 208-885-7602
Fax: 208-882-8939
E-Mail: jeff@uidaho.edu
Web:
Address May Change:

PUBLICATION GUIDELINES:

Manuscript Length: 11-15
Copies Required: Four
Computer Submission: Yes
Format: For Final Draft Only
Fees to Review: 40.00 US$

Manuscript Style:
    See Manuscript Guidelines

CIRCULATION DATA:

Reader: Academics
Frequency of Issue: 2 Times/ Year
Copies per Issue: Less than 1,000
Sponsor/Publisher: No Reply
Subscribe Price: 30.00 US$ Individual
    40.00 US$ Institution
    50.00 US$ Foreign

REVIEW INFORMATION:

Type of Review: Blind Review
No. of External Reviewers: 2
No. of In House Reviewers: 0
Acceptance Rate: 21-30%
Time to Review: 4 - 6 Months
Reviewers Comments: Yes
Invited Articles: 0-5%
Fees to Publish: 0.00 US$

MANUSCRIPT TOPICS:
Accounting Education; Accounting Information Systems; Accounting Theory & Practice

MANUSCRIPT GUIDELINES/COMMENTS:

Manuscripts should be double-spaced on white 8½ x 11" paper. The cover page should include the title of manuscript, authors' full names, affiliations and complete mailing address. The second page should include the title of the manuscript and an abstract of not more than 200 words. The third page should include the manuscript title and the first page of text.

Instruments, cases of forms used to gather data should be included at the back of the paper. They need not be referenced nor published, but should be available for the reviewers to evaluate.

References to other works should be in square brackets in the body of the text and include author's name and year of publication. Include page numbers when references are to works of over 25 pages. The list of references should be in alphabetical order at the end of the text and include all referenced literature. Footnotes should be used for discussions that would disrupt the flow of the text. They should be numbered sequentially and be placed at the end of the

24

text. Authors are encouraged to include materials that will assist the reviewers, such as copies of difficult to locate materials referenced in the text and discussions of essential issues that would be excessive if included in the text. The inclusion of these materials will facilitate the review process.

Tables and figures should appear on separate pages and be placed at the end of the text. They should be numbered at the top of the page and referenced in the text. Indicate in the text where tables should be placed. Tables and figures included in manuscripts accepted for publication must be submitted in camera-ready form. Normally proportional spacing and printing on a laser printer is adequate.

Authors should send three copies of their manuscripts to the Editor.

Policy On Reproduction
Permission is hereby granted to reproduce any of the contents of the *Accounting Educator's Journal* for classroom use by faculty members. Please indicate the source and our copyright on any reproduction.

Written permission is required to reproduce any of these copyrighted material in other publications.

Mail requests for subscriptions to the Editor.

Accounting Enquiries

ADDRESS FOR SUBMISSION:

The Editor
Accounting Enquiries
2344 Canterbury Crescent
Pickering, Ontario, L1X 2T6
Canada
Phone:
Fax: 905-686-3439
E-Mail:
Web:
Address May Change:

PUBLICATION GUIDELINES:

Manuscript Length: 40 or less
Copies Required: Four
Computer Submission: No
Format: N/A
Fees to Review: 25.00 US$

Manuscript Style:
        See Manuscript Guidelines

CIRCULATION DATA:

Reader: Academics
Frequency of Issue: 2 Times/ Year
Copies per Issue: Less than 1,000
Sponsor/Publisher: Stanversal Publishing
Subscribe Price: 40.00 US$ Individual
        80.00 US$ Institution

REVIEW INFORMATION:

Type of Review: Blind Review
No. of External Reviewers: 2
No. of In House Reviewers: 1
Acceptance Rate: 33%
Time to Review: 4 - 6 Months
Reviewers Comments: Yes
Invited Articles: 6-10%
Fees to Publish: 0.00 US$

MANUSCRIPT TOPICS:

Accounting History; Accounting Information Systems; Accounting Theory & Practice; Auditing; Capital Budgeting; Cost Accounting; Government & Non Profit Accounting; Tax Accounting

MANUSCRIPT GUIDELINES/COMMENTS:

Editor and Location

Stanley C. W. Salvary
Canisius College
Wehle School of Business
Buffalo, NY 14208
Tel: 716-888-2869
Fax: 716-888-2248
salvary@CCVMSA

Editorial Policy

Accounting Enquiries is devoted to the study of accounting and accounting related issues. This journal will publish articles in, but not limited to, the following areas: accounting theory and practice, accounting history, auditing theory and practice, standard setting, and behavioral issues in accounting and auditing. The journal should prove to be a forum for scholarly debate and exchange of ideas. No paradigm will be espoused by this journal: competing theories are to be examined; contradictions are to be exposed for scrutiny; and ideas are to be explored for the purpose of theory building.

Articles will be refereed double blind. Only well researched, logically developed and properly articulated articles will be considered for publication. Both theoretical and empirical research are equally acceptable and highly desirable. Mathematical papers will be considered if those papers either demonstrate applications for solving real problems rather than assume away the problems that they are to solve, or are pedagogical notes which demonstrate for classroom purposes means of solving accounting problems. Papers which are designed to demonstrate mathematical elegance of particular models are not acceptable, since they are better suited for publication in mathematics journals. Of interest would be historical research that traces the origins of accounting ideas and examines the causes of divergence from their original conceptualization and the effect of such divergence on current day accounting practice.

Submissions
Four copies of manuscripts should be submitted to the editor at the editor's location. An abstract must accompany the manuscript. The review period takes from twelve to sixteen weeks. Manuscript style-instructions are mailed upon request.

Style Instructions
Author Information: Provide the following information: On the first page of the manuscript, (1) title, (2) author, (3) institutional affiliation, (4) address, and (5) telephone number. Reviewers will not receive this page. On the next page of the manuscript, include the title and the abstract.

Abstract: A single paragraph abstract of no more than 100 words must be included. Do not include references, footnotes, or abbreviations in the abstract.

Typing Format: The text, the footnotes, and the references are to be double-spaced. Leave wide margins for ease of editing and of typesetting.

Headings And Subheadings: No more than three levels of headings should be used. Center first-level headings and capitalize. Second-level headings are to be indented five spaces from the left margin and capitalize the first letter of the first word and of major words. Third-level headings are to be indented five spaces from the left margin and capitalize the first letter, and end these with a period. Do not use letters or numbers before headings (e.g., I, II, or A, B, etc.).

Footnotes: The initial footnote, identifying the author's(s') affiliation, should be marked with an asterisk. **Avoid footnotes in the text. Use endnotes.**

Equations: Only those equations that are referenced in the text are to be numbered consecutively. Indent equations and place numbers at the right margin. Type equations clearly with one space before and after mathematical function signs except in subscripts and superscripts. Type the main components, the equal signs, and the fraction bar on the main line of typing. Spell out in the right margin any handwritten Greek letters used in equations. Write on one line mathematical expressions used within a paragraph.

Number Of Significant Digits: In results of calculations, keep numbers of significant digits constant, not exceeding four.

Tables: Tables are to appear immediately in the text of the paper after they have been introduced. Center the word "TABLE" followed by an arabic numeral above the body of the table. Separate headings in a table from the title of the table and from the body of the table with solid lines. Use a solid line to end the table or to separate the body of the table from table footnotes. Mark table footnotes with asterisks. Capitalize only the first letter of the word "Table" (e.g., Table 1) when referring to a specific table in the text of the paper.
FIGURES: Camera-ready form of a professional quality for figures should be provided. Photocopies are acceptable at the initial stage. In the text when referring to specific figures, capitalize only the first letter (e.g., Figure 1). When labeling figures, capitalize the first letter in the word and number with arabic numerals (e.g., Figure 1). In the title of each figure, capitalize the first letter of the first word and of major words.

References: List references alphabetically by author's last name at the end of the paper. Include only those references cited in the text. Cite references in the text by enclosing the last name of the author, year, and page(s) number(s).

Style Of References: The following facts are to be included in the list of references:
   Books: (1) full name of author(s), editor(s), or institution/business responsible for writing the book; (2) full title; (3) series (if any); (4) volume number; (5) edition; (6) city of publication; (7) publisher's name; and (8) date of publication.
   Articles: (1) full name of author(s), (2) title, (3) name of periodical, (4) volume number and date, and (5) pages occupied by article. Use *full name* rather than initials whenever possible.

Presentation: To minimize editorial changes, check the manuscript for clarity, grammar, spelling, punctuation, and consistency of references.

Accounting Forum

ADDRESS FOR SUBMISSION:

Glen Lehman, Joint Chief Editor
Accounting Forum
University of South Australia
School of Accounting
North Terrace
Adelaide, SA 5000
Australia
Phone: 61-08-8302 2309
Fax: 61-08-8302 0102
E-Mail: glen.lehman@unisa.edu.au
Web:
Address May Change:

CIRCULATION DATA:

Reader: Business Persons, Academics
Frequency of Issue: Quarterly
Copies per Issue: Less than 1,000
Sponsor/Publisher: Basil Blackwell Ltd.
Subscribe Price: 45.00 AUS$ Individual
    55.00 AUS$ Institution/ Company
    80.00 AUS$ Library

PUBLICATION GUIDELINES:

Manuscript Length: Open
Copies Required: Two
Computer Submission: Yes
Format: Word for Windows/IBM compat.
Fees to Review: 0.00 US$

Manuscript Style:
    Uniform System of Citation (Harvard
    Blue Book)

REVIEW INFORMATION:

Type of Review: Blind Review
No. of External Reviewers: 3
No. of In House Reviewers: 0
Acceptance Rate: 11-20%
Time to Review: 2 - 3 Months
Reviewers Comments: Yes
Invited Articles: 0-5%
Fees to Publish: 0.00 US$

MANUSCRIPT TOPICS:

Accounting Information Systems; Accounting Theory & Practice; Auditing; Cost Accounting;
Fiscal Policy; Government & Non Profit Accounting; Social and Environmental Accounting

MANUSCRIPT GUIDELINES/COMMENTS:

Tony Tinker, Joint Chief Editor
City University Of New York
Baruch College Box E 0723
17 Lexington Avenue
New York, NY 10010 USA
Phone: 212-802-6436, Fax: 212-802-6435
Email: tony.tinker@MSN.com

Accounting Forum is a quarterly journal covering all aspects of accounting. *Accounting Forum* is a vehicle for scholastic papers of quality which have the potential to advance the knowledge of theory and practice in all areas of accounting, business finance and associated areas.

1. Only manuscripts not currently under consideration by another publisher will be considered.

2. A maximum length of 5,000 words will generally be required and the Editor reserves the right to modify articles to increase readability. Articles will also be considered in sections for consecutive issues of AF.

3. Authors should indicate their position and affiliation and provide an address to which two complimentary copies of AF will be posted.

4. Three copies of each manuscript (and on IBM Compatible Word for Windows 6.0 disk if possible) should be typed, double-spaced and have wide margins. **An abstract not exceeding 50 words should be included**.

5. All diagrams and graphs should be prepared on separate sheets and be of a professional quality ready for reproduction.

6. The Harvard (author-date) System should be used:

(1) In citing works quote the author followed by the date of publication, and if relevant, page numbers eg. (Brown 1988, p.3).

(2) A list of references is required, containing only cited references, in alphabetical order by author. This should include the author's name, year of publication in round brackets, the publisher and place of publication. For articles, the periodical, volume number, month of issue and page numbers are required.

7. Address all contributions to Glen Lehman, Joint Chief Editor.

Subscription Rates: Australia, add $5 for postage, International, add $15 for postage

Accounting Historians Journal

ADDRESS FOR SUBMISSION:

Richard Fleischman, Editor
Accounting Historians Journal
John Carroll University
Department of Accounting
University Heights, OH 44118
USA
Phone: 216-397-4443
Fax: 216-397-3063
E-Mail: fleischman@jcu.edu
Web:
Address May Change: 12/31/00

PUBLICATION GUIDELINES:

Manuscript Length: 7000 Words Maximum
Copies Required: Three
Computer Submission: No
Format: N/A
Fees to Review: 0.00 US$

Manuscript Style:
    See Manuscript Guidelines

CIRCULATION DATA:

Reader: Academics
Frequency of Issue: 2 Times/ Year
Copies per Issue: 1,001 - 2,000
Sponsor/Publisher: Professional Assoc.
Subscribe Price: 40.00 US$

REVIEW INFORMATION:

Type of Review: Blind Review
No. of External Reviewers: 2
No. of In House Reviewers: 0
Acceptance Rate: 20-25%
Time to Review: 3 Months
Reviewers Comments: Yes
Invited Articles: 0-5%
Fees to Publish: 0.00 US$

MANUSCRIPT TOPICS:

Accounting History; Accounting Information Systems; Accounting Theory & Practice; Auditing; Cost Accounting; Economic History; Gender Issues in Accounting; Government & Non Profit Accounting; International Accounting; International Economics & Trade; Public Policy Accounting; Tax Accounting

MANUSCRIPT GUIDELINES/COMMENTS:

Manuscripts should be in English and of acceptable style and organization for clarity of presentation. Submit three copies, typewritten, double-spaced on one side of 8 ½ X 11 inch (approx. 28.5 cm X 28.0 cm) white paper; paragraphs should be indented. The manuscript should not exceed 7,000 words and margins should be wide enough to facilitate editing and duplication. All pages, including bibliographic pages, should be serially numbered. Manuscripts should be run through a spellcheck software program or similar review prior to submission. [**Type of Review is double blind**]

Cover Sheet. The cover sheet should state the title of the paper, name(s) of author(s), affiliation(s), the address for future correspondence and the FAX number or EMAIL address (or both) of the author designated as the contact person for the manuscript.

Abstract. An abstract of not more than 100 words should accompany the manuscript on a separate page. The title, but not the name(s) of the author(s) should appear on the abstract page and on the first page of the manuscript.

Major Headings within the manuscript should be centered, unnumbered and capitalized. Subheadings should be on a separate line beginning flush with the left margin, italicized, with the first letter of major words capitalized. Text should follow immediately on the same line, separated from the header by a colon.

Tables, Figures And Exhibits should be numbered (arabic), titled, and, when appropriate, referenced. Limited use of original documents can be accommodated in the Journal if authors can provide good quality reproductions. Important textual materials may be presented in both the original language and the English translation. Tables, and similar items must be discussed in the text and will not be included unless they lend support to the text.

Literature References
Footnotes should not be used for literature references. The work cited should be referenced using the author's name and date of publication in the body of the text, inside square brackets, i.e., Garner [1954, p. 33]. If the author's name is mentioned in the text, it need not be repeated, i.e., Garner [1954, p. 33] concluded.... If a reference has more than three authors, only the first name and "et al" should be used in the text citation. References to statutes, legal treatise or court cases should follow the accepted form of legal citation. All references to direct quotations should contain page numbers.

Content Footnotes
Content footnotes may be used sparingly to expand upon or comment upon the text itself. These should numbered consecutively throughout the manuscript and should appear at the bottom of the page on which the reference appears.

Bibliography
A bibliography of works cited should appear at the end of the manuscript. The works cited should be listed alphabetically according to the surname of the first author. Information about books and journals should include the following information
Books—author(s), date of publication, title italicized, place of publication, and publisher (in parentheses); **Articles**—author(s), date of publication, title (with quotation marks), journal italicized, volume and number, page numbers. **Multiple works by an author** should be listed in chronological order; if multiple works appear in a single year, the suffix a, b, etc. should be used to identify each work.

For questions of style not covered above, authors should consult a style manual such as Turabian, Kate L. *A Manual For Writers Of Term Papers, Theses And Dissertations*, published by the University of Chicago Press.

Diskette. When a manuscript has been accepted for publication, authors will be asked to submit a diskette with the final manuscript. The diskette should be prepared in IBM compatible ASCII file format.

Complimentary Copies And Reprints. Author(s) will be provided with 3 copies of the Journal issue in which the manuscript is published. Reprints may be ordered from the printer; the minimum order is 100. The printer will establish the price and bill the author(s) directly for the cost of the reprints.

Accounting History

ADDRESS FOR SUBMISSION:

Garry D. Carnegie, Editor
Accounting History
Deakin University
School of Accounting and Finance
Geelong, Victoria, 3217
Australia
Phone: 61 3 5227 2733
Fax: 61 3 5227 2264
E-Mail: carnegie@deakin.edu.au
Web:
Address May Change:

PUBLICATION GUIDELINES:

Manuscript Length: 26-30
Copies Required: Three
Computer Submission: No
Format: N/A
Fees to Review: 0.00 US$

Manuscript Style:
    See Manuscript Guidelines

CIRCULATION DATA:

Reader: Academics
Frequency of Issue: 2 Times/ Year
Copies per Issue: Less than 1,000
Sponsor/Publisher: Academic Association
Subscribe Price: 68.00 AUS$
    80.00 AUS$ Airmail

REVIEW INFORMATION:

Type of Review: Blind Review
No. of External Reviewers: 2
No. of In House Reviewers: 0
Acceptance Rate: 21-30%
Time to Review: 2 - 3 Months
Reviewers Comments: Yes
Invited Articles: 11-20%
Fees to Publish: 0.00 US$

MANUSCRIPT TOPICS:
Accounting History; Accounting Theory & Practice; Auditing; Cost Accounting; Economic History

MANUSCRIPT GUIDELINES/COMMENTS:

Accounting History is sponsored by Accounting History Special Interest Group of the Accounting Association of Australia and New Zealand.

Editorial Policies
Accounting History aims to publish quality historical papers. These could be concerned with exploring the advent and development of accounting bodies, conventions, ideas, practices and rules. They should attempt to identify the individuals and also the local, time-specific environmental factors which affected accounting, and should endeavour to assess accounting's impact on organisational and social functioning.

Editorial Procedures
1. Address copies of all manuscripts and editorial correspondence to the Editor.

2. The cover of the manuscript should contain the following:
- (i)　　Title of manuscript.
- (ii)　　Name of author(s).
- (iii)　　Institutional affiliation of author(s) including telephone, fax and email address(es).
- (iv)　　Month of submission.
- (v)　　Any acknowledgment, not exceeding 50 words. An acknowledgment should not be included in the consecutive number of other notes.

3. An abstract of no more than 150 words should be presented on a separate page immediately preceding the text of the manuscript.

4. Three copies of all manuscripts should be submitted for review. Manuscripts should be typed on one side of the paper only, double-spaced and all pages should be numbered. Manuscripts currently under review for publication in other outlets should not be submitted.

5. Headings should be formatted so that major headings are flush left, bold, lower case and two font sizes larger than the main text. Second level headings should be flush left, bold, lower case and same size as main text. Third level headings should be flush left, italics, lower case and same size as main text. For example:

1. **Flush left, bold, lower case, two font sizes larger than main text**
2. **Flush left, bold, lower case, same size font as main text**
3. *Flush left, italics, lower case, same size font as main text.*

6. Figures, tables, diagrams and appendices should be numbered consecutively and titled.

7. Notes should appear as endnotes and be numbered consecutively. They should begin on a separate page at the end of the manuscript.

8. References should appear in the text as Walker (1998) or Walker (1998, p.35). The full references should be typed on separate sheets and appear after any notes at the end of the manuscript. The following rules should be adopted:
Periodicals:
Walker, S.P., (1998), "More Sherry and Sandwiches? Incrementalism and the Regulation of Late Victorian Bank Auditing", *Accounting History*, NS Vol. 3, No. 1, May, pp.33-54.
Books:
Crosby, A.W., (1997), *The Measure of Reality. Quantification and Western Society, 1250-1600*, Cambridge: Cambridge University Press.

9. When a paper is accepted for publication the authors are requested to provide a copy of the paper on a 3 1/2" diskette as well as a printed copy of the accepted version of the paper. Submissions saved in text format (specifically ASCII text) are preferred. Microsoft Word (for Macintosh or PC compatibles) is the preferred word processing format.

Accounting Horizons

ADDRESS FOR SUBMISSION:

Eugene A. Imhoff, Jr., Editor
Accounting Horizons
University of Michigan
Business School
701 Tappan Street
Ann Arbor, MI 48109-1234
USA
Phone: 734-763-1192
Fax: 734-647-2871
E-Mail: imhoff@umich.edu
Web:
Address May Change:

CIRCULATION DATA:

Reader: Business Persons, & Academic
Frequency of Issue: Quarterly
Copies per Issue: More than 25,000
Sponsor/Publisher: American Accounting
   Association
Subscribe Price: 75.00 US$

PUBLICATION GUIDELINES:

Manuscript Length: 7000 words maximum
Copies Required: Five
Computer Submission: Yes
Format: WordPerfect,ASCII,Microsoft
Fees to Review: 75.00 US$
   100.00 US$ Nonmembers of AAA

Manuscript Style:
   Chicago Manual of Style

REVIEW INFORMATION:

Type of Review: Blind Review
No. of External Reviewers: 2
No. of In House Reviewers: 1
Acceptance Rate: 11-20%
Time to Review: 2 - 3 Months
Reviewers Comments: Yes
Invited Articles: 6-10%
Fees to Publish: 0.00 US$

MANUSCRIPT TOPICS:

Accounting & Tax Policy; Accounting Theory & Practice; Auditing; Cost Accounting;
Government & Non Profit Accounting; Tax Accounting

MANUSCRIPT GUIDELINES/COMMENTS:

Accounting Horizons is a publication of the American Accounting Association (AAA)
designed primarily to disseminate papers of an applied nature. *Accounting Horizons* represents
the AAA's partnership between the profession of accounting and accounting education,
serving as the principle vehicle for written scholarly communication between and among its
constituents. Accordingly, papers submitted for publication should address topics of interest to
accounting educators, practicing accountants and students of accounting, and should
communicate effectively to all three groups.

Publishing original scholarly research, or "discovery" research, is the primary objective of
many accounting journals, including the AAA's own *The Accounting Review*. *Accounting
Horizons* does not have discovery research as its primary focus. In an effort to communicate
effectively with its readership, *Accounting Horizons* will encourage the submission and

publication of a wide variety of applied forms of scholarship. These forms of scholarship include:

1. Papers which summarize and synthesize original discovery-based research whose findings may have already been published or accepted for publication by other scholarly journals which publish primarily for academic audiences. Such papers should help accounting educators, practicing accountants and students of accounting to understand the important implications of scientific-based discovery research. Such papers may summarize or synthesize one or more discovery articles, and may be prepared by an author who conducted some portion of the original discovery or by others who are able to craft a paper that contributes to the literature by communicating the relevance of contributions from discovery research to a broader audience.

2. Original scientific-based research of discovery which employs state-of-the-art methodologies and is communicated in a form that is comprehensible to a substantial portion of the readership of *Accounting Horizons*.

3. Papers that provide discussions or illustrations of important, useful or interesting accounting issues that are informative to educators, practitioners and students of accounting. Such applied or pedagogical efforts might contribute to the literature by using illustrative cases from practice, small sample studies which document the practical aspects of important accounting policy issues such as tax rules or accounting and auditing standards.

4. Both solicited and unsolicited commentaries designed to enhance the communication between practitioners and academe.

The common thread which ties these four forms of scholarship together is that they all should provide contributions which are relevant to a large majority of all three constituents. Accounting Horizons can best achieve its objectives by disseminating relevant information in one of these forms to its readership. We hope that authors will keep these objectives in mind when submitting manuscripts to *Accounting Horizons*.

Submission Of Manuscripts
Authors should note the following guidelines for submitting manuscripts:

1. Manuscripts currently under consideration by another journal or other publisher should not be submitted. The author must state that the work is not submitted or published elsewhere.

2. In the case of manuscripts reporting on field surveys or experiments, five copies of the instrument (questionnaire, case, interview plan or the like) should be submitted.

3. Five copies should be submitted together with a check in U.S. funds for $75.00 for members or $100.00 for nonmembers of the AAA, made payable to the American Accounting Association and sent to Professor Eugene A. Imhoff, Jr., University of Michigan Business School, 701 Tappan Street, Ann Arbor, MI 48109-1234. The submission fee is nonrefundable.

4. The author should retain a copy of the paper.

5. Revisions must be submitted within 12 months from request, otherwise they will be considered new submissions.

Comments

Comments on articles previously published in *Accounting Horizons* will be reviewed (anonymously) by two reviewers in sequence. The first reviewer will be the author of the original article being subjected to critique. If substance permits, a suitably revised comment will be sent to a second reviewer to determine its publishability in *Accounting Horizons*. If a comment is accepted for publication, the original author will be invited to reply. All other editorial requirements, as enumerated above, also apply to proposed comments.

Manuscript Preparation And Style

The *Accounting Horizons* manuscript preparation guidelines follow (with a slight modification) documentation 2 of the *Chicago Manual Of Style* (14th ed.; University of Chicago Press). Another helpful guide to usage and style is *The Elements Of Style*, by William Strunk, Jr., and E. B. White (Macmillan). Spelling follows *Webster's International Dictionary*.

Format

1. All manuscripts should be typed on one side of 8 1/2 x 11" good quality paper and be double spaced, except for indented quotations.

2. Manuscripts should be as concise as the subject and research method permit, generally not to exceed 7,000 words.

3. Margins should be at least one inch from top, bottom and sides to facilitate editing and duplication.

4. To assure anonymous review, authors should not identify themselves directly or indirectly in their papers. Single authors should not use the editorial "we."

5. A cover page should include the title of the paper, the author's name, title and affiliation, any acknowledgments, and a footnote indicating whether the author would be willing to share the data (see last paragraph in this statement).

6. All pages, including tables, appendices and references, should be serially numbered.

7. Spell out numbers from one to ten, except when used in tables and lists, and when used with mathematical, statistical, scientific or technical units and quantities, such as distances, weights and measures. For example: three days; 3 kilometers; 30 years. All other numbers are expressed numerically. Generally when using approximate terms spell out the number, for example, approximately thirty years.

8. In text use the word percent; in tables and figures, the symbol % is used.

9. Use a hyphen to join unit modifiers or to clarify usage. For example: *a well-presented analysis; re-form*. See *Webster's* for correct usage.

10. Headings should be arranged so that major headings are centered, bold and capitalized. Second level headings should be flush left, bold, and both upper and lower case. Third level headings should be flush left, bold, italic, and both upper and lower case. Fourth level headings should be paragraph indent, bold and lower case. Headings and subheadings should not be numbered. For example:

A CENTERED, BOLD, ALL CAPITALIZED, FIRST LEVEL HEADING
A Flush Left, Bold, Upper and Lower Case, Second Level Heading
A Flush Left, Bold, Italic, Upper and Lower Case, Third Level Heading
A paragraph indent, bold, lower case, fourth level heading. Text starts...

Synopsis
A synopsis of about 150-200 words should be presented on a separate page immediately preceding the text. The synopsis should be nonmathematical and include a readable summary of the research question, method, and the significance of the findings and contribution. The title, but not the author's name or other identification designations, should appear on the synopsis page.

Tables And Figures
The author should note the following general requirements:

1. Each table and figure (graphic) should appear on a separate page and should be placed at the end of the text. Each should bear an arabic number and a complete title indicating the exact contents of the table or figure.

2. A reference to each table or figure should be made in the text.

3. The author should indicate by marginal notation where each table or figure should be inserted in the text, e.g., (Insert Table X here).

4. Tables or figures should be reasonably interpreted without reference to the text.

5. Source lines and notes should be included as necessary.

6. Figures must be prepared in a form suitable for printing.

Mathematical Notation
Mathematical notation should be employed only where its rigor and precision are necessary, and in such circumstances authors should explain in the narrative format the principal operations performed. Notation should be avoided in footnotes. Unusual symbols, particularly if handwritten, should be identified in the margin when they first appear. Displayed material should clearly indicate the alignment, superscripts and subscripts. Equations should be numbered in parentheses flush with the right-hand margin.

Documentation

Citations: Work cited should use the "author-date system" keyed to a list of works in the reference list (see below). Authors should make an effort to include the relevant page numbers in the cited works.

1. In the text, works are cited as follows: author's last name and date, without comma, in parentheses: for example (Jones 1987); with two authors: (Jones and Freeman 1973); with more than two: (Jones et al. 1985); with more than one source cited together: (Jones 1987; Freeman 1986); with two or more works by one author: (Jones 1985, 1987).

2. Unless confusion would result, do not use "p." or "pp." before page numbers, for example (Jones 1987, 115).

3. When the reference list contains more than one work of an author published in the same year, the suffix *a, b*, etc. follows the date in the text citation: for example (Jones 1987a) or (Jones 1987a; Freeman 1985b).

4. If an author's name is mentioned in the text, it need not be repeated in the citation: for example "Jones (1987, 115) says..."

5. Citations to institutional works should use acronyms or short titles where practicable: for example, (AAAASOBAT 1966); (AICPA *Cohen Commission Report* 1977). Where brief, the full title of an institutional work might be shown in a citation: for example (ICAEW *The Corporate Report* 1975).

6. If the manuscript refers to statutes, legal treatises or court cases, citations acceptable in law reviews should be used.

Reference List: Every manuscript must include a list of references containing only those works cited. Each entry should contain all data necessary for unambiguous identification. With the author-date system, use the following format recommended by the *Chicago Manual*:

1. Arrange citations in alphabetical order according to surname of the first author or the name of the institution responsible for the citation.

2. Use authors' initials instead of proper names.

3. Dates of publication should be placed immediately after authors' names.

4. Titles of journals should not be abbreviated.

5. Multiple works by the same author(s) should be listed in chronological order of publication. Two or more works by the same author(s) in the same year are distinguished by letters after the date.

40

Sample entries are as follows:

American Accounting Association, Committee on Concepts and Standards for External Financial Reports. 1977. *Statement on Accounting Theory and Theory Acceptance*. Sarasota, FL: AAA.

Becker, H., and D. Fritsche. 1987. Business ethics: A cross-cultural comparison of managers' attitudes. *Journal of Business Ethics* 6: 289-295.

Bowman, R. 1980a. The importance of market-value measurement of debt in assessing leverage. *Journal of Accounting Research* 18 (Spring): 617-630.

_____. 1980b. The debt equivalence of leases: An empirical investigation. *The Accounting Review* 55 (April): 237-253.

Cohen, C. 1991. Chief or indians-Women in accountancy. *Australian Accountant* (December): 20-30.

Harry, J., and N. S. Goldner. 1972. The null relationship between teaching and research. *Sociology of Education* 45 (1): 47-60.

Jensen, M. C., and C. W. Smith. 1985. Stockholder, manager, and creditor interests: Applications of agency theory. In *Recent Advances in Corporate Finance*, edited by E. Altman and M. Subrahmanyam. Homewood, IL: Richard D. Irwin.

Munn, G. G., F. L. Garcia, and C. J. Woelfel, eds. 1991. *Encyclopedia of Banking and Finance*, 9th ed. Chicago, IL: St. James Press.

Ohlson, J. A. 1991. Earnings, book values, and dividends in security valuation. Working paper, Columbia University.

Footnotes: Footnotes are not to be used for documentation. Textual footnotes should be used only for extensions and useful excursions of information that if included in the body of the text might disrupt its continuity. Footnotes should be consecutively numbered throughout the manuscript with superscript Arabic numerals. Footnote text should be double-spaced and placed at the end of the article.

Policy On Reproduction

An objective of *Accounting Horizons* is to promote the wide dissemination of the results of systematic scholarly inquiries into the broad field of accounting.

Permission is hereby granted to reproduce any of the contents of *Horizons* for use in courses of instruction, as long as the source and American Accounting Association copyright are indicated in any such reproductions.

Written application must be made to the Editor for permission to reproduce any of the contents of *Horizons* for use in other than courses of instruction e.g., inclusion in books of readings or in any other publications intended for general distribution. In consideration for the grant of permission by *Horizons* in such instances, the applicant must notify the author(s) in writing of the intended use to be made of each reproduction. Normally, *Horizons* will not assess a charge for the waiver of copyright.

Except where otherwise noted in articles, the copyright interest has been transferred to the American Accounting Association. Where the author(s) has (have) not transferred the copyright to the Association, applicants must seek permission to reproduce (for all purposes) directly from the author(s).

Policy On Data Availability
The following policy has been adopted by the Executive Committee in its April 1989 meeting. "An objective of (*The Accounting Review, Accounting Horizons, Issues In Accounting Education*) is to provide the widest possible dissemination of knowledge based on systematic scholarly inquiries into accounting as a field of professional, research and educational activity. As part of this process, authors are encouraged to make their data available for use by others in extending or replicating results reported in their articles. Authors of articles which report data dependent results should footnote the status of data availability and, when pertinent, this should be accompanied by information on how the data may be obtained."

Accounting Instructors' Report

ADDRESS FOR SUBMISSION:

Belverd E. Needles, Jr., Editor
Accounting Instructors' Report
Depaul University
School of Accountancy
1 East Jackson Blvd.
Chicago, IL 60604-2287
USA
Phone: 312-362-5130
Fax: 312-362-6208
E-Mail: bneedles@wppost.depaul.edu
Web:
Address May Change:

PUBLICATION GUIDELINES:

Manuscript Length: 1-5
Copies Required: Two
Computer Submission: Yes
Format: N/A
Fees to Review: 0.00 US$

Manuscript Style:
    No Reply

CIRCULATION DATA:

Reader: Academics
Frequency of Issue: 2 Times/ Year
Copies per Issue: 5,001 - 10,000
Sponsor/Publisher: Profit Oriented Corp.
Subscribe Price: No Reply

REVIEW INFORMATION:

Type of Review: Blind Review
No. of External Reviewers: 1
No. of In House Reviewers: 1
Acceptance Rate: 21-30%
Time to Review: 4 - 6 Months
Reviewers Comments: No
Invited Articles: 6-10%
Fees to Publish: 0.00 US$

MANUSCRIPT TOPICS:
Accounting Education; Accounting Theory & Practice

MANUSCRIPT GUIDELINES/COMMENTS:

Accounting Management & Information Technologies

ADDRESS FOR SUBMISSION:

Richard J. Boland, Editor
Accounting Management & Information
   Technologies
Case Western University
Weatherhead School of Management
10900 Euclid Avenue
Cleveland, OH 44106-7235
USA
Phone: 216-368-6022
Fax: 216-368-4776
E-Mail: rjb7@po.cwru.edu
Web:
Address May Change:

PUBLICATION GUIDELINES:

Manuscript Length: Any
Copies Required: Four
Computer Submission: No
Format: N/A
Fees to Review: 0.00 US$

Manuscript Style:
   See Manuscript Guidelines

CIRCULATION DATA:

Reader: Academics
Frequency of Issue: Quarterly
Copies per Issue: No Reply
Sponsor/Publisher: Pergamon Press
Subscribe Price: 478.00 US$

REVIEW INFORMATION:

Type of Review: Blind Review
No. of External Reviewers: 3
No. of In House Reviewers: 0
Acceptance Rate: 11-20%
Time to Review: 2 - 3 Months
Reviewers Comments: Yes
Invited Articles: 0-5%
Fees to Publish: 0.00 US$

MANUSCRIPT TOPICS:

Accounting Information Systems; Accounting Theory & Practice; Strategic Management Policy; Technology Impact

MANUSCRIPT GUIDELINES/COMMENTS:

Submission of Papers

Authors are requested to submit their original manuscript and figures with four copies to: Richard J. Boland, Jr., Weatherhead School of Management, Case Western Reserve University, 10900 Euclid Avenue, Cleveland, OH 441067235, U.S.A. Cleveland, USA. Tel: +1 216 368 6022; Fax: +1 216 368 4776: E-mail: rjb@po.cwru.edu

Manuscripts should be carefully prepared using the *Publication Manual of* the American Psychological Association, 4th ed., Washington, DC: American Psychological Association. Submission of a paper implies that it has not been published previously, that it is not under consideration for publication elsewhere, and that if accepted it will not be published elsewhere in the same form, in English or in any other language, without the written consent of the publisher.

Manuscript Preparation

General: Manuscripts must be typewritten, double-spaced with wide margins on one side of white paper. Good quality printouts with a font size of 12 or 10 pt are required. The corresponding author should be identified (include a Fax number and E-mail address). Full postal addresses must be given for all co-authors. Authors should consult a recent issue of the journal for style if possible. An electronic copy of the paper should accompany the final version. The Editors reserve the right to adjust style to certain standards of uniformity. Authors should retain a copy of their manuscript since we cannot accept responsibility for damage or loss of papers. Original manuscripts are discarded one month after publication unless the Publisher is asked to return original material after use. If the manuscript refers to questionnaires or other research instruments which are not fully reproduced in the text, authors must also submit three copies of the complete research instrument.

Abstracts: Four copies of an abstract not exceeding 150 words should accompany each manuscript submitted. Authors are also asked to supply a maximum of 10 "key" words or phrases which will be useful for indexing purposes.

Text: Follow this order when typing manuscripts: Title, Authors, Affiliations, Abstract, Keywords, Main text, Acknowledgements, Appendix, References, Vitae, Figure Captions and then Tables. Do not import the Figures or Tables into your text. The corresponding author should be identified with an asterisk and footnote. All other footnotes (except for table footnotes) should be identified with superscript Arabic numbers.

References: All publications cited in the text should be presented in a list of references following the text of the manuscript. In the text refer to the author's name (without initials) and year of publication (e.g. "Since Peterson (1993) has shown that ..." or "This is in agreement with results obtained later (Kramer, 1994)"). For 2-6 authors, all authors are to be listed at first citation, with "&" separating the last two authors. For more than six authors, use the first six authors followed by et al. Subsequent citations for three of more authors use author et al. The list of references should be arranged alphabetically by authors' names. The manuscript should be carefully checked to ensure that the spelling of authors' names and dates are exactly the same in the text as in the reference list. References should be given in the following form:

Jarvenpaa, S.L., & Dickson, G.W. (1988). Graphics and managerial decision making Research based guidelines. *Communications of* the ACM, 31, 764-774.

Zuboff, S. (1988). In the age *of* the smart *machine. New* York: Basic Books.

Bijker, W.E., Hughes, T.P., & Pinch, T. (Eds.). (1987). *The social construction of technological systems.* Cambridge, MA: MIT Press.

Boland, R.J. (1989). Metaphorical traps in developing information systems for human progress. In K. Klein & K. Kumar, *Systems development* for *human progress* (pp. 277-290). New York: North Holland Press.

Research Instruments: Because of space limitations, questionnaires and other research instruments sometimes may not be fully reproduced in the published paper. When they are not fully reproduced a note must be inserted in the text of the paper indicating the address from which copies of the complete instrument are available.

Illustrations: All illustrations should be provided in camera-ready form, suitable for reproduction (which may include reduction) without retouching. Photographs, charts and diagrams are all to be referred to as "Figure(s)" and should be numbered consecutively in the order in which they are referred. They should accompany the manuscript, but should not be included within the text. All illustrations should be clearly marked on the back with the figure number and the author's name. All figures are to have a caption. Captions should be supplied on a separate sheet. *Line drawings:* Good quality printouts on white paper produced in black ink are required. All lettering, graph lines and points on graphs should be sufficiently large and bold to permit reproduction when the diagram has een reduced to a size suitable for inclusion in the journal. Dye-line prints or photocopies are not suitable for reproduction. Do not use any type of shading on computer-generated illustrations. *Photographs:* Original photographs must be supplied as they are to be reproduced (e.g. black and white or colour). If necessary, a scale should be marked on the photograph. Please note that photocopies of photographs are not acceptable. Colour: Authors will be charged for colour at current printing costs.

Tables: Tables should be numbered consecutively and given a suitable caption and each table typed on a separate sheet. Footnotes to tables should be typed below the table and should be referred to by superscript lowercase letters. No vertical rules should be used. Tables should not duplicate results presented elsewhere in the manuscript, (e.g. in graphs).

Electronic Submission
Authors should submit an electronic copy of their paper with the final version of the manuscript. The electronic copy should match the hardcopy exactly. Always keep a backup copy of the electronic file for reference and safety. Full details of electronic submission and formats can be obtained from http://www.elsevier.nl/locate/disksub or from Author Services at Elsevier Science.

Proofs
Proofs will be sent to the author (first-named author if no corresponding author is identified for multi-authored papers) and should be returned within 48 hours of receipt. Corrections should be restricted to typesetting errors; any others may be charged to the author. Any queries should be answered in full. Please note that authors are urged to check their proofs carefully before return, since the inclusion of late corrections cannot be guaranteed. Proofs are to be returned to the Log-in Department, Elsevier Science, Stover Court, Bampfylde Street, Exeter, Devon EM 2AH, U.K.

Offprints

Twenty-five offprints will be supplied free of charge. Additional off prints and copies of the issue can be ordered at a specially reduced rate using the order form sent to the corresponding author after the manuscript has been accepted. Orders for reprints (produced after publication of an article) will incur a 50% surcharge.

Copyright

All authors must sign the "Transfer of Copyright" agreement before the article can be published. This transfer agreement enables Elsevier Science Ltd to protect the copyrighted material for the authors, but does not relinquish the author's proprietary rights. The copyright transfer covers the exclusive rights to reproduce and distribute the article, including reprints, photographic reproductions, microfilm or any other reproductions of similar nature and translations. It includes the right to adapt the article for use in conjunction with computer systems and programs, including reproduction or publication in machine-readable form and incorporation in retrieval systems. Authors are responsible for obtaining from the copyright holder permission to reproduce any figures for which copyright exists.

Author Services

For queries relating to the general submission of manuscripts (including electronic text and artwork) and the status of accepted manuscripts, please contact Author Services, Log-in Department, Elsevier Science, The Boulevard, Langford Lane, Kidlington, Oxford OX5 1GB, UK. E-mail: authors@elsevier.co.uk, Fax: +44 (0) 1865 843905, Tel: +44 (0) 1865 843900. Authors can also keep track of the progress of their accepted article through our OASIS system on the Internet. For information on an article go to this Internet page and key in the corresponding author's name and the Elsevier reference number.

Accounting Research Journal

ADDRESS FOR SUBMISSION:

Robert Faff, Joint Editor
Accounting Research Journal
RMIT Business
Economics & Finance
GPO Box 2476V
Melbourne, VIC,, 3001
Australia
Phone: 03 9925-5905
Fax: 03 9925-5986
E-Mail: robertf@bf.rmit.edu.au
Web:
Address May Change:

PUBLICATION GUIDELINES:

Manuscript Length: N/A
Copies Required: Three
Computer Submission: Yes
Format: 3.5 disk
Fees to Review: 0.00 US$

Manuscript Style:
  See Manuscript Guidelines

CIRCULATION DATA:

Reader: Academics
Frequency of Issue: 2 Times/Year
Copies per Issue: Less than 1,000
Sponsor/Publisher: N/A
Subscribe Price: 30.00 AUS$
    25.00 AUS$ New Zealand

REVIEW INFORMATION:

Type of Review: N/A
No. of External Reviewers: 2
No. of In House Reviewers: 1
Acceptance Rate: 21-30%
Time to Review: 2 - 3 Months
Reviewers Comments: Yes
Invited Articles: 0-5%
Fees to Publish: 0.00 US$

MANUSCRIPT TOPICS:

Accounting Information Systems; Accounting Theory & Practice; Auditing; Corporate Finance; Cost Accounting; Government & Non Profit Accounting; International Finance; Portfolio & Security Analysis; Tax Accounting

MANUSCRIPT GUIDELINES/COMMENTS:

Joint Editor: Scott Holmes
        University of Newcastle
        Department of Commerce
        University Drive
        Callaghan NSW 2308
        Phone: 049 215 036
        Fax: 049 216 905

Editorial Policy
The objective of the *Accounting Research Journal* is to provide a valuable forum for communication between the profession and academics on the research and practice of

accounting, finance, auditing, commercial law and cognate disciplines. The editors would encourage submissions in any of the above areas, which have a practical and/or applied focus. However, this policy does not exclude the publication of theoretical works. The journal is committed to the dissemination of research findings to as wide an audience as possible. As a result, we strongly encourage authors to consider a wide and varied readership when writing papers.

Three types of articles are published in the *Accounting Research Journal*:
(1) Main articles; (2) Notes and Comments; and (3) Educational articles.

Main Articles. These papers are written in an academic style, providing considerable detail about the issues at hand. The paper may be either theoretical or empirical or a combination of both. Work involving a case study approach is acceptable. In addition, well balanced review articles covering fundamental and/or topical areas relevant to the accounting and finance disciplines will be encouraged.

Notes And Comments. These papers are shorter pieces of work that, for example, focus on a specific topical issue or critique a previously published paper.

Educational Articles. These papers would involve issues or experiments which have accounting education (broadly defined) as their central focus. While these papers would normally be shorter than main articles, longer pieces may be justified depending on the specific topic area.

Manuscript Award
An annual prize of $500 and a certificate will be awarded to the best manuscript published in the *Accounting Research Journal*.

Preparation Of Manuscripts
1. Manuscripts should be typed on one side of the paper only, double-spaced; all pages should be numbered.

2. Headings, Figures, Tables and Diagrams should be numbered consecutively and titled.

3. Footnotes should be numbered consecutively with superscript arabic numerals. Footnotes must appear on the page they refer to and not on a separate sheet at the end of the manuscript.

4. References should appear in the text as Brown (1988) or Brown (1988, p. 120). The full references should be typed on separate sheets at the end of the manuscript. The following rules should be adopted:

Monographs
Brown, X.Y. (1988), Advanced Commercial Law, Brett Publishing Co., Brisbane.
Periodicals
Brown, X.Y. and Black, A.B. (1988), 'The Current Tax Law,' Journal of   Taxation, June, vol 1, pp. 15-50.

Accounting Review

ADDRESS FOR SUBMISSION:

Gerald L. Salamon, Editor
Accounting Review
Indiana University
School of Business
Bloomington, IN 47405
USA
Phone: 812-855-2612
Fax: 812-855-4985
E-Mail: areview@indiana.edu
Web:
Address May Change:

PUBLICATION GUIDELINES:

Manuscript Length: 26-30
Copies Required: Four
Computer Submission: No
Format: N/A
Fees to Review: 75.00 US$
          100.00 US$ Nonmembers of AAA

Manuscript Style:
    See Manuscript Guidelines

CIRCULATION DATA:

Reader: Academics
Frequency of Issue: Quarterly
Copies per Issue: 5,001 - 10,000
Sponsor/Publisher: American Accounting
   Association
Subscribe Price: 100.00 US$

REVIEW INFORMATION:

Type of Review: Blind Review
No. of External Reviewers: 2
No. of In House Reviewers: 0
Acceptance Rate: 11-20%
Time to Review: 2 - 3 Months
Reviewers Comments: Yes
Invited Articles: 0-5%
Fees to Publish: 0.00 US$

MANUSCRIPT TOPICS:

Accounting Information Systems; Accounting Theory & Practice; Auditing; Cost Accounting; Government & Non Profit Accounting; Tax Accounting

MANUSCRIPT GUIDELINES/COMMENTS:

Editorial Policy

According to the policies set by the Publications Committee (which were endorsed by the Executive Committee and were published in *The Accounting Education News*, June 1987), *The Accounting Review* "should be viewed as the premier journal for publishing articles reporting the results of accounting research and explaining and illustrating related research methodology. The scope of acceptable articles should embrace any research methodology and any accounting-related subject, as long as the articles meet the standards established for publication in the journal.... No special sections should be necessary. The primary, but not exclusive, audience should be -as it is now- academicians, graduate students, and others interested in accounting research."

The primary criterion for publication in *The Accounting Review* is the significance of the contribution an article makes to the literature.

The efficiency and effectiveness of the editorial review process is critically dependent upon the actions of both authors submitting papers and the reviewers. Authors accept the responsibility of preparing research papers at a level suitable for evaluation by independent reviewers. Such preparation, therefore, should include subjecting the manuscript to critique by colleagues and others and revising it accordingly prior to submission. The review process is not to be used as a means of obtaining feedback at early stages of developing the research.

Reviewers and associate editors are responsible for providing critically constructive and prompt evaluations of submitted research papers based on the significance of their contribution and on the rigor of analysis and presentation. Associate editors also make editorial recommendations to the editor.

Manuscript Preparation And Style
The Accounting Review's manuscript preparation guidelines follow (with a slight modification) the B-format of the *Chicago Manual Of Style* (14th ed.; University of Chicago Press). Another helpful guide to usage and style is *The Elements Of Style*, by William Strunk, Jr., and E. B. White (Macmillan). Spelling follows *Webster's International Dictionary*.

Format
1. All manuscripts should be typed on one side of 8 1/2 x 11" good quality paper and be double spaced, except for indented quotations.

2. Manuscripts should be as concise as the subject and research method permit, generally not to exceed 7,000 words.

3. Margins of at least one inch from top, bottom and sides should facilitate editing and duplication.

4. To assure anonymous review, authors should not identify themselves directly or indirectly in their papers. Single authors should not use the editorial "we."

5. A cover page should show the title of the paper, the author's name, title and affiliation, any acknowledgments, and a footnote indicating whether the author would be willing to share the data (see last paragraph in this statement).

Pagination: All pages, including tables, appendices and references, should be serially numbered. The first section of the paper should be untitled and unnumbered. Major sections may be numbered in Roman numerals. Subsections should not be numbered.

Numbers: Spell out numbers from one to ten, except when used in tables and lists, and when used with mathematical, statistical, scientific, or technical units and quantities, such as distances, weights and measures. For example: three days; 3 kilometers; 30 years. All other numbers are expressed numerically. Generally when using approximate terms spell out the number, for example, approximately thirty years.

Percentages And Decimal Fractions: In nontechnical copy use the word percent in the text; in technical copy the symbol % is used. (See the *Chicago Manual* for discussion of these usages.)

Hyphens: Use a hyphen to join unit modifiers or to clarify usage. For example: a well-presented analysis; re-form. See *Webster's* for correct usage.

Key Words: The abstract is to be followed by four key words that will assist in indexing the paper.

Abstract / Introduction

An Abstract of about 100 words should be presented on a separate page immediately preceding the text. The Abstract should concisely inform the reader of the manuscript's topic, its methods and its findings. Keywords and the Data Availability statements should follow the Abstract. The text of the paper should start with a section labeled "I. Introduction," which provides more details about the paper's purpose, motivation, methodology and findings. Both the abstract and the introduction should be relatively non-technical, yet clear enough for an informed reader to understand the manuscript's contribution. The manuscript's title, but neither the author's name nor other identification designations, should appear on the Abstract page.

Tables And Figures

The author should note the following general requirements:

1. Each table and figure (graphic) should appear on a separate page and should be placed at the end of the text. Each should bear an Arabic number and a complete title indicating the exact contents of the table or figure.

2. A reference to each graphic should be made in the text.

3. The author should indicate by marginal notation where each graphic should be inserted in the text.

4. Graphics should be reasonably interpreted without reference to the text.

5. Source lines and notes should be included as necessary.

Equations: Equations should be numbered in parentheses flush with the right-hand margin.

Documentation

Citations: Work cited should use the "author-date system" keyed to a list of works in the reference list (see below). Authors should make an effort to include the relevant page numbers in the cited works.

1. In the text, works are cited as follows: authors' last name and date, without comma, in parentheses: for example, (Jones 1987); with two authors: (Jones and Freeman 1973); with more than two: (Jones et al. 1985); with more than one source cited together (Jones 1987; Freeman 1986); with two or more works by one author: (Jones 1985, 1987).

2. Unless confusion would result, do not use "p." or "pp." before page numbers: for example, (Jones 1987, 115).

3. When the reference list contains more than one work of an author published in the same year, the suffix a, b, etc. follows the date in the text citation: for example, (Jones 1987a) or (Jones 1987a; Freeman 1985b).

4. If an author's name is mentioned in the text. it need not be repeated in the citation; for example, "Jones (1987, 115) says...."

5. Citations to institutional works should use acronyms or short titles where practicable; for example, (AAA ASOBAT 1966); (AICPA Cohen Commission Report 1977). Where brief, the full title of an institutional work might be shown in a citation: for example, (ICAEW The Corporate Report 1975).

6. If the manuscript refers to statutes, legal treatises or court cases, citations acceptable in law reviews should be used.

Reference List: Every manuscript must include a list of references containing only those works cited. Each entry should contain all data necessary for unambiguous identification. With the author-date system, use the following format recommended by the *Chicago Manual*:

1. Arrange citations in alphabetical order according to surname of the first author or the name of the institution responsible for the citation.

2. Use author's initials instead of proper names.

3. Dates of publication should be placed immediately after author's name.

4. Titles of journals should not be abbreviated.

5. Multiple works by the same author(s) should be listed in chronological order of publication. Two or more works by the same author(s) in the same year are distinguished by letters after the date.

6. Inclusive page numbers are treated as recommended in *Chicago Manual* section 8.67. Sample entries are as follows:

American Accounting Association, Committee on Concepts and Standards for External Financial Reports. 1977. Statement on Accounting Theory and Theory Acceptance. Sarasota, FL: AAA.

Demski, J. S., and D. E. M. Sappington. 1989. Hierarchical structure and responsibility accounting. Journal of Accounting Research 27 (Spring): 40-58.

Dye, R., B. Balachandran, and R. Magee. 1989. Contingent fees for audit firms. Working paper, Northwestern University, Evanston, IL.

Fabozzi, F., and I. Pollack, eds. 1987. The Handbook of Fixed Income Securities. 2d ed. Homewood, IL: Dow Jones-Irwin.

Kahneman, D., P. Slovic, and A. Tversky, eds. 1982. Judgment Under Uncertainty: Heuristics and Biases. Cambridge, United Kingdom: Cambridge University Press.

Porcano, T. M. 1984a. Distributive justice and tax policy. The Accounting Review 59 (October): 619-36.

_____. 1984b. The perceived effects of tax policy on corporate investment intentions. The Journal of the American Taxation Association 6 (Fall): 7-19.

Shaw, W. H. 1985. Empirical evidence on the market impact of the safe harbor leasing law. Ph.D. Dissertation, University of Texas at Austin.

Sherman, T. M., ed. 1984. Conceptual Framework for Financial Accounting. Cambridge, MA: Harvard Business School.

Footnotes: Footnotes are not used for documentation. Textual footnotes should be used only for extensions and useful excursions of information that if included in the body of the text might disrupt its continuity.

Footnotes should be consecutively numbered throughout the manuscript with superscript Arabic numerals.

Footnote text should be doubled-spaced and placed at the end of the article.

Submission Of Manuscripts
Authors should note the following guidelines for submitting manuscripts:

1 . Manuscripts currently under consideration by another journal or publisher should not be submitted. The author must state that the work is not submitted or published elsewhere.

2. In the case of manuscripts reporting on field surveys or experiments. four copies of the instrument (questionnaire, case, interview plan or the like) should be submitted.

3. Four copies should be submitted together with a check in U.S. funds for $75.00 for members or $100.00 for nonmembers of the AAA made payable to the American Accounting Association. Effective January 1990, the submission fee is nonrefundable.

4. The author should retain a copy of the paper.

5. Revisions must be submitted within 12 months from request, otherwise they will be considered new submissions.

54

Comments
Comments on articles previously published in *The Accounting Review* will be reviewed (anonymously) by two reviewers in sequence. The first reviewer will be the author of the original article being subjected to critique. If substance permits, a suitably revised comment will be sent to a second reviewer to determine its publishability in *The Accounting Review*. If a comment is accepted for publication, the original author will be invited to reply. All other editorial requirements, as enumerated above, also apply to proposed comments.

Policy On Reproduction
An objective of *The Accounting Review* is to promote the wide dissemination of the results of systematic scholarly inquiries into the broad field of accounting.

Permission is hereby granted to reproduce any of the contents of the Review for use in courses of instruction, as long as the source and American Accounting Association copyright are indicated in any such reproductions.

Written application must be made to the Editor for permission to reproduce any of the contents of the Review for use in other than courses of instruction--e.g., inclusion in books of readings or in any other publications intended for general distribution. In consideration for the grant of permission by the Review in such instances, the applicant must notify the author(s) in writing of the intended use to be made of each reproduction. Normally, the Review will not assess a charge for the waiver of copyright.

Except where otherwise noted in articles, the copyright interest has been transferred to the American Accounting Association. Where the author(s) has (have) not transferred the copyright to the Association, applicants must seek permission to reproduce (for all purposes) directly from the author(s).

Policy On Data Availability
The following policy has been adopted by the Executive Committee in its April 1989 meeting.

"An objective of (*The Accounting Review*, *Accounting Horizons*, *Issues In Accounting Education*) is to provide the widest possible dissemination of knowledge based on systematic scholarly inquiries into accounting as a field of professional research, and educational activity. As part of this process, authors are encouraged to make their data available for use by others in extending or replicating results reported in their articles. Authors of articles which report data dependent results should footnote the status of data availability and, when pertinent, this should be accompanied by information on how the data may be obtained."

Accounting, Organizations and Society

ADDRESS FOR SUBMISSION:

Anthony G. Hopwood, Editor
Accounting, Organizations and Society
University of Oxford
Said Business School
59 George Street
Oxford, OX1 2BE
UK
Phone: 44 (0) 1865-288650
Fax: 44 (0) 1865-288651
E-Mail: Anthony.Hopwood@osbs.ox.ac.uk
Web:
Address May Change:

PUBLICATION GUIDELINES:

Manuscript Length: Any
Copies Required: Three
Computer Submission: No
Format: N/A
Fees to Review: 0.00 US$

Manuscript Style:
    See Manuscript Guidelines

CIRCULATION DATA:

Reader: Academics
Frequency of Issue: 8 Times/Year
Copies per Issue: 1,001 - 2,000
Sponsor/Publisher: Elsevier Science
    Publishing Co.
Subscribe Price: 1255.00 US$ U.S.
    238.00 US$ Associated Personal
    US$

REVIEW INFORMATION:

Type of Review: Blind Review
No. of External Reviewers: 2
No. of In House Reviewers: 0
Acceptance Rate: 11-20%
Time to Review: 2 - 3 Months
Reviewers Comments: Yes
Invited Articles: 0-5%
Fees to Publish: 0.00 US$

MANUSCRIPT TOPICS:

Accounting Information Systems; Accounting Theory & Practice; Auditing; Cost Accounting; Economic History; Government & Non Profit Accounting; Industrial Organization; Organization Theory; Social Aspects of Accounting

MANUSCRIPT GUIDELINES/COMMENTS:

Associate Editors
Robert Libby, Johnson Graduate School of Management, Cornell University, NY.
Peter Miller, Department of Accounting and Finance, London School of Economics and Political Science, Houghton Street, London WC2A 2AE, UK.
Michael Shields, Michigan State University.

Aims And Scope
Accounting, Organizations & Society is a major international journal concerned with all aspects of the relationship between accounting and human behaviour, organizational structures and processes, and the changing social and political environment of the enterprise. Its unique focus covers such topics as: the social role of accounting, social accounting, social audit and

56

accounting for scarce resources; the provision of accounting information to employees and trade unions and the development of participative information systems; processes influencing accounting innovations and the social and political aspects of accounting standard setting; behavioural studies of the users of accounting information; information processing views of organizations, and the relationship between accounting and other information systems and organizational structures and processses; organizational strategies for designing accounting and information systems; human resource accounting; cognitive aspects of accounting and decision-making processes, and the behavioural aspects of budgeting, planning and investment appraisal.

Audience:
Researchers and students involved in behavioural, organisational and social aspects of accounting, personnel managers, information technologists.

Abstracted/Indexed In:
Current Contents, Research Alert, Social Sciences Citation Index.

Published material will range from original theoretical and empirical contributions to review articles describing the state of the art in specific areas. Shorter critical assessments of experiments related to the behavioural and social aspects of accounting will also be published. Other features of the journal are book reviews and other bibliographical materials. The objectives of the journal are:

1. To provide a specialized forum for the publication of research on the behavioural, organizational and social aspects of accounting.

2. To foster new thinking, research and action on the social and behavioural aspects of accounting.

3. To report on experiments on the behavioural and social aspects of accounting in a way that explains how the experiment was developed, the process by which it was implemented and its consequences, both planned and unplanned. The journal is particularly interested in discussions of the interplay between theory, practice and social and individual values.

4. To accelerate the transfer from research to practice by promoting an international dialogue between researchers, accountants, managers and administrators.

The journal will be concerned with all aspects of the relationship between accounting and human behaviour, organizational structures and processes, and the changing social and political environment of the enterprise. Its unique focus will cover such topics as:

- the social role of accounting, social accounting, social audit and accounting for scarce resources
- the provision of accounting information to employees and trade unions and the development of participative information systems
- processes influencing accounting innovations and the social and political aspects of

- accounting standard setting
- behavioural studies of the users of accounting information
- information processing views of organizations, and the relationship between accounting and other information systems and organizational structures and processes
- organizational strategies for designing accounting and information systems
- human resource accounting
- cognitive aspects of accounting and decision-making processes
- the behavioural aspects of budgeting, planning and investment appraisal.

Submission of Papers

Authors are requested to submit their original manuscript and figures plus two copies to the Editor-in-Chief of *Accounting, Organizations and Society:* Anthony G. Hopwood, Said Business School, 59 George Street, Oxford OX1 2BE, UK.

Submission of a paper implies that it has not been published previously, that it is not under consideration for publication elsewhere, and that if accepted it will not be published elsewhere in the same form, in English or in any other language, without the written consent of the publisher. The contribution of the author(s) should be an original one and should in no way violate any existing copyright, and it should contain nothing of a libellous or scandalous nature.

Types of Contributions

Original papers; review articles; short communications; reports of conferences and meetings; book reviews; letters to the editor; forthcoming meetings; selected bibliography.

Manuscript Preparation

General: Manuscripts must be typewritten, double-spaced with wide margins on one side of white paper. Good quality printouts with a font size of 12 or 10 pt are required. A cover page should give the title of the manuscript, the author's name, position and institutional affiliation, and an acknowledgement, if desired. The title of the manuscript, but not the authors names, should appear on the first page of the text. The corresponding author should be identified (include a Fax number and E-mail address). Full postal addresses must be given for all co-authors on the cover sheet. Authors should consult a recent issue of the journal for style if possible. An electronic copy of the paper should accompany the final version. The Editors reserve the right to adjust style to certain standards of uniformity. Authors should retain a copy of their manuscript since we cannot accept responsibility for damage or loss of papers. Original manuscripts are discarded one month after publication unless the Publisher is asked to return original material after use.

Abstract and Index: Three copies of an abstract not exceeding 80 words should accompany each manuscript submitted. Authors are also asked to supply a maximum of 10 keywords or phrases which will be used for indexing purposes.

Text: Follow this order when typing manuscripts: Title, Authors, Affiliations, Abstract, Keywords, Main text, Acknowledgements, Appendix, References, Vitae, Figure Captions and then Tables. Do not import the Figures or Tables into your text but supply them as separate

58

files. The corresponding author should be identified with an asterisk and footnote. All other footnotes (except for table footnotes) should be identified with superscript Arabic numbers. Footnotes for clarification or elaboration should be used sparingly.

Research Instruments: If the manuscript refers to questionnaires or other research instruments which are not fully reproduced in the text, authors must also submit three copies of the complete research. Because of space limitations, questionnaires and other research instruments sometimes may not be fully reproduced in the published paper. When they are not fully reproduced a note must be inserted in the text of the paper indicating the address from which copies of the complete instrument are available.

References: All publications cited in the text should be present in a list of references following the text of the manuscript. The work should be cited by author's name and year of publication in the body of the text, e.g. (Watson, 1975); or when reference is made to a specific page (Wilkes & Harrison, 1975, p. 21). Where the author's name is included in the text, the name should not be repeated in the reference citation: e.g. "Angrist (1975, p. 79) says...". For identification purposes, the suffix a, b, etc. should follow the date when the bibliography contains more than one work published by an author in a single year. For 2-6 authors, all authors are to be listed at first citation, with "&" separating the last two authors. For more than six authors, use the first six authors followed by et al. In subsequent citations for three or more authors use author et al. in the text. The list of references should be arranged alphabetically by authors' names. The manuscript should be carefully checked to ensure that the spelling of authors names and dates are exactly the same in the text as in the reference list. Each reference should contain full bibliographical details and journal titles should not be abbreviated. References should be given in the following form:

Abernathy, M., & Stoelwinder, J. (1996). The role of professional control in the management of complex organizations. *Accounting, Organizations and Society 20*, 1-17.
Bowen, D.E., & Schneider, B. (1988). Services, marketing and management: implications for organisational behaviour. In B.M. Straw, & L.L. Cummings, *Research in organisational behaviour, vol. 10*. Greenwich, CT: JAI Press.
Ericsson, K., & Simon, H. (1984). *Protocol analysis*. Cambridge, MA: The MIT Press.
Harper, R. (1989). An ethnography of accountants. Ph D Thesis. Department of Sociology, Manchester University.

Illustrations: All illustrations should be provided in camera-ready form, suitable for reproduction (which may include reduction) without retouching. Photographs, charts and diagrams are all to be referred to as "Figure(s)" and should be numbered consecutively in the order to which they are referred. They should accompany the manuscript, but should not be included within the text. All illustrations should be clearly marked on the back with the figure number and the author's name. All figures are to have a caption. Captions should be supplied on a separate sheet at the end of the paper. The author should clearly indicate in the text where he or she would like each figure to be placed.

Line drawings: Good quality printouts on white paper produced in black ink are required. All lettering, graph lines and points on graphs should be sufficiently large and bold to permit reproduction when the diagram has been reduced to a size suitable for inclusion in the journal.

Dye-line prints or photocopies are not suitable for reproduction. Do not use any type of shading on computer-generated illustrations.

Photographs: Original photographs must be supplied as they are to be reproduced (e.g. black and white or colour). If necessary, a scale should be marked on the photograph. Please note that photocopies of photographs are not acceptable.

Colour: Authors will be charged for colour at current printing costs.

Tables: Tables should be numbered consecutively and given a suitable caption and each table typed on a separate sheet. Footnotes to tables should be typed below the table and should be referred to by superscript lowercase letters. No vertical rules should be used. Tables should not duplicate results presented elsewhere in the manuscript, (e.g. in graphs). The author should clearly indicate in the text where he or she would like each table to be placed.

Electronic Submission
Authors should submit an electronic copy of the final version of their paper with the final version of the manuscript. The electronic copy should match the hardcopy exactly. Please specify what software was used, including which release, and what computer was used (IBM compatible PC or Apple Macintosh). Always keep a backup copy of the electronic file for reference and safety. Full details of electronic submission and formats can be obtained from http://www.elsevier.nl/locate/disksub or from Author Services at Elsevier Science.

Proofs
Proofs will be sent to the author (first named author if no corresponding author is identified of multi-authored papers) and should be returned within 48 hours of receipt. Corrections should be restricted to typesetting errors; any others may be charged to the author. Any queries should be answered in full. Please note that authors are urged to check their proofs carefully before return, since the inclusion of late corrections cannot be guaranteed. Proofs are to be returned to the Log-in Department, Elsevier Science, Stover Court, Bampfylde Street, Exeter, Devon EX1 2AH, UK.

Offprints
Twenty-five offprints will be supplied free of charge. Offprints and copies of the issue can be ordered at a specially reduced rate using the order form sent to the corresponding author after the manuscript has been accepted. Orders for reprints (after publication) will incur a 50% surcharge.

Copyright
All authors must sign the "Transfer of Copyright" agreement before the article can be published. This transfer agreement enables Elsevier Science Ltd to protect the copyrighted material for the authors, but does not relinquish the author's proprietary rights. The copyright transfer covers the exclusive rights to reproduce and distribute the article, including reprints, photographic reproductions, microfilm or any other reproductions of similar nature and translations. This Includes the right to adapt the article for use in conjunction with computer systems and programs, including reproduction or publication in machine-readable form and

60

incorporation in retrieval systems. Authors are responsible for obtaining from the copyright holder permission to reproduce any figures for which copyright exists.

Author Services

For queries relating to the general submission of manuscripts (including electronic text and artwork) and the status of accepted manuscripts, please contact Author Services, Log-in Department, Elsevier Science, The Boulevard, Langford Lane, Kidlington, Oxford OX5 1GB, UK. Email: authors@elsevier.co.uk. Fax: 44 (0) 1865 843905 Phone: 44 (0) 1865 843900.

Authors can also keep track of the progress of their accepted article through (our) OASIS System on the internet.

Elsevier Science Ltd., 660 White Plains Road, Tarrytown, NY 10591-5153, USA.
Tel: +1-914-524-9200, Fax: +1-914-333-2444.

Acquisition Review Quarterly

ADDRESS FOR SUBMISSION:

Debbie Gonzalez, Editor
Acquisition Review Quarterly
Defense Systems Management College
Attn: AS-VAP
9820 Belvoir Road, Suite 3
Fort Belvoir, VA 22060-5565
USA
Phone: 703-805-4284
Fax: 703-805-2917
E-Mail: gonzalez@dsmc.dsm.mil
Web: www.dsmc.mil
Address May Change:

PUBLICATION GUIDELINES:

Manuscript Length: 21-25
Copies Required: Two
Computer Submission: Yes
Format: MSWord 6.0,WP
   6.0,MSPowerpoint
Fees to Review: 0.00 US$

Manuscript Style:
   American Psychological Association

CIRCULATION DATA:

Reader: Academics
Frequency of Issue: Quarterly
Copies per Issue: 5,001 - 10,000
Sponsor/Publisher: Defense Systems
  Management College
Subscribe Price: 0.00 US$

REVIEW INFORMATION:

Type of Review: Blind Review
No. of External Reviewers: 3
No. of In House Reviewers: 1
Acceptance Rate: 11-20%
Time to Review: 4 - 6 Months
Reviewers Comments: Yes
Invited Articles: 0-5%
Fees to Publish: 0.00 US$

MANUSCRIPT TOPICS:
Accounting Information Systems; Acquisition Related Topics; Fiscal Policy; Weapons (Procurement)

MANUSCRIPT GUIDELINES/COMMENTS:

The *Acquisition Review Quarterly* (ARQ) is a scholarly peer-reviewed journal published by the Defense Acquisition University. All submissions receive a masked review to ensure impartial evaluation.

Submissions
Submissions are welcomed from anyone involved in the Defense acquisition process. Defense acquisition is defined as the conceptualization, initiation, design, development, test, contracting, production, deployment, logistic support, modification, and disposal of weapons and other systems, supplies, or services to satisfy Defense Department needs, or intended for use in support of military missions.

Research Articles

Manuscripts should reflect research or empirically-supported experience in one or more of the aforementioned areas of acquisition. Research or tutorial articles should not exceed 4,500 words. Opinion pieces should be limited to 1,500 words.

Research articles are characterized by a systematic inquiry into a subject to discover or revise facts, theories, etc.

Definitions of Research and Acquisition Research

Research requires studious inquiry or examination, especially an investigation or experiment aimed at discovering and interpreting facts, revising accepted theories or laws in light of new facts, or practically applying such new or revised theories or laws. Acquisition research might investigate the acquisition process and its management from development of an initial concept through final disposition of a product. The product may be a system, item of hardware and/or software, or technical/professional services. Research examines source selection, acquisition planning and strategy, contract administration, technical management, business administration, costing and pricing, performance measurement, transition to production, manufacturing and production, test and evaluation, product assurance, product support, joint program management, and multinational program management. Our evaluation criteria for reviewing submitted articles will consider the quality of research and writing, the relevancy and currency of research to acquisition management and reform, and current interest in the topic.

Manuscript Sections

The introduction should state the purpose of the article and concisely summarize the rationale for the undertaking.

The methods section should include a detailed methodology that clearly describes work performed. Although it is appropriate to refer to previous publications in this section, the author should provide enough information so that the experienced reader need not read earlier works to gain understanding of the methodology.

The results section should concisely summarize findings of the research and follow the train of thought established in the methods section. This section should not refer to previous publications, but should be devoted solely to the current findings of the author.

The discussion section should emphasize the major findings of the study and its significance. Information presented in the aforementioned sections should not be repeated.

Research Considerations

Contributors should also consider the following questions in reviewing their research-based articles prior to submission:

- Is the research question significant?
- Are research instruments reliable and valid?
- Are outcomes measured in a way clearly related to the variables under study?
- Does the research design fully and unambiguously test the hypothesis?
- Did you build needed controls into the study?

Contributors of research-based submissions are also reminded they should share any materials and methodology necessary to verify their conclusions.

Criteria for Tutorials
Tutorials should provide special instruction or knowledge relevant to an area of defense acquisition to inform the Defense Acquisition Workforce.

Topics for submissions should rely on or be derived from observation or experiment, rather than theory. The submission should provide knowledge in a particular area for a particular purpose.

Opinion Criteria
Opinion articles should reflect judgments based on the special knowledge of the expert. Opinion articles should be based on observable phenomena and presented in a factual manner; that is, submissions should imply detachment. The observation and judgment should not reflect the author's personal feelings or thoughts. Nevertheless, opinion pieces should clearly express a fresh point of view, rather than negatively criticize the view of another previous author.

Manuscript Style
We will require you to recast your last version of the manuscript, especially citations (e.g., footnotes or endnotes) into the format required in two specific style manuals. The ARQ follows the author (date) form of citation. We expect you to use the *Publication Manual of the American Psychological Association* (4th Edition), and the *Chicago Manual of Style* (14th Edition). The *ARQ* follows the author (date) form of citation.

Contributors are encouraged to seek the advice of a reference librarian in completing citations of government documents. Standard formulas of citations may give only incomplete information in reference to government works. Helpful guidance is also available in Garner, D.L. and Smith, D.H., 1993, *The Complete Guide to Citing Government Documents: A Manual for Writers and Librarians* (Rev. Ed.), Bethesda, MD: Congressional Information Service, Inc.

Copyright Information
The ARQ is a publication of the United States Government and as such is not copyrighted. Contributors of copyrighted works and copyright holders of works for hire are strongly encouraged to request that a copyright notification be placed on their published work as a safeguard against unintentional infringement. The work of federal employees undertaken as part of their official duties is not subject to copyright.

In citing the work of others, it is the contributor's responsibility to obtain permission from a copyright holder if the proposed use exceeds the fair use provisions of the law (see U.S. Government Printing Office, 1994, *Circular 92: Copyright Law of the United States of America , p. 15,* Washington, DC: Author). Contributors will be required to submit a copy of the written permission to the editor before publication.

DSMC Press requires the author to complete a copyright release form which gives DSMC permission to use material in print, for courses, and on the internet. The same form is necessary if you have used copyrighted material within a submitted article.

The other side of the form certifies work was done for the government and as such is not copyrightable. DSMC reserves the right to reject articles with questionable or unattainable copyright permission.

Please print out copyright forms from web site
http://www.dsmc.dsm.mil/pubs/arq/arqart.htm
and fax to DSMC Press (703) 8052917, or mail them to:
DEFENSE SYST MGMT COLLEGE
ATTN DSMC PRESS
9820 BELVOIR ROAD STE 3
FT BELVOIR VA 22060-5565

Manuscript Format
Pages should be double-spaced and organized in the following order: title page, abstract, body, reference list, author's note (if any), and figures or tables. Figures or tables should not be inserted (or embedded, etc.) into the text, but segregated one to a page following the text. If material is submitted on a computer diskette, each figure or table should be recorded in a separate, exportable file (i.e., a readable .eps file). For additional information on the preparation of figures or tables, see CBE Scientific Illustration Committee, 1988, *Illustrating Science: Standards for Publication* , Bethesda, MD: Council of Biology Editors, Inc. Please restructure briefing charts and slides to a look similar to those in previous issues of ARQ.

The author (or corresponding author in the case of multiple authorship) should attach to the manuscript a signed cover letter that provides the author's name, address, and telephone number (fax and Internet addresses are also appreciated). The letter should verify that the submission is an original product of the author; that it has not been published before; and that it is not under consideration by another publication. Details about the manuscript should also be included in this letter: for example, its title, word length, the need for copyright notification, the identification of copyrighted material for which permission must be obtained, a description of the computer application programs and file names used on enclosed diskettes, etc.

The letter, one copy of the printed manuscript, and any diskettes should be sturdily packaged and mailed to: Defense Systems Management College, Attn: DSMC Press (ARQ), 9820 Belvoir Road, Suite 3, Fort Belvoir, VA 22060-5565.

In most cases, the author will be notified that the submission has been received within *48* hours of its arrival. Following an initial review, submissions will be referred to referees and be given subsequent consideration by the ARQ Editorial Board. Contributors may direct their questions to the Editor, ARQ, at the address shown above, by calling (703) 805-4290 (fax 805-2917), or via the Internet Debbie Gonzalez.

Advances in Accounting

ADDRESS FOR SUBMISSION:

Philip M. J. Reckers, Editor
Advances in Accounting
Arizona State University
College of Business
Tempe, AZ 85287
USA
Phone: 602-965-2283
Fax: 602-965-5277
E-Mail: philip.reckers@asu.edu
Web:
Address May Change:

PUBLICATION GUIDELINES:

Manuscript Length: Any
Copies Required: Four
Computer Submission: No
Format: N/A
Fees to Review: 50.00 US$

Manuscript Style:
    See Manuscript Guidelines

CIRCULATION DATA:

Reader: Academics
Frequency of Issue: Yearly
Copies per Issue: Less than 1,000
Sponsor/Publisher: JAI Press, Inc./Elsevier
    Publishing
Subscribe Price: 28.25 US$

REVIEW INFORMATION:

Type of Review: Blind Review
No. of External Reviewers: 2
No. of In House Reviewers: 1
Acceptance Rate: 11-20%
Time to Review: 3 - 4 Months
Reviewers Comments: Yes
Invited Articles: 0-5%
Fees to Publish: 0.00 US$

MANUSCRIPT TOPICS:
Accounting Information Systems; Accounting Theory & Practice; Auditing; Cost Accounting; Tax Accounting

MANUSCRIPT GUIDELINES/COMMENTS:

Advances In Accounting (AIA) is a professional publication whose purpose is to meet the information needs of both practitioners and academicians. We plan to publish thoughtful, well-developed articles on a variety of current topics in financial and management accounting, accounting education, auditing and accounting information systems.

Articles may range from empirical to analytical, from practice-based to the development of new techniques. Articles must be readable, relevant, and articles must be understandable and concise. To be relevant, articles must be related to problems facing the accounting and business community. To empirical reports, sound design and execution are critical. For theoretical treatises, reasonable assumptions and logical development are essential.

AIA welcomes all comments and encourages articles from practitioners and academicians. Editorial correspondence pertaining to manuscripts should be sent to Phillip M. J. Reckers

Editorial Policy And Manuscripts Form Guidelines

1. Manuscripts should be typewritten and double-spaced on 8" x 11" white paper. Only one side of a page should be used. Margins should be set to facilitate editing and duplication except as noted:

A. Tables, figures and exhibits should appear on a separate page. Each should be numbered and have a title.

B. Footnotes should be presented by citing the author's name and the year of publication in the body of the text, e.g., Schwartz [1981]; Reckers and Pany [1980].

2. Manuscripts should include a cover page which indicated the author's name and affiliation.

3. Manuscripts should include on a separate lead page an abstract not exceeding 200 words. The author's name and affiliation should not appear on the abstract.

4. Topical headings and subheadings should be used. Main headings in the manuscript should be centered, secondary headings should be flush with the left-hand margin. (As a guide to usage and style, refer to William Strunk, Jr. and E.B. White, *The Elements Of Style*.)

5. Manuscripts must include a list of references which contain only those works actually cited. (As a helpful guide in preparing a list of references, refer to Kate L. Turabian. *A Manual For Writers Of Term Papers, Theses, And Dissertations*.)

6. In order to be assured of an anonymous review, authors should not identify themselves directly or indirectly. Reference to unpublished working papers and dissertations should be avoided. If necessary, authors may indicate that the reference is being withheld for the reasons cited above.

7. The author will be provided one complete volume of the AIA issue in which his or her manuscript appears and ten off-prints of the article.

8. Manuscripts currently under review by other publications should not be submitted. Complete reports of research presented at a national or regional conference of a professional association (e.g. AAA, DSI, etc.) and "State of the Art" papers are acceptable.

9. **Four** copies of each manuscript should be submitted to the Editor-in-Chief at the Virginia Commonwealth University address. Copies of any and all research instruments also should be included.

For additional information regarding the type of manuscripts that are desired, see AIA Statement of Purpose.

Advances in Accounting Behavioral Research (AABR)

ADDRESS FOR SUBMISSION:

James E. Hunton, Editor
Advances in Accounting Behavioral
    Research (AABR)
University of South Florida
School of Accountancy
4202 East Fowler Avenue, BSN 3403
Tampa, FL 33620
USA
Phone: (813) 974-6523
Fax: (813) 974-6528
E-Mail: jhunton@coba.usf.edu
Web:
Address May Change:

PUBLICATION GUIDELINES:

Manuscript Length: 30+
Copies Required: Four
Computer Submission: No
Format: N/A
Fees to Review: 25.00 US$

Manuscript Style:
    American Psychological Association

CIRCULATION DATA:

Reader: Academics
Frequency of Issue: Yearly
Copies per Issue: 1,001 - 2,000
Sponsor/Publisher: JAI Press, Inc.
Subscribe Price: 78.50 US$

REVIEW INFORMATION:

Type of Review: Blind Review
No. of External Reviewers: 3
No. of In House Reviewers: 0
Acceptance Rate: 6-10%
Time to Review: 2 - 3 Months
Reviewers Comments: Yes
Invited Articles: 0-5%
Fees to Publish: 0.00 US$

MANUSCRIPT TOPICS:

Accounting Information Systems; Accounting Theory & Practice; Applied, Psych.-based, Experiment. Research; Auditing; Cost Accounting; Tax Accounting

MANUSCRIPT GUIDELINES/COMMENTS:

Advances in Accounting Behavioral Research (AABR) publishes articles encompassing all areas of accounting that incorporate theory from and contribute new knowledge and understanding to the fields of applied psychology, sociology, management science, and economics. The journal is primarily devoted to original empirical investigations; however, critical review papers, theoretical analyses, and methodological contributions are welcome.

Manuscripts should be double-spaced, formatted with one-inch margins all around, typeset using a 12 point proportional font (such as Times-Roman), and printed on one side of high quality white paper. Authors are requested to follow the instructions provided by the *Publication Manual of the American Psychological Association*, 4th ed., 1994 (see the *Journal of Applied Psychology* for formatting examples).

Four copies of the manuscript should be submitted, along with four copies of any experimental materials or survey instruments. The first page of the manuscript should contain the article title, names and affiliations of all authors, and complete mailing address, e-mail address, and telephone number of the corresponding author. The second page should contain the article title and an abstract. Pages should be consecutively numbered, beginning with the abstract page. Manuscripts will be blind-reviewed by an associate editor and two reviewers.

Please send submissions and a $25.00 processing fee (make checks payable to AABR/USF) to the above address.

Advances in Accounting Education (Research in Accounting Ethics)

ADDRESS FOR SUBMISSION:

Bill Schwartz, Co-editor (Non-empirical)
Advances in Accounting Education
   (Research in Accounting Ethics)
Virginia Commonwealth University
School of Business
Department of Accounting
1015 Floyd Ave.
Richmond, VA 23284-4000
USA
Phone: 804-828-7194
Fax: 804-828-8884
E-Mail: bnschwar@vcu.edu
Web:
Address May Change:

PUBLICATION GUIDELINES:

Manuscript Length: No Reply
Copies Required: Three
Computer Submission: No
Format: N/A
Fees to Review: 35.00 US$

Manuscript Style:
   See Manuscript Guidelines

CIRCULATION DATA:

Reader: Academics
Frequency of Issue: Yearly
Copies per Issue: No Reply
Sponsor/Publisher: JAI Press, Inc.
Subscribe Price: 78.50 US$

REVIEW INFORMATION:

Type of Review: Blind Review
No. of External Reviewers: 2
No. of In House Reviewers: 0
Acceptance Rate: 21-30%
Time to Review: 1 Month or Less
Reviewers Comments: Yes
Invited Articles: 0-5%
Fees to Publish: 0.00 US$

MANUSCRIPT TOPICS:
Accounting Education; Pedagogy and Curriculum Issues

MANUSCRIPT GUIDELINES/COMMENTS:

1. Manuscripts should be typewritten and double-spaced on 8½" by 11" white paper. Only one side of the page should be used.

2. Manuscripts should include a cover page which indicates the author's name, address, affiliation and any acknowledgements. The author should **not** be identified anywhere else in the manuscript.

3. Manuscripts should include on a separate lead page an abstract not exceeding 250 words. The author's name and affiliation should **not** appear on the abstract. It should contain a

concise statement of the purpose of the manuscript, the primary methods or approaches used (if applicable), and the main results, conclusions, or recommendations.

4. Topical headings should be in caps and centered. Subheadings should be flush with the left margin, underlined, and **not** in caps. Headings and subheadings should **not** be numbered.

5. Tables, figures and exhibits should appear on separate pages. Each should be numbered and have a title.

6. Footnotes and references should appear at the end of the manuscript. However, every effort should be made to incorporate material into the body of the paper. The list of references should include only works actually cited.

7. In order to be assured of an anonymous review, authors should **not** identify themselves directly or indirectly in the text of the paper. Reference to unpublished working papers and dissertations should be avoided. If necessary,. authors may indicate the reference is being withheld for the reasons cited here.

8. Authors are expected to use a spell check and a grammar check. Accepted manuscripts ultimately must be submitted on an IBM compatible disk in ASCII file format.

9. Manuscripts currently under review by other publications or manuscripts that already have been published (including proceedings from regional or national meetings) should **not** be submitted. Please include a statement to that effect in the cover letter accompanying your submission. Complete reports of research presented at a regional or national meeting, which have not been published in the proceedings, are acceptable for submission.

10. **Three** copies of each manuscript should be submitted. Empirical manuscripts should be submitted to J. Edward Ketz at The Pennsylvania State University. Copies of any and all research instruments also should be included. Non-empirical manuscripts should be submitted to Bill N. Schwartz at Virginia Commonwealth University.

11. The author should send a check for $35 made payable to *Accounting Education* each submission, whether it is the initial submission or a revision.

Advances in Environmental Accounting and Management

ADDRESS FOR SUBMISSION:

Bikki Jaggi, Co-Editor
Advances in Environmental Accounting and
    Management
Rutgers University
School of Business
Department of Accounting
Levin Building
New Brunswick, NJ 08903
USA
Phone: 732-445-3540
Fax: 732-445-3201
E-Mail:
Web:
Address May Change:

PUBLICATION GUIDELINES:

Manuscript Length: 16-20
Copies Required: Three
Computer Submission: No
Format: N/A
Fees to Review: 0.00 US$

Manuscript Style:
    Chicago Manual of Style, Accounting
    Review

CIRCULATION DATA:

Reader: Academics
Frequency of Issue: Yearly
Copies per Issue: Less than 1,000
Sponsor/Publisher: JAI Press, Inc.
Subscribe Price: No Reply

REVIEW INFORMATION:

Type of Review: Blind Review
No. of External Reviewers: 2
No. of In House Reviewers: 1
Acceptance Rate: 0-5%
Time to Review: 1 - 2 Months
Reviewers Comments: Yes
Invited Articles: 0-5%
Fees to Publish: 0.00 US$

MANUSCRIPT TOPICS:

Accounting Theory & Practice; Cost Accounting; Environmental Accounting; Public Policy
Economics

MANUSCRIPT GUIDELINES/COMMENTS:

Manuscripts, in triplicate, should be sent to **address for submission** above or to:

Marty Freedman, Co-Editor
School of Management
Binghamton University
Binghamton, NY 13902-6015
E-mail: mfreed@binghamton.edu
Phone: (607) 777-2440
Fax: (607) 777-4422

Advances In Environmental Accounting And Management invites manuscripts dealing with accounting and management perspectives of environmental issues. The Journal is devoted to examining different environmental aspects of manuscript decisions to meet the environmental information needs of various stakeholders, such as investors, creditors, employers, suppliers, customers, environmentalists, and the community. The Journal welcomes papers using traditional or alternative approaches, such as theoretical, empirical, applied, or critical approaches. Manuscripts dealing with case studies are also welcome.

Advances in International Accounting

ADDRESS FOR SUBMISSION:

Timothy J. Sale, Editor
Advances in International Accounting
University of Cincinnati
Department of Accounting Info Systems
Mail Location 211
Cincinnati, OH 45221-0211
USA
Phone: 513-556-6062
Fax: 513-556-4891
E-Mail: tim.sale@uc.edu
Web:
Address May Change:

PUBLICATION GUIDELINES:

Manuscript Length: 26-30
Copies Required: Three
Computer Submission: Yes
Format: ASCII/only on acceptance
Fees to Review: 0.00 US$

Manuscript Style:
     See Manuscript Guidelines

CIRCULATION DATA:

Reader: Academics
Frequency of Issue: Yearly
Copies per Issue: Less than 1,000
Sponsor/Publisher: JAI Press, Inc./Elsevier
   Publications
Subscribe Price: 63.00 US$

REVIEW INFORMATION:

Type of Review: Blind Review
No. of External Reviewers: 2
No. of In House Reviewers: 1
Acceptance Rate: 50%
Time to Review: 2 - 3 Months
Reviewers Comments: Yes
Invited Articles: 0-5%
Fees to Publish: 0.00 US$

MANUSCRIPT TOPICS:

Accounting Information Systems; Accounting Theory & Practice; Auditing; Cost Accounting; Government & Non Profit Accounting; International Finance; Tax Accounting

MANUSCRIPT GUIDELINES/COMMENTS:

GENERAL INSTRUCTIONS

Paper: Type or print the manuscript on one side of standard-size, or European equivalent, paper. Do not use half sheets or strips of paper glued, taped, or stapled to the pages.

Type Element: The type must be dark, clear, and legible.

Double Spacing: Double space between all lines of the manuscript including headings, notes, references, quotations, and figure captions. Single-spacing is acceptable only on tables.

Permission To Reprint: If you are using material from a copyrighted work (e.g., tables, figures), you will need written permission from the copyright holder (in most cases the publish to use this material. **It is the author's responsibility to obtain the reprint permission.** A copy o the permission letter must accompany the manuscript.

Title Page: The title page includes 4 elements: (1) The title and subtitle, if any; (2) The author(s); (3) abbreviated title to be used as a running head consisting of a maximum of 70 characters, which includes all letters, punctuation, and spaces; (4) complete mailing address, phone, and fax numbers of each author.

Text: Begin the next on a new page. The sections of the text follow each other without a break.

Appendices: Begin each Appendix on a separate page, with the word "Appendix" and identifying capital letters centered at the top of the page. If there is only one Appendix, it is .n necessary to use an identifying letter.

Notes: Notes that are mentioned in text are numbered consecutively throughout the chapter. Begin notes on a separate page and **double space** them.

References: Each series has its own reference style, whether it be APA, ASA, or a style unique to its discipline. For the style you should use, please consult a previously published volume it the series.

References cited in text **must** appear in the reference list; conversely, each entry in the reference list **must** be cited in text. It is the author's responsibility to be sure that the text citation and reference list are identical.

Important: Foreign language volumes, parts, numbers, editions, and so on **must** be translated into their English equivalents. Both the original language and the English translation will appear in the references. Authors **must** transliterate or romanize languages that do not use Latin characters (e.g., Greek, Russian, Chinese, Arabic, etc.), along with their English translation. A comprehensive resource for this is a publication issued by the Library of Congress, titled: *ALA-LC Romanization Tables: Transliteration Schemes for Non-Roman Scripts.*

Tables: Tables are numbered consecutively in the order in which they are first mentioned in text. Begin each table on separate page. Do not write "the table above/below" or "the table on p. 32" because the position and page number of a table cannot be determined until the page is typeset. In text, indicate the approximate placement of each table by a clear break in the text, inserting: .

TABLE 1 ABOUT HERE

set off by double-spacing above and below.

Figures: Figures are also numbered consecutively in the order in which they are first mentioned in text. Indicate the approximate placement of each figure by a clear break, inserting:

FIGURE 1 ABOUT HERE

set off by double-spacing above and below. All figures must be submitted in a form suitable for reproduction by the printer without redrawing or retouching. Figures should be no larger than 4 x 6". If a figure exceeds this size, it should be large enough and sharp enough to be legible when reduced to fit the page.

Type all figure numbers and captions, double-spaced, on a separate page. When enclosing a figure in a box, please do not include the figure number and caption within the box, as these are set separately.

For identification by the production editor and the printer, please indicate your name and the figure number on the back of each figure. "Top" should be written on any figure that might accidently be reproduced wrong side up. Staples nor paper clips should be used on any figure. Scotch tape should never !--.used to attach figure copy t^ another page as tape edges show up as black line in reproduction. Art will not be returned unless otherwise indicated.

DISK PREPARATION

1. Use a word processing program that is able to create an IBM compatible file. For technical (math, chemistry, etc.) Macintosh files are acceptable. (Macintosh files should be submitted on **high density** disks only.)

2. Use 3 1/2 inch, double (low) density or high density disks (preferably high density.
Note: If you use double (low) density disks, be sure that the disk is formatted for double (low) density. If you use high density, be sure that the disk is formatted for high density. Unformatted or incorrectly formatted disks are unusable.

3. Structure the manuscript according to the Guidelines. Print one (1) copy for copy-editing/styling purposes. Be sure to **Double-Space** this copy. That includes the notes and references.

4. The entire chapter should be in one (1) file. **Do not** make separate files for text, notes, and references. If necessary, tables may go in a separate file.

5. All manuscripts must have **numbered pages**; all tables and figures must be placed **at the end of the chapters**; placement lines must be indicated for all tables and figures (e.g., PLACE FIGURE/TABLE X HERE).

6. Submit the word processing file with your printed copy. Please indicate on the disk which word processing program and version you have used (e.g., MS Word, WordPerfect 5.1, 6.0, 7.0, etc. Word Star, WordPerfect for Windows, MS Word for Windows, etc.).

7. All text files must be spell checked and stripped of any and all graphics (graphs, equations, charts, line drawings, illustrations, or tables). Text files must be marked as to the placement of **all** graphics. Please send a **separate** graphics file as either **tiff** (tagged image file format) or

eps (encapsulated postscript) and indicate which format has been used on the disk. We will still require **camera-ready copy**, whether or not material is also supplied in a graphics file.

8. **PLEASE** be sure that the manuscript and disk submitted match. If the material on the disk has been updated, please print out a new copy of the manuscript to be sure you are submitting the correct version.

JAI PRESS INC., Publishers of Professional and Research Works in Pure, Applied, and Social Sciences, 100 Prospect Street, North Tower, P.O. Box 811, Stamford, Connecticut 06904-0811. Tel: (203) 323-9606, Fax: (203) 357-8826.

Advances in Management Accounting

ADDRESS FOR SUBMISSION:

John Y. Lee, Editor
Advances in Management Accounting
Pace University
Lubin School of Business
Goldstein Center 218
861 Bedford Road
Pleasantville, NY 10570
USA
Phone: (914) 773-3443
Fax: (914) 773-3908
E-Mail: jylee@pace.edu
Web:
Address May Change:

PUBLICATION GUIDELINES:

Manuscript Length: 21-25
Copies Required: Four
Computer Submission: No
Format: N/A
Fees to Review: 25.00 US$

Manuscript Style:
  See Manuscript Guidelines

CIRCULATION DATA:

Reader: Business Persons, Academics
Frequency of Issue: Yearly
Copies per Issue: 2,001 - 3,000
Sponsor/Publisher: JAI Press, Inc.
Subscribe Price: 75.00 US$

REVIEW INFORMATION:

Type of Review: Blind Review
No. of External Reviewers: 2
No. of In House Reviewers: 1
Acceptance Rate: 21-30%
Time to Review: 1 - 2 Months
Reviewers Comments: Yes
Invited Articles: 0-5%
Fees to Publish: 0.00 US$

MANUSCRIPT TOPICS:
Accounting Information Systems; Cost Accounting; Managerial Accounting

MANUSCRIPT GUIDELINES/COMMENTS:

Statement of Purpose and Review Procedures
Advances in Management Accounting (AIMA) a professional journal whose purpose is to meet the information needs of both practitioners and academicians. We plan to publish thoughtful, well developed articles on a variety of current topics in management accounting, broadly defined.

Advances in Management Accounting is to be an annual publication of quality applied research in management accounting. The series will examine areas of management accounting, including performance evaluation systems, accounting for product costs, behavioral impacts on management accounting, and innovations in management accounting. Management accounting includes all systems designed to provide information for management decision making. Research methods will include survey research, field tests, corporate case studies, and modeling. Some speculative articles and survey pieces will be included where appropriate.

AIMA welcomes all comments and encourages articles from both practitioners and academicians.

Review Procedures
AIMA intends to provide authors with timely reviews clearly indicating the acceptance status of their manuscripts. The results of initial reviews normally will be reported to authors within eight weeks from the date the manuscript is received. Once a manuscript is tentatively accepted, the prospects for publication are excellent. The author(s) will be accepted to work with the corresponding Editor, who will act as a liaison between the author(s) and the reviewers to resolve areas of concern. To ensure publication, it is the author's responsibility to make necessary revisions in a timely and satisfactory manner.

Editorial Policy and Manuscript Form Guidelines
1. Manuscripts should be type written and double-spaced on 81/2 " by 11" white paper. Only one side of the paper should be used. Margins should be set to facilitate editing and duplication except as noted:

a. Tables, figures, and exhibits should appear on a separate page. Each should be numbered and have a title. b. Footnote should be presented by citing the author's name and the year of publication in the body of the text; for example, Ferreira (1998); Cooper and Kaplan (1998).

2. Manuscripts should include a cover page that indicates the author's name and affiliation.

3. Manuscripts should include on a separate lead page an abstract not exceeding 200 words. The author's name and affiliation should not appear on the abstract.

4. Topical headings and subheadings should be used. Main headings in the manuscript should be centered, secondary headings should be flush with the left hand margin. (As a guide to usage and style, refer to the William Strunk, Jr., and E.B. White, *The Elements of Style.)*

5. Manuscripts must include a list of references which contain only those works actually cited. (As a helpful guide in preparing a list of references, refer to Kate L. Turbian, *A Manual for Writers of Term Papers, Theses, and Dissertations.)*

6. In order to be assured of anonymous review, authors should not identify themselves directly or indirectly. Reference to unpublished working papers and dissertations should be avoided. If necessary, authors may indicate that the reference is being withheld for the reason cited above.

7. The author will be provided one complete volume of AIMA issue in which his or her manuscript appears and the senior author will receive 25 offprints of the article.

8. Manuscripts currently under review by other publications should not be submitted. Complete reports of research presented at a national or regional conference of a professional association and "State of the Art" papers are acceptable.

9. Four copies of each manuscript should be submitted to John Y. Lee at the address below under Guideline 13.

10. A submission fee of $25.00, made payable to Advances in Management Accounting, should be included with all submissions.

11. For additional information regarding the type of manuscripts that are desired, see "AIMA Statement of Purpose."

12. Final acceptance of all manuscripts requires typed and computer disk copies in the publisher's manuscript format.

13. Inquires concerning *Advances in Management Accounting* may be directed to either one of the two editors:

Marc J. Epstein
Jones Graduate School of Administration
Rice University
Houston, Texas 77251-1892

John Y. Lee
Lubin School of Business
Pace University
Pleasantville, NY 10570-2799

Advances in Public Interest Accounting

ADDRESS FOR SUBMISSION:

Cheryl R. Lehman, Editor
Advances in Public Interest Accounting
Hofstra University
Department of Accounting
Weller Hall
Hempstead, NY 11549
USA
Phone: 516-463-6986 or 5684
Fax: 516-463-4834
E-Mail: actcrl@hofstra.edu
Web:
Address May Change:

PUBLICATION GUIDELINES:

Manuscript Length: Any
Copies Required: Five
Computer Submission: No
Format: N/A
Fees to Review: 0.00 US$

Manuscript Style:
  See Manuscript Guidelines

CIRCULATION DATA:

Reader: Academics
Frequency of Issue: Yearly
Copies per Issue: Less than 1,000
Sponsor/Publisher: JAI Press, Inc./Elsevier
  Publishing
Subscribe Price: 27.50 US$
  54.50 US$ Institution

REVIEW INFORMATION:

Type of Review: Editorial Review
No. of External Reviewers: 2
No. of In House Reviewers: 0
Acceptance Rate: 21-30%
Time to Review: 2 - 3 Months
Reviewers Comments: Yes
Invited Articles: 21-30%
Fees to Publish: 0.00 US$

MANUSCRIPT TOPICS:

Accounting Education; Accounting Theory & Practice; Auditing; Cost Accounting; Gender Issues in Accounting; Government & Non Profit Accounting

MANUSCRIPT GUIDELINES/COMMENTS:

1. *Advances In Public Interest Accounting* is a publication with two major aims. First to provide a forum for the growing body of researchers who are concerned with critically appraising and radically transforming conventional accounting theory and practice. And second, to increase the social self-awareness of accountants and encourage them to assume a greater responsibility for the profession's social role.

2. We are seeking original manuscripts that explore all facets of this broad agenda. For example, we would welcome manuscripts from authors who are trying to:

- expand accounting's focus beyond the behavior of individual corporate entities;

- explore alternatives to the neo-classical economic model that currently grounds much of accounting theory;

- find alternatives to conventional efficiency and profitability measures of corporate performance;

- investigate the ways accounting contributes to the allocative, distributive, social and ecological consequences of corporate activities;

- incorporate into the reporting system the costs that corporations externalize by imposing them on their employees, their communities, and future generations;

- explore the ways in which both financial and managerial accounting participate in resolving the social tensions that surround corporate activities;

- expand the profession's reporting responsibilities beyond investors and creditors to encompass the broader set of those who interact with and are acted upon by the corporation;

- recognize the heterogeneity of interests and conflicts within investors and creditor groups;

- address the implications of the changing market structure of the accounting profession and the diminution of auditing services in relation to tax and consulting practices.

3. Send five copies of prospective manuscripts to Cheryl Lehman, Hofstra University.

4. All manuscripts should be typewritten and double-spaced on 8-1/2" x 11" white paper. Only one side of a page should be set to facilitate editing and publication except as noted:
a. Tables, figures and exhibits should appear on a separate page. Each should be numbered and have a title,
b. Footnotes should be presented by citing the author's name and the year of publication in the body of the text, e.g. Schwartz (1981); Reckers and Pany (1980).

6. Manuscripts should include a cover page which indicates the author's name and affiliation.

7. Manuscripts should include on a separate lead page an abstract not exceeding 200 words. The author's name and affiliation should not appear on the abstract.

8. Topical headings and subheadings should be used. Main headings in the manuscript should be centered, secondary headings should be flush with the left-hand margin. (As a guide to usage and style, refer to William Strunk Jr. and E.B. White, *The Elements Of Style*.)

9. Manuscripts must include a list of references which contain only those works actually cited. (As a helpful guide in preparing a list of references, refer to Kate L. Turabian, *A Manual For Writers Of Term Papers, Theses, And Dissertations*.)

10. In order to be assured of an anonymous review, authors should not identify themselves directly or indirectly. Reference to unpublished working papers and dissertations should be avoided. If necessary, authors may indicate that the reference is being withheld for the reasons cited above.

11. The author will be provided one complete volume of the issue in which his or her manuscript appears and ten off-prints of the article.

12. Manuscripts currently under review by other publications should not be submitted. Complete reports of research presented at a national or regional conference of a professional association (e.g. AAA, AIDS etc.) and "State of the Art" papers are acceptable.

13. Five copies of each manuscript should be submitted to the General Editor, Cheryl R. Lehman. Ph.D.

14. Copies of any and all research instruments should be included.

Advances in Taxation

ADDRESS FOR SUBMISSION:

Thomas M. Porcano, Editor
Advances in Taxation
Miami University
Richard T. Farmer Sch. of Bus. Admin.
Department of Accountancy
Oxford, OH 45056
USA
Phone: 513-529-6221
Fax: 513-529-4740
E-Mail: porcantm@muohio.edu
Web:
Address May Change:

PUBLICATION GUIDELINES:

Manuscript Length: More than 20
Copies Required: Three
Computer Submission: No
Format: N/A
Fees to Review: 30.00 US$

Manuscript Style:
    See Manuscript Guidelines

CIRCULATION DATA:

Reader: Academics
Frequency of Issue: Yearly
Copies per Issue: Less than 1,000
Sponsor/Publisher: JAI Press, Inc./Elsevier
    Publishing
Subscribe Price: 49.95 US$
    78.50 US$ Institution

REVIEW INFORMATION:

Type of Review: Blind Review
No. of External Reviewers: 2
No. of In House Reviewers: 0
Acceptance Rate: 21-30%
Time to Review: 2 - 3 Months
Reviewers Comments: Yes
Invited Articles: 0-5%
Fees to Publish: 0.00 US$

MANUSCRIPT TOPICS:
Fiscal Policy; Public Policy Economics; Tax Accounting

MANUSCRIPT GUIDELINES/COMMENTS:

Advances In Taxation is a refereed academic tax journal published annually. Academic articles on any aspect of federal, state, or local taxation will be considered. These include, but are not limited to, compliance, computer usage, education, law, planning, and policy. Interdisciplinary research involving economics, finance, or other areas also is encouraged. Acceptable research methodologies include any analytical, behavioral, descriptive, legal, quantitative, survey, or theoretical approach appropriate to the project.

Manuscripts must be readable, relevant, and reliable. To be readable, articles must be understandable and concise. To be relevant, articles must be directly related to problems inherent in systems of taxation. To be reliable, conclusions must follow logically from the evidence and arguments presented. For empirical papers, sound research design and execution are critical. For theoretical papers, reasonable assumptions and logical development are essential.

Three copies of the typed manuscript should be submitted together with a check for $30.00 in U.S. funds made payable to *Advances In Taxation*. The manuscript should be double spaced on 8½" x 11" paper. The submission fee is nonrefundable. On the cover page the author(s) should include name, affiliation, address, phone number, fax number, and e-mail address (if available). In the case of manuscripts reporting on field surveys or experiments, three copies of the instrument also should be submitted. Manuscripts currently under consideration by another journal or publisher should not be submitted.

Advances In Taxation is published by JAI Press, which is a well-regarded publisher of academic literature in a number of business and non-business fields. Subscription information may be obtained by calling the publisher at (203) 661-7602.

1. Manuscripts should be typewritten and double-spaced on 8-1/2" x 11" white paper. Only one side of a page should be used. Margins should be set to facilitate editing and duplication except as noted:

a. Tables, figures and exhibits should appear on a separate page. Each should be numbered and have a title.

b. Literature citations should be presented by citing the author's name and the year of publication in the body of the text, for example, Schwartz (1981); Reckers and Pany (1980).

c. Textual footnotes should be used only for extensions, the inclusion of which in the text might disrupt its continuity. Footnotes should be numbered consecutively throughout the manuscript with subscript Arabic numbers, and placed at the end of the text.

2. Manuscripts should include a cover page which indicates the author's name and affiliation.

3. Manuscripts should include on a separate lead page an abstract not exceeding 200 words. The author's name and affiliation should not appear on the abstract.

4. Topical headings and subheadings should be used. Main headings in the manuscript should be centered and typed in uppercase, secondary headings should be centered with initial capital letters, tertiary headings should be lefthand justified, italicized (underlined), with capital letters. (As a guide to usage and style, refer to William Strunk, Jr. and E.B. White, *The Elements Of Style*.)

5. Manuscripts must include a list of references which contain only those works actually cited. The entries should be arranged in alphabetical order according to the surname of the first author. Samples of entries are as follows:

Swenson, C.W., and M.L. Moore, "Use of Input-Output Analysis in Tax Research". Advances in Taxation, Vol. 1 (1987), pp. 49-84.

Pocano, T.M., "The Perceived Effects of Tax Policy on Corporate Investment Intentions", The Journal of the American Taxation Association, (Fall 1984), pp. 7-19.

6. In order to be assumed of an anonymous review, authors should not identify themselves directly or indirectly. Reference to unpublished working papers and dissertations should be avoided. If necessary, authors may indicate that the reference is being withheld for the reasons cited above.

7. The author will be provided one complete volume of the AIT volume which his or her manuscript appears and ten offprints of the article.

8. Manuscripts currently under review by other publications should not be submitted. Complete reports of research presented at a national or regional conference of a professional association (e.g., AAA, DSJ, etc.) and "State of the Art" papers are acceptable.

9. Three copies of each manuscript should be submitted to the Editor. Copies of any and all research instruments should be included.

10. For additional information regarding the type of manuscripts that are desired, see AIT Statement of Purpose.

Application of Fuzzy Logic and the Theory of Evidence in Accounting

ADDRESS FOR SUBMISSION:

Philip H. Siegel, Editor
Application of Fuzzy Logic and the Theory
    of Evidence in Accounting
Long Island University - C.W. Post
School of Professional Accounting
Brookville, NY 11548
USA
Phone:
Fax: 516-299-3221
E-Mail: psiegel@titan.liu.edu
Web:
Address May Change:

CIRCULATION DATA:

Reader: Academics
Frequency of Issue: Yearly
Copies per Issue: 1,001 - 2,000
Sponsor/Publisher: Elsevier Science
    Publishing Company
Subscribe Price: 45.00 US$ Individual
    75.00 US$ Institution

PUBLICATION GUIDELINES:

Manuscript Length: 21-25
Copies Required: Three
Computer Submission: No
Format: N/A
Fees to Review: 45.00 US$

Manuscript Style:
    American Psychological Association

REVIEW INFORMATION:

Type of Review: Blind Review
No. of External Reviewers: 2
No. of In House Reviewers: 1
Acceptance Rate: 15-20%
Time to Review: 4 - 6 Months
Reviewers Comments: Yes
Invited Articles: 0-5%
Fees to Publish: 0.00 US$

MANUSCRIPT TOPICS:
Accounting Information Systems; Accounting Theory & Practice; Auditing; Cost Accounting;
Nevral Networks; Portfolio & Security Analysis; Quantitative Methods; Tax Accounting

MANUSCRIPT GUIDELINES/COMMENTS:

Author's Responsibilities
The author is responsible for correct spelling and punctuation, accurate quotations with page
numbers, complete and accurate references, relevant content, coherent organization, legible
appearance, and so forth. The author must proofread the manuscript after it is typed, making
all corrections and changes before submitting the manuscript. Before submitting the
manuscript to the editor please use the checklist on last page of pamphlet to be sure all
necessary material is included.

The author is also responsible for preparing the manuscript on a computer. Just as word
processing eliminates a good amount of retyping, submitting a disk provides an opportunity to

eliminate duplicate keyboarding by the typesetter. One key to success is **compatibility**. Therefore, the following steps should be followed closely.

1. Use a word processing program that is able to create an IBM compatible file. For technical material (math, etc.) Macintosh files are acceptable. (Macintosh files should be submitted on **high density** disks only.)

2. Use either 5 1/4 or 3 1/2 inch, double (low) density or high density disks. **Note**: If you use double (low) density disks, be sure that the disk is formatted for double (low) density. If you use high density, be sure that the disk is formatted for high density. Unformatted or incorrectly formatted disks are unusable.

3. Structure the manuscript according to the Guidelines. Print one (1) copy of the manuscript for copy editing/styling purposes. Be sure to **double-space** this copy. That includes the notes and references.

4. Keep each chapter on one (1) file if possible. Do not make separate files for text, notes, and references. Tables may go in a separate file. A single file should contain no more than 200,000 characters. Please do not store in subdirectories.

5. **Do not** use a footnote feature. All notes should be typed in a separate section at the end of the chapter.

6. Eliminate manuscript page numbers and identifying abbreviated title from disk **after** the chapter has been printed out.

7. Submit the word processing file with your printed copy. Please indicate on the disk which word processing program and version you have used (e.g., WordPerfect 4.0, 5.1, 6.0; Word Star; WordPerfect for Windows 5.1, 6.0; Microsoft Word for Windows, etc.).

8. If using a graphics program (for art only), please put in a **separate** file in either:
.tiff
eps image (encapsulated post script)
.ps (post script)
Please **do not** include tables in the graphics program.

9. **Please** be sure that the manuscript and disk submitted match. If the material on the disk has been updated, please print out a new copy of the manuscript to be sure you are submitting the correct version.

Volume Editor's Responsibility
The volume editor is responsible for reviewing all printed manuscripts and disks before submission for publication.

Printed manuscripts should be checked for original artwork, tables, and, where necessary, letters of permission to reprint.

GENERAL INSTRUCTIONS

Paper
Type or print the manuscript on one side of standard-sized (8 1/2 x 11"), or European equivalent, paper. Do not use onionskin or erasable paper. All pages must be of the same size. Do not use half sheets or strips of paper glued, taped, or stapled to the pages.

Type Element
The type must be dark, clear, and readable. A typeface that is made up of dots, as generated by some printers, is acceptable only if it is clear and legible.

Double Spacing
Double space between all lines of the manuscript, which includes the title, headings, notes, quotations, and references, figure captions. Never use single-spacing or one-and-a-half line spacing except on tables.

Margins
Leave uniform margins of 1 1/2" at the top, bottom, right, and left of every page. The length of each typed line is 5 1/2". Do not justify lines; leave the right margin uneven. Do not hyphenate words at the end of a line; let a line run short or long rather than break a word. Type no more than 25 lines of text on a manuscript page.

Headings
Most manuscripts use from one to four headings. The four levels should appear as:

CENTERED ALL UPPERCASE HEADING

Centered Uppercase and Lowercase Heading

Flush Left, Underlined, Uppercase and Lowercase Side Heading

Indented, underlined, lowercase paragraph heading ending with a period.

Paragraphs And Indentation
Indent the first line of every paragraph and the first line of every note five spaces. Type the remaining lines of the manuscript to a uniform left-hand margin.

Quotations
Direct quotations must be accurate. Quotations of 40 words or less should be incorporated into the text and enclosed by double quotation marks ("). Display quotations of more than 40 words should appear as a double-spaced block with no quotation marks. Do not single-space. Indent 5 spaces from the left margin and 5 spaces from the right margin.

Permission To Quote

Any direct quotation, regardless of length must be accompanied by a reference citation that includes the author, year of publication, and page number(s). If you quote at length from a copyrighted work, you will also need written permission from the owner of the copyright. It is the author's responsibility to obtain the reprint permission. A copy of the letter of permission must accompany the manuscript.

Statistical And Mathematical Copy

Type all signs and symbols in mathematical copy that you can. Either type a character that resembles the symbol or draw the symbol in by hand. Identify symbols that may be hard to read or ambiguous to the copy editor or typesetter. The first time the ambiguous symbol appears in the manuscript, spell out and circle the name next to the symbol. Space mathematical copy as you would space words. Align signs and symbols carefully. Type subscripts half a line below the symbol and superscripts half a line above the symbol. Display a mathematical equation by setting it off from the text by double-spacing twice above and below the equation. If the equation is identified by a number, type the number in parentheses flush against the right margin. Do not underline: (1) greek letters, subscripts, and superscripts that function as identifiers, and (2) abbreviations that are not variables. Mark symbols for vectors with a wavy line to indicate bold typeface. Underline all other statistical symbols.

Parts Of A Manuscript

Order of manuscript pages: Number all pages consecutively. Arrange the pages of the manuscript as follows:

title page (page 1)
abstract (page 2)
text (page 3)
appendices (start each on a separate page)
author acknowledgment
notes (start on a new page)
references (start on a new page)
tables (start each on a separate page)
figures (start each on a separate page)

This arrangement is not the way the printed paper will appear; it is necessary for handling by the copy editor and the typesetter.

After the manuscript pages are arranged in the correct order, number them consecutively, beginning with the title page. Number all pages. Type the number in the upper right-hand corner using arabic numbers. Identify each manuscript page by typing an abbreviated title above the page number.

Title Page

The title page includes 4 elements:

The title in uppercase (capital) letters.
The author(s) in uppercase and lowercase letters.

An abbreviated title to be used as a running head. The running head should be a maximum of 70 characters, which includes all letters, punctuation, and spaces between words.
Complete mailing address, phone, and fax numbers of each author.

Abstract
Begin the abstract on a new page. Type the word "ABSTRACT" in all uppercase letters, centered at top of page. Type the abstract itself as a single paragraph, double-spaced, indent 5 spaces from the left margin and 5 spaces from the right margin.

Text
Begin the text on a new page. The sections of the text follow each other without a break.

Appendices
Begin each Appendix on a separate page. Type the word "APPENDIX" in all uppercase letters and identifying capital letters in the order in which they are mentioned in text, centered at the top of the page. If there is only one Appendix, it is not necessary to use an identifying letter.

Author Acknowledgment
This note is neither numbered nor is it mentioned in text. In all uppercase letters, type the word "ACKNOWLEDGMENT" centered at top of a new page. Type the acknowledgment itself as a double-spaced single paragraph.

Notes
Notes that are mentioned in text are numbered consecutively throughout the chapter. Double-space the notes and begin on a separate page. Center the word "NOTES" in all uppercase letters at the top of the page. Indent the first line of each note 5 spaces and type the notes in the order in which they are mentioned in text.

References
Each series has its own individual style, whether it be APA, ASA, reference notes, or a style unique to its discipline. For the style that you must follow, consult the *Publication Manual Of The American Psychological Association* (Fourth Edition), *The Chicago Manual Of Style* (14th Edition), or a previously published volume in the series.

References cited in text **must** appear in the reference list; conversely, each entry in the reference list must be cited in text. It is the author's responsibility to make certain that each source referenced appears in both places and that the text citation and reference list are identical.

Important: (1) Foreign language volumes, parts, numbers, editions, and so on **must** be translated into their English equivalents. Both the original language and the English translation will appear in the references. Authors **must** transliterate or romanize languages that do not use Latin characters (e.g., Greek, Russian, Chinese, Arabic, etc.), along with their English translation. A comprehensive resource for this is a publication issued by the Library of Congress, titled *ALA-LC Romanization Tables: Transliteration Schemes For Non-Roman Scripts*. (2) JAI Press does not use either op. cit. or loc. cit. A short-title form is required. Ibid. is acceptable.

Items to be included in a full reference are:

Book:
Author's full name
Complete title of the book
Editor, compiler, or translator, if any
Series, if any, and volume or number in series
Edition, if not the original
Number of volumes
Facts of publication: city where published, publisher, date of publication
Volume number, if any
Page number(s) of the particular citation

Article In A Periodical:
Author's full name
Title of the article
Name of the periodical
Volume (and number) of the periodical
Date of the volume or issue
Page number(s) of the particular citation

Unpublished Material:
Title of document, if any, and date
Folio number or other identifying material
Name of collection
Depository and city where it is located

Tables
Tables are numbered consecutively in the order in which they are first mentioned in text and are identified by the word "Table" and an arabic numeral. Begin each table on a separate page. Type the short title of the manuscript and the page number in the upper right-hand corner of every page of a table. Tables are complicated to set in type and more expensive to publish than text. Therefore, they should be reserved for important data directly related to the content of the paper. Refer to every table and its data in text. Do not write "the table above/below" or "the table on p. 32" because the position and page number of a table cannot be determined until the text is typeset. In text, indicate the approximate placement of each table by a clear break in the text, inserting:

TABLE 1 ABOUT HERE

set off double-spaced above and below. Do not abbreviate table headings. Limit the use of rules to horizontal rules only. Draw all rules in pencil.

Figures

Figures are also numbered consecutively in the order in which they are first mentioned in text. Use the word "Figure" and an arabic numeral. Indicate the location of each figure by a clear break, inserting:

INSERT FIGURE 1 ABOUT HERE

set off double-spaced above and below.

All **figures, charts, illustrations, and halftones** are figures and must be submitted in a form suitable for reproduction by the printer without redrawing or retouching. Careful adherence to the following instructions will ensure the high quality appearance of your paper.

1. All figures must be submitted as either camera-ready original ink drawings or laser quality copy.

2. All lettering must be done professionally. Three methods of lettering are acceptable: professional lettering, stencil, or dry-transfer sheets. Freehand and typewritten lettering is not acceptable. It is best not to use all capital lettering. Lettering should be large enough so that it is completely legible after photo reduction. Lettering in all figures should be the same size.

3. When planning a figure, take into consideration that all published figures must fit the dimensions of a book page. Figures should be no larger than 4 x 6" If a figure exceeds this size, it should be large enough and sharp enough to be legible when reduced to fit the page. Please remember that reducing the width of a figure will reduce the length by the same percentage.

4. Graphs and charts: Keep lines clean and simple and eliminate all extraneous detail. Graph paper should never be used.

5. Illustrations: Illustrations should be prepared by a professional artist. The least amount of detail necessary should be used.

6. Halftones: Original photos of professional quality are a necessity. Place overlays on all halftones to prevent scratches and damage from handling. Please keep in mind that halftones require a complicated printing process, which makes them more expensive than line drawings to reproduce.

Important: Color halftones are very costly to print. If color halftones are submitted, they will be printed in black and white. If any halftones must be printed in color, the cost will be charged to the author.

7. Unlike the figure, which is reproduced from the glossy print, the figure number and legend is typeset and placed outside the figure. Therefore, type all figure numbers and legends double-spaced on a separate page.

8. When enclosing a figure in a box, do not include figure caption within the box. The figure number and captions are set separately.

9. For identification by the production editor and printer, please indicate on the back of each photo the author, title of paper, number and figure legend. All information should be written lightly in soft pencil, using as little pressure as possible. "Top" should be written on any illustration that might accidentally be reproduced wrong side up.

10. Staples, of course, should never be used on any illustration copy, nor should paper clips unless they are well padded with several thicknesses of paper to prevent scratching and indentation. Scotch tape should never be used to attach illustration copy to another page as tape edges show up as black lines in reproduction.

11. Prints should never be folded. They should be put in a separate envelope and protected by a sheet or sheets of stiff cardboard.

12. The author is responsible for obtaining permission to reproduce a figure from a copyrighted source. A photocopy of the permission must be submitted with the manuscript.

13. We will naturally assume that the print(s) have been thoroughly checked for accuracy before submission to JAI Press.

14. All prints will be considered final and no corrections will be allowed.

15. Unless otherwise indicated, prints will not be returned to the author.

Manuscript Checklist

—Is the manuscript typed on 8 1/2 X 11" paper?

—Is the entire manuscript-including quotations, references, notes, figure captions, and all parts of tables- double-spaced?

—Is the manuscript neatly prepared and clean?

—Are the margins 1 1/2 inch?

—Are the title page, abstract, notes, references, tables, and figures on separate pages?

—Are all pages numbered in sequence, starting with the title page?

—Are all headings of the same level typed in the same format?

—Are Greek letters and all but the most common mathematical symbols identified?

—Are all non-Greek letters that are used as statistical symbols or algebraic variables underlined?

—Are all notes indicated in text and are the note numbers correctly located?

—Are references cited both in text and in the reference list?

—Do the text citations and reference list entries agree both in spelling and in date?

—Are journal titles in the reference list spelled out fully?

—Are inclusive page numbers for all articles or chapters in books provided in the reference list?

—Does every table column have a heading?

—Are tables horizontally ruled with light pencil lines only?

—Have all vertical table rules been omitted?

—Have all figures been submitted as camera-ready?

—Are the elements in the figures large enough to remain legible after the figure has been reduced to fit a printed page?

—Is each figure labeled on its back with the author's name, title of paper, figure number, and figure legend?

—Are all figures and tables mentioned in text?

__ Is the placement of each table and figure indicated in text?

—Is written permission to use previously published text, tables, or figures enclosed with the manuscript?

—Are page numbers provided in text for all quotations?

Asia-Pacific Financial Markets

ADDRESS FOR SUBMISSION:

Tsunemasa Shiba, Editor
Asia-Pacific Financial Markets
Hitotsubashi University
Faculty of Economics
2-1 Naka
Kunitachi-shi, Tokyo, 186-8601
Japan
Phone: 81 425-80-8786
Fax: 81 425-80-8882
E-Mail: tshiba@stat,hit-u.ac.jp
Web:
Address May Change:

PUBLICATION GUIDELINES:

Manuscript Length: 21-25
Copies Required: Four
Computer Submission: No
Format: N/A
Fees to Review: 0.00 US$

Manuscript Style:
    See Manuscript Guidelines

CIRCULATION DATA:

Reader: Academics, Business Persons
Frequency of Issue: Quarterly
Copies per Issue: Less than 1,000
Sponsor/Publisher: Japanese Assn. of
    Financial Economics and
    Econometrics/Kluwer Publishers
Subscribe Price: 267.50 US$

REVIEW INFORMATION:

Type of Review: Editorial Review
No. of External Reviewers: 1-2
No. of In House Reviewers: 1-2
Acceptance Rate: 40%
Time to Review: 6 Months
Reviewers Comments: Yes
Invited Articles: Zero
Fees to Publish: 0.00 US$

MANUSCRIPT TOPICS:
Derivative Securities; Econometrics; Finance & Investments; Financial Engineering;
Insurance; International Finance; Mathematical Finance; Portfolio & Security Analysis

MANUSCRIPT GUIDELINES/COMMENTS:

Asia-Pacific Financial Markets publishes empirical and/or theoretical research articles on
financial time series, pricing models for various financial assets including derivatives, global
asset allocation, trading strategies for investment, optimization methods etc. Papers with
empirical analysis using the Asian market data are preferred.

Asia-Pacific Financial Markets is published by Kluwer Academic Publishers, P.O. Box 17,
330 AH Dordrecht, The Netherlands. Phone (31) 78 524400, fax (31) 78 52447.

Manuscript Submission
Kluwer Academic Publishers prefer the submission of manuscripts and figures in electronic
form in addition to a hard-copy printout. The preferred storage medium for your electronic
manuscript is a 3 1/2 inch diskette. Please label your diskette properly, giving exact details on

the name(s) of the file(s), the operating system and software used. Always save your electronic manuscript in the word processor format that you use; conversions to other formats and versions tend to be imperfect. In general, use as few formatting codes as possible. For safety's sake, you should always retain a backup copy of your file(s). **After acceptance,** please make absolutely sure that you send the latest (i.e., revised) version of your manuscript, both as hard-copy printout and on diskette.

Kluwer Academic Publishers prefer articles submitted in word processing packages such as MS Word, WordPerfect, etc. running under operating systems MS DOS, Windows and Apple Macintosh, or in the file format LaTeX. Articles submitted in other software programs, as well as articles for conventional typesetting, can also be accepted.

For submission in LaTeX, *Kluwer Academic Publishers* have developed a Kluwer LaTeX class file, which can be downloaded from: www.wkap.nl/kaphtml.hftn/IFAHOME. Use of this class file is highly recommended. Do not use versions downloaded from other sites. Technical support is available at: texhelp@wkap.nl. If you are not familiar with TeX/LaTeX, the class file will be of no use to you. In that case, submit your article in a common word processor format.

To be considered for publication in *Asia-Pacific Financial Markets* each paper should contain some empirical analysis of Asia-Pacific financial data, even when its main part is theoretical or methodological. For the purpose of reviewing, articles for publication should be submitted as hard-copy printout (4-fold) and on diskette, along with a cover letter, to:

Professor Tsunemasa Shiba, Faculty of Economics,
Hitotsubashi University, 2-1 Naka, Kunitachi-shi, Tokyo 186-8601, Japan
Phone: 81 42 580 8786, Fax: 81 42 580 8882, E-mail: tshiba@stat.hit-u.ac.jp

Manuscript Presentation

The journal's language is English. British English or American English spelling and terminology may be used, but either one should be followed consistently throughout the article. Manuscripts should be printed or typewritten on A4 or US Letter bond paper, one side only, leaving adequate margins on all sides to allow reviewers' remarks. Please double-space all material, including notes and references. Quotations of more than 40 words should be set off clearly, either by indenting the left-hand margin or by using a smaller typeface. Use double quotation marks for direct quotations and single quotation marks for quotations within quotations and for words or phrases used in a special sense.

Number the pages consecutively with the first page containing:
- running head (shortened title)
- title
- author(s)
- affiliation(s)
- full address for correspondence, including telephone and fax number and email address

Abstract

Please provide a short abstract containing a maximum of 300 words. The abstract should not contain any undefined abbreviations or unspecified references. The author should make sure that the abstract is readable to those who are unfamiliar with the subject matter.

Key Words
Please provide 5 to 10 key words or short phrases in alphabetical order.

Symbols and Units
Units. Any numerical results in dimensional form should be presented in SI units. Indicate clearly the differences between 0 (zero) en **O**, o (the letters), between the numeral 1 and the letter 1, between *a* and alpha, k and kappa, p and rho, a and mu, v and nu, *n* and eta, etc. The author should also see to it that the level of subscripts, subscripts to subscripts, exponents as well as exponents in exponents, cannot be misunderstood. Fractions to be printed in the body of the text (not in display formulae) should make use of the solidus. The use of negative exponents will save both space and typesetting costs. Attention should be paid to the consistent use of braces, brackets, and parentheses. *Equations.* Number consecutively only those equations that are referred to in the text.

Figures and Tables

Submission of electronic figures

In addition to hard-copy printouts of figures, authors are encouraged to supply the electronic versions of figures in either Encapsulated PostScript (EPS) or TIFF format. Many other formats, e.g., Microsoft Postscript, PICT (Macintosh) and WMF (Windows), cannot be used and the hard copy will be scanned instead.

Figures should be saved in separate files *without* their captions, which should be included with the text of the article. Files should be named according to DOS conventions, e.g., 'figurel.eps'. For vector graphics, EPS is the preferred format. Lines should not be thinner than 0.25pts and in-fill patterns and screens should have a density of at least 10%. Font-related problems can be avoided by using standard fonts such as Times Roman and Helvetica. For bitmapped graphics, TIFF is the preferred format but EPS is also acceptable. The following resolutions are optimal: black-and-white line figures - 600 - 1200 dpi; line figures with some grey or coloured lines - 600 dpi; photographs - 300 dpi; screen dumps - leave as is. Higher resolutions will not improve output quality but will only increase file size, which may cause problems with printing; lower resolutions may compromise output quality. Please try to provide artwork that approximately fits within the typeset area of the journal-Especially screened originals, i.e. originals with grey areas, may suffer badly from reduction by more than 10-15%.

AVOIDING PROBLEMS WITH EPS GRAPHICS
Please always check whether the figures print correctly to a PostScript printer in a reasonable amount of time. If they do not, simplify your figures or use a different graphics program.

If EPS export does not produce acceptable output, try to create an EPS file with the printer driver (see below). This option is unavailable with the Microsoft driver for Windows NT, so if you run Windows NT, get the Adobe driver from the Adobe site (www.adobe.com).

If EPS export is not an option, e.g., because you rely on OLE and cannot create separate files for your graphics, it may help us if you simply provide a PostScript dump of the entire document.

HOW TO SET UP FOR EPS AND POSTSCRIPT DUMPS UNDER WINDOWS
Create a printer entry specifically for this purpose: install the printer 'Apple Laserwriter Plus' and specify 'FILE': as printer port. Each time you send something to the 'printer' you will be asked for a filename. This file will be the EPS file or PostScript dump that we can use.

The EPS export option can be found under the PostScript tab. EPS export should be used only for single-page documents. For printing a document of several pages, select 'Optimise for portability' instead. The option 'Download header with each job' should be checked.

Submission of hard-copy figures

If no electronic versions of figures are available, submit only highquality artwork that can be reproduced as is, i.e., without any part having to be redrawn or re-typeset. The letter size of any text in the figures must be large enough to allow for reduction. Photographs should be in black-and-white on glossy paper. If a figure contains colour, make absolutely clear whether it should be printed in black-and-white or in colour. Figures that are to be printed in black-and-white should not be submitted in colour. Authors will be charged for reproducing figures in colour.

Each figure and table should be numbered and mentioned in the text. The approximate position of figures and tables should be indicated in the margin of the manuscript. On the reverse side of each figure, the name of the (first) author and the figure number should be written in pencil; the top of the figure should be clearly indicated. Figures and tables should be placed at the end of the manuscript following the Reference section. Each figure and table should be accompanied by an explanatory legend. The figure legends should be grouped and placed on a separate page. Figures are not returned to the author unless specifically requested.

In tables, footnotes are preferable to long explanatory material in either the heading or body of the table. Such explanatory footnotes, identified by superscript letters, should be placed immediately below the table.

Section Headings
Section headings should be numbered (e.g., 1., 1.1., 1.1.1., 2., 2.1., etc.).

Appendices
Supplementary material should be collected in an Appendix and placed before the Notes and Reference sections.

Notes

Please use endnotes rather than footnotes. Notes should be indicated by consecutive superscript numbers in the text and listed at the end of the article before the References. A source reference note should be indicated by means of an asterisk after the title. This note should be placed at the bottom of the first page.

Cross-Referencing

In the text, a reference identified by means of an author's name should be followed by the date of the reference in parentheses and page number(s) where appropriate. When there are more than two authors, only the first author's name should be mentioned, followed by 'et al.'. In the event that an author cited has had two or more works published during the same year, the reference, both in the text and in the reference list, should be identified by a lower case letter like 'a' and 'b ` after the date to distinguish the works.

Examples:

Winograd (1986, p. 204)

(Winograd, 1986a, b)

(Winograd, 1986; Flores et al., 1988)

(Bullen and Bennett, 1990)

Acknowledgements

Acknowledgements of people, grants, funds, etc. should be placed in a separate section before the References.

References

References to books, journal articles, articles in collections and conference or workshop proceedings, and technical reports should be listed at the end of the article in **alphabetical** order (see examples below). Articles in preparation or articles submitted for publication, unpublished observations, personal communications, etc. should not be included in the reference list but should only be mentioned in the article text (e.g., T. Moore, personal communication).

References to books should include the author's name; year of publication; title; page numbers where appropriate; publisher; place of publication, in the order given in the example below.

Duffle, D. (1989) *Future Markets,* Prentice Hall, Englewood Cliffs, N. J.

References to articles in an edited collection should include the author's name; year of publication; article title; editor's name; title of collection; first and last page numbers; publisher; place of publication, in the order given in the example below.

Ross, S. A. (1976) Risk, return and arbitrage. In I. Friend and J. S. Bicksler (eds), *Risk and Return in Finance,* Ballinger, Cambridge, Mass.

References to articles in conference proceedings should include the author's name; year of publication; article title; editor's name (if any); title of proceedings; first and last page numbers; place and date of conference; publisher and/or organization from which the proceedings can be obtained; place of publication, in the order given in the example below.

Skiba, Yu. N. (1995) Pollution concentration estimates in ecologically important zones. In *Proceedings of X World Clean Air Congress "Growing Challenges - From Local To Global"*, May 28-June 2, 1995, Helsinki, Finland, Vol. 3, paper 525.

References to articles in periodicals should include the author's name; year of publication; article title; abbreviated title of periodical; volume number (issue number where appropriate); first and last page numbers, in the order given in the example below.

Canina, L. and Figlewski, S. (1993) The informational content of implied volatility, *Rev. Financ. Stud. 6,* 659-681.

References to technical reports or doctoral dissertations should include the author's name; year of publication; title of report or dissertation; institution; location of institution, in the order given in the example below.

Stone, W. A., Thorp, J. M., Grifford, O. P., and Hoitink, D. J.: Climatological summary for the Hanford area, Technical Report, PNL-4622, Pacific Northwest Laboratory, Richland, Washington.

Proofs
Proofs will be sent to the corresponding author. One corrected proof, together with the original, edited manuscript, should be returned to the Publisher [Editor] within three days of receipt by mail (airmail overseas).

Offprints .
Twenty-five offprints of each article will be provided free of charge. Additional offprints can be ordered by means of an offprint order form supplied with the proofs.

Page Charges and Colour Figures
No page charges are levied on authors or their institutions. Colour figures are published at the author's expense only.

Copyright
Authors will be asked, upon acceptance of an article, to transfer copyright of the article to the Publisher. This will ensure the widest possible dissemination of information under copyright laws.

Permissions
It is the responsibility of the author to obtain written permission for a quotation from unpublished material, or for all quotations in excess of 250 words in one extract or 500 words in total from any work still in copyright, and for the reprinting of figures, tables or poems from unpublished or copyrighted material.

Auditing: A Journal of Practice and Theory

ADDRESS FOR SUBMISSION:

Arnold Wright, Editor
Auditing: A Journal of Practice and Theory
Boston College
Carroll School of Management
Department of Accounting
Chestnut Hill, MA 02167-3808
USA
Phone: 617-552-0876
Fax: 617-552-2097
E-Mail: wrighta@bc.edu
Web:
Address May Change:

PUBLICATION GUIDELINES:

Manuscript Length: 20+
Copies Required: Four
Computer Submission: No
Format: N/A
Fees to Review: 50.00 US$
    100.00 US$ International Submission

Manuscript Style:
    See Manuscript Guidelines

CIRCULATION DATA:

Reader: Academics, Auditors
Frequency of Issue: 2 Times/ Year
Copies per Issue: 1,001 - 2,000
Sponsor/Publisher: American Accounting
    Association
Subscribe Price: 25.00 US$

REVIEW INFORMATION:

Type of Review: Editorial Review
No. of External Reviewers: 2
No. of In House Reviewers: 0
Acceptance Rate: 11-20%
Time to Review: 2 - 3 Months
Reviewers Comments: Yes
Invited Articles: 0-5%
Fees to Publish: 0.00 US$

MANUSCRIPT TOPICS:
Auditing

MANUSCRIPT GUIDELINES/COMMENTS:

Editorial Philosophy
The purpose of this journal is to contribute to improving the theory and practice of auditing. The term "auditing" is to be interpreted broadly. Thus this journal invites articles on internal and external auditing as well as comprehensive and financial (attest) audits. Practices and developments in auditing in different countries, either in corporate or governmental contexts, are appropriate topics, and so are uses of auditing in new ways and for different purposes. Discussion and analysis of current problems and issues in auditing will constitute an important part of the journal's contents. This will include surveys which summarize and evaluate developments in related fields which have an important bearing on auditing. Papers reporting results or original research which have improvements in auditing theory or auditing methodology as a central focus are also invited. The objective is to promote a two-way flow between research and practice which will influence developments in auditing education as well as auditing research and auditing practice.

Manuscript Preparation And Style
Auditing: A Journal Of Practice & Theory's manuscript preparation guidelines follow closely that used in *The Accounting Review*, another American Accounting Association publication. These guidelines follow (with slight modification) the B-format of the *Chicago Manual Of Style* (13th ed.; University of Chicago Press). Another helpful guide to usage and style is *The Elements Of Style*, by William Strunk, Jr., and E.B. White (Macmillan). Spelling follows *Webster's International Dictionary*.

Format

1. All manuscripts should be typed on one side of 8 1/2 x 11" paper and be double-spaced, except for indented quotations, footnotes, and references.

2. Manuscripts should be as concise as the subject and research method permit, and as a general rule, should not exceed 7,000 words.

3. Margins of at least one inch on top, bottom, and sides will facilitate editing and duplication.

4. A cover page should show the title of the paper, the author's name, title, affiliation, complete mailing address, and any acknowledgements. The title of the paper, but not the author's name, should appear on the Summary page and on the first page of the text.

5. All pages, including tables, appendices, and references, should be serially numbered.

6. When not in lists, numbers from one through ten should be spelled out, except where decimals are used. All others should be written numerically.

7. Hyphens are preferred to the compounding or to the coining of words. Authors should avoid using first person.

8. Mathematical notation should be employed only where its rigor and precision are indispensable, and in such circumstances authors should explain in narrative format the principal operations performed. Notation should be avoided in footnotes. Unusual symbols, particularly if handwritten, should be identified in the margin when they first appear. Displayed material should clearly indicate the alignment, superscripts, and subscripts. Equations should be numbered in parentheses flush with the right-hand margin.

9. Headings should be arranged so that major headings are centered and capitalized. Second level headings should be flush with the side of the page and subsequent levels appropriately indented. For example:

A CENTERED, ALL CAPITALIZED, FIRST LEVEL HEADING

A flush Side Second Level Heading
A Third Level Heading
A Fourth Level Heading

Tables And Figures

Each table and figure should appear on a separate page and bear an arabic number and a complete title indicating the exact contents. A reference to each table or figure should appear in the text. The author should indicate by marginal notation where each table or figure is to be inserted in the text, e.g., [Insert table X here].

Summary

A summary, of approximately (but not in excess of) 300 words, should be on a separate page immediately preceding the text. This summary should be non-mathematical and easily readable, with an emphasis on the significant findings or conclusions of the article. The intent is to enable the target audience--practitioners and academics--to quickly determine the relevance of the article to their own interests. Thus, the language should be less formal than that used in the article itself, and discussion of method should be brief, unless that is the main focus of the article.

Documentation

Literature Citations: Work cited should be in the body of the text, by the author's name and the year of publication.

1. With one author, use author's last name and date, without comma, in parentheses: for example (Shank 1975); with two authors: (Storey and Moonitz 1976); with more than two: (Jones et al. 1985); with more than one source cited together: (Shank 1975; Chambers 1976); with two or more works by one author: (Jones 1985, 1987).

2. Citations to institutional works should employ acronyms or short titles, where practicable; for example (AAAASOBAT 1966) or (AICPA Cohen Commission Report 1977). Where brief, the full title of an institutional work may be used; for example (ICAEW The Corporate Report 1975).

3. Unless confusion would result, do not use "p." or "pp." before page numbers; for example (Khun 1970, 20).

4. If an author's name is mentioned in the text, it need not be repeated in the citation; for example, "Khun (1970, 20) says...."

5. When the reference list contains more than one work of an author published in a single year, the suffix a, b, etc. follows the date in the text citation; for example (Demski 1973a).

6. If the manuscript refers to statutes, legal treaties, or court cases, citations acceptable in law reviews should be used.

Footnotes: Textual footnotes are used only for extensions and explanations whose inclusion in the body of the manuscript might disrupt the continuity. Footnotes should be numbered consecutively throughout the manuscript with superscript arabic numbers. Footnotes are placed at the end of the text.

104

Reference List: The list of references follows the text, and contains only those works actually cited. Each entry should contain all of the data necessary for unambiguous identification, in the following format

1. Arrange citations in alphabetical order according to the surname of the first author, or the name of the institution responsible for a work with no author listed.

2. Multiple works by the same author(s) should be listed in chronological order of publication: two or more works by the same author(s) in the same year are distinguished by letters after the date.

3. Use authors' initials instead of proper names.

4. Do not abbreviate titles of journals.

5. Dates of publication should be placed immediately after author's name.

Sample entries:

American Accounting Association, Committee on Concepts and Standards for External Financial Reports. 1977. Statement on Accounting Theory and Theory Acceptance. Sarasota, FL: AAA.

Dye, R., B. Balachandran, and R. Magee. 1989. Contingent fees for audit firms. Working paper, Northwestern University, Evanston, IL.

Garrison, R. 1988. Managerial Accounting. Homewood, IL: BPI/Irwin.

Revsine, L. 1970a. Data expansion and conceptual structure. The Accounting Review (October): 704-11.

_____, 1970b. Change in budget pressure and its impact on supervisor behavior. Journal of Accounting Research (Autumn): 90-91.

Bank Accounting & Finance

ADDRESS FOR SUBMISSION:

Claire Greene, Editor
Bank Accounting & Finance
129 Everett Street
Concord, MA 01742
USA
Phone: 978-369-6285
Fax: 978-371-2961
E-Mail: cgreene@world.std.com
Web:
Address May Change:

PUBLICATION GUIDELINES:

Manuscript Length: 16-25
Copies Required: Two
Computer Submission: Yes
Format: IBM PC Compat, Microsoft Word
Fees to Review: 0.00 US$

Manuscript Style:
    Chicago Manual of Style

CIRCULATION DATA:

Reader: Business Persons
Frequency of Issue: Quarterly
Copies per Issue: 2,001 - 3,000
Sponsor/Publisher: Institutional Investor,
    Inc.
Subscribe Price: 220.00 US$
    66.00 US$ Academics

REVIEW INFORMATION:

Type of Review: Blind Review
No. of External Reviewers: 2
No. of In House Reviewers: 1
Acceptance Rate: 50%
Time to Review: 1 - 2 Months
Reviewers Comments: Yes
Invited Articles: 50% +
Fees to Publish: 0.00 US$

MANUSCRIPT TOPICS:
Accounting Theory & Practice; Auditing; Cost Accounting

MANUSCRIPT GUIDELINES/COMMENTS:

How To Submit A Manuscript
Bank Accounting & Finance welcomes articles to be considered for publication. *Bank Accounting & Finance* is the first in-depth, practical journal for bank accounting and financial officers. Readers are CFOs, treasurers controllers, accountants, auditors, cashiers, and financial VPs.

Readers are interested in articles on topics including, but not limited to, the following:
• financial accounting,
• management accounting,
• capital planning,
• profitability measurement,
• asset/liability management,
• liquidity issues,
• treasury management and investment policy,

- new financial instruments and capital markets products,
- bank stock analysis,
- risk management,
- portfolio management,
- cost control,
- mergers and acquisitions,
- technology,
- reporting systems,
- auditing and internal control,
- regulation,
- taxes.

For example, the following types of articles would be appealing to the practitioners who read *Bank Accounting & Finance:*

Description and analysis of implementation issues for new standards and rules issued by FASB, the EITF , bank regulators, the SEC, and the IRS.

Case studies showing how a particular bank designed a new management accounting system, implemented new techniques of A/L management, combined operations after a merger, or improved controls for derivatives.

Surveys showing how a group of banks implemented a new accounting standard or correlating banks' stock prices to strategy or reporting practices.

Articles should be practical, with concrete advice, illustrative anecdotes and examples, and a description of results readers might expect if they follow the author's recommendations. Articles generally run from 3,000 to 7,500 words (12 to 30 double-spaced typewritten pages). The how and case study approach is particularly appropriate for *Bank Accounting & Finance.*

Submission Guidelines

To propose an article, please contact editor Claire Greene before you start to write (voice 978-369-6285; fax 978-371-2961. She will enjoy talking over your idea with you and can help you tailor it to *Bank Accounting & Finance's* specific needs for manuscripts.

Bank Accounting & Finance is published by Institutional Investor, Inc., 488 Madison Avenue, New York, NY 10022. Tel: 212-224-3545 Fax: 212-224-3527.

Behavioral Research in Accounting

ADDRESS FOR SUBMISSION:

Susan Haka, Editor
Behavioral Research in Accounting
Michigan State University
Eli Broad College of Business
N270, North Business
East Lansing, MI 48824
USA
Phone: 517-432-2920
Fax: 517-432-1101
E-Mail: suehaka@pilot.msu.edu
Web:
Address May Change:

PUBLICATION GUIDELINES:

Manuscript Length: 21-25
Copies Required: Four
Computer Submission: No
Format: N/A
Fees to Review: 50.00 US$

Manuscript Style:
    See Manuscript Guidelines

CIRCULATION DATA:

Reader: Academics
Frequency of Issue: 2 Times/ Year
Copies per Issue: 1,001 - 2,000
Sponsor/Publisher: Accounting, Behavior
    and Organizations Section of American
    Accounting Assn.
Subscribe Price: 20.00 US$ AAA Members
        20.00 US$ ABO Members

REVIEW INFORMATION:

Type of Review: Blind Review
No. of External Reviewers: 2
No. of In House Reviewers: 0
Acceptance Rate: 11-20%
Time to Review: 4 - 6 Months
Reviewers Comments: Yes
Invited Articles: 0-5%
Fees to Publish: 0.00 US$

MANUSCRIPT TOPICS:

Accounting Information Systems; Accounting Theory & Practice; Auditing; Behavioral Accounting Research; Cost Accounting; Econometrics; Government & Non Profit Accounting; Micro Economics; Tax Accounting

MANUSCRIPT GUIDELINES/COMMENTS:

Editorial Policies

Behavioral Research In Accounting is published by the Accounting, Behavior and Organizations Section of the American Accounting Association. Original research relating to accounting and how it affects and is affected by individuals and organizations will be considered by the journal. Theoretical papers and papers based upon empirical research (e.g., field, survey, and experimental research) are appropriate. Replications of previously published studies will be considered. The primary audience of the journal is the membership of the Accounting, Behavior and Organizations Section of the American Accounting Association.

For a manuscript to be acceptable for publication, the research question should be of interest to the intended readership, the research project should be well designed and well executed, and arguments or findings should be presented effectively and efficiently.

The Review Process
Each manuscript submitted to *Behavioral Research In Accounting* is subject to the following review procedures:

Review Process
1. Each manuscript is reviewed by the editor for general suitability for this journal.

2. For those that are judged suitable, at lease two reviewers are selected and a double blind review process takes place.

3. Using the recommendations of the reviewers, the editor will decide whether the particular manuscript should be accepted as is, revised, or rejected for publication.

The process described above is a general process. In any particular case, deviations may occur from the steps described.

Submission Of Manuscripts
Authors should note the following guidelines for submitting manuscripts:

1. Manuscripts currently under consideration by another journal or other publisher should not be submitted. The author must state that the work is not submitted or published elsewhere.

2. In the case of manuscripts reporting on field surveys or experiments, four copies of the instrument (questionnaire, case, interview plan, or the like) should be submitted.

3. Four copies should be submitted together with a check for $50.00 in U.S. funds payable to the American Accounting Association and sent to Don W. Finn, Texas Tech University, COBA, P.O. Box 42101, Lubbock Texas 79409-2101. The submission fee is nonrefundable.

4. The author should retain a copy of the paper.

5. Revisions must be submitted within 12 months from request, otherwise they will be considered new submissions.

Mathematical Notation
Mathematical notation should be employed only where its rigor and precision are necessary, and in such circumstances authors should explain in the narrative format the principal operations performed. Notation should be avoided in footnotes. Unusual symbols, particularly if handwritten, should be identified in the margin when they appear. Displayed material should clearly indicate the alignment, superscripts, and subscripts. Equations should be numbered in parentheses flush with the right-hand margin.

Documentation

Citations: Work cited should use the "author-date system" keyed to a list of works in the reference list (see below). Authors should make an effort to include the relevant page numbers in the cited works.

1. In the text, works are cited as follows: author's last name and date, without comma, in parentheses: for example (Jones 1987); with two authors: (Jones and Freeman 1973); with more than two: (Jones et al. 1985): with more than one source cited together (Jones 1987; Freeman 1986); with two or more works by one author: (Jones 1985, 1987).

2. Unless confusion would result, do not use "p." or "pp." before page numbers, for example Jones 1987, 115).

3. When the reference list contains more than one work of an author published in the same year, the suffix a, b, etc. follows the data in the text citation, for example (Jones 1987a) or Jones 1987a; Freeman 1985b).

4. If an author's name is mentioned in the text, it need not be repeated in the citation, for example "Jones (1987, 115) says..."

5. Citations to institutional works should use acronyms or short titles where practicable, for example (AAA ASOBAT 1966); (AICPA Cohen Commission Report 1977). Where brief, the full title of an institutional work might be shown in a citation, for example (ICAEW The Corporate Report 1975).

6. If the manuscript refers to statutes, legal treatises, or court cases, citations acceptable in law reviews should be used.

Reference List: Every manuscript must include a list of references containing only those works cited. Each entry should contain all data necessary for unambiguous identification. With the author-date system, use the following format recommended by *The Chicago Manual*:

1. Arrange citations in alphabetical order according to surname of the first author or the name of the institution responsible for the citation.

2. Use author's initials instead of proper names.

3. In listing more than one name in references (Rayburn, L., and B. Harrelson,...), there should always be a comma before "and."

4. Dates of publication should be placed immediately after author's names.

5. Titles of journals should not be abbreviated.

6. Multiple works by the same author(s) should be listed in chronological order of publication. Two or more works by the same author(s) in the same year are distinguished by letters after the date.

Sample entries are as follows:

American Accounting Association, Committee on Concepts and Standards for External Financial Reports. 1977. Statement on Accounting Theory and Theory Acceptance. Sarasota, FL: AAA.

Bohrnstedt, G. W. 1970. Reliability and Validity Assessment in Attitude Measurement. In Attitude Measurement, edited by G. Summers, 80-99. Chicago, IL: Rand McNally.

Burgstahler,D. 1987. Inference from Empirical Research The Accounting Review 62 (January): 203-214. Chow, C. 1983. The impacts of Accounting Regulation on Bondholder and Shareholder Wealth: The Case of the Securities Act. The Accounting Review 58 (3): 4845-520.

Hunt, S. D.; L. B. Chonko and J. B. Wilcox. 1984. Ethical Problems of Marketing Researchers. Journal of Marketing Research (August):304-324. Maranell, G., ed. 1974. Scaling A Sourcebook of Behavioral Scientist. Chicago, IL: Aldine Publishing Company.

Saaty, T. L., and L. G. Vargas. 1984a. The Legitimacy of Rank Reversal. Omega 12: 513-516.

_____and_____. 1984b. Inconsistency and Rank Reversal. Journal of Mathematical Psychology 28: 205-214.

Waterhouse, J., and A. Richardson. 1989. Behavioral Research Implications of the New Management Accounting Environment. Working paper, University of Alberta.

Footnotes: Footnotes are not to be used for documentation. Textual footnotes should be used only for extensions and useful excursions of information that, if included in the body of the text, might disrupt its continuity. Footnotes should be double-spaced and numbered consecutively throughout the manuscript with superscript Arabic numerals. Footnotes are placed at the end of the text.

Policy On Reproduction

An objective of *Behavioral Research In Accounting* is to promote the wide dissemination of the results of systematic scholarly inquires into the broad field of accounting.

Permission is hereby granted to reproduce any of the contents of BRIA for use in courses of instruction, as long as the source and American Accounting Association copyright are indicated in any such reproductions.

Written application must be made to the Editor for permission to reproduce any of the contents of BRIA for use in other than courses of instruction-e.g., inclusion in books of readings or in any other such instances, the applicant must notify the author(s) in writing of the intended use of each reproduction. Normally, BRIA will not assess a charge for the waiver of copyright.

Except as otherwise noted in articles, the copyright has been transferred to the American Accounting Association for all items appearing in this journal. Where the author(s) has (have) not transferred the copyright to the American Accounting Association, applicants must seek permission to reproduce (for all purposes) directly from the author(s).

Manuscript Preparation And Style

Behavioral Research In Accounting's manuscript preparation guidelines follow (with a slight modification) documentation 2 of *The Chicago Manual Of Style* (14th ed.; University of

Chicago Press). Another helpful guide to usage and style is *The Elements Of Style*, by William Strunk, Jr., and E. B. White (Macmillan). Spelling follows *Webster's International Dictionary*.

Format

1. All manuscripts should be typed on one side of 8 1/2 x 11" good quality paper and be double-spaced, except for indented quotations.

2. Manuscripts should be as concise as the subject and research method permit, generally not to exceed 7,000 words.

3. Margins should be at least one inch from top, bottom, and sides to facilitate editing and duplication.

4. To assure anonymous review, authors should not identify themselves directly or indirectly in their papers. Single authors should not use the editorial "we."

5. A cover page should include the title of the paper, the author's name, title, and affiliation, any acknowledgments, and a footnote indicating whether the author would be willing to share the data (see last paragraph in this statement).

6. All pages, including tables, appendices, and references, should be serially numbered.

7. Spell out numbers from one to ten, except when used in tables and lists, and when used with mathematical, statistical, scientific, or technical units and quantities, such as distances, weights, and measures. For example: three days; 3 kilometers; 30 years. All other numbers are expressed numerically. Generally, when using approximate terms, spell out the number, for example, approximately thirty years.

8. In nontechnical text use the word percent; in technical text the symbol % is used (See *The Chicago Manual* for discussion of the correct usage.

9. a. Use a hyphen (-) to join unit modifiers or to clarify usage. For example: a well-presented analysis; re-form. See *Webster's* for correct usage.
b. En dash (-) is used between words indicating a duration, such as hourly time or months or years. No space on either side.
c. Em dash(—) is used to indicate an abrupt change in thought, or where a period is strong and a comma is too weak. No space on either side.

10. The following will be Roman in all cases: i.e., e.g., ibid., et al., op.cit.

11. Initials: A. B. Smith (space between): States, etc.: U.S., U.K. (no space)

12. When using "Big 6" or "Big 8" use Arabic figures (don't spell out).

13. Ellipsis should be used not periods, example: .... not. . . .

14. Use "SAS" No. #" no "SAS #."

15. Use only one space after periods, colons, exclamation points, question marks, quotation marks—any punctuation that separates two sentences.

16. a. Use real quotation marks--never inch marks: "and" not and.
b. Use apostrophes, not footmarks: 'not'.

17. Punctuation used with quote marks:
a. Commas and periods are always placed inside the quotation marks.
b. Colons and semicolons go outside the quotation marks.
c. Question marks and exclamation points go in or out, depending on whether they belong to the material inside the quote or not. If they belong to the quoted material, they go inside the quote marks, and vice versa.

18. Punctuation and parentheses: Sentence punctuation goes after the closing parenthesis if what is inside the parentheses is part of the sentence (as this phrase is). This also applies to commas, semicolons, and colons. If what is inside the parentheses is an entire statement of its own, the ending punctuation should also be inside the parentheses.

19. Headings should be arranged so that major headings are centered, bold, and capitalized. Second level headings should be flush left, bold, and both upper and lower case. Third level headings should be flush left bold, italic, and both upper and lower case. Fourth level headings should be paragraph indent, bold, and lower case. Headings and subheadings should not be numbered. For example:

A CENTERED, BOLD, ALL CAPITALIZED, FIRST LEVEL HEADING

A Flush Left, Bold, Upper and Lower Case, Second Level Heading
A Flush Left, Bold, Italic, Upper and Lower case, Third Level Heading
    A paragraph indent, bold, lower case, fourth level heading. Text starts...

Abstract
An abstract of about 100-150 words should be presented on a separate page immediately preceding the text. The abstract should be nonmathematical and include a readable summary of the research question, method, and the significance of the findings and contribution. The title, but not the author's name or other identification designations, should appear on the abstract page.

Tables And Figures
The author should note the following general requirements:

1. Each table and figure (graphic) should appear on a separate page and should be placed at the end of the text. Each should bear an Arabic number and a complete title indicating the exact contents of the table or figure.

2. A reference to each table or figure should be made in the text.

3. The author should indicate by marginal notation where each table or figure should be inserted in the text, e.g., (Insert Table X here).

4. Tables or figures should be reasonably interpreted without reference to the text.

5. Source lines and notes should be included as necessary.

6. When information is not available, use "NA" capitalized with no slash between.

7. Figures must be prepared in a form suitable for printing.

Policy On Data Availability
The following policy, adopted by the Executive Committee of the AAA in April 1989, is applicable to all manuscripts submitted to *Behavioral Research In Accounting*:

....authors are encouraged to make their data available for use by others....
Authors of articles which report data dependent results should footnote the status of data availability and, when pertinent, this should be accomplished by information on how the data may be obtained.

British Accounting Review (The)

ADDRESS FOR SUBMISSION:

Cheryl Jones, Editor
British Accounting Review (The)
University of Manchester
Manchester School of Accounting
Oxford Road
Manchester, M13 9PL
UK
Phone: +44 161 275 4276
Fax: +44 161 275 4023
E-Mail: bar@man.ac.uk
Web:
Address May Change:

PUBLICATION GUIDELINES:

Manuscript Length: Up to 10,000 Words
Copies Required: Four
Computer Submission: No
Format: N/A
Fees to Review: 0.00 US$

Manuscript Style:
    See Manuscript Guidelines

CIRCULATION DATA:

Reader: Academics
Frequency of Issue: Quarterly
Copies per Issue: 1,001 - 2,000
Sponsor/Publisher: Academic Press, Inc.
Subscribe Price: 195.00 US$
    40.00 US$ Brit. Acct. Assn.Mem

REVIEW INFORMATION:

Type of Review: Blind Review
No. of External Reviewers: 2
No. of In House Reviewers: 0
Acceptance Rate: 21-30%
Time to Review: 2 - 3 Months
Reviewers Comments: Yes
Invited Articles: 0-5%
Fees to Publish: 0.00 US$

MANUSCRIPT TOPICS:

Accounting Information Systems; Accounting Theory & Practice; Auditing; Capital Budgeting; Corporate Finance; Cost Accounting; Government & Non Profit Accounting; International Finance; Portfolio & Security Analysis; Tax Accounting

MANUSCRIPT GUIDELINES/COMMENTS:

Editorial Policy
The *British Accounting Review* is pleased to publish original scholarly papers across the whole spectrum of Accounting and Finance. The Journal is eclectic and pluralistic and contributions are welcomed across a wide range of research methodologies and topics. Each paper will be judged according to international standards within its topic area, the originality of its contribution, its relevance to development of the subject and its quality of exposition. Published papers will normally be expected to be informed theoretically and empirically. Authoritative state-of-the-art reviews that provide significant insight for future research progress are, however, welcome. Papers should be comprehensible to colleagues with a specialist or informed interest in the general area to which the paper relates but who may, however, not be experts in the specific issues dealt with in the paper.

All papers are subject to a minimum of double blind refereeing. The Journal seeks to serve the aims of the *British Accounting Association* and the broader international accounting community by publishing research of the highest quality possible and of interest to an international audience. Contributions from all parts of the world are welcomed though, where appropriate, submissions are expected to be cognisant of relevant research and issues in Britain, Europe and the Commonwealth.

The editors are pleased to receive any enquiries from authors about papers they are considering submitting to *BAR* but the editors will not provide detailed comments upon papers prior to submission to the journal. The editors reserve the right to return manuscripts directly to authors without them being put through the refereeing process. Reasons for this will include situations in which, in the editors' judgement, the paper falls outside the editorial policy or the author(s) have not complied with the *Notes to Contributors* (inside the back cover).

Notes For Contributors
Four copies of any manuscripts for consideration by BAR should be sent to:

Mrs. Cheryl A Jones   The Manchester School of Accounting and Finance
Editorial Assistant   The University of Manchester,
                       Crawford House, Booth Street East,
                       Manchester, M13 9PL
                       Tel: 0161 275 4276   Fax: 0161 275 402
                       email BAR@MAN.AC.UK

Acceptance criteria BAR, is particularly concerned with the readability of papers. Prospective authors are asked to pay attention to the clarity of their communication. Authors are reminded that the most common root causes for the rejection of a manuscript are the failure to expose the material as widely as possible before submission and failure to comply with the *Editorial Policy* and *Notes for Contributors*. Authors are asked to use mathematics only if it contributes to the clarity and economy of presentation. Authors are encouraged to put the mathematics in an appendix whenever possible.

Submission of a paper to *BAR* automatically implies that the manuscript is not concurrently under consideration for publication elsewhere. All papers submitted to *BAR* will normally only be published subject to review by double blind referee. In the interests of a fair review, authors should try and avoid the use of anything which would make their identity obvious. Referees are asked to comment upon the *originality, authority, comprehensiveness, contribution, interest* and *usefulness* of a submitted paper. All papers are also subjected to editorial review which covers style, quality of communication, and academic and scholarly content. The editors make every effort to give a decision on manuscripts as soon as possible.

When supplying your final article please include, where possible, a disc of your manuscript prepared on PC compatible or Apple Macintosh computers, along with the hard copy print-out. 5¼" or 3½ " sized discs and most word processing packages are acceptable, although any version of WordPerfect or Microsoft Word are preferred.

Preparation of copy, Manuscripts must be typed in journal style on one side only of the paper (preferably A4 or 8½ in x 11 in), double spaced (including notes and references), with a margin of at least 1½ in on the left-hand side. Essential notes should be indicated by superscript figures in the text and collected in a single section placed before the references under a heading 'Notes'. Tables and figures should be attached on separate sheets at the end of the manuscript: their position should be indicated in the text. A short abstract should be included at the head of the paper.

Citations in the text should read thus: (Brown & Smith (1975), or, Brown & Smith, 1975), or for specific quotations, (Brown & Smith, 1975, pp. 63-64). The conventions White (1975a), White (1975b) should be used if more than one publication by the same authors) in a particular year is cited. Where there are three authors or more, all names should be given in the first citation; subsequently use *et al.* References should be listed in full, alphabetically at the end of the paper in the following style:

Arnold, J., Carsberg, B. & Scapens, R. (1980). *Topics in Management Accounting,* Oxford, Philip Allan.

Benston, G. (1981). 'Are accounting standards necessary?' In R. Leach & E. Stamp (eds), *British Accounting Standards, The First 10 Years,* pp. 201-214, Cambridge, Woodhead-Faulkener.

Bromwich, M. (1977). 'The use of present value valuation models in published accounting reports', *The Accounting Review,* July, pp. 587-596.

Proofs and offprints. Authors are expected to correct proofs quickly and not to make revisions on proofs; revisions made on proofs may be charged for by the editors. No payments are made to authors.

Authors submitting a manuscript do so on the understanding that if it is accepted for publication, exclusive copyright in the paper shall be assigned to the Publisher. In consideration for the assignment of copyright, the Publisher will supply 50 offprints of each paper. Further offprints may be ordered at extra cost; the copyright assignment/offprint order form will be sent with the proofs. The Publisher will not put any limitation on the personal freedom of the author to use material contained in the paper in other works which may be published.

CA Magazine

ADDRESS FOR SUBMISSION:

Christian Bellavance, Editor-in-Chief
CA Magazine
Canadian Inst. of Chartered Accountants
277 Wellington Street, W.
Toronto, Ontario, M5V 3H2
Canada
Phone: 416-204-3246
Fax: 416-204-3409
E-Mail: camagazine@cica.ca
Web:
Address May Change:

PUBLICATION GUIDELINES:

Manuscript Length: 11-15
Copies Required: One
Computer Submission: Yes
Format: Wd for Win,WdPer,Text only
Fees to Review: 0.00 US$

Manuscript Style:
    See Manuscript Guidelines

CIRCULATION DATA:

Reader: , Canadian Chartered Accountants
Frequency of Issue: 10 Times/ Year
Copies per Issue: More than 70,000
Sponsor/Publisher: Canadian Institute of
    Chartered Accountants
Subscribe Price: 47.00 CAN$
    37.00 CAN$ Member, Student, Faculty
    72.00 US$ Outside Canada

REVIEW INFORMATION:

Type of Review: Editorial Review
No. of External Reviewers: 1
No. of In House Reviewers: 2
Acceptance Rate: 6-10%
Time to Review: 1 - 2 Months
Reviewers Comments: No
Invited Articles: 50% +
Fees to Publish: 0.00 US$

MANUSCRIPT TOPICS:

Accounting Information Systems; Accounting Theory & Practice; Auditing; Business Law & Public Responsibility; Capital Budgeting; Cost Accounting; Econometrics; Economic History; Government & Non Profit Accounting; Industrial Organization; Insurance; International Finance; Portfolio & Security Analysis; Public Policy Economics; Tax Accounting

MANUSCRIPT GUIDELINES/COMMENTS:

Material must be of specific interest to Canadian Chartered Accountants.

Canadian Tax Journal

ADDRESS FOR SUBMISSION:

Laurel Amalia, Editor-In-Chief
Canadian Tax Journal
595 Bay Street, Suite 1200
Toronto, M5G 2N5
Canada
Phone: 416-599-0283 Ext. 214
Fax: 416-599-9283
E-Mail: lamalia@ctf.ca
Web: www.ctf.ca
Address May Change:

PUBLICATION GUIDELINES:

Manuscript Length: Any
Copies Required: Three
Computer Submission: Yes
Format: Any
Fees to Review: 0.00 US$

Manuscript Style:
  See Manuscript Guidelines

CIRCULATION DATA:

Reader: Academics, Tax Professionals,
  Gov't Offic.
Frequency of Issue: Bi-Monthly
Copies per Issue: 8.4 Million
Sponsor/Publisher: Canadian Tax
  Foundation
Subscribe Price: 150.00 CAN$
  275.00 CAN$ (Free to Indv. Member)
  495.00 CAN$ (Free to Corp. Member)

REVIEW INFORMATION:

Type of Review: Blind Review
No. of External Reviewers: 2
No. of In House Reviewers: 0
Acceptance Rate: 21-30%
Time to Review: 1 - 2 Months
Reviewers Comments: Yes
Invited Articles: 0-5%
Fees to Publish: 0.00 US$

MANUSCRIPT TOPICS:
Business Law; Economics; Fiscal Policy; International Business; Tax Accounting

MANUSCRIPT GUIDELINES/COMMENTS:

The Canadian Tax Foundation invites interested parties to submit manuscripts for possible publication in the *Canadian Tax Journal*, a forum for the dissemination of research in and informed comment on taxation and public finance, with **particular relevance to Canada**.

Manuscripts may be written in either French or English, should present an **original analysis** of the topic, and should not have been published elsewhere. All manuscripts submitted are subject to review by an Editorial Board. Manuscripts may be (1) accepted outright, (2) accepted if recommended revisions are made, or (3) revised by the author as recommended by the Editorial Board, and resubmitted for further consideration, or (4) rejected, with reasons.

It is recommended that a detailed draft proposal be submitted before writing commences to ensure that the topic is of interest. Proposals that are accepted are not to be viewed as a commitment on the foundation's part to publish the resulting manuscripts; these manuscripts are subject to the same review procedures as are all other manuscripts.

Contributors are responsible for submitting detailed abstracts of their manuscripts, for providing complete and accurate citations to reference materials used, and for preparing manuscripts in the prescribed format. A style and format guide for literature citation and manuscript preparation may be obtained from the editor.

Prospective contributors should submit a current curriculum vitae and three copies of their draft proposals or manuscripts to Ms. Laurel Amalia, Editor. Telephone or written inquiries are welcome.

Style And Format Guide For Papers Submitted for Publication
Please submit three (3) hard copy printouts and a copy of your disk (with the file name and name of the word-processing package clearly indicated).

Formatting: Use 12 pt. Courier typeface only (do not use a proportional font), double-spaced (including extracts and notes), with an unjustified right margin. Notes must be coded as "endnotes," not as plain text. (In WordPerfect and Word choose "Endnotes" from the "Insert" menu when creating notes.) Ensure that all styles coding (other than bold-face, italic, and one-tab paragraph indention) is removed. Number pages of chapter or paper consecutively in the upper right-hand corner.

Title page: Include title of paper or chapter, author's name, firm or affiliation, and (if applicable) name of conference at which the paper was presented.

Subheadings: Differentiate levels of headings so that the organization of the content of the work is apparent.

> Level 1 subhead: full caps, centred
> Level 2 subhead: cap and lower-case, centred, underlined
> Level 3 subhead: cap and lower-case, flush left, underlined
> Level 4 subhead: cap and lower-case, flush left

Abstract: Papers submitted for publication in the *Canadian Tax Journal* are to include a detailed abstract that emphasizes the conclusions.

References to literature: Authors are responsible for providing complete and accurate quotations and citations. All references must be in foundation style (refer to *Canadian Tax Foundation Style Guide*, 1995 ed.). If you are in doubt about how much information to include, provide a copy of the title page of the work in question. Following is a list of sample citations illustrating foundation style.

Statute: Income Tax Act, RSC 1985, c. 1, (5th Supp.), as amended. Case: *Multiview Inc. v. The Queen,* 97 DTC 1489 (TCC). Book: Howard J. Kellough and Peter E. McQuillan, *Taxation of Private Corporations and Their Shareholders,* 3d ed. (Toronto: Canadian Tax Foundation, 1999). Journal article: Bert Waslander, "Government Expenditures on Aboriginal People: The Costly Status Quo" (1997), vol. 45, no. 5 *Canadian Tax Journal* 959-78, at 960.

Graphs: If your paper includes graphical representation of data, supply values for the data points in a separate ASCII text file.

Please direct any inquiries to Laurel Amalia, Editor, or Leesa Armstrong, Production Coordinator.

CGA Magazine

ADDRESS FOR SUBMISSION:

Lesley Wood, Editor
CGA Magazine
Certified Gen. Accountants' Assn. of Can
700-1188
West George Street
Vancouver, BC V6E 4A2
Canada
Phone: 604-669-3555
Fax: 604-689-5845
E-Mail: editcga@cga-canada.org
Web:
Address May Change:

PUBLICATION GUIDELINES:

Manuscript Length: 6-10
Copies Required: Two
Computer Submission: Yes
Format: Any
Fees to Review: 0.00 US$

Manuscript Style:
    See Manuscript Guidelines

CIRCULATION DATA:

Reader: Business Persons, Professional
    Accountants
Frequency of Issue: Monthly
Copies per Issue: More than 25,000
Sponsor/Publisher: CGA- Canada
Subscribe Price: 45.00 US$

REVIEW INFORMATION:

Type of Review: Blind Review
No. of External Reviewers: 1
No. of In House Reviewers: 1
Acceptance Rate: 0-5%
Time to Review: 2 - 3 Months
Reviewers Comments: Yes
Invited Articles: 50% +
Fees to Publish: 0.00 US$

MANUSCRIPT TOPICS:

Accounting Information Systems; Accounting Theory & Practice; Auditing; Cost Accounting; Insurance; Tax Accounting

MANUSCRIPT GUIDELINES/COMMENTS:

Background

CGA Management Magazine is the official publication of the Certified General Accountants' Association of Canada (CGA-Canada). Published monthly, the bilingual magazine reaches an audience of over 40,000 CGAs and CGA students across Canada, in the Caribbean, Hong Kong and Macau.

Content

Articles published deal with topics of interest to professional accountants—accounting, auditing, taxation, law, finance, business and aspects of computers. A certain number of background, general interest articles are included from time to time. Frequent "focus" issues contain several articles dealing with different aspects of a special topic.

Queries

Potential authors should send a query letter to the editor discussing the proposed article. Your letter should explain the relevance of the topic, include a brief outline of the areas to be covered and explain how the article will differ from others published on the same topic. Queries should state whether an article is original or has been previously published. A length should also be proposed.

In your letter, tell us a bit about yourself. What makes you the right person to do this article? Have you published before, and if so, for whom? If you have published previously, you might want to include a sample of your work.

The editorial team generally considers article ideas during our monthly meeting, so it may be a few weeks before you receive a response to your query.

Queries should be sent to Editor, *CGA Management Magazine*, 700 1188 West Georgia St., Vancouver V6E 4A2.

Writing

If your query is successful, the editor will commission you to write the article. At this point, a deadline will be established and a target length determined.

Once an article has been approved, do not change the topic without consulting with the editor. Your new topic may not fit into editorial plans or may have already been assigned to someone else.

Any article that you write for *CGA Management Magazine* should not be shown to anyone else prior to publication. This includes the manufacturer of any product you may review, the subject of an interview or any other publication. Should you encounter difficulties with this policy, refer the matter to your editor.

"I prefer to write in French"

Not a problem! Our French editor will be happy to work with you.

Style

All articles must be thoroughly researched and you are ultimately responsible for accuracy. Use graphs, tables or charts and examples where appropriate. Remember that the readers are professionals with good grounding in all accounting and many business areas -- writing at too low a level is inappropriate. However, esoteric jargon should always be avoided. First and second person ("I", "you") can be used, providing the resulting tone is not condescending. The best way to get a "feel" for the magazine's style is to study a few back issues.

All articles are edited, and some changes are inevitable. When you write an article, it becomes your "baby"—it is often difficult to view it objectively. The "outside" eye of an editor can sometimes see ways of making your presentation even clearer. Remember that writing a magazine article is a joint effort—you and the editor are a team! You will be contacted should any points require clarification, and the article, after editing, will be returned to you for final approval before publication.

Deadlines

Deadlines are sacred. We need enough time to edit the article, obtain your final approval and do a translation. Always give the editor plenty of notice if you anticipate problems meeting the deadline.

What To Submit

Please submit your article both on diskette in any version of WordPerfect and in "hard copy." At this time, send along a head and shoulders style photo and a one or two-sentence biography, both of which will be published with the article.

Rights

Our acceptance of your original material assumes first-time world rights in French and English. After that, you are free to republish your original article elsewhere. As a courtesy, we ask that, on republication, mention be made of the *CGA Management Magazine* issue in which the article first appeared. If you choose to republish the edited version, mention of prior publication in *CGA Management Magazine* is essential.

CGA Management Magazine is sent to universities, colleges and professional associations across Canada. We often get requests to reprint material for educational purposes. You will be contacted for approval before such a request is granted whenever possible. If we cannot reach you, however, we will grant permission ourselves. Please note that no money exchanges hands in these arrangements, so you will not miss out on any revenues!

Likewise, requests to reprint in another publication will be referred back to you, though again, we will co-ordinate the permission-granting process. Anyone reprinting material from *CGA Management Magazine* is required to credit the magazine and author, and indicate that reprint permission was obtained.

Thank you for your interest in *CGA Management Magazine*.

Chartered Accountants' Journal of New Zealand

ADDRESS FOR SUBMISSION:

Editor
Chartered Accountants' Journal of New
   Zealand
Inst. Chartered Accountants/New Zealand
National Office--Cigna House
PO Box 11 342
40 Mercer Street
Wellington, 6034
New Zealand
Phone: 64 04 474 7840
Fax: 64 04 499 8033
E-Mail:
Web: www.icanz.co.nz
Address May Change:

PUBLICATION GUIDELINES:

Manuscript Length: 6-10
Copies Required: Two
Computer Submission: Yes
Format: See Guidelines
Fees to Review: 0.00 US$

Manuscript Style:
   See Manuscript Guidelines

CIRCULATION DATA:

Reader: Business Persons
Frequency of Issue: 11 Times/Year
Copies per Issue: 10,001 - 25,000
Sponsor/Publisher: Institute of Chartered
   Accountants of New Zealand
Subscribe Price: 90.00 $ Member
   100.00 $ Non-Member
   55.00 $ Student

REVIEW INFORMATION:

Type of Review: Editorial Review
No. of External Reviewers: 2
No. of In House Reviewers: 2
Acceptance Rate: 50%
Time to Review: 2 - 3 Months
Reviewers Comments: No
Invited Articles: 21-30%
Fees to Publish: 315.00 $
   420.00 $ Depending on length

MANUSCRIPT TOPICS:

Accounting Information Systems; Accounting Theory & Practice; Auditing; Cost Accounting;
Econometrics; Fiscal Policy; Micro Economics

MANUSCRIPT GUIDELINES/COMMENTS:

Subscription Price: An additional charge for overseas postage is payable.

Number of Reviewers: The number of internal reviewers varies from one to two, as does the
number of external reviewers. A copy of the reviewer's comments is not sent unless the author
asks to be contacted.

For information on author guidelines and publication style for manuscripts see previously
published articles in the journal and the following guidelines.

Thank you for your interest in contributing to the *Chartered Accountants Journal of New Zealand*, the monthly publication of the New Zealand Society of Accountants.

Before you commence work, or as you consider the suitability of an article you have already written, you will need to consider your potential audience carefully.

You should be aware that under the Society's new structure, members have elected which of the three "Colleges" they will belong to. Their interests are separate and distinct in some ways, and overlap in others.

Briefly, the College structure can be described as follows:

- The College of Chartered Accountants-Society members working in all sectors whose primary focus is accounting, including holders of Public Practice Certificates.

- The College of Associate Chartered Accountants-Members whose primary focus is other than accounting-general management and education, for example.

- The College of Accounting Technicians-A new group of members who are trained to provide accounting support services in all types of organizations. Their work is largely of practical, "hands-on" nature.

Like the Society as a whole, the Journal seeks to cater for the interests of all three groups as fully as possible.

Further information on the College structure and ways in which the Journal seeks to meet the different markets is available from the Editor.

Your first task in preparing an article will therefore be to decide which target group or groups your material is aimed at, and to write accordingly.

Our reviewers (see below) will consider the potential audience(s) of submitted material as an important part of their function in deciding suitability for publication. A copy of the reviewers' evaluation guidelines is attached.

Respondents to our recent readership survey emphasized strongly that they seek in the Journal practical information of direct value to their work.

If appropriate, case studies, worked examples and brief summaries are very popular with readers. These can be presented apart from the main flow of the text.

Some further pointers:

1. Articles should not exceed 1200 words (or if they do, they should be divided into parts).

2. If the article has not yet been written, a brief synopsis should be forwarded to the Editor for consideration and comment.

3. Manuscripts should preferably be typed double-spaced on one side of A4 paper.

4. Disks are also acceptable, particularly if graphs or tables are included. The followings points should be noted if forwarding material on disk:

- Indicate whether the disk is high or medium density.
- Indicate the program it is written in (Microsoft Word is preferred).
- Do not use typist's return at the end of lines.
- Do not space paragraphs.
- Do not use Microsoft Word table for tables but tab limited text.
- If you are using PC file, save in RTF format and also send the original text.
- If you are sending graphs or figures, also forward the data on which the illustration is based.
- E-mail is available.

Further information is available from the Production Manager.

5. Provide a brief, preferably bullet-pointed, summary at the head of the article to indicate its content.

6. Layout and style - see previous issues for examples.

7. Deadlines fall in the middle of each month for publication in the second succeeding month - for example, a 15 June deadline for publication in the first week of August (subject to time taken for review - see (9), below).

8. If a deadline is looming, articles should be faxed with original script plus disks and any additional material being sent by post.

9. All articles are subject to a formal review procedure, which is likely to take between 2 and 6 weeks. Reviewers consider (among other things) level of coverage - see above, topicality, readability and accessibility.

Articles will be accepted for publication (always subject to editorial input, however), returned for amendment or rejected (with reasons).

10. Photographs (preferably 6 x 4 colour prints), graphs and other illustrations are welcome so long as they are high-quality.

11. Payment - whether articles are paid for is by negotiation with the Editor. There are two flat rates, depending on length.

Please contact the Editor for further information. We look forward to working with you.

CMA Management Magazine

ADDRESS FOR SUBMISSION:

David J. Fidler, Publisher
CMA Management Magazine
Society of Mgmt. Accountants of Canada
P.O. Box 176
Hamilton, Ontario, L8N 3C3
Canada
Phone: 905-525-4100
Fax: 905-525-4533
E-Mail: dfidler@managementmag.com
Web:
Address May Change:

PUBLICATION GUIDELINES:

Manuscript Length: 11-15
Copies Required: Two
Computer Submission: Yes
Format: N/A
Fees to Review: 0.00 US$

Manuscript Style:
See Manuscript Guidelines, Canadian
Press Style Book

CIRCULATION DATA:

Reader: Business Persons, Financial
Executives
Frequency of Issue: 10 Times/ Year
Copies per Issue: 75,000 +
Sponsor/Publisher: CMA Canada
Subscribe Price: 49.95 CAN$
50.00 US$ Overseas

REVIEW INFORMATION:

Type of Review: Blind Review
No. of External Reviewers: 1
No. of In House Reviewers: 1
Acceptance Rate: 21-30%
Time to Review: 2 - 3 Months
Reviewers Comments: No
Invited Articles: 50% +
Fees to Publish: 0.00 US$

MANUSCRIPT TOPICS:

Economic Development; Economic History; Fiscal Policy; Government & Non Profit Accounting; International Economics & Trade; International Finance; Monetary Policy; Public Policy Economics; Regional Economics; Strategic Management Policy

MANUSCRIPT GUIDELINES/COMMENTS:

1. Management accountants are involved in most aspects of business from an accounting and managerial perspective.

2. Articles should be brief (about 1500 words), readable and practical, illustrating how organizations can do things better (more cheaply, with good quality and economy of personnel). Management accountants are members of the management team providing information (not necessarily financial) for strategic, tactical and operational decisions. Their contribution is based on in-depth knowledge about what information is required and how it must be organized and presented to improve such decisions. Therefore, most aspects of business are of interest to them.

3. We especially like case study types of articles, featuring interviews with management, accounting and other authorities; articles of new developments in computers and software, management methods, accounting practices, etc.; articles on news and trends in management accounting and management, taxes, legislation, etc.

4. Articles should be readable and interesting, with the minimum of footnotes and references, as well as business jargon.

Commentaries on the Law of Accounting & Finance

ADDRESS FOR SUBMISSION:

Robert W. McGee, Editor
Commentaries on the Law of Accounting &
   Finance
Dumont Inst. of Public Policy Research
71 South Orange Avenue, Ste.260
South Orange, NJ 07079
USA
Phone:
Fax:
E-Mail: bob@dumontinst.com
Web:
Address May Change:

PUBLICATION GUIDELINES:

Manuscript Length: 16-30+
Copies Required: Three
Computer Submission: No
Format: N/A
Fees to Review: 0.00 US$

Manuscript Style:
   Uniform System of Citation (Harvard
   Blue Book)

CIRCULATION DATA:

Reader: Academics
Frequency of Issue: Yearly
Copies per Issue: Less than 1,000
Sponsor/Publisher: Dumont Institute for
   Public Policy Research
Subscribe Price: 30.00 US$ Individual
   85.00 US$ Institution

REVIEW INFORMATION:

Type of Review: Blind Review
No. of External Reviewers: 2
No. of In House Reviewers: 1
Acceptance Rate: 50%
Time to Review: 1 Month or Less
Reviewers Comments: Yes
Invited Articles: 11-20%
Fees to Publish: 0.00 US$

MANUSCRIPT TOPICS:

Accounting Law, Finance Law; Accounting Theory & Practice; Fiscal Policy; International Finance; Public Policy Economics; Tax Accounting

MANUSCRIPT GUIDELINES/COMMENTS:

Construction Management and Economics

ADDRESS FOR SUBMISSION:

Will P. Hughes, Editor
Construction Management and Economics
University of Reading
Department of Construction Management
  and Engineering
PO Box 219
Whiteknights, Reading, RG6 6AW
UK
Phone: 44 118 931 8201
Fax: 44 118 931 3856
E-Mail: w.p.hughes@reading.ac.uk
Web:
Address May Change:

CIRCULATION DATA:

Reader: Academics
Frequency of Issue: Bi-Monthly
Copies per Issue: Less than 1,000
Sponsor/Publisher: Routledge Journals
Subscribe Price: 785.00 US$
        220.00 US$ CIB,CIOB,ARCON,AUBE
        66.00 US$ Student Share Rate

PUBLICATION GUIDELINES:

Manuscript Length: 11-15
Copies Required: Four
Computer Submission: Yes
Format: Microsoft Wd / Wd Perfect
Fees to Review: 0.00 US$

Manuscript Style:
        Uniform System of Citation (Harvard
        Blue Book), for References

REVIEW INFORMATION:

Type of Review: Blind Review
No. of External Reviewers: 4
No. of In House Reviewers: 0
Acceptance Rate: 50%
Time to Review: 2 - 3 Months
Reviewers Comments: Yes
Invited Articles: 0-5%
Fees to Publish: 0.00 US$

MANUSCRIPT TOPICS:

Construction Management; Cost Accounting; Econometrics; Economic Development;
Economic History; Industrial Organization; International Economics & Trade; Macro
Economics; Micro Economics; Real Estate

MANUSCRIPT GUIDELINES/COMMENTS:

1. Submission

Authors should submit their paper as an e-mail attachment (in Word 97 or Rich Text Format)
to: W.P.Hughes@ reading.ac.uk. Alternatively, authors should send four copies of their papers
(with floppy disk) to facilitate refereeing with original artwork to: Professor Ranko Bon or Dr
Will Hughes, Department of Construction Management and Engineering, University of
Reading, PO Box 219, Whiteknights, Reading RG6 6AW, UK. It will be assumed that the
authors will keep a copy. Papers will be anonymously refereed by acknowledged experts in
the subject. Only those receiving favourable recommendations from the referees will be
accepted for publication. If an author is uncertain about whether a paper is suitable for
publication in the Journal, it is acceptable to submit a synopsis first.

2. Effective communication

The paper should be written and arranged in a style that is succinct and easily followed. An informative but short title, a concise abstract with keywords, and a well-written introduction will help to achieve this. Simple language, short sentences and a good use of headings all help to communicate information more effectively. Discursive treatment of the subject matter is discouraged. Figures should be used to aid the clarity of the paper. The reader should be carefully guided through the paper. Always think about your reader.

3. Manuscript - papers

(a) *Length:* although there is no length limitation, papers should fall within the range of 2000-5000 words. Authors are requested to state how many words their paper contains. The manuscript must be in English, typed in double spacing on one side of A4 paper only, with a 4 cm margin on the left-hand side. The pages should be numbered consecutively. There should be no loose addenda or notes or other explanatory material. The manuscript should be arranged under headings and subheadings.

(b) *Title page:* the first page of the manuscript must contain the full title, the affiliation(s) and address(es) of the author(s), a running title of not more than 75 characters and spaces, and the name and address of the author who will be responsible for correspondence and correcting proofs.

(c) *Abstract and* keywords: an abstract and up to five keywords for the purposes of indexing should be included, preferably on the title page. The abstract must not exceed 200 words and must precise the paper giving a clear indication of the conclusions it contains. Keywords must be carefully selected to facilitate readers' search.

(d) *Illustrations:* illustrations must accompany the manuscript but should not be included in the text. Photographs, standard forms, and charts should be referred to as `Fig. 1', `Fig. 2' etc. They should be numbered in the order in which they are referred to in the text.

Illustrations should be submitted in a form ready for reproduction. Diagrams and drawings should be drawn in black indian ink on white card or tracing paper. Figures will normally be reduced in size on reproduction and authors should draw with this in mind. With a reduction scale of 2:1 in mind the authors should use lines not less than 0.25 mm thick, and upper and lower case lettering, the capital of which should be 4 mm high. To keep within the type area of the journal, drawings for a 2:1 reduction should not exceed 280 mm in width. If you draw for any reduction other than 2:1 please indicate your intentions. Stencil lettering or Letraset should be used; typewritten annotations are not acceptable.

Forms should be completed in black indian ink. Photographs should be black and white glossy prints. Each should

have written lightly on the back the author's name, the figure number and an indication of which is top. Where lettering is to appear on the photograph, two prints should be supplied, one of which should be left unlettered.

(e) *Measurements:* metric units should be used; if other units are used then metric equivalents should be given in parentheses.

(f) *References:* the Harvard system is used. References in the text should be quoted in the following manner: Smith (1975) or (Brown and Green, 1976) or if there are more than two authors, Jones *et al.* (1980). References should be collected at the end of the paper in alphabetical order by the first author's surname. If references to the same author have the same year, they should be differentiated by using 1980a and 1980b etc. The style should follow the examples below:

Ranasinghe, M. and Russeil, A.D. (1993) Elicitation of subjective probabilities for economic risk analysis. *Construction Management and Economics,* 11(5), 326-40.

Reynolds, C.E. and Steedman, J.C. (1988) *Reinforced ConcreteDesigner's Handbook,* 10th Edn. E & FN Spon, London.

Barrett, S. (1981) Implementation of public policy, in Policy *and Action,* Barrett, S. and Fudge, C. (eds), Chapman & Hall, London, pp. 1-33.

If no person is named as the author the body should be used - for example: Royal Institution of Chartered Surveyors (1980) *Report on Urban Planning Methods,* London.

(g) *Endnotes:* a limited number of explanatory endnotes is permissible. These should be numbered 1, 2, 3, consecutively in the text and denoted by superscripts. They should be typed on a separate sheet of paper at the end of the text. Endnotes should not be used for academic or project citations.

4. Manuscripts - short papers or notes
Short papers or notes should be as short as possible, and should not be longer than 2000 words. The specifications from the previous section apply in all respects. Short papers or notes may offer comments on other papers published by this Journal, as well as offer original contributions.

5. Proofs
Proofs will be sent to the corresponding author for correction. The difficulty and expense involved in making amendments at proof stage makes it essential for authors to prepare their manuscript carefully: any alterations to the original text are strongly discouraged. Our aim is rapid publication: this will be helped if authors provide good copy following the above instructions, and return their proofs as quickly as possible.

6. Offprints
The corresponding author will be sent 25 free offprints as well as a bound copy of the journal.

7. Copyright
Submission of an article to this Journal is taken to imply that it represents original, unpublished work, not under consideration for publication elsewhere. Authors will be asked to transfer the copyright for their papers to the publisher if and when the article is accepted for

publication, using the form provided. The copyright covers the exclusive rights to reproduce and distribute the article, including reprints, photographic reproductions, microfilm or any reproduction of a similar nature, and translations. Permission to publish illustrations must be obtained by the author before submission and any acknowledgements should be included in the figure captions.

Contemporary Accounting Research

ADDRESS FOR SUBMISSION:

Editorial Assistant
Contemporary Accounting Research
University of British Columbia
Faculty of Commerce
2053 Main Mall
Vancouver, BC V6T 1Z2
Canada
Phone: 604-822-8534
Fax: 604-822-9470
E-Mail: car@commerce.ubc.ca
Web:
Address May Change: 1/15/01

PUBLICATION GUIDELINES:

Manuscript Length: 20-80
Copies Required: Three
Computer Submission: No
Format: N/A
Fees to Review: 75.00 US$ C.A.A.Assn.
    125.00 US$ Non-Members

Manuscript Style:
    Chicago Manual of Style

CIRCULATION DATA:

Reader: Academics
Frequency of Issue: Quarterly
Copies per Issue: 1,001 - 2,000
Sponsor/Publisher: Canadian Academic
    Accounting Assn.
Subscribe Price: 75.00 CAN$ Members
    125.00 CAN$ Non Members

REVIEW INFORMATION:

Type of Review: Blind Review
No. of External Reviewers: 2
No. of In House Reviewers: 0
Acceptance Rate: 11-20%
Time to Review: 2 - 3 Months
Reviewers Comments: Yes
Invited Articles: 0-5%
Fees to Publish: 0.00 US$

MANUSCRIPT TOPICS:
Accounting Information Systems; Accounting Theory & Practice; Auditing; Capital Budgeting; Cost Accounting; Government & Non Profit Accounting; Tax Accounting

MANUSCRIPT GUIDELINES/COMMENTS:

Paul Granatstein, Managing Editor
12 Donwoods Drive
Toronto, ON M4N 2G1 Canada
Tel: 416-486-5361, Fax: 416-486-6158
Email: pdgetal@interlog.com

Editor's Policy Statement
As editors of *Contemporary Accounting Research* since July 1, 1997, we feel it is appropriate to share with our readers and fellow researchers our vision for the journal, as well as information on how our editorial structure operates. A change in editorship often creates questions in these areas, particularly among researchers choosing a potential publication outlet.

While *CAR* is the journal of the Canadian Academic Accounting Association, its success is very much due to its being, from its inception, a North American journal, and increasingly, an international journal. Currently, 35 percent of our 1,184 subscribers are in Canada, 48 percent are in the United States, and 17 percent are international. Moreover, the proportion of non-Canadian subscribers is increasing. The pattern of manuscript submissions is similar, with an even larger percentage coming from outside Canada. Our goal is to build upon and enhance this diversity, while making *CAR* and the annual *CAR* Conference a first choice among Canadian and non-Canadian accounting researchers seeking an outlet for their best work.

To help accomplish this, we use a decentralized editorial structure that draws upon the deep and diverse expertise of our Associate Editors and Editorial Board. Our Associate Editors are empowered to make editorial decisions up to and through the final acceptance or rejection of a manuscript. Moreover, while they are encouraged to work with authors to improve a paper, our goal is to accept or reject a paper early in the review process - after one or two review rounds – rather than to protract the process. After all, it is the author's(s') manuscript that appears in print - not that of the editors or the reviewers. This type of crisp decision-making process has traditionally been applied with success to *CAR* Conference submissions. Our intent is to maintain and expand that tradition.

Finally, we encourage authors to submit their best work in all accounting research areas, written in English or French. Please note that *CAR* incorporates a long abstract in the other language for each article. We welcome interesting and intellectually rigorous work, whether it be analytical, empirical, or experimental; based in economics, psychology, or other disciplines. We believe our editorial structure enables us to evaluate papers in all fields in a thorough, fair, and timely manner. Simply put, our goal for *Contemporary Accounting Research is* that it be an excellent research journal of which the editorial team, the authors, subscribers, CAAA members, and our sustaining patrons and other sponsors, can all be proud.

Instructions To Authors
Papers should be written either in English or in French

Format
Manuscripts should be typed, doubled-spaced, on one side of 8 ½ x 11 inch paper. Margins should be wide enough to facilitate editing and duplication. All pages, including endnotes, tables, figures, illustrations, appendices, and references should be serially numbered. In the text, when not in lists, numbers from one through nine should be spelled out, except when decimals are used.

A cover page should contain the following information: title, author's name and affiliation, the present address, e-mail, telephone, and fax number of the author to whom correspondence should be addressed, and acknowledgements and information on grants received. Authors should not identify themselves in the paper.

An abstract of not more that 250 words should be presented on the second page immediately preceding the text. The abstract should include the research question, method of examination, and principal findings.

Endnotes should be used for extensions where inclusion in the body of the text might disrupt continuity. All endnotes should be numbered consecutively, presented together separately on pages immediately following the text, and referred to throughout the text with superscript Arabic numerals - **not** by using the automated endnote/footnote command. Each table, figure, or illustration should be presented on a separate page and bear an Arabic number and title.

Accepted papers are to be prepared on disk using software acceptable to the managing editor, but disks need not be included at the point of initial submission.

Disclosure
Together with the paper being submitted, authors are asked to include a copy of any other paper, whether or not published elsewhere, that shares data or modelling analysis with the submitted paper. The contribution of the submitted paper must be clearly distinguished from other such papers. If the submitted paper is based on an experiment, survey, or other data manipulations, participants or variables involved in that collection are reflected in the paper, authors are asked to include a memo describing and explaining the circumstances and estimating any effects on the results. The memo may be sent to reviewers.

Submission
Papers that contain original unpublished work, and are not being considered for publication elsewhere, should be mailed in quadruplicate to Professor Gerald Feltham or Professor Dan Simunic, *Contemporary Accounting Research,* Faculty of Commerce, University of British Columbia, 2053 Main Mall, Vancouver, B.C., Canada, V6T IZ2. A submission fee of $75 for CAAA members, and $125 for nonmembers, payable to *Contemporary Accounting Research* should accompany the manuscript.

Manuscripts reporting on field surveys or experiments should be accompanied by copies of the instrument (questionnaire, case, interview plan, etc.)

Corporate Finance Review

ADDRESS FOR SUBMISSION:

Alisa Salamon, Associate Editor
Corporate Finance Review
RIA Group
395 Hudson Street
New York, NY 10014
USA
Phone: 212-367-6582
Fax: 212-367-6718
E-Mail: alisa.salamon@riag.com
Web:
Address May Change:

PUBLICATION GUIDELINES:

Manuscript Length: 6-10
Copies Required: Three
Computer Submission: Yes
Format: Microsoft Word, WordPerfect
Fees to Review: 0.00 US$

Manuscript Style:
    Chicago Manual of Style

CIRCULATION DATA:

Reader: Business Persons, Academics
Frequency of Issue: Bi-Monthly
Copies per Issue: 2,001 - 3,000
Sponsor/Publisher: RIA Group/Thomson
    Corporate Finance
Subscribe Price: 150.00 US$

REVIEW INFORMATION:

Type of Review: Editorial Review
No. of External Reviewers: 2
No. of In House Reviewers: 1
Acceptance Rate: 21-30%
Time to Review: 1 - 2 Months
Reviewers Comments: No
Invited Articles: 6-10%
Fees to Publish: 0.00 US$

MANUSCRIPT TOPICS:

Accounting Information Systems; Accounting Theory & Practice; Auditing; Cost Accounting; Econometrics; Economic Development; Economic History; Fiscal Policy; Government & Non Profit Accounting; International Economics & Trade; International Finance; Macro Economics; Micro Economics; Monetary Policy; Regional Economics

MANUSCRIPT GUIDELINES/COMMENTS:

Articles focus on strategies, policies, and ideas of interest to financial executives. The style should be consistent with Harvard citations. Include a brief author bio. Disks should be submitted with hard copy of article, figures and tables.

Cost Engineering

ADDRESS FOR SUBMISSION:

Kathy Deweese, Managing Editor
Cost Engineering
AACE International
209 Prairie Avenue, Suite 100
Morgantown, WV 26501
USA
Phone: 304-296-8444/ 800-858-COST
Fax: 304-291-5728
E-Mail: info@aacei.org
Web:
Address May Change:

CIRCULATION DATA:

Reader: Academics, Construction/
   Engineering
Frequency of Issue: Monthly
Copies per Issue: 5,001 - 10,000
Sponsor/Publisher: Professional Assoc./
   Non Profit Corp.
Subscribe Price: 57.00 US$
      73.00 US$ All Non-US Countries
      99.00 US$ Airmail

PUBLICATION GUIDELINES:

Manuscript Length: 11-15
Copies Required: Four
Computer Submission: Yes
Format: N/A
Fees to Review: 0.00 US$

Manuscript Style:
   Chicago Manual of Style

REVIEW INFORMATION:

Type of Review: Blind Review
No. of External Reviewers: 3
No. of In House Reviewers: 1
Acceptance Rate: 60%
Time to Review: 2 - 3 Months
Reviewers Comments: Yes
Invited Articles: 0-5%
Fees to Publish: 0.00 US$

MANUSCRIPT TOPICS:
Cost Accounting

MANUSCRIPT GUIDELINES/COMMENTS:

About *Cost Engineering* magazine and the manuscript review process...
Cost Engineering magazine is a monthly publication of the AACE International. The first issue was published in 1958 and served as a forum for the accumulation and exchange of cost engineering knowledge; i.e., cost estimating, cost control, business planning and management science, profitability analysis, project management, and planning and scheduling. *Cost Engineering* magazine continues to invite manuscripts on these topics.

Cost Engineering is a highly respected, refereed, technical journal. The technical articles published in the magazine serve as a reference for the magazine's 6,000+ subscribers. *Cost Engineering's* Board of Reviewers consists of international consultants; professors and researchers; AACE's technical directors and committee chairs; and professional cost engineers with many Canadian, American, and international firms. Many of the reviewers are well-known authors themselves.

Approximately 30 to 35 technical articles are published each year in the magazine. The review process for each manuscript takes an average of 3 to 4 months. Everyone who submits a manuscript will be notified of its receipt and of its acceptance or rejection when the review is complete. If a paper is accepted for publication, it is scheduled on the magazine's editorial calendar. Publication, then, is within 1 year of acceptance. *Cost Engineering* will rarely consider publishing more than one manuscript by any author in one year's volume of the magazine. *Cost Engineering* does not pay for manuscripts, nor is it interested in commercial or marketing-type articles on a particular product, method, or company. Please follow the enclosed author guidelines when preparing and submitting your manuscript to *Cost Engineering* magazine.

If you have any questions about *Cost Engineering* magazine or would like to talk with an editor about preparing your manuscript, call (304) 296-8444.

PREPARING YOUR MANUSCRIPT

Since we use a blind review process, **do not** use your name in the paper. The title page should contain your name and address.

Previously published work - you must notify us if the work you are submitting has previously been published elsewhere.

Format - please submit a clean, professional-looking copy, either a good xerox or a clear computer printout. Only print on the front page. Please number all pages.

References - we require proper credit and documentation of any information that is not the author's original work. Include complete bibliographic information for every reference in your paper. References should be numbered and listed at the end of the paper, in alphabetical order, by the author's last name. Include the title, publisher, place of publication, publication date, and page numbers, (if necessary). When something mentioned in your paper must be referenced, cite the reference by its number in the reference section, and enclose the number in brackets. We follow *The Chicago Manual Of Style*, 14th edition.

Equations - All equations must be typed or included in your software program. Do not hand-letter equations.

Illustrations - All tables and figures must be laser-printed or typeset. We cannot accept hand-drawn figures. Your figures and tables must be legible and integrated with the text, not lumped together in an appendix at the end.

Units Of Measure - We use metric units. If other units are used, metric equivalents must be given in parenthesis.

Abbreviations And Acronyms - spell out the words the first time you use an abbreviation or acronym. Make sure that any "jargon" or special terms are defined.

SUBMITTING YOUR MANUSCRIPT

Send 4 (**four**) copies of your manuscript, along with an IBM-compatible disk (preferably WordPerfect 5.2, Microsoft Word for Windows 2.0, or ASCII).

Clearances - all papers dealing with subjects containing information that could be construed as company confidential or private must be accompanied by written clearance from the author's company.

Manuscripts and disks cannot be returned.

You will be notified by mail when we have received your manuscript and on its status.

If Your Paper Is Accepted
An editor will contact you about the specifics of the production and scheduling of your work.

Title And Copyright - you will be sent a copyright form to sign and have notarized. Title and copyright of your paper become vested in AACE International upon acceptance of the paper. Once a paper is accepted for publication in *Cost Engineering* and the author(s) signs the publication agreement, the paper may not be published elsewhere unless authorized by AACE International Reproduction elsewhere in whole or in part is welcomed, provided that proper credit is given to the author and to AACE International. If *Cost Engineering* publishes a manuscript that has previously been copyrighted, the copyright must be transferred to AACE International.

Responsibility - statements and opinions expressed are the responsibility of the author. AACE international publishes articles in *Cost Engineering* for the benefit of its members and to make public and preserve skills and knowledge of cost engineering and cost management. Publication does not necessarily imply endorsement by AACE International.

If Your Are Asked To Revise Your Paper
If revisions are deemed necessary, an editor will contact you.

Minor Revisions - you will be asked to supply one copy of the revised paper. If our editor determines that the revisions have been made, you will be notified.

Major Revisions - if the reviewers feel that your paper needs substantial reworking, four copies of the revised paper must be submitted. The paper will then go out to the same reviewers. You will be notified of the result.

If Your Paper Is Rejected
If your work is rejected, you will be notified by mail.

Send your manuscripts to: AACE International (see address above).

CPA Journal

ADDRESS FOR SUBMISSION:

James L. Craig, Jr.,CPA, Editor-In-Chief
CPA Journal
530 Fifth Avenue
New York, NY 10036-5101
USA
Phone: 212-719-8300
Fax: 212-719-3364
E-Mail: cpaj@luca.com
Web:
Address May Change:

CIRCULATION DATA:

Reader: Business Persons, CPAs
Frequency of Issue: Monthly
Copies per Issue: More Than 35,000
Sponsor/Publisher: New York State Society
of CPAs
Subscribe Price: 42.00 US$

PUBLICATION GUIDELINES:

Manuscript Length: 2500-4000 Words
Copies Required: Three
Computer Submission: Yes
Format: WP 5.1, 6.1; Wd or RTF
Fees to Review: 0.00 US$

Manuscript Style:
    Chicago Manual of Style

REVIEW INFORMATION:

Type of Review: Blind Review
No. of External Reviewers: 3+
No. of In House Reviewers: 3
Acceptance Rate: 21-30%
Time to Review: 2 - 3 Months
Reviewers Comments: No
Invited Articles: 6-10%
Fees to Publish: 0.00 US$

MANUSCRIPT TOPICS:

Accounting Information Systems; Accounting Theory & Practice; Auditing; Cost Accounting; Government & Non Profit Accounting; International Economics & Trade; Online Services; Portfolio & Security Analysis; Regional Economics; Tax Accounting

MANUSCRIPT GUIDELINES/COMMENTS:

1. *Chicago Manual Of Style*

2. We publish original articles of interest to practitioners, those in business, and in educational fields. Submitted articles should offer: Help in resolving questions that arise in practice, advice in implementing published standards and guides, insight to problems with, preferably, workable solutions, or report on the status of developing issues. Our articles should be of broad interest, although some could relate to specific industries or techniques. Article should be of immediate interest and timely to the profession. The Journal also allots space to theoretical discussion and viewpoints and will consider brief articles of this genre.

3. Please write clearly, concise and to the point--avoid numerous footnotes and citations. What we look for is originality and logic. We reserve the right to edit manuscripts for lucidity and grammar.

4. Manuscripts of 2500-4000 words are desirable. Short articles may be considered for use in our monthly departments (accounting, auditing, etc.) All major headings should be flush left, with initial uppercase letters. Subheads should also be flush left, with initial uppercase letters. Subheads are a writer's tool to logically present thought and introduce ideas in a minimal amount of space. Use subheads wisely.

5. Tables and figures should be numbered, titled so references made within the text can refer to the key. Tables and figures should be on separate sheets. Please submit clear and accurate renderings of the tables and figures.

6. Include a brief biography (about 25 words) with your name, title, affiliation, address, and telephone number.

7. Authors are notified when an article is accepted as a feature or department article. The acceptance letter also serves as a copyright permission form which grants The CPA Journal copyright privileges, including the right to authorize reprints.

8. Manuscripts should be submitted typed, double-spaced on 8 ½" x 11" white paper. We ask that three copies be submitted along with the computer disk. Send manuscript package, including two copies and bio to the above address. Manuscripts will be returned upon written request. Any question re: topic, idea development, presentation, etc., please contact The Journal.

Manuscripts may also be E-mailed to cpaj@luca.com

Critical Perspectives on Accounting

ADDRESS FOR SUBMISSION:

Tony Tinker, Editor
Critical Perspectives on Accounting
City Univesity of New York
Baruch College
Box E- 273
17 Lexington Avenue
New York, NY 10010
USA
Phone: 212-802-6435
Fax: 212-802-6423
E-Mail: tonytinker@msn.com
Web:
Address May Change:

PUBLICATION GUIDELINES:

Manuscript Length: 20+
Copies Required: Four
Computer Submission: Yes
Format: N/A
Fees to Review: 0.00 US$

Manuscript Style:
    Chicago Manual of Style

CIRCULATION DATA:

Reader: Academics
Frequency of Issue: 6 Times/ Year
Copies per Issue: Less than 1,000
Sponsor/Publisher: Harcourt Brace
Subscribe Price: 137.00 US$

REVIEW INFORMATION:

Type of Review: Blind Review
No. of External Reviewers: 3
No. of In House Reviewers: 3
Acceptance Rate: 6-10%
Time to Review: 2 - 3 Months
Reviewers Comments: Yes
Invited Articles: 0-5%
Fees to Publish: 0.00 US$

MANUSCRIPT TOPICS:
Accounting Information Systems; Accounting Theory & Practice; Auditing; Behavioral
Accounting Research; Cost Accounting; Critical Research; Economic Development;
Economic History; Government & Non Profit Accounting; Industrial Organization;
International Economics & Trade; International Finance; Macro Economics; Micro
Economics; Public Policy Economics

MANUSCRIPT GUIDELINES/COMMENTS:

Critical Perspectives On Accounting aims to provide a forum for the growing number of
accounting researchers and practitioners who realize that conventional theory and practice is
ill-suited to the challenges of the modern environment, and that accounting practices and
corporate behaviour are inextricably connected with many allocative, distributive, social and
ecological problems of our era. From such concerns, a new literature is emerging that seeks to
reformulate corporate, social and political activity, and the theoretical practical means by
which we apprehend and affect that activity.

Specific issues that the journal will address include, but are not limited to, the following:

- Studies involving the political economy of accounting, critical accounting, radical accounting, and accounting's implication in the exercise of power
- Financial accounting's role in the processes of international capital formation, including its impact on stock market stability and international banking activities
- Management accounting's role in organizing the labour process
- The relationship between accounting and the state in various social formation
- Studies of accounting's historical role, as a means of "remembering" the subject's social and conflictual character
- The role of accounting in establishing "real" democracy at work and other domains of life
- Accounting's adjudicative function in international exchanges, such as that of the third world debt
- Antagonisms between the social and private character of accounting, such as conflicts of interest in the audit process
- The identification of new constituencies for radical and critical accounting information
- Accounting's involvement in gender and class conflicts in the workplace
- The interplay between accounting, social conflict, industrialization, bureaucracy and technocracy
- Reappraisals of the role of accounting as a science and technology
- Accounting's implication in the management conflict around state enterprises
- Critical reviews of "useful" scientific knowledge about organizations

Instructions To Authors

Notes of Guidance To Contributors
Authors submitting papers for publication warrant that the work does not infringe any existing copyright and does not contain material of a libelous or scandalous nature. Further, the author indemnifies the publisher and editors against any branch of such warranty.

Format And Style

Chicago Manual of Style
Manuscripts are to be typewritten double spaced on one side (preferably international-size A4). Authors should include four copies of:

- an abstract not exceeding 150 words - it should summarize the purpose, methodology, and major conclusions of the article;
- 10 key words or phrases that can be used for indexing purposes;
- a short biographical sketch for each of the authors, together with their addresses and phone numbers.

The cover page of the manuscript should include the title, the author's name(s), position and institutional affiliation, and any acknowledgements. Only the title should appear on the next page of the manuscript and on the abstract. Footnotes, identified in the text by a numeral that is superscripted, should not include literature citations, and should be listed at the end of the paper, before the bibliography.

Literature citations in the text should include the author's name, the year of publication, and the specific page numbers if required (e.g., Mickey and Donald, 1968; p. 24). For more than two authors, the citation should be abbreviated as follows: (Kramdon et al., 1988, p. 1). Multiple citations of the same author(s) in the same year should be distinguished in the text (and in the bibliography) by a, b, c, etc. and followed by the year of publication. The bibliography should only include references cited in the text and should be arranged in the alphabetical order according to the surname of the first author. Full bibliographical details are required. The following style is required for

1. articles;
2. books;
3. citations from edited books;
4. translated books;
5. reference to a report.

1. DuBoff, R.B., and Herman, E.S., "Alfred Chandler's New Business History: A Review", Politics & Society, Vol. 10, No. 1, 1980, pp. 87-110.
2. Anderson, P., *Considerations On Western Marxism* (London: New Left Review Books,1976).
3. Hall, S., "The Little Caesars of Social Democracy", in Hall, S. and Jacques, M., (eds) The Politics of Thatcherism, pp. 309-322, (London: Lawrence & Wishart, 1983).
4. Adorno, T.W., Negative Dialektic (Frankfurt: Suhrkamp, 1968). Negative Dialectics, E.B. Ashton (trans) (New York: Seabury Press,1973).
5. Joint WHO Committee on Multinational Expansion. *The Role Of The Multinational In Health And Safety Developments* (Geneva: World Health Organisation, 1982, Technical Report Series 503).

Charts, Diagrams And Figures
These should all be called figures, numbered consecutively in Arabic numerals, with a brief title in capitals and labeled axes. The text should clearly indicate where the figure is to appear. Each figure should be submitted on a separate sheet of paper and be suitable for direct reproduction.

Tables
Tables should be numbered consecutively and independently of figures. Tables should be labeled with Roman numerals, a brief descriptive title, and headings down and across. The text should indicate clearly where each table is to appear. Each table should be submitted on a separate sheet of paper and be suitable for direct reproduction.

Proofs And Copies
Page proofs should be checked by the author and returned to the publisher within 48 hours. Only printer's typographical errors should be corrected at this stage; any substantive changes other than these will be charged to the author. The Editors reserve the right to publish a paper without the author's own corrections in cases of undue delay in returning the proofs.

Notes For Reviewers And Authors
The journal aims to provide a prompt and informative response to authors. Manuscripts that pass an initial preliminary screening will be sent to two blind reviews. It is policy to offer authors constructive and supportive reviews and thus, as far as possible, reviewers will be encouraged to stress in their review what additional work would be necessary to bring a submission to publication standard.

Reprints
50 reprints of each paper are supplied free of charge. In the case of multiple authored papers, they will be sent to the first named author. Additional quantities may be ordered at the time the proofs are checked, on the form provided. There are no page charges.

Submission Requirements
Only manuscripts not under consideration elsewhere should be submitted. Copies of questionnaires and other research instruments should be included with the submission. However, space limitations may preclude the publication of this material. When they are not reproduced a note should be included indicating an address where readers may obtain a complete copy of the instruments.

Four copies of each manuscript should be submitted to the Editor.

European Accounting Review

ADDRESS FOR SUBMISSION:

Kari Lukka, Editor
European Accounting Review
Turku School of Economics and
   Business Administration
Rehtorinpellonkatu 3
FIN 20500 Turku,
Finland
Phone: 35 8 2 3383 315
Fax: 35 8 2 3383 350
E-Mail: kari.lukka@tukkk.fi
Web: www.tandf.co.uk
Address May Change:

PUBLICATION GUIDELINES:

Manuscript Length: Any
Copies Required: Four
Computer Submission: No
Format: N/A
Fees to Review: 0.00 US$

Manuscript Style:
   Uniform System of Citation (Harvard
   Blue Book)

CIRCULATION DATA:

Reader: Academics
Frequency of Issue: Quarterly
Copies per Issue: 1,001 - 2,000
Sponsor/Publisher: Routledge
   Journals/Taylor and Francis
Subscribe Price: 215.00 US$

REVIEW INFORMATION:

Type of Review: Blind Review
No. of External Reviewers: 2
No. of In House Reviewers: 0
Acceptance Rate: 11-20%
Time to Review: 2 - 3 Months
Reviewers Comments: No Reply
Invited Articles: 6-10%
Fees to Publish: 0.00 US$

MANUSCRIPT TOPICS:
Accounting Theory & Practice; Auditing; Econometrics; International Accounting; Micro Economics

MANUSCRIPT GUIDELINES/COMMENTS:

Editorial changes to The European Accounting Review
As of 1.1.2000 there will be a reorganisation in the editorial structure of *The European Accounting Review (EAR)*. The editorial team will consist of an Editor, seven Associate Editors and an Assistant Editor.

Professor Kari Lukka from the Turku School of Economics and Business Administration, Finland, will start as the new Editor of EAR. Of the current two joint Editors, Professors Peter Walton and Anne Loft, Prof. Walton will step down at the end of 1999, whilst Prof. Loft will continue as an Editor the first few months of the year 2000, jointly with Prof. Lukka, and will step down from her current position at the EAA Congress to be held in Munich next March. After that she will yet continue as a member of the newly organised editorial team as one of the Associate Editors.

The new Associate Editors of EAR will be Begona Giner, John Christensen, Frank Hartmann, Christian Leuz, Anne Loft, Yannick Lemarchand and Stuart McLeay. Markus Granlund will start as the Assistant Editor of EAR.

From the start of 2000, all paper submissions (still as hard copies) and other editorial correspondence linked to EAR should be directed to Kari Lukka (address below). Prof. Anne Loft will deal with all articles submitted before the end of 1999, and correspondence regarding these should still be sent to her (also after the Munich Congress).

Relevant contact information:

Professor Kari Lukka, Turku School of Economics and Business Administration, Rehtorinpellonkatu 3, FIN-20500 Turku, FINLAND. tel. +358 2 3383 315. fax. +358 2 3383 350. e-mail: kari.lukka@tukkk.fi

Professor Anne Loft, (new address from November 1999) Copenhagen Business School, Department of Accounting and Auditing, Solbjerg Plads 3, DK 2000 F, DENMARK. tel. +45 3815 2343. fax. +45 3815 2321. e-mail: al.acc cbs.dk

Submission of Articles
Authors should submit *four* complete copies of their article, including an abstract and six *keywords* suitable for indexing and online search purposes. Original copies of any illustrations should be provided. It will be assumed that the authors will keep a copy of their paper.

Submission of a paper to the journal will be taken to imply that it presents original, unpublished work not under consideration for publication elsewhere. By submitting a manuscript, the authors agree that the copyright has been assigned to the European Accounting Association. All articles will be double blind refereed.

The journal has two regular sections for articles: The main section (for articles which fulfill the highest standards of academic accounting research) and the Accounting in Europe section (for primarily descriptive articles and articles commenting on current developments). Authors can specify the section of the journal for which they are submitting their work, if they wish.

In addition, special sections of articles may be published on topics of particular interest. The journal also has a book review section.

Articles should be submitted as hardcopies (not by e-mail) to Prof. Kari Lukka, Turku School of Economics and Business Administration, Rehtorinpellonkatu 3, FIN-20500 Turku, Finland.

The Manuscript
Submissions may be made in any major European language, although publication is in English. They should be typed in double spacing with wide margins, on one side only of the paper, preferably of A4 size. The title, but not the author's name, should appear on the first page of the manuscript. Furthermore, to assist objectivity, the author should avoid any reference to himself or herself which would enable identification by referees.

Articles should normally be as concise as possible and preceded by an abstract of not more than 200 words.

Tables and figures should not be inserted in the pages of the manuscript but should be on separate sheets. They should be numbered consecutively in arabic numerals with a descriptive caption. The desired position in the text for each table and figure should be indicated in the manuscript. Permission to reproduce copyright material must be obtained by the authors before submission and any acknowledgements should be included in the typescript or captions as appropriate.

Notes should be used only where necessary to avoid interrupting the continuity of the text. They should be numbered consecutively and placed at the end of the article before the bibliographic references.

If an article is accepted for publication, authors are requested to send an electronic version of their paper to Dr Markus Granlund, either via e-mail as an attached file (markus.granlund@tukkk.fi) or on disk by ordinary mail (Turku School of Economics and Business Administration, Rehtorinpellonkatu 3, FIN-20500 Turku, Finland). They are asked to ensure that the electronic version is exactly the same as the accepted final version of the article, and to provide details of the make and model of the computer and the name and version of the word-processing package used.

References
The Harvard system uses the name of the author and the date of publication as a key to the full bibliographical details which are set out in the references.

When the author's name is mentioned in the text, the date is inserted in parentheses immediately after the name, as in 'Fitchew (1990)'. When a less direct reference is made to one or more authors, both name and date are bracketed, with the references separated by a semi-colon, as in 'several authors have noted this trend 'Roberts, 1990; Brunsson, 1990; Johnson, 1987)'.

When the reference is to a work of dual or multiple authorship, use only surnames or the abbreviated form, as in 'Johnson and Kaplan (1987)' or 'Jones, et al. (1976)'. If an author has two references published in the same year, add lower-case letters after the date to distinguish them, as in 'Roberts (1990a, 1990b)'.

The date of publication used is the date of the source you have referred to. However, when using a republished book, a translation or a modern edition of an older edition, also give the date of the original publication, as in Flint (1988/1968), in order to place the work chronologically and locate it in the reference list. When using a reprinted article, cite date of original publication only, as this both places the work chronologically and locates it in the reference list. (See Format of reference lists for forms of citation in reference list.)

Page numbers are indicated by inserting the relevant numbers after the date, separated from the date by a colon and with no other punctuation, as in 'Provasoli (1989: 56)' or 'Casey and

Bartczak (1985: 423)'. Always use the minimum number of figures in page numbers, dates, etc., e.g. 22-4, 101-2, 1968-9; but for 'teen numbers use 13-14, 1914-18, etc.

When references are made to institutions or works whose official title is not English, the following procedure should apply:

(a) institutions should always be referred to by their full official native title when first mentioned in the text, and by that title or an abbreviation of it thereafter. An English translation may be included, if appropriate, at the first mention, e.g. 'standard setting is the responsibility of the Conseil National de la Comptabilité (CNC - National Accounting Council). The CNC consists of . . . ';

(b) articles, book titles, etc., which have been published other than in English should be referred to, where appropriate, using their original title [with English translation provided in brackets];

(c) where a quotation is used in the text, this should be an English translation, with the foreign language appended as a footnote if this is essential for an understanding of the point, e.g. 'It is a little different to the extent that it does not consider accounting exclusively as a technique of capturing, recording and manipulating information' (Colasse, 1991 translation).

Format of Reference Lists and Bibliographies

Submissions should include a reference list whose content and format conforms to the following examples. Note: secondary lines are indented; authors' names are given in full; page numbers are required for articles in readers, journals and magazines; where relevant, translator and date of first publication of a book, and original date of reprinted article, are noted.

Book Bromwich, M. (1985) The *Economics of Standard Setting*. London: Prentice-Hall/ICAEW.

Multiple author Bruns, W. J. and Kaplan, R. S. (eds) (1987) *Accounting and Management: Field Study Perspectives*. Boston, MA: Harvard Business School Press.

Article in edited volume Kaplan, R. S. (1985) 'Accounting lag: the obsolescence of cost accounting systems', in Clark, K. and Lorenze, C. (eds) *Technology and Productivity: the Uneasy Alliance*. Boston, MA: Harvard Business School Press, pp. 195-226.

Article in journal Ordelheide, D. (1993) 'The true and fair view: impact on and of the Fourth Directive', *European Accounting Review,* 2(1): 81-90.

Report Fitchew, G. E. (1990) 'Summing up', in Commission of the European Communities, *The Future of Harmonization of Accounting Standards Within the European Communities*. Brussels.

Article in newspaper The Times Literary Supplement (1991) 'The year that shook the world', 23 August 1991: 9.

Unpublished Zito, A. (1994) 'Epistemic communities in European policymaking', Ph.D. dissertation, Department of Political Science, University of Pittsburgh.

NB: If referring to a revised or second edition, cite only edition used.

Proofs
Page proofs will be sent for correction to the first-named author, unless otherwise requested. The difficulty and expense involved in making amendments at the page-proof stage make it essential for authors to prepare their typescript carefully: any alteration to the original text is strongly discouraged. Authors should correct printers' errors in red; minimal alterations of their own should be in black.

Offprints
25 offprints and a copy of the journal will be supplied free of charge for each main article. In the case of joint authorship, offprints must be shared.

Exempt Organization Tax Review (The)

ADDRESS FOR SUBMISSION:

Carolyn D. Wright, Editor
Exempt Organization Tax Review (The)
Tax Analysts
6830 N. Fairfax Drive
Arlington, VA 22213
USA
Phone: 703-533-4419
Fax: 703-533-4425
E-Mail: cwright@tax.org
Web: www.tax.org
Address May Change:

PUBLICATION GUIDELINES:

Manuscript Length: Any
Copies Required: One
Computer Submission: Yes
Format: MS Word, Wd Perfect
Fees to Review: 0.00 US$

Manuscript Style:
Chicago Manual of Style

CIRCULATION DATA:

Reader: , Tax law practitioners
Frequency of Issue: Monthly
Copies per Issue: Less than 1,000
Sponsor/Publisher: Tax Analysts
Subscribe Price: 649.00 US$

REVIEW INFORMATION:

Type of Review: Editorial Review
No. of External Reviewers: 0
No. of In House Reviewers: 1
Acceptance Rate: 50%
Time to Review: 1 Month or Less
Reviewers Comments: No
Invited Articles: 11-20%
Fees to Publish: 0.00 US$

MANUSCRIPT TOPICS:
Government & Non Profit Accounting; Nonprofit Tax Law

MANUSCRIPT GUIDELINES/COMMENTS:

Financial Counseling and Planning

ADDRESS FOR SUBMISSION:

Sherman Hanna, Editor
Financial Counseling and Planning
Ohio State University
Room 265 Cambell Hall
Consumer and Textile Sciences Department
1787 Neil Avenue
Columbus, OH 43210-1295
USA
Phone: 614-292-4584
Fax: 614-292-7536
E-Mail: hanna.1@osu.edu
Web: http://afcpe.org
Address May Change:

PUBLICATION GUIDELINES:

Manuscript Length: 16-20
Copies Required: Four
Computer Submission: Yes after accepted
Format: MsWord 97, WdPerfect 7
Fees to Review: 0.00 US$

Manuscript Style:
    American Psychological Association

CIRCULATION DATA:

Reader: Academics, Business Persons,
    Agencies
Frequency of Issue: 2 Times/Year
Copies per Issue: Less than 1,000
Sponsor/Publisher: Association for
    Financial Couseling and Planning
    Education
Subscribe Price: 80.00 US$ Membership
    40.00 US$ Membership/Student
    120.00 US$ Membership/Corporate

REVIEW INFORMATION:

Type of Review: Blind Review
No. of External Reviewers: 3
No. of In House Reviewers: 0
Acceptance Rate: 25%
Time to Review: 2 - 3 Months
Reviewers Comments: Yes
Invited Articles: 0-5%
Fees to Publish: 0.00 US$

MANUSCRIPT TOPICS:
Econometrics; Financial Counseling Theory; Insurance; Portfolio & Security Analysis; Real Estate; Retirement Planning; Tax Accounting

MANUSCRIPT GUIDELINES/COMMENTS:

Guidelines for Submission of Manuscripts
Submissions related to some aspect of financial counseling and planning are welcome. Manuscripts submitted should not be currently under review by another journal, but it is acceptable to submit papers that have been presented at conferences, even if they have been published in conference proceedings. If journal publication might precede the conference, you should check with the conference chair before submission to this journal.

Submissions should **always** have four paper copies, with author names not included in the body of the manuscript. There should be a title page, with author names and detailed contact information, including an e-mail address. If the authors do not have an e-mail address, a fax number or a telephone number with an answering machine or voice mail should be included. Include as many methods of contact as possible.

Format:
Cover page with title and authors (including mailing address, phone and fax numbers, an email address of contact author).
Manuscript, with title on same page as manuscript (including abstract) but no information identifying the authors.

Body of manuscript.

Note: to save time after acceptance, it may be worthwhile to study the **Guidelines for Submission of Accepted Manuscripts**. For instance, a version of APA style is used in the journal. However, it is acceptable to submit manuscripts for review in other formats.

It the manuscript is accepted for publication, it is the author's responsibility to submit a manuscript file in a standard word processing format (e.g., WordPerfect or Word) as an attached file in an email, or on a PC disk. The Guidelines for Submission of Accepted Manuscripts should be followed as closely as possible, including the journal's version of APA style for references.

Guidelines for Preparation of Accepted Manuscripts
Sherman Hanna , Sept. 3, 1998

Note! **Initial submissions should always have four paper copies, with author names not included in the body of the manuscript.**
Format:
Cover page with title and authors (including mailing address, phone and fax numbers, and email address of contact author.
Manuscript, with title on same page as manuscript (including abstract) but no information identifying the authors.

For submission of files of accepted manuscripts
We will be using WordPerfect 7 for Windows, and that or WordPerfect 6 (Windows or DOS) would be the **ideal** word processing software. Most word processing packages should be OK, but if you are unsure, email me at hanna.1@osu.edu. If you have a choice, please use WordPerfect rather than Word. If, however, you have prepared your manuscript in Word, just send me the Word file. I have Word 97, so that will be better than saving as a WordPerfect file. *If you do not use WordPerfect, please use as little formatting as possible. Spacing between paragraphs should **not** be with paragraph formatting -- instead, hit an extra hard return.*

If you have communications software that can send an attached document using the MIME, BinHex or UUDECODE protocol, you do not have to send me a disk, just email me and use the "attach document" procedure for your communications software. Otherwise, send me any type of PC disk (not Mac!) with your word processing file.

APA Style We will use the Fourth Edition of the *Publication Manual of the American Psychological Association.* For some minor differences and other details, see the 1995 issue of *Financial Counseling and Planning.* **NOTE!** Please consult the following Web site for a proposed standard for citation of Web documents: http://www.nyct.net/~beads/weapas/.

Note that the APA guidelines include some suggestions that are NOT appropriate for submission of accepted manuscripts for *Financial Counseling and Planning.* For instance, do **not** use double spacing.

Font: Set your initial font to Times Roman, 10 point.

Margins. All margins should be 0.9 inches.

Footnote options: Set the footnote space= 0.05 inches.

Headers. The headers should be set **only** at the top of the manuscript. DO NOT set headers at any other place in the document. Make sure that you set 0.9 inch margins within the headers. Headers should be in Times Roman 8 point italics.
1. Odd pages: Brief synopsis of title. **NOTE**: put Flush Right command after the font.
2. Even pages: [Flush Right (Alt F6)], *Financial Counseling and Planning,* Volume 8 (2), 1997
Suppress the headers for the first page. **DO NOT USE "delay"**

Footers The footers should be set **only** at the top of the manuscript. DO NOT set footers at any other place in the document. Make sure that you set 0.9 inch margins within the headers. The footers should contain:
©1997, Association for Financial Counseling and Planning Education *All rights of reproduction in any form reserved.* flush right page# function
The footers should be in a Swiss font, in 8 point,
1. Odd pages. The formatted page number command should be inserted flush right.
2. Even pages. The formatted page number command should be inserted before everything else, then ©1997, Association for Financial Counseling and Planning Education should be flush right.

Title. (Times Roman 16pt Bold). Center the title. Use upper and lower case letters, capitalizing the first letter of **every word. (Note that this rule has changed from previous issues.)** - Put one [HRt] before the title Put 1 [HRt] after the title.
Author(s). **(Times Roman 14pt bold).** Be sure to create footnotes with the author(s) name (s). Only include the authors' names. Do not include affiliations. List author names on one line if possible.

Footnotes. Create a footnote for each author. Type the name, title, address, phone number, FAX number if there is one, and email address if there is one. See an article from the first issue of the 1997 volume.

Abstract. Place 1 [HRt] after the author(s) name(s) and type the abstract. The abstract should be typed in Times Roman 12pt and not be more than 100 words. Try to write an interesting abstract that a practitioner without special training can understand. Be as descriptive as possible, e.g., do not state that "race was significantly related to stock ownership" -- state "Blacks were less likely to own stocks than otherwise similar whites." (We will assume you would only include statistically significant results in the abstract!)

Key Words

Please include 1 to 5 key words or phrases below your abstract. Carefully check the index of key words in the 1994 issue or on the web site to find appropriate key words. If you feel that new key words (i.e., not previously used) are needed for your article, please attach a note to the editor. Also, if you feel that some previously published articles should be listed under your new key words, please include those references in your attached note to the editor.

Text

Format. After the abstract, turn on columns (2, with 0.5 inches between -- usually the default anyway.)

Font: Times Roman 10 pt.) Single-space the final draft. Double-space between paragraphs, but do not indent at the beginning of the paragraphs. Make sure that all returns are soft returns. However, make sure that there are hard returns at the end of each paragraph.

Order

The order of parts of the article should be (if each is included):
- text (including tables, figures, and diagrams)
- appendices (Times Roman 8 point)
- endnotes (Times Roman 8 point Italicized, note # is not italicized, Do not use WordPerfect endnote function, unless you are using WordPerfect 6.1 or 7.
- references

Headings

Note this example, because it is different from the usual instructions for headings:

Methods
Description of Data and Sample
The data used for the analysis are from a public use tape

- Skip only one line before centering the main headings. Main, centered headings should be in bold.
- Do not skip a line after a main heading. (This is different from issues of the journal before 1995.)
- Place second level headings of sections at the left margin in italics. Do not skip a line before the text.
- All headings should be in Upper and Lower Case Letters.
- Third level headings should be in italics, with 2 spaces but no period before starting the first sentence of the paragraph. Note that the enclosed article is slightly different from these instructions, because third level headings were used for variable definitions, and I am not sure if we did it in the most logical way.

Footnotes
The only footnotes in the article should be for the author identifications on the first page. Please extract all other footnotes and change insert them in an endnote section. In the 1995 issue, we started using lower case letters to number endnotes.

If you have notes for a particular table or figure, use a different system, with neither alphabetic nor numeric superscripts, e.g., * or symbols, not superscripted. If a note is not specific to a particular item in the table, just put it below the table.

Figures
If a graphic is embedded in your Wordperfect or Word file, there should be no problem. Under no circumstances should you send me a separate graphics file! If you cannot insert it in your word processing file, the chances are pretty good that I will not be able to. If you feel you must include a hand done graphic, it is your responsibility to send a dark enough copy in an appropriate size, so that I do not have to reduce it and further decrease the quality of the reproduction.

Tables
No landscape tables will be printed and few multi-page tables will be allowed. Usually we can manage to change your landscape tables to portrait, but we would appreciate your efforts at this!

All contents of a table other than the title should be in 8 point Times Roman. If you use tabs, use "relative" tabs in tables, not "absolute" tabs. For columns of numbers, please use decimal tabs. Unless you can format the tables in the final dimensions of the journal, you MUST create all tables using the table function of your word processing software. Also, if your table has more than 3 columns, you must use the table function to create the table.

References

We use the latest APA book for references, with one important difference -- we use italics when APA uses underline. *There is also one minor difference -- no comma just before an &.*

Checking the references cited in the text, with the reference list is very important. Using the search feature and spell check feature, check forward and backwards for errors in spelling or omissions.

For WordPerfect 5 or 6 DOS: The references should have the following codes: Tab setting, relative, 0 and 0.2. Before each reference place an indent (F4) and a hanging indent (Shift Tab).

For everyone: Please learn how to create true hanging indents. **Never** shove over second lines to create hanging indents.

WordPerfect 7: Format, Paragraph, Hanging Indent; or, Control F7 to create a hanging indent.

Word. Use CTRL+T (Windows) or COMMAND+T (Macintosh). to create a hanging indent. For other help with Word, check out <u>and search the knowledge bas</u>e

You must set the first tab to 0.2 inches from the left margin.

Under no circumstances should you use a table to simulate hanging indents, as suggested in the Microsoft instructions.

The reference list should be in 9 point Times Roman.

Underline. Search for underline commands. These should be changed to italics (e.g., for journal titles) or bold (e.g., for emphasis in your text.) **There should be no underlines in your manuscript.**

Global Business and Economic Review

ADDRESS FOR SUBMISSION:

Demetri Kantarelis, Editor
Global Business and Economic Review
64 Holden Street
Worcester, MA 01605-3109
USA
Phone: 508-767-7557
Fax: 508-756-1780
E-Mail: dkantar@assumption.edu
Web:
Address May Change:

PUBLICATION GUIDELINES:

Manuscript Length: 11-15
Copies Required: Four
Computer Submission: Yes
Format: MS Word
Fees to Review: 30.00 US$

Manuscript Style:
    No Reply

CIRCULATION DATA:

Reader: Academics, Pracitioners
Frequency of Issue: 3 Times/Year
Copies per Issue: Less than 1,000
Sponsor/Publisher: Business & Economics
    Society International
Subscribe Price: 120.00 US$

REVIEW INFORMATION:

Type of Review: Blind Review
No. of External Reviewers: 3+
No. of In House Reviewers: 3+
Acceptance Rate: 22-25%
Time to Review: 2 - 3 Months
Reviewers Comments: Yes
Invited Articles: 0-5%
Fees to Publish: 0.00 US$

MANUSCRIPT TOPICS:
Accounting Information Systems; Accounting Theory & Practice; Auditing; Cost Accounting;
Government & Non Profit Accounting

MANUSCRIPT GUIDELINES/COMMENTS:

The *Global Business & Economics Review* (GBER)* is an international refereed journal,
published semi-annually (June and December) by the Business & Economics Society
International, for the presentation, discussion and analysis of advanced concepts, initial
treatments and fundamental research in all fields of Business and Economics. Priority is given
to insightful policy oriented articles that deal with the implications of the increasingly global
business activity, especially written for the educated lay-person.

The GBER welcomes contributions from academicians, corporate executives, staff members
of research institutions, international organizations and government officials. Interested
authors should submit four (4) copies of original manuscripts in English, with authorship
identified on a removable cover page, accompanied by a submission fee of $30 payable to
B&ESI. Manuscripts and editorial communications should be directed to the Editor.

Manuscripts submitted to the Review must be original contributions and should not be under consideration for any other publication at the same time. The reviewing is based on the anonymity of the authors) and the confidentiality of reviewers' and editors' reports. Authorship should be identified only on a removable cover page. Manuscripts should, normally, not exceed 12 single-spaced pages (Font:Times, Size: 10) inclusive of graphs, tables, endnotes/footnotes and references. Detailed Format Instructions will be attached to the acceptance for publication letter.

ISSN: 1097-4954
Copyright © 1998 by the Business & Economics Society International
Printed in Worcester, Massachusetts, USA
All rights reserved
Web Site: http//www.assumption.eduihtmi/faculty/kantar/niissbl.htrnl

* Each previous issue of the GBER is available at $20 (inside continental US) or $26 (outside continental US).

Government Accountants Journal

ADDRESS FOR SUBMISSION:

Marie Force, Editor
Government Accountants Journal
2208 Mount Vernon Avenue
Alexandria, VA 22301
USA
Phone: 703-684-6931 ext.203
Fax: 703-548-9367
E-Mail: mforce0610@aol.com
Web:
Address May Change:

PUBLICATION GUIDELINES:

Manuscript Length: 15-18
Copies Required: Three
Computer Submission: Yes
Format: WordPerfect 5.1
Fees to Review: 0.00 US$

Manuscript Style:

CIRCULATION DATA:

Reader: , Gov't Accountants, Auditors,
   Budget Analysts
Frequency of Issue: Quarterly
Copies per Issue: 16,000
Sponsor/Publisher: Association of
   Government Accountants
Subscribe Price: 60.00 US$

REVIEW INFORMATION:

Type of Review: Blind Review
No. of External Reviewers: 2
No. of In House Reviewers: No Reply
Acceptance Rate: 40%
Time to Review: 2 - 3 Months
Reviewers Comments: Yes
Invited Articles: 0-5%
Fees to Publish: 0.00 US$

MANUSCRIPT TOPICS:

Accounting Information Systems; Accounting Theory & Practice; Auditing; Cost Accounting;
Government & Non Profit Accounting; Tax Accounting

MANUSCRIPT GUIDELINES/COMMENTS:

Harvard Business Review

ADDRESS FOR SUBMISSION:

Editor
Harvard Business Review
60 Harvard Way
Boston, MA 02163
USA
Phone: 617-495-6800
Fax: 617-495-9933
E-Mail: hbr_editorial@hbsp.harvard.edu
Web: www.hbsp.harvard..edu
Address May Change:

CIRCULATION DATA:

Reader: Business Persons
Frequency of Issue: Bi-Monthly
Copies per Issue: More than 25,000
Sponsor/Publisher: Harvard University
Subscribe Price: 95.00 US$ USA
   105.00 US$ Canada

PUBLICATION GUIDELINES:

Manuscript Length: See Guidelines
Copies Required: See Guidelines
Computer Submission:
Format:
Fees to Review: 0.00 US$

Manuscript Style:
   Chicago Manual of Style

REVIEW INFORMATION:

Type of Review: Editorial Review
No. of External Reviewers: 0
No. of In House Reviewers: 3+
Acceptance Rate: 0-5%
Time to Review: 1 - 2 Months
Reviewers Comments: No
Invited Articles: 31-50%
Fees to Publish: 0.00 US$

MANUSCRIPT TOPICS:
Accounting Information Systems; Accounting Theory & Practice; Auditing; Cost Accounting; Government & Non Profit Accounting; Tax Accounting

MANUSCRIPT GUIDELINES/COMMENTS:

Author Guidelines

The purpose of the *Harvard Business Review is* to advance the theory and practice of management. *Harvard Business Review* articles fulfill this purpose in several ways:

- They offer important new ideas and original thinking to help senior managers establish an intellectual agenda for discussion within their companies.
- They provide best-practice models and hands-on techniques from companies around the world.
- They report on cutting-edge research by academics, consultants, and management analysts. They give firsthand insight into how companies work and how managers respond to demanding challenges in the workplace.

Published articles cover a wide range of management topics and practices in different industries, sectors, management functions, and geographic locations. They develop themes such as globalization, business and social issues, service and quality, corporate restructuring, and managing change. But regardless of the subject, *Harvard Business Review* articles share certain characteristics. They are written for senior managers by experts whose authority comes from careful analysis and study of an issue or from deep personal experience, and who demonstrate a mastery of the material presented. Their ideas have been tested in the real world of business and can be translated into management action in most instances.

Harvard Business Review readers are overwhelmingly managers: almost 95 percent of *Harvard Business Review*'s 200,000-plus subscribers are managers in organizations of all sizes and kinds. Their interests—in improving their performance, in learning and benefiting from the thinking and experience of experts—shape what *Harvard Business Review* editors look for in reviewing submissions. Proposals for articles that demonstrate clear and bold thinking, fresh and useful ideas, accessible and jargon-free expression, and unambiguous authority and expertise are most likely to meet such readers' needs.

The best way to inquire about *Harvard Business Review*'s potential interest in a topic is to send a letter with a two-page proposal and a full sentence outline. Because of the volume of inquiries about publishing in *Harvard Business Review*, it is not our policy to read complete manuscripts, and we cannot guarantee a response if they are submitted. The proposal should clearly and succinctly answer the following questions:

What is the message of the article you propose to write? What are the implications of the message? Or, as *Harvard Business Review* editors often say, What's the "so what"? Why should a busy manager stop and read your article? What is new, unusual, useful, counterintuitive, or important about your message? Who is the targeted audience? What research have you conducted to support the argument or logic in your article? What company examples can you cite to support your argument? What is the authority or expertise that you will draw on to make your argument convincing?

After you have answered these questions, outline the manuscript, offering enough detail for an editor to be able to understand the article's main points and the evidence or examples that will support those points. You should also write a draft of the first few paragraphs of the article, which contains the central message of the piece.

Send the letter, the outline, and the introduction to
Harvard Business Review
60 Harvard Way
Boston, MA 02163

We will review the proposal and get back to you as quickly as we can. The volume of proposals is so large, however, that it can take four to six weeks for *Harvard Business Review* to complete the review of a proposal. We appreciate your interest in *Harvard Business Review* and ask for your patience.

Unsolicited materials will be returned only if accompanied by a self-addressed, stamped envelope.

Internal Auditing

ADDRESS FOR SUBMISSION:

Alisa Salaman, Editor
Internal Auditing
RIA Group
395 Hudson Street
New York, NY 10014
USA
Phone: 212-367-6582
Fax: 212-367-6718
E-Mail:
Web:
Address May Change:

CIRCULATION DATA:

Reader: Business Persons, Academics, &
   Internal Auditors
Frequency of Issue: Bi-Monthly
Copies per Issue: 4,001 - 5,000
Sponsor/Publisher: Thompson Corp.
   Finance
Subscribe Price: 150.00 US$
   195.00 US$ Canada

PUBLICATION GUIDELINES:

Manuscript Length: 5,000 Words
Copies Required: Two & disk
Computer Submission: Yes
Format: MS Word 6.0 or '97
Fees to Review: 0.00 US$

Manuscript Style:
   Chicago Manual of Style

REVIEW INFORMATION:

Type of Review: Blind Review
No. of External Reviewers: 2
No. of In House Reviewers: 2
Acceptance Rate: 45%
Time to Review: 1 - 2 Months
Reviewers Comments: No
Invited Articles: 31-50%
Fees to Publish: 0.00 US$

MANUSCRIPT TOPICS:
Auditing; Econometrics

MANUSCRIPT GUIDELINES/COMMENTS:

Subscription Price: Academic discounts are given.

Internal Auditing seeks articles that are primarily practice oriented and that will be of interest to directors of internal auditing and their staff. The intent of *Internal Auditing* is to provide operational and implementational guidance to internal auditors.
The major areas for articles are:
- Operations auditing
- Financial auditing
- EDP auditing
- Audit department administration
- Relationships with external auditors, management and the Board
- Risk assessment
- Oral and written reporting

It is expected that most articles will fall in the 3000 to 5000 word range. The subject matter should be the final determinant of length, and this range may be broken in either direction in individual cases.

Authors should bear in mind that articles published will be read by busy people. The article should get to the point and not digress into extraneous areas.

While a how-to approach is preferred, we are interested in receiving articles that are controversial or unusual in their viewpoint so long as the topic should be of interest to our audience.

The Editor-in-Chief and the editors initially screen articles. Promising manuscripts are sent to two external reviewers for their comments and review. The editors make final decisions of acceptance.

Manuscript Style
Every publication seeks a certain degree of uniformity of style in the papers written by its several authors. We, too, seek a certain level of writing that, though not so heavy handed as *The New Yorker* or the *Harvard Business Review*, which make all articles seem to have been written by the same person, will create an impression of unity in a reader's mind.

Technical writers use too much punctuation, too much emphasis, and too many stops and starts in their writing. Some, though not all, of our authors have been infested with the disease. Some examples follow:

Parentheses. Parentheses should be used to insert data that is not part of the discussion. Parentheses are not designed to permit an author to carry on two unrelated discussions simultaneously.

Correct:
The American Institute of CPA's (AICPA) has decreed...

Incorrect:
Some of the characteristics of the standard accountants report (e.g., the uncertainty qualification) are under review.

Can an accountant apply poolings of interest accounting (as defined in APB Opinion 15) without first...?

Quotation Marks. Quotation marks are used to identify words used by others, not to cast doubt or to emphasize and to identify words being used as words instead of ideas. When quotation marks are used to identify a term being defined, this should be done only the first time and not throughout the discussion.

Correct:
The term "window period" means the period after issuance of a report during which...

Incorrect:
    An event during the "window period" may require dual dating.

Underlining. A fair quota of words to be underlined would be two words per article. Emphasis is a matter of phraseology and writing, not typography.

Footnotes. Identify sources of material in References. As to footnotes with additional information, a fair quota is five footnotes for contra discussions. If a thing is worth saying, put it in the text.

Titles of Published Works. Some publications call for underlined titles indicating to the printer that italics should be used. We use this form in the reference notes but in the text the correct title surrounded by quotation marks is used the first time a publication is identified, thus:

    In 1984 the SEC issued Financial Reporting Release 17. (FRR 17) "Oil and Gas Producers—Full Cost Accounting Practices." Thereafter refer simply to FRR 17.

As to other publications:

    Full Title
    Abbreviation

    Statement of Financial Accounting
    Standards No. 80   SFAS 80

    Statement of Auditing
    Standards 49   SAS 49

    Statement of Internal Auditing Standards
    No. 3   SIAS 3

Preparation Of Manuscripts:
1. Use only 8-1/2 x 11" white bond paper. Do not use "erasable" paper.

2. **All manuscript copy**—text, footnotes, charts, quotations and everything else—**must be typed double-spaced**, on one side of the paper only.

3. All footnotes are to be double-spaced and typed on a separate page at the end of the manuscript. They should be numbered consecutively throughout the article starting from 1.

4. Footnotes should be limited to identification of sources referred to in the text. We believe that anything worth saying should be said in the text of the paper although occasionally small exceptions will be made. We do not ordinarily publish bibliographies.

5. Minor changes should be made between the lines of the typescript, not in the margins. That is, typographical errors and slight corrections of the text or footnotes may be written (please print) on the manuscript in pen. If corrections are lengthy or complex, retype the entire manuscript page.

6. Illustrations accompanying manuscripts should be numbered, provided with suitable legends (again, typed double-spaced on 8-1/2 x 11" sheets), and marked lightly in pencil on the back with the name of the author and the title of the article. Illustrations such as original drawings or graphs are to be drawn in black India ink. Typewritten or freehand lettering is not acceptable. All lettering must be done professionally. Do not staple or paper clip illustrations between sheets of cardboard before mailing.

7. Tables and exhibits should be numbered consecutively.

8. Use headings and subheadings extensively. Center main headings within the article, type secondary headings flush left with the left-hand margin.

9. Keep the punctuation simple. Most authors overuse parentheses, italics and quotations marks, which are simply edited out in the publication process.

10. If an article includes any previously copyrighted material (other than short quotations), the publisher must have letters of permission to reprint from the copyright holder and from the author if he or she is not the copyright holder. These letters must be submitted at the same time as the manuscript.

11. *Internal Auditing* normally publishes articles only if they have not yet appeared or since been accepted for publication elsewhere. There is generally no objection, however, to having articles that appear in *Internal Auditing* reprinted in other publications at a later date, if appropriate permission is requested from the publisher.

12. Three copies of each manuscript should be submitted for review.

Manuscripts should be sent to: Urton Anderson, Editor-in-Chief
Accounting Department
University of Texas at Austin
CBA 4M 202
Austin, TX 78712-1172

or to: David C. Burns
Mall Location 211
CBA
University of Cincinnati
Cincinnati, OH 45221

Internal Auditor

ADDRESS FOR SUBMISSION:

Christy Chapman, Editor
Internal Auditor
The Institute of Internal Auditors
249 Maitland Avenue
Altamonte Springs, FL 32701-4201
USA
Phone: 407-830-7600
Fax: 407-830-4832
E-Mail: dsalierno@theiia.org
Web:
Address May Change:

PUBLICATION GUIDELINES:

Manuscript Length: 10
Copies Required: Four
Computer Submission: Yes
Format: Word, e-mail, disk
Fees to Review: 0.00 US$

Manuscript Style:
    American Psychological Association

CIRCULATION DATA:

Reader: Business Persons
Frequency of Issue: Bi-Monthly
Copies per Issue: 45,000
Sponsor/Publisher: The Institute of Internal
    Auditors
Subscribe Price: 60.00 US$
    108.00 US$ 2 Years
    156.00 US$ 3 Years

REVIEW INFORMATION:

Type of Review: Blind Review
No. of External Reviewers: 3
No. of In House Reviewers: 3
Acceptance Rate: 21-30%
Time to Review: 2 - 3 Months
Reviewers Comments: No Reply
Invited Articles: 20%
Fees to Publish: 0.00 US$

MANUSCRIPT TOPICS:
Auditing; Corporate Governance; Internal Control; Risk

MANUSCRIPT GUIDELINES/COMMENTS:

1. AP Style

2. Our primary audience is the internal auditing professional in practice all over the globe. Our readers hold top management positions in the multicorporate world and the public sector; they are found in private industry, nonprofit organizations, and local and national governments. From vice presidents to entry-level staff auditors, the majority are members of the Institute and actively support the development of their profession.

3. The Journal has secondary audiences of professionals in such fields as public accounting, education, information systems, and security. The steady growth of these audiences plus a broadening membership base has increased the total readership each year. A respected reference, the Journal's articles are reprinted and translated in books and periodicals around the world.

4. Each issue of the Journal carries special interest material much of which comes from our readers. If you wish to send an item, look for the address published in that department or send it directly to the Journal and we will forward it to the department editor.

5. The Roundtable. One of our most popular departments, it includes "short stories" from auditors who tell how they discovered and solved problems in their companies. Submit one or two typewritten, double-spaced pages describing the problem, how it was discovered, what was done to fix it, and include the benefit to the company such as a monetary saving. Individual anonymity is voluntary and assured; the sources are usually listed as an IIA Chapter or an anonymous offering.

6. Fraud Findings. Only discovery and resolution of fraud are presented here. Events must be based on actual facts, but names of individuals or companies involved will not be mentioned. Submissions are usually a few pages long and include a brief narrative of the case, the key clue uncovering the fraud, steps taken to facilitate the audit, motivation of the perpetrator, control weaknesses, and action taken to prevent recurrence.

7. Letters. We encourage readers to write letters to comment on published articles. Letters must be signed and should be no longer than 700 words because space is limited. All letters will be edited for purposes of clarity or space.

8. Readings include reviews of books or periodicals we believe to be of interest to internal auditors. If you know of a book that we have not yet reviewed, but that you would like to read an opinion on before purchasing, please send us the name of the book and its publisher's name and address.

9. "Computers & Auditing" provides audit professionals with information about how other audit organizations have integrated the personal computer into their operations. The column features software product reviews, tips from end-user auditors, and examples of auditor-developed applications.

10. "Risk Watch" discusses an emerging business. The Column includes practical tips on how internal auditors can help their organization address risk.

11. "Around the Globe" profiles the practice of internal auditing in countries around the world.

12. In addition to our Outstanding Contributor Certificates, which are given for the finest articles we publish, each year we honor the article judged best by our review board by awarding the author the coveted John B. Thurston Award for literary excellence. The author also travels to IIA's international conference—all expenses paid.

13. Write clearly and concisely. Get directly to the point, make your point in as few words as possible, and use simple language.

14. Define terms that may not be well known. Avoid jargon and cliches that may confuse the reader or send them running for the dictionary. On first mention, spell out abbreviations or

initials such as IIA, GAO, USPS. Remember: While some computer terms are "universal" not all computer systems use the same term to mean the same thing. If in doubt, define!

15. For crisp writing, use the active voice. Too often a passive voice statement such as "it was decided" leaves the reader questioning "who decided?" Anticipate your readers' questions and give them reasonable and useful answers.

16. Subheads give the reader a break between main sections of a manuscript and provide points of quick reference for a reader searching for a particular thought or concept.

17. Be sure all direct quotes are accurate and contribute to your topic. Be aware of what constitutes libel. Indicate your source. If you cannot attribute a quote to a publication, we may have to rephrase the idea or delete the quote and any reference to it altogether. When quoting a speech, identify the speaker, the date of delivery and the event.

18. The average published article is five or six pages, so limit the length of your manuscript to 8000 words. The manuscript should be **typed** and **double-spaced**.

19. Exhibits should be concise, separated from the body of the manuscript, and detailed enough to make their message clear. Our staff will prepare them to fit the publications' specifications, so original art is necessary only for unique items.

20. We discourage the use of footnotes.

21. Submit the original and three copies of the manuscript. We need the name, address, and telephone number of the author, even when the manuscript is submitted through the local IIA chapter.

22. Mail your material to *Internal Auditor*, 249 Maitland Avenue, Altamonte Springs, FL 32715-1119.

23. The review process for the *Internal Auditor* generally takes about 10-12 weeks. Three members of our editorial advisory board, selected for their compatibility to your topic, will receive a "blind" copy of your manuscript and evaluate it for its interest to auditors, quality of writing, technical soundness, timeliness, and originality.

24. Although every manuscript we receive is judged on its own merits, we follow these general criteria:

- Does the manuscript deal with a problem, issue, or condition that is the concern of people in the auditing profession?

- Is this a new concern or a new approach to a continuing concern?

- Does the author discuss it in enough depth to help the reader (who is, more often that not, an internal auditor)?

- Does the author support the discussion with examples drawn from actual experience?

- Does the manuscript offer any solutions to the problem discussed?

- Does the manuscript stand as a carefully reasoned presentation?

- Does the manuscript add significantly to what has already been published about the subject in the IA about elsewhere?

- Does the manuscript have a global perspective? **Avoid** using a North American focus.

25. Not every manuscript must cover all of these criteria, but inclusion of them increases the chances for acceptance of a manuscript.

International Journal of Accounting

ADDRESS FOR SUBMISSION:

Young Kwon, Editor
International Journal of Accounting
University of Illinois
320 West Building, Box 109
1206 South Street
Champaign, IL 61820
USA
Phone: 217-333-4545
Fax: 217-244-6565
E-Mail: gillham@uiuc.edu
Web:
Address May Change:

PUBLICATION GUIDELINES:

Manuscript Length: 30-40
Copies Required: Three
Computer Submission: Yes
Format: Word
Fees to Review: 0.00 US$

Manuscript Style:
    Chicago Manual of Style

CIRCULATION DATA:

Reader: Academics
Frequency of Issue: Quarterly
Copies per Issue: 1,001 - 2,000
Sponsor/Publisher: Elsevier Science
    Publishing Co.
Subscribe Price: 105.00 US$ Individuals
    250.00 US$ Institutions

REVIEW INFORMATION:

Type of Review: Blind Review
No. of External Reviewers: 2
No. of In House Reviewers: 0
Acceptance Rate: 30%
Time to Review: 1 - 2 Months
Reviewers Comments: Yes
Invited Articles: 0-5%
Fees to Publish: 0.00 US$

MANUSCRIPT TOPICS:
Accounting Information Systems; Accounting Theory & Practice; Auditing; Cost Accounting; Econometrics; Economic Development; Economic History; Fiscal Policy; Government & Non Profit Accounting; Industrial Organization; Insurance; International Business; International Economics & Trade; International Finance; Macro Economics; Micro Economics

MANUSCRIPT GUIDELINES/COMMENTS:

Aims and Scope The aims of *The International Journal of Accounting* are to advance the academic and professional understanding of accounting theory and practice from the international perspective and viewpoint. The Journal recognizes that international accounting is influenced by a variety of forces. e.g.. governmental. political and economic.

The Journal attempts to assist in the understanding of the present and potential ability of accounting to aid in the recording and interpretation of international economic transactions. These transactions may be within a profit or nonprofit. environment. The Journal deliberately encourages a broad view of the origins and development of accounting with an emphasis on its functions in an increasingly interdependent global economy, and welcomes manuscripts that help explain current international accounting practices. with related theoretical justifications. and identify criticisms of current practice. Other than occasional commissioned papers or special issues, all the manuscripts published in the Journal are selected by the editors after the normal refereeing process. [**Type of Review is double blind**.]

Instructions For Authors

1. Manuscripts should be submitted in triplicate to the Editor, Professor Young Kwon *The International Journal of Accounting,* University of Illinois, 320 Commerce West, 1206 S. Sixth Street, Champaign, IL 61820. U.S.A.

2. All manuscripts must be typewritten or word processed. double spaced on one side only and numbered consecutively, including an abstract of approximately 100 words, and 6 key words for indexing. Papers muss either be neither previously published nor submitted elsewhere simultaneously. Authors are responsible for obtaining permission from the copyright owner (usually the publisher) to use any quotations. illustration. or tables from another source.

3. The author's full name, affiliation, and when applicable, e-mail address should appear on the title page.

4. All tables, figures and illustrations should accompany the manuscript on separate sheets. Captions should clearly identify all separate matter. and all figures must be submitted in camera ready copy, or electronic program specifies files, such as EPS or Post Script. All should be called out in text and indication given as to location. For example.

TABLE 1 ABOUT HERE.

5.Footnotes should be numbered consecutively throughout the manuscript with superscript Arabic numerals. They should be collected in a separate file at the end of the text.

6. References should be cited in the text as follows:

Schweikart and O'Conner (1989) agree with this method. Other studies have found similar results (Schweikart and O'Conner, 1989; Smith, 1991).

On a separate Reference page(s), each citing should appear, double-spaced, in alphabetical order as follows:

Journal Articles
Langlois, Catherine C. and Bodo B. Schlegelmilch. 1990. "Do Corporate Codes of Conduct Reflect National Character?" Journal of *International Business Studies,* (Fourth Quarter): 519-539

Books
Hampden-Turner Charles and Alfons Trompenaars. 1993. *The Seven Cultures of Capitalism.* New York: Doubleday.

7. Upon acceptance the author is to submit one copy of the approved manuscript on a spell checked IBM compatible. program specific disk to the editor. The accuracy of the disk and proofs is the responsibility of the author. Macintosh submissions are limited to high density disks.

Book Review Section. The book review section is interested in works published in any language, as long as they are comparative or international in character. The author or publisher of such works should furnish either book review editor with two (2) copies of the work, including information about its price and the address where readers may write for copies. Reviews will be assigned by the book review editors. No unsolicited reviews will be accepted- Suggestions of works that might be reviewed are welcomed.

Professor Stephen A. Zeff, Rice University - MS 531, P. O. Box 1892, Houston. TX 77251-1892; Tel: +1-713-527-6066; Fax: +1-713-285-5251: E-Mail: sazeff@rice.edu; Dr. habil. Axel Holler, Universität Augsburg, Lehrstuhl fur Wirtschaftspriüfung, 86135 Augsburg, Germany; Tel: +49 821 5984127; Fax: +49 821 5984224: EMail: axel.haller@wiso.uni-augsburg.de.

More subscription rates (postage included):

Institutions: Foreign Surfaced mail $275
Foreign Air mail $300

Individuals: Foreign Surface Mail $130
Foreign Air Mail $155

International Journal of Accounting Information Systems

ADDRESS FOR SUBMISSION:

Steve G. Sutton, Editor
International Journal of Accounting
    Information Systems
Texas Tech University
Send Electronic Submission to:
    sutton@ba.ttu.edu
COBA-MS2101
Lubbock, TX 79409
USA
Phone: 806-742-2038
Fax: 806-742-3182
E-Mail: ijais@coba.ttu.edu
Web:
Address May Change:

PUBLICATION GUIDELINES:

Manuscript Length: 21-25
Copies Required: Four
Computer Submission: Yes Preferred
Format: Word File: MS Word compatible
Fees to Review: 0.00 US$

Manuscript Style:
    Chicago Manual of Style

CIRCULATION DATA:

Reader: Academics, Practitioners
Frequency of Issue: 2 Times/Year
Copies per Issue: New Journal
Sponsor/Publisher: Elsevier Science
    Publishing Co.
Subscribe Price: 60.00 US$ Individual
    200.00 US$ Institution

REVIEW INFORMATION:

Type of Review: Blind Review
No. of External Reviewers: 2
No. of In House Reviewers: 1
Acceptance Rate: 11-20%
Time to Review: 2 - 3 Months
Reviewers Comments: Yes
Invited Articles: 0-5%
Fees to Publish: 0.00 US$

MANUSCRIPT TOPICS:
Accounting Information Systems; Intelligent Systems

MANUSCRIPT GUIDELINES/COMMENTS:

IJAIS Statement Of Purpose
Statement of purpose *International Journal of Accounting Information Systems* is a professional publication whose purpose is to meet the information needs of both practitioners and academicians. We plan to publish thoughtful, well-developed articles that examine the rapidly evolving relationship between accounting and information technology. Articles may range from empirical to analytical, from practice-based to the development of new techniques. Articles must be readable and logically integrated. To be reliable, conclusions must follow logically from the evidence and arguments presented. For empirical reports sound design and execution are critical. For theoretical treatises, reasonable assumptions and logical development are essential. Relevant articles must be related to problems facing the integration

of accounting and information technology. Specific issues that the journal will address include, but are not limited to, the following:

- Information systems assurance
- Control and auditability of information systems
- Management of information technology
- Artificial intelligence research in accounting
- Development issues in accounting and information systems
- Human factors issues related to information technology
- Development of theories related to information technology
- Methodological issues in information technology research
- Information systems validation
- Human-computer interaction research in accounting information systems.

IJAIS welcomes all comments and encourages articles from practitioners and academicians.

Editorial correspondence pertaining to manuscripts should be forwarded to the Editor.

Editorial Policy And Manuscript Form Guidelines

1. Manuscripts should be word processed for spacing on 8 1/2" x 11" white paper. Margins should be set to facilitate editing and duplication except as noted:

a. Tables, figures, and exhibits should appear on a separate page. Each should be numbered and have a title.

b. Footnotes should be presented by citing the author's name and the year of publication in the body of the text, for example, Sutton (1990) and Arnold, et.al. (1995).

2. Manuscripts should include a cover page which indicates the author's name and affiliation.

3. Manuscripts should include on a separate lead page an abstract not exceeding 200 words. The author's name and affiliation should not appear on the abstract.

4. Topical headings and subheadings should be used. Main headings in the manuscript should be centered, secondary headings should be flush with the left-hand margin. (As a guide to usage and style, refer to William Strunk, Jr. and E.B. White, *The Elements Of Style*.)

5. Manuscripts must include a list of references which contain only those works actually cited. (As a helpful guide in preparing a list of references, refer to Kate L. Turabian, *A Manual For Writers Of Term Papers, Theses, And Dissertations*.)

6. In order to be assured of an anonymous review, authors should not identify themselves directly or indirectly. Reference to unpublished working papers and dissertations should be avoided. If necessary, authors may indicate that the reference is being withheld for the reasons cited above.

7. The author will be provided offprints of their paper from the IJAIS issue in which his or her manuscript appears.

8. Manuscripts currently under review by other publications should not be submitted. Complete reports and research presented at a national or regional conference of a professional association (e.g., AAA, DSI, etc.) and "State of the Art" papers are acceptable.

9. **Four** copies of each manuscript should be submitted to the Editor. Copies of any and all research instruments also should be included.

10. For additional information regarding the type of manuscripts that are desired, see **IJAIS Statement Of Purpose**.

International Journal of Auditing

ADDRESS FOR SUBMISSION:

Andrew Chambers, General Editor
International Journal of Auditing
Management Audit Ltd.
6 Market Street
Sleaford, Lincolnshire, NG34 7SF
England
Phone: 44 (0) 1529-413344
Fax: 44 (0) 1529-413355
E-Mail: ProfADC@aol.com
Web:
Address May Change:

CIRCULATION DATA:

Reader: Academics
Frequency of Issue: 3 Times/Year
Copies per Issue: Less than 1,000
Sponsor/Publisher: John Wiley & Sons
Subscribe Price: 205.00 US$ Individual
275.00 US$ Institution
75.00 Pounds , BAA Auditing Group

PUBLICATION GUIDELINES:

Manuscript Length: 21-25
Copies Required: Two
Computer Submission: Yes
Format: Word or WordPerfect
Fees to Review: 0.00 US$

Manuscript Style:
See Manuscript Guidelines

REVIEW INFORMATION:

Type of Review: Blind Review
No. of External Reviewers: 0
No. of In House Reviewers: 2
Acceptance Rate: 43%
Time to Review: 1 - 2 Months
Reviewers Comments: No Reply
Invited Articles: 6-10%
Fees to Publish: 0.00 US$

MANUSCRIPT TOPICS:
Auditing

MANUSCRIPT GUIDELINES/COMMENTS:

Announcing a new international forum for academics, professionals and policy makers with research interests in new ideas, techniques and approaches within all aspects of auditing...

1. *International Journal of Auditing* sets out to be a high quality specialist journal carrying articles over a broad spectrum of auditing. Its primary aim is to communicate clearly to an international readership the results of original auditing research conducted in practice and in research institutions. The results of research conducted jointly by academics and practitioners are particularly welcome. Submitted articles should have an international appeal either due to the research topic transcending national frontiers, or due to the clear potential for readers to apply the results, perhaps with adaptation, to their local environments.

2. While articles must be methodologically sound, any research orientation is acceptable - for instance papers may have a behavioural, economics, agency, sociological or historical basis.

3. *International Journal of Auditing's* scope is eclectic with regard to auditing. As such the editors consider articles for publication which fit into one or more of the following subject categories:
- The audit of financial statements
- Public sector/governmental auditing
- Internal auditing
- Audit education, including case studies
- Audit aspects of corporate governance, including audit committees
- The new audit agendas (including quality, environment, social and vfm auditing, ethical issues and State: profession relationships)

4. With the exception of governmental auditing the scope of *International Journal o f Auditing* does not extend to sector-specific audit topics (such as academic audits, circulation audits, etc) unless the content of the research has more general applicability across sectors.

5. Articles which are reflective rather than empirical in nature are considered for publication, if they fall into one of the above categories - so long as they extend the frontiers of knowledge and understanding about audit theory or practice.

6. *International Journal of Auditing* may also carry comment on articles previously published.

7. The first issue was published in February 1997.

Papers or enquiries about submissions should be addressed to:
Jackie Bishop, Editorial Assistant, Management Audit Ltd, 6 **Market Street, Sleaford, Lincolnshire, NG34 7SF, England** *Tel:* (0)1529 413344; *fax:* (0)1529 413355; *e-mail:* e-mail@management-audit.com

Submission of articles
Two copies of any manuscript for consideration should be sent on single-sided paper to Jackie Bishop, Editorial Assistant, at the above address. The author's name(s), title(s) of their academic department(s), institution(s) of affiliation and mini profile(s) (maximum three sentences for each profile) should appear on a sheet separate from the title of the paper and separate from any text. No responsibility is taken for damages or loss of papers submitted. Papers will not normally be returned unless this is specially requested.

Submitted and resubmitted ms's are "blind read" by two referees reporting to one of the journal's editors.

It is a condition of our consideration of a ms for inclusion in *International Journal of Auditing* that the author(s) fax or write a covering note confirming that it will not be simultaneously under consideration for publication elsewhere. In return, we undertake, wherever possible to give a decision on a ms within eight weeks of receipt. It is important the author(s)' covering note includes full address, phone and fax numbers.

Authors submitting a ms do so on the basis that if it is accepted for publication, exclusive copyright in the paper shall be assigned to the Publisher; no article will be accepted for publication without satisfactory completion of a standard form which will be supplied for this purpose. In consideration for the assignment of copyright, the Publisher will supply 25 offprints of each paper and further offprints may be ordered at extra cost. Authors are free to use their own material in other publications written or edited by themselves provided that when they do this they make proper acknowledgements to the Journal and to the Publisher.

Preparation of copy
The ms *(including notes arid references)* should be 12 line spacing in A4 (210 x 297mm) or Letter (82 x 11 inches) format and should commence with:

- 10 *Key words* or *phrases* which can be used for indexing.
- An *Abstract* of not more than 150 words summarizing the purpose, methodology and major conclusions.
- A *Summary* of not more than 500 words to provide the reader with a non-technical overview of the contents of the article.

Readability is a key criterion for acceptance in *International Journal of Auditing*. Mathematics should only be included if it is essential–in which case preferably in *Appendix* form. Essential *Notes* should be indicated by superscripts in the text and provided in a single section just before the *References* at the end of the ms. Citations in the text should be given in abbreviated form allowing the-,reader to readily relate the citation to the full reference at the end of the article. A citation in the text should be embedded in the text in one of these forms:

'Innes *(1990)* showed that   ' 'It has been shown that   (Innes, *1990)*

Until recently   (Ng & Tai *(1994))'*

The last section of the ms should be the *References* -in alphabetical order by first word, in this form:

Boritz JE. (1992). The use of artificial intelligence in auditing. *In Proceedings of the XIV World Congress of Accountants on the Accountant's Role in a Global Economy* (Washington, October), New York, The International Federation of Accountants. pp 19E-1-19E-48.

Innes, J. (1990), 'External management auditing of companies: a survey of bankers', *Accounting, Auditing & Accountability Journal,* Vol.3, No. 1, pp. 18-37.

Lee, T.A. (1993), *Corporate Audit Theory,* (1" edn) London: Chapman & Hall, p. 174.

Ng P.P.H. & Tai, B.Y.K. *(1994),* An empirical examination of the determinants of audit delay in Hong Kong. *The British Accounting Review,* **26**, March, pp. 43-59.

It is the responsibility of the authors to obtain and supply with the manuscript written permission to use material from copyrighted sources.

Proofs
Authors are given sight of the proofs of their articles and are expected to make corrections quickly. Changes at the proof stage should be limited to correcting typesetting errors.

Payments
No payments are made to authors and no charges to authors are made with the exception that revisions to content at the proof stage may be charged to the authors.

International Journal of Government Auditing

ADDRESS FOR SUBMISSION:

Don R. Drach, Editor
International Journal of Government
   Auditing
Int'l Organiz. Of Supreme Audit Instit.
U.S. General Accounting Office
441 G Street, N.W., Room 7806
Washington, DC, 20548
USA
Phone: 202-512-4707
Fax: 202-512-4021
E-Mail: chases@gao.gov, drachd@gao.gov
Web:
Address May Change:

PUBLICATION GUIDELINES:

Manuscript Length: 6-10
Copies Required: Two
Computer Submission: Yes
Format: MS Word 97
Fees to Review: 0.00 US$

Manuscript Style:
   No Reply

CIRCULATION DATA:

Reader: Business Persons,
   Auditors/Financial Managers
Frequency of Issue: Quarterly
Copies per Issue: 1,001 - 2,000
Sponsor/Publisher: Int'l. Organization of
   Supreme Audit Institutions
Subscribe Price: 5.00 US$

REVIEW INFORMATION:

Type of Review: Editorial Review
No. of External Reviewers: 2
No. of In House Reviewers: 1
Acceptance Rate: 11-20%
Time to Review: 2 - 3 Months
Reviewers Comments: No Reply
Invited Articles: 11-20%
Fees to Publish: 0.00 US$

MANUSCRIPT TOPICS:
Accounting Information Systems; Auditing; Econometrics; Fiscal Policy

MANUSCRIPT GUIDELINES/COMMENTS:

International Journal of Intelligent Systems in Accounting, Finance & Management

ADDRESS FOR SUBMISSION:

Daniel E. O'Leary, Editor
International Journal of Intelligent Systems
   in Accounting, Finance & Management
University of Southern California
School of Business Administration
Expert Systems Program
Los Angeles, CA 90089-1421
USA
Phone: 213-790-4856
Fax: 213-747-2815
E-Mail: oleary@usc.edu
Web:
Address May Change:

PUBLICATION GUIDELINES:

Manuscript Length: 16-25
Copies Required: Four
Computer Submission: Yes
Format: Word, PDF, etc
Fees to Review: 0.00 US$

Manuscript Style:
   American Psychological Association

CIRCULATION DATA:

Reader: Academics
Frequency of Issue: Quarterly
Copies per Issue: 1,001 - 2,000
Sponsor/Publisher: John Wiley & Sons
Subscribe Price: 230.00 US$ Individual
   465.00 US$ Full
   110.00 US$ Society Membership

REVIEW INFORMATION:

Type of Review: Blind Review
No. of External Reviewers: 3+
No. of In House Reviewers: 1
Acceptance Rate: 11-20%
Time to Review: 2 - 3 Months
Reviewers Comments: Yes
Invited Articles: 0-5%
Fees to Publish: 0.00 US$

MANUSCRIPT TOPICS:

Accounting Information Systems; Auditing; Capital Budgeting; Cost Accounting; Econometrics; Electronic Commerce; Enterprise Information Systems; Finance Information Systems; Tax Accounting

MANUSCRIPT GUIDELINES/COMMENTS:

Initial Manuscript Submission. Submit five copies of the manuscript (including copies of tables and illustrations) to Daniel E. O'Leary, Editor IJ.ISAFM, School of Business, University of Southern California, Los Angeles, CA 90089-1421, USA.

Authors must also supply

* a Copyright Transfer Agreement with original signature - without this, we are unable to accept the submission,

- permission letters - it is the author's responsibility to obtain written permission to reproduce (in all media, including electronic) material which has appeared in another publication and
- an electronic copy of the final version (see section below).

Submission of a manuscript will be held to imply that it contains original unpublished work and is not being submitted for publication elsewhere at the same time. Submitted material will not be returned to the author, unless specifically requested.

Electronic submission. The electronic copy of the final, revised manuscript must be sent to the Editor **together with** the paper copy. Disks should be PC or Mac formatted; write on the disk the software package used, the name of the author and the name of the journal. We are able to use most word processing packages, but prefer Word or WordPerfect and TeX or one of its derivatives.

Illustrations must be submitted in electronic format where possible. Save each figure as a separate file, in **TIFF** or **EPS** format preferably, and include the source file. Write on the disk the software package used to create them; we favor dedicated illustration packages over tools such as Excel or PowerPoint.

Manuscript style. The language of the journal is English. All submissions including book reviews must have a title, be printed on one side of the paper, be double-line spaced and have a margin of 3cm all round. Illustrations and tables must be printed on separate sheets, and not be incorporated into the text.

- The **title page** must list the full title, short title of up to 70 characters and names and affiliations of all authors. Give the full address, including email, telephone and fax, of the author who is to check the proofs.
- Include the name(s) of any sponsor(s) of the research contained in the paper, along with **grant number(s).**
- Supply an abstract of up to 150 words for all articles [except book reviews]. An abstract is a concise summary of the whole paper, not just the conclusions, and is understandable without reference to the rest of the paper. It should contain no citation to other published work.
- Include up to five **keywords** that describe your paper for indexing purposes.
- Include also a brief autobiography (50 to 100 words) for each author, together with a black and white glossy photograph suitable for reproduction within the journal.

Reference style. References should be quoted in the text as name and year and listed at the end of the paper alphabetically. Where reference is made to more than one work by the same author published in the same year, identify each citation in the text as follows: (Collins, 1998a), (Collins, 1998b). Where three or more authors are listed in the reference list, please cite in the text as (Collins *et al.,* 1998)

All references must be complete and accurate. Online citations should include date of access. If necessary, cite unpublished or personal work in the text but do not include it in the reference list. References should be listed in the following style:

Denna EL, Hansen JV, Meservy RD, Wood LE. 1992. Case-based reasoning and risk assessment in audit judgment. *Intelligent Systems in Accounting, Finance and Management* 1(3): 163-171.

Chan S, Govindan M, Picard JY, Leschiutta E. 199 3. *EDI for Managers, and Auditors.* Electronic Data Interchange Council of Canada: Toronto, Ontario.

Sprague R, Benbast I, El Sawy O, King D Hill TR Sol H Todd P. 1992. Technology environments to support decision processes. In *Information arid Decision Processes,* Stohr E, Konsynski B (eds). IEEE Computer Society Press: Los Alamitos, CA; 167-204.

The Geriatric Website. 1999. http://www.wiley.com/oap/ [1 April 1999]

Illustrations. Supply each illustration on a separate sheet, with the lead author's name and the figure number, with the top of the figure indicated, on the reverse. Supply original **photographs;** photocopies or previously printed material will not be used. Line artwork must be high-quality laser output (not photocopies). Tints are not acceptable; lettering must be of a reasonable size that would still be clearly legible upon reduction, and consistent within each figure and set of figures. Supply artwork at the intended size for printing. The artwork must be sized to the text width of 7cm (single column) and 15cm (double column).

The cost of printing **color** illustrations in the journal will be charged to the author. There is a charge for printing color illustrations of approximately £700 per page. If color illustrations are supplied electronically in either **TIFF** or **EPS** format, they **may** be used in the PDF of the article at no cost to the author, even if this illustration was printed in black and white in the journal. The PDF will appear on the *Wiley InterScience* site.

Copyright. To enable the publisher to disseminate the author's work to the fullest extent, the author must sign a Copyright Transfer Agreement, transferring copyright in the article from the author to the publisher, and submit the original signed agreement with the article presented for publication. A copy of the agreement to be used (which may be photocopied) can be found in the first issue of each volume of *International Journal of Intelligent Systems in Accounting, Finance & Management.* Copies may also be obtained from the journal editor or publisher., or may be printed from this website.

Further Information. Proofs will be sent to the author for checking. This stage is to be used only to correct errors that may have been introduced during the production process. Prompt return of the corrected proofs, preferably within two days of receipt, will minimize the risk of the paper being held over to a later issue. 25 complimentary offprints will be provided to the author who checked the proofs, unless otherwise indicated. Further offprints and copies of the journal may be ordered. There is no page charge to authors.

International Journal of Strategic Cost Management

ADDRESS FOR SUBMISSION:

Il-Woon Kim, Managing Editor
International Journal of Strategic Cost
   Management
University of Akron
College of Business Administration
Building 262, Accountancy
259 South Broadway
Akron, OH 44325-4802
USA
Phone: 330-972-7461
Fax: 330-972-3597
E-Mail: ikim@uakron.edu
Web:
Address May Change:

PUBLICATION GUIDELINES:

Manuscript Length: 16-20
Copies Required: Five
Computer Submission: No
Format: N/A
Fees to Review: 0.00 US$

Manuscript Style:
   See Manuscript Guidelines

CIRCULATION DATA:

Reader: Business Persons
Frequency of Issue: Quarterly
Copies per Issue: 2,001 - 3,000
Sponsor/Publisher: John Wiley & Sons, Inc.
Subscribe Price: 128.00 US$

REVIEW INFORMATION:

Type of Review: Blind Review
No. of External Reviewers: 2
No. of In House Reviewers: 1
Acceptance Rate: 21-30%
Time to Review: 2 - 3 Months
Reviewers Comments: Yes
Invited Articles: 0-5%
Fees to Publish: 0.00 US$

MANUSCRIPT TOPICS:
Business Topics related to Cost Mgt. Acctg.; Cost Accounting

MANUSCRIPT GUIDELINES/COMMENTS:

Aims and Scope
The *International Journal of Strategic Cost Management* is directed to corporate financial executives with an interest in cost management, as well as consultants and academics. Areas that this Journal will focus on include: activity-based costing, activity-based management, performance measurement, benchmarking, best practices, target costing, continuous improvement, and total quality management.

Articles should address the readership and be informative, analytical, and practical. We seek material that will offer our readership new insights into and new approaches toward cost management issues. Manuscripts are considered for publication with the understanding that they represent original material, and are offered exclusively and without fee to the *International Journal of Strategic Cost Management.*

Articles must not have been published previously and may not be simultaneously submitted elsewhere.

Submission Instructions

A cover letter must accompany each submission indicating the name, address, telephone number, facsimile number, and e-mail address of the author to whom all correspondence is to be addressed. An affiliation must be supplied for each author. If the manuscript has been presented, published, or submitted for publication elsewhere, please inform the Editor.

Prospective authors should submit five copies of the complete manuscript, including tables and illustrations.

Format

Manuscripts should contain: title, names and complete affiliations of authors, including phone number, facsimile number, and e-mail address. Please provide an informative 100- to 200-word abstract at the beginning of your manuscript. The abstract should provide an overview of your paper and not a statement of conclusions only. If applicable, please provide keywords, contract grant sponsors, and contract grant number(s). Articles are normally about 15 published journal pages in length or shorter. Columns are generally no more than 10 journal pages in length.

Instructions for Typists

Manuscripts must be typed double-spaced on a single side only on standard 8 ½ x 11-inch (21.5 X 28-cm) white paper with one-inch margins. Material intended for footnotes should be inserted in the text as parenthetical material whenever possible.

All mathematical symbols, equations, formulas, Greek, or unusual symbols should be typed. If they must be handwritten, please write clearly and leave ample space above and below for printer's marks. When handwritten symbols are necessary, please provide a separate sheet listing and defining such symbols. This list will help to distinguish between characters that may otherwise be confused (e.g., b, B, β). If italic type is unavailable to the typist, underscore with a straight line anything to be printed in italic type. Note that the use of italics for emphasis should be used with extreme discretion.

References

Compile references on a separate sheet at the end of the main body of the text. References to published literature should be quoted in the text by giving author's name and year of publication, such as Smith (1995) or (Smith, 1995). The format for multiple references is either Smith (1997) and Jones and Black (1996), or (Smith, 1997; Jones and Black, 1996).

References should be listed alphabetically in the last section of the article titled "References." Journal references must be complete and include authors' initials, year of publication in parentheses, title of the paper, name of the journal, volume, and pages on which the article appears. Book references must include city of publication, publisher, and year of publication. Anthologies and collections must include names of editors and pages on which the reference appears. Books in a series must include series title and number/volume if applicable. Because

188

of the many conference proceedings available, it is critical to give as much information as possible when citing references from proceedings. The complete title of the meeting, symposium, etc. *(do not abbreviate titles),* and the city and dates of the meeting must be included. If a proceeding has been published, provide the editors' names, publisher, city, year of publication, and pages on which the article appears. If a proceeding has *not* been published, indicate so. Examples follow:

Article in a Journal:
Beatty, C.A., "Implementing Advanced Manufacturing Technology." *Business Quarterly* (Autumn 1990), 46-50.

Proceedings:
Bessant, J. (1998). Organization Adaptation and Manufacturing Technology. *Proc. Final HASA Conf. CIM: Technologies, Organizations, and People in Transition* (Luxembourg, Austria), pp. 351-360.

Book:
Usher, J.M., Roy, U., and Parsaei, H.R. *Integrated Product and Process Development: Methods, Tools, and Technologies.* (New York: John Wiley & Sons, 1998.)

Contributed Book:
Kadirkamanathan, V, Niranjan, M., and Fallside, F. "Sequential Adaptation of Radial Basis Function Neural Networks and its Applications to Time-Series Prediction," in R. Lippman, J. Moody, and D. Touretzky, Eds., *Neural Information Processing,* Vol. 3, San Mateo, CA: Morgan Kaufman, 1991: 721-727.

Exhibits
Exhibits (such as tables and figures) should not be incorporated into the text, but grouped separately after the references. All exhibits should be numbered consecutively with Arabic numerals (1, 2, 3, etc.) and should include an explanatory heading. A list of exhibit captions on a separate sheet should be supplied.

Line Drawings. Figures should be professionally prepared and submitted in a form suitable for reproduction (camera-ready copy). Computer-generated graphs are acceptable only if they have been printed with a high-quality laser printer. Authors are cautioned to provide lettering of graphs and figure labels that are large clear, and "open" so that letters and numbers do not become illegible when reduced. Likewise, authors are cautioned that very thin lines and other fine details in figures may not successfully reproduce. Original figures should be drawn with these precautions in mind.

Halftones. High-quality photographs are necessary for clear halftone reproduction.

Electronic Submissions
In addition to providing hard copy, authors are requested to submit the final, accepted version of their manuscript on diskette to the Editor.

Text

Storage medium. 3 ½" high-density disk in IBM MS-DOS, Windows, or Macintosh format.

Software and format. Microsoft Word *6.0* is preferred, although manuscripts prepared using any other microcomputer word processor are acceptable. Sending a Rich Text Format (RTF) file will be very helpful also. Refrain from complex formatting; the Publisher will style your manuscript according to the *International Journal of Strategic Cost Management* design specifications. Do not use desktop publishing software such as Aldus Pagemaker or Quark XPress. If you prepared your manuscript using one of these programs, export the text to a word processing format. Make sure your word processing program's "fast save" feature is turned off.

File names. Submit the text and tables of each manuscript as a single file. Name each file with your last name (up to eight letters). Text files should be given the three-letter extension that identifies the file format. Macintosh users should maintain the MS-DOS "eight dot three" file-naming convention.

Labels. Label all diskettes with your name, the file name, and the word processing program and version used.

Paper copy. Accompany all electronic files with five identical printed paper copies.

Illustrations

Storage medium. Submit as separate files from text files, on separate diskettes or cartridges, *32"* diskettes, Iomega Zip, and 5 ¼" 44- or 88-MB SyQuest cartridges can be submitted. At the author's request, cartridges and diskettes will be returned after publication.

Software and format. The preferred formats are TIFF or EPS with pict or tiff preview, although any format that is in general use that is not application-specific is acceptable.

Resolution. Journal-quality reproduction will require greyscale and color files at resolutions yielding approximately 300 ppi. Bitmapped line art should be submitted at resolutions yielding 600-1200 ppi. These resolutions refer to the output size of the file; if you anticipate that your images will be enlarged or reduced, resolutions should be adjusted accordingly.

File names. Illustration files should be given the 2- or 3-letter extension that identifies the file format used (i.e., TIFF, EPS, RGB, etc.).

Labels. Label all diskettes and cartridges with your name, the file names, formats, sizes, and compression schemes (if any) used. Hard copy output must accompany all files.

Authors of accepted papers will be asked to submit to the Editor three copies of their revised manuscripts, tables, original illustrations, floppy disk with an electronic copy of their material, copyright release form, and permissions. Additional information concerning this will be sent with acceptance letters.

Copyright Information

No article can be published unless accompanied by a signed publication agreement, which serves as a transfer of copyright from author to publisher. A publication agreement may be obtained from the editor or the publisher. A copy of the publication agreement appears in most issues of the journal.

Only original papers will be accepted, and copyright in published papers will be vested in the publisher. It is the author's responsibility to obtain written permission to reproduce material that has appeared in another publication. A form for this purpose is sent with the manuscript acceptance letter.

International Tax and Public Finance

ADDRESS FOR SUBMISSION:

Jack Mintz, Editor
International Tax and Public Finance
Kluwer Academic Publishers
c/o Melissa Sullivan
101 Philip Drive
Norwell, MA 02061
USA
Phone: 416-978-3985
Fax: 416-978-5433
E-Mail: mintz@fmgmt.utoronto.ca
Web:
Address May Change:

PUBLICATION GUIDELINES:

Manuscript Length: 26-30
Copies Required: Four
Computer Submission: No Reply
Format: N/A
Fees to Review: 0.00 US$

Manuscript Style:
See Manuscript Guidelines

CIRCULATION DATA:

Reader: Academics
Frequency of Issue: 5 Times/ Year
Copies per Issue: No Reply
Sponsor/Publisher: Kluwer Academic
    Publishers
Subscribe Price: 900.00 DFL Institution
    150.00 DFL Individual

REVIEW INFORMATION:

Type of Review: Blind Review
No. of External Reviewers: 3
No. of In House Reviewers: 0
Acceptance Rate: 11-20%
Time to Review: 4 - 6 Months +
Reviewers Comments: Yes
Invited Articles: 0-5%
Fees to Publish: 0.00 US$

MANUSCRIPT TOPICS:
Fiscal Policy; International Economics & Trade; Public Policy Economics; Tax Accounting

MANUSCRIPT GUIDELINES/COMMENTS:

Aims and Scope
International Tax and Public Finance serves as an outlet for and seeks to stimulate, first-rate research on both theoretical and empirical aspects of tax policy, broadly interpreted to include expenditure and financial policies. A special emphasis will be open economy issues: the coordination of policies across jurisdictions, or the effects of taxation on capital and trade flows. This international focus is not, however, an exclusive one: high quality work in any area of policy (e.g., single-country tax reform analysis) will also be welcome.

A central feature of *International Tax and Public Finance* will be the inclusion in each issue of a special section – called Policy Watch – discussing a current policy issue, or reviewing some recent developments. Facilitating communication between academic work and practice in this way serves many purposes – researchers need to know priorities and policy-makers need to absorb the products of research.

International Tax and Public Finance is peer-reviewed and published four times per year. Reflecting its international focus, one editor is from North America and the other in Europe. An active Editorial Board will reinforce this diversity and, more importantly, play a central role in establishing the journal as an essential resource for policy analysis.

Editor's Address: Jack Mintz, Editor, International Tax and Public Finance, University of Toronto, Rotman School of Management, 105 St. George Street, Toronto, ON, M5S 3E6, Canada.

Submissions for the Policy Watch section should be indicated as such in the covering letter. Unless requested otherwise, the editors will consider all submissions for both the regular and Policy Watch sections.

Electronic Delivery of Accepted Papers

Please send only the electronic version (of ACCEPTED paper) via one of the methods listed below. Note, in the event of minor discrepancies between the electronic version and hard copy, the electronic file will be used as the final version.

Via electronic mail

1. Please e-mail electronic version to: KAPfiles@wkap.com
   Recommended formats for sending files via e-mail:
   - Binary files - uuencode or binhex
   - Compressing files - compress, pkzip, or gzip
   - Collecting files - tar
2. The e-mail message should include the author's last name, the name of the journal to which the paper has been accepted, and the type of file (e.g., LaTeX or ASCII).

Via anonymous ftp

ftp: ftp.wkap.com
cd: /incoming/production

Send email to KAPfiles@wkap.com to inform Kluwer that electronic version is at this FTP site.

Via disk

1. Label a 3.5 inch floppy disk with the operating system and word processing program along with the authors' names, manuscript title, and name of journal to which the paper will be published.
2. Mail disk to:
   Kluwer Academic Publisher
   Desktop Department
   101 Philip Drive
   Assinippi Park
   Norwell, MA 02061, USA

Any questions about the above procedures please send e-mail to: dthelp@wkap. com

Manuscript Preparation
Submitted papers should typically be less than 20 double-spaced typewritten pages, and should in no event exceed 40 pages. Final versions of accepted manuscripts (including notes, references, tables, and legends) should be typed double-spaced on 8 1/2 x 11" (22cm x 29cm) white paper with 1" (2.5cm) margins on all sides. Sections should appear in the following order: title page, abstract, text, notes, references, tables, figure legends, and figures. Comments or replies to previously published articles should also follow this format with the exception of abstracts, which are not required.

We encourage electronic delivery of accepted papers. It is important that hard copy of the accepted paper (along with separate, original figures in camera-ready form) should accompany the electronic version. The hard copy must match the electronic version, and any changes made to the hard copy must be incorporated into the electronic version. Label a 3.5-inch floppy disk with the operating system and word processing program e.g., DOS/WordPerfect, along with the author,, names, manuscript title, and name of journal to which the paper has been accepted.

Title Page. The title page should include the article title, authors' names and permanent affiliations, and the name, current address, and telephone number of the person to whom page proofs and reprints should be sent.

Abstract. The following page should include an abstract of not more than 100 words and a list of two to six keywords.

Text. The text of the article should begin on a new page. Section headings (including appendices) should be designated by arabic numerals (1, 2, etc.), and subsection headings should be numbered 1. 1, 1.2, etc. Figures, tables, and displayed equations should be numbered consecutively throughout the text (1, 2, etc.). Equation numbers should appear flush left in parentheses and running variables for equations (e.g., $i=1,...,n$) flush right in parentheses.

Notes. Acknowledgments and related information should appear in a note designated by an asterisk after the last author's name, and subsequent notes should be numbered consecutively and designated by superscripts (1, 2, etc.) in the text. All notes should be typed double-spaced beginning on a separate page following the text.

References. References in the text should follow the author-date format (e.g., Brown (1986), Jones (1978a, 1978b), Smith and Johnson (1983)). References should be typed double-spaced beginning on a separate page following the notes, according to the following samples (journal and book titles may be underlined rather than italicized). References with up to three authors should include the names of each author; references with four or more authors should cite the first author and add "et al." It is the responsibility of the authors to verify all references.

Sample References
- Becker, Gordon, Morris DeGroot, and Jacob Marschak. (1964). "Measuring Utility by a Single-Response Sequential Method." Behavioral Science 9, 226-232.

- Schoemaker, Paul. (1980). Experiments in Decisions Under Risk: The Expected Utility Hypothesis. Boston: Kluwer-Nijhoff Publishing.
- Smith, V. Kerry. (1986). "A Conceptual Overview of the Foundations of Benefit-Cost Analysis." In Judith Bentkover, Vincent Covello, and Jeryl Mumpower (eds.), Benefits Assessment: The State of the Art. Dordrecht: D. Reidel Publishing Co.

Tables. Tables should be titled and typed double-spaced, each on a separate sheet, following the references. Notes to tables should be designated by superscripted letters. a, b, etc.., within each table and typed double-spaced on the same page as the table. Use descriptive labels rather than computer acronyms, and explain all abbreviations. When tables are typed on oversized paper, please submit both the original and a reduced copy.

Figures. Figures for accepted manuscripts should be submitted in camera-ready form, i.e., clear glossy prints or drawn in India ink on drafting paper or high quality white paper. Lettering in figures should be large enough to be legible after half-size reduction. Authors should submit one 5" x 7" (13cm x 18cm) original and two photocopies of each figure, with authors' names, manuscript title, and figure number on the back of each original and copy (used gummed labels if necessary to avoid damaging originals). Figures should be enclosed in a separate envelope backed by cardboard and without staples or paper clips. Figure legends should be typed double-spaced on a separate sheet following the tables.

Page Proofs and Reprints
Corrected page proofs must be returned within three days of receipt, and alterations other than corrections may be charged to the authors. Authors will receive 50 free reprints, and may order additional copies when returning the corrected proofs.

International Tax Journal

ADDRESS FOR SUBMISSION:

Walter F. O'Connor, Editor
International Tax Journal
Fordham University
Grad. School of Business Administration
113 West 60th Street
New York, NY 10023
USA
Phone: 212-636-6122
Fax: 212-765-5573
E-Mail: See Manuscript Guidelines
Web:
Address May Change:

PUBLICATION GUIDELINES:

Manuscript Length: 16-20+
Copies Required: Three
Computer Submission: Yes
Format: WordPerfect 5.1 or ASCII
Fees to Review: 0.00 US$

Manuscript Style:
    See Manuscript Guidelines

CIRCULATION DATA:

Reader: Business Persons
Frequency of Issue: Quarterly
Copies per Issue: 1,001 - 2,000
Sponsor/Publisher: Aspen Publishers
Subscribe Price: 136.00 US$

REVIEW INFORMATION:

Type of Review: Blind Review
No. of External Reviewers: 2
No. of In House Reviewers: 1
Acceptance Rate: 50%
Time to Review: 1 Month or Less
Reviewers Comments: No
Invited Articles: 0-5%
Fees to Publish: 0.00 US$

MANUSCRIPT TOPICS:

Accounting Information Systems; Accounting Theory & Practice; Auditing; Capital Budgeting; International Finance; International Tax; Portfolio & Security Analysis; Tax Accounting

MANUSCRIPT GUIDELINES/COMMENTS:

Editor's E-mail: woconnor@bschool.bnet.fordham.edu

1. Articles should provide practical information and ideas about international tax practice. Articles should cover matters of importance to practitioners, and cover tax, legal, and business planning aspects affecting clients with international tax situations.

2. Be sure to include both your address and telephone number where you may be reached during business hours. While the utmost care will be given to all manuscripts, we cannot accept responsibility for unsolicited manuscripts. Article accepted for publication are subject to editorial revision. There is no payment for articles; authors will receive 10 copies (to be shared by multiple authors) of their published articles.

3. Type manuscript on one side of the paper only, on 8-1/2" x 11" good-quality white bond. Please do not use "erasable" paper. Use one-inch margins and double spacing. Generally, article manuscript should be approximately 15 to 35 typed pages. On acceptance, submit a computer disk of the article in WordPerfect 5.1 or ASCII.

4. Within your article use headings and subheadings to break up and emphasize your points. Type headings and subheadings flush left.

5. Type footnotes separately, double spaced, at the end of the main manuscript. Footnote and reference citations should generally follow the *Harvard Blue Book*.

6. With your article, please include a brief biographical note.

7. Any artwork, e.g., flow charts, original drawings, or graphs, must be provided in camera-ready form. Typewritten or free-hand lettering is not acceptable; all lettering must be done professionally. Do not staple or paper clip illustrations and put all illustrations between sheets of cardboard before mailing, to prevent folds. Note: We will typeset tubular material, which you may provide in typewritten form as part of your manuscript.

8. Except in rare cases, *International Tax Journal* publishes articles only if they have not yet appeared or been accepted for publication elsewhere. If you are considering submission of previously published material, please correspond with the Editor first to determine if such submission is suitable. We will generally be pleased to consider articles for prior publication adapted from book-length works in progress but, again, request advance notice so that we may work out necessary copyright arrangements.

9. If you are reprinting any previously copyrighted material in your article, other than short quotations, you must submit with your manuscript letters of permission from the copyright holder and from the author (if he or she is not the copyright holder).

10. We will own and retain the copyright to all of the articles we publish, together with the right to reprint them in any republication of the Journal in any form or media. You may reprint your article for personal use, provided you do not do so for resale and provided the Journal, and Panel Publishers, a division of Aspen Publishers, Inc. as the Journal's publisher, are given appropriate credit if and when you reprint the article. We will be happy to provide you with appropriate credit-line language. (Should you wish to have your own article reprinted or reissued in a book or periodical to be sold or distributed by another publisher or organization, you must obtain prior written permission from us.)

IS Audit & Control Journal

ADDRESS FOR SUBMISSION:

Janet Perry, Editor
IS Audit & Control Journal
Info. Systems Audit and Control Assoc.
3701 Algonquin Road, Suite 1010
Rolling Meadows, IL 60008
USA
Phone: 847-253-1545 ext.458
Fax: 847-253-1443
E-Mail: publication@isaca.org
Web:
Address May Change:

PUBLICATION GUIDELINES:

Manuscript Length: 11-15
Copies Required: Three
Computer Submission: Yes
Format: ASCII,MS Word,WP:PC or MAC
Fees to Review: 0.00 US$

Manuscript Style:
    See Manuscript Guidelines

CIRCULATION DATA:

Reader: Business Persons
Frequency of Issue: Bi-Monthly
Copies per Issue: 10,001 - 25,000
Sponsor/Publisher: Info. Systems Audit and
    Control Assoc.
Subscribe Price: 40.00 US$
    50.00 US$ Outside U.S

REVIEW INFORMATION:

Type of Review: Editorial Review
No. of External Reviewers: 3+
No. of In House Reviewers: 2
Acceptance Rate: 50%
Time to Review: 2 - 3 Months
Reviewers Comments: See Below
Invited Articles: 50% +
Fees to Publish: 0.00 US$

MANUSCRIPT TOPICS:
Accounting Information Systems; Auditing; Computer Security

MANUSCRIPT GUIDELINES/COMMENTS:

Reviewer's Comments: Yes – if major revisions. No – if not major revisions.

Thank you for your interest in the *IS Audit & Control Journal,* the official journal of the Information Systems Audit and Control Association (formerly the EDP Auditors Association). The Journal provides important information on industry advancements and professional development to those involved in the IS audit, control and security community. Each issue focuses on a new technical topic relevant to our readers.

The Journal is published bi-monthly and combines short columns with longer feature articles.

Why Invest In Becoming Published?
Publishing an article in the *IS Audit & Control Journal* offers you several benefits. It places your name in front of your peers, establishes you as an expert in a technical area of IS audit and control, and enables you to exchange ideas with your colleagues.

Who May Write?

Authors should cover either new developments in the field or in-depth technically oriented subjects. Major feature should have broad appeal and focus on practical matters; purely theoretical material is not solicited. Authors are not required to be Association members.

Original submissions should be offered exclusively to the *IS Audit & Control Journal*. However, finished manuscripts are also considered. Advertising and public relations agency submissions generally are not accepted for feature articles, but are for the "Product Overview" or "Case Study" columns.

Our Reader Profile

The *IS Audit & Control Journal*'s 25,000 readers are a combination of Association members and paid subscribers in 92 countries around the world. The paid subscribers include university libraries worldwide, and copies are circulated within organizations in a wide range of industries and government.

According to a recent reader survey, more than 98 percent of those responding report reading each bimonthly issue of the Journal. The majority of our readers refer to back issues and can recall specific information found in past issues within the last several years.

Types Of Articles Accepted

All manuscripts on subjects relevant to the Journal's readers will be considered for publication.

We accept and consider articles for the following sections: Guest Editorial, Perspectives, and Case Study. Articles submitted for these departments should be from two to four double-spaced pages in length, and must adhere to the Journal's style conventions. Articles may be edited for length.

A strong article will co-mingle the pertinent facts with references to personal experience, and use anecdotes to illustrate the author's key points. Quotations from other experts involved also add to the article's depth.

An article should not simply repeat information gleaned from existing literature. Instead, it should draw lessons from such material and include the author's conclusions about the impact of this information on the practice of IS auditing.

Articles based on surveys or questionnaires must include a brief analysis of the results, with evaluations as to the significance of the responses and tabulations. Include the number of respondents and indicate when and where the study was done. We strongly encourage you to include exhibits, graphics and artwork for an article. These will assist the reader in comprehending and retaining the information in your article, and will make the layout of the Journal more appealing. Such items are treated as text manuscripts requiring the same warranties and assignments.

The New Products/Book Review sections provide an impartial evaluation to our readers. While we generally assign reviews, we do accept review submissions from an independent source. Articles submitted for this section should be from one to two double-spaced pages. Product illustrations or photographs are helpful.

Submission Requirements

The following guidelines must be followed when formatting your document for submission to the Journal:

Typewritten (matrix printer output is acceptable if it is letter or near-letter quality); double-spaced between paragraphs; one side to a page; and on pages that measure 8 1/2 x 11 inches or are A4 sized.

Submit Two Hard Copies of the article and one disk formatted in Word Perfect (IBM compatible), Microsoft Word (IBM or Macintosh), or ASCII on a 3 1/2-inch diskette. Diskettes should be dearly labeled with the author's name, article title, date, software and version used.

Also, when saving the document, choose the **save as** option in the File Menu. Select **save** AS "Mac 5.1 format." Or, **save as** "Text Only."

These documents parameters must be followed when formatting your file:
* Hyphenation **off**;
* Double spacing,
* Margins - 1 and 80;
* Page numbering - Upper Right;
* Right justify - OFF;
* No automation headers/footers (type them manually);
* Standard Printer Spec; and
* **Avoid** special characters or keys (e.g., indents - instead use **tab** for the indent key).

Graphics And Artwork should be submitted both in hard copy and on disk.

Article Length should be from 2,500 to 3,000 words. Even major articles are seldom more than 4,000 words. (Articles may be edited for length.)

Article Style should be structured as explained in the box on p. 3, as well as follow *The Chicago Manual Of Style.*

Use endnotes at the end of your article, rather than footnotes, to credit your sources.

Authors should include a brief biography including current position, background, professional affiliations, and books or articles published.

Material should be written in English. Other languages will be accepted only after discussion with the editor.

Review Process
Manuscripts submitted to the Journal are acknowledged by the staff upon receipt. Manuscripts are subject to review by one or more members of the Editorial Board of the Information Systems Audit and Control Association.

The review process generally takes eight weeks, depending on the length of the article and its complexity. When the review process is complete, the author will be informed whether the manuscript has been accepted for publication (with or without revisions).

Each article published in the Journal becomes part of our overall copyright. We request authors ask for permission to reprint their articles and include a statement "Reprinted with permission of the *IS Audit & Control Journal*, Vol. X, year, pages xx-xx."

Accepted articles are placed in the inventory of unpublished articles until scheduled for publication. In general articles are published within three to nine months of their acceptance.

The Association sends authors five copies of the issue in which the article appears. There is no honorarium for Journal authors.

Manuscripts for publication in the *IS Audit & Control Journal* are edited according to *The Chicago Manual Of Style*. Revisions are made by the author.

The *IS Audit & Control Journal* is published by the Information Systems Audit and Control Association. For more information, call the associate publisher at + 1.708.253.1545.

Copyright And Reprints
The Information Systems Audit and Control Association obtains first International serial rights to any published manuscript in the *IS Audit & Control Journal*. While every effort is made to preserve the author's (or authors') style, the Journal Editorial Board and staff reserves the right to edit articles.

Article reprints are available after publication. For more information, contact the Journal's associate publisher.

Send Your Article To:
Please send your manuscripts or direct your questions regarding editorial policy to:
    Patricia K. Dahlberg, Associate Publisher
    IS Audit & Control Journal
    Information Systems Audit and Control Association
    3701 Algonquin Road, Suite 1010
    Rolling Meadows, IL 60008, USA
    + 1.708.253.1545, ext.453.

Style Conventions -*IS Audit & Control Journal*
I. **Headings**
A. Major headings should be flush left and capitalized.

Example: SECURITY AUDITS OF IMS

B. Subheadings should also begin at the left margin (flush left), but should have an initial capital letter, rather than be all caps.
Example: Importance of Program Control Procedures

C. Sub subheads under subheads should be indented five spaces. In this case, only the first word needs to be capitalized.

II. Endnotes
A. Endnotes in text should be numbered sequentially and listed on a separate page(s) at the end of the article. Each endnote should include the full name of the reference, e.g., author, book, date, and page number(s).
Example:
In the United States, forgers started with a counterfeit check drawn on a Los Angeles business account, and proceeded with an elaborate scheme that defrauded a Midwestern bank out of $700,000.

Bradford, Michael. "Thieves Sting Banks with High-Tech Forgeries." Business Insurance. March 2, 1992. p.14.

III. Tables, Exhibits, Figures And Illustrations
These should be on separate pages, properly labeled. In the text of the article, please indicate where each table, exhibit, or figure should be placed, e.g., "Place Exhibit I here." Exhibits and Tables should have Roman numerals (I, II, III); figures should take Arabic numerals (1,2,3).

A Checklist for Success
Helpful Hints For Getting Published In The Journal

Drafting a manuscript takes time and practice. Crafting your article to fit each publication's style requires an eye for editorial detail. Here are some tips regarding the *IS Audit & Control Journal* that will help you in becoming published:

Keep your colleagues in mind. Remember that while you are writing for a sophisticated audience, both in technical training and in education, they also are busy. So be concise when expressing your ideas. Use subheadings to break up the text and make skimming easier.

Follow a journalistic style. Keep your writing concise, provide details that illustrate your position and follow a logical progression of ideas. Vary your sentence lengths to make reading easier and to help engage the reader.

Write in the active voice using active verbs.

Use specific examples and case histories to illustrate points. (But be careful not to promote an individual, company, product or service.)

Address your readers in a friendly, conversational tone. Avoid unnecessarily complex vocabulary, clichés and excessive jargon.

Add subheads to signal topic changes and use bullets to make points easier to read.

Provide a summary of the major points of your article at the end.

If your article becomes too long, consider separating some of the copy to form a sidebar. Sidebars should include supporting facts or data and should be no longer than 300-350 words.

Provide supporting tables, figures, charts or artwork along with your manuscript. Tables and charts should be sent on separate pages. Captions should be included that explain the relevance and significance of these supporting items.

Give your article a final edit to eliminate unnecessary words. Make sure paragraphs flow smoothly and logically.

And be sure to double-check facts and figures.

Thank you for your interest! And good luck!!

Issues in Accounting Education

ADDRESS FOR SUBMISSION:

David E. Stout, Editor
Issues in Accounting Education
Villanova University
College of Commerce & Finance
Department of Accounting
800 Lancaster Avenue
Villanova, PA 19085
USA
Phone: 610-519-4048
Fax: 610-519-5204
E-Mail: stout@cf-faculty.vill.edu
Web:
Address May Change:

PUBLICATION GUIDELINES:

Manuscript Length: 20
Copies Required: Five
Computer Submission: No
Format: N/A
Fees to Review: 75.00 US$
   100.00 US$ Non-members

Manuscript Style:
   See Manuscript Guidelines

CIRCULATION DATA:

Reader: Academics
Frequency of Issue: Quarterly
Copies per Issue: 5,001 - 10,000
Sponsor/Publisher: American Accounting
   Association
Subscribe Price: 45.00 US$

REVIEW INFORMATION:

Type of Review: Blind Review
No. of External Reviewers: 2-3
No. of In House Reviewers: 1
Acceptance Rate: 15%
Time to Review: 2 - 3 Months
Reviewers Comments: Yes
Invited Articles: 0-5%
Fees to Publish: 0.00 US$

MANUSCRIPT TOPICS:

Accounting Education; Accounting Information Systems; Accounting Theory & Practice;
Auditing; Capital Budgeting; Cost Accounting; Curriculum Issues; Government & Non Profit
Accounting; Instructional Cases; Pedagogical Articles; Tax Accounting

MANUSCRIPT GUIDELINES/COMMENTS:

1. The purpose of *Issues In Accounting Education* is to provide useful information to
accounting faculty to assist in the teaching of accounting courses and in the understanding of
student and faculty performance and behavior. Papers that present research related to this
purpose, that provide insights into the teaching function, or that describe methods or materials
that can be used in the classroom will be considered for publication. Cases for classroom use
are also welcomed. Authors should communicate in a direct and easily understood manner.
Examples and illustrations are frequently helpful. Papers should contain descriptions of the
methods used to support and validate the conclusions reached by the authors.

2. Authors should submit five copies of their papers along with the submission fee to the editor. Checks should be made payable to The American Accounting Association. A submission must provide a representation by the author that the paper is not currently under review by any other journal.

3. The editor will screen papers submitted to the Journal. Those papers that are considered inappropriate or for which there appears to be a low probability of acceptance will be returned to the author promptly. The submission fee will not be returned.

4. Those papers that pass the initial screening will be sent to two to three reviewers for evaluation. A double blind review procedure is used. The reviewers are asked to provide a recommendation to accept or reject the paper, or to return it for revision. This review process takes approximately eight weeks. Approximately 15 percent of the papers submitted to the journal are eventually accepted for publication. Most of these papers are revised one or more times before acceptance. The lag between submission of a paper and publication generally is between eight and twelve months.

Authors are requested to use the following guidelines in preparing manuscripts for submission:

- An abstract of no more than 150 words should accompany the manuscript. The abstract should contain a concise statement of the purpose of the paper, the primary methods or approaches used, and the main results or conclusions.

- The paper should be double-spaced throughout, including abstract, notes, and references.

- Footnotes, references, tables, and figures should appear on separate pages.

- Tables and figures should be numbered serially using Arabic numerals. The table number (TABLE 1) and a title should appear at the top of the page in caps. The tables and figures should stand alone. Abbreviations should be avoided, and when used, should be explained in footnotes. Headings should be clear. Vertical lines normally should not be used. Horizontal lines should separate the title from the headings and the headings from the body. Figures should be prepared in a form suitable for printing.

- Headings and subheadings should be used throughout the paper. The title and major headings should be in caps, bold, and centered. Subheadings should be flush with the left margin, bold, and not in caps. Headings and subheadings should not be numbered.

- Notes should be used sparingly. References should be noted in the text using the date of publication in parentheses. For example: Wright (1986, 27). The reference list should use the following format:

Fleming, C.C., and B. von Halle. 1990. An overview of logical data modeling. *Data Resource Management* 1 (Winter): 5-15.

The title page should list the authors' names, titles, affiliations, telephone numbers, **email addresses** and any acknowledgements. The authors and their affiliations should not be identified anywhere else in the paper.

5. Permission is granted to reproduce any of the contents of *Issues* for use in courses of instruction, so long as the source and American Accounting Association copyright are indicated in any such reproductions.

6. Written application must be made to the Editor for permission to reproduce any of the contents of *Issues* for use in other than courses of instruction, e.g., books of readings. The applicant must notify the author(s) in writing of the intended use of each reproduction.

7. Except as otherwise noted, the copyright has been transferred to the American Accounting Association for articles appearing in this journal. For those articles for which the copyright has not been transferred, permission to reproduce must be obtained directly from the author.

Journal of Accountancy

ADDRESS FOR SUBMISSION:

Colleen Katz, Editor
Journal of Accountancy
American Institute of CPAs
Harborside Financial Center
201 Plaza Three
Jersey City, NJ 07311-9801
USA
Phone: 201-938-3292
Fax: 201-938-3329
E-Mail: ckatz@aicpa.org
Web:
Address May Change:

CIRCULATION DATA:

Reader: Business Persons, Accountants
   (CPAs)
Frequency of Issue: Monthly
Copies per Issue: Over 35,000
Sponsor/Publisher: American Institute of
   CPAs
Subscribe Price: 59.00 US$

PUBLICATION GUIDELINES:

Manuscript Length: 8 Max
Copies Required: Five
Computer Submission: Yes disks only
Format: MS Word, WdPerfect, Most Others
Fees to Review: 0.00 US$

Manuscript Style:
   Chicago Manual of Style

REVIEW INFORMATION:

Type of Review: Blind Review
No. of External Reviewers: 3+
No. of In House Reviewers: 1
Acceptance Rate: 11-20%
Time to Review: 2 - 3 Months
Reviewers Comments: Yes
Invited Articles: 50% +
Fees to Publish: 0.00 US$

MANUSCRIPT TOPICS:

Accounting Information Systems; Accounting Theory & Practice; Auditing; Cost Accounting; Econometrics; Fiscal Policy; Government & Non Profit Accounting; Industrial Organization; Insurance; International Economics & Trade; International Finance; Micro Economics; Portfolio & Security Analysis; Tax Accounting

MANUSCRIPT GUIDELINES/COMMENTS:

The *Journal of Accountancy* is a monthly magazine for the accounting profession. It covers everything that accountants should know. The subjects include accounting, financial reporting, auditing, taxation, personal financial planning, technology, professional developments, ethics, liability issues, consulting, practice management, education and related business and international issues.

Because *Journal* readers have a variety of interests that require diverse editorial content, **articles should have broad appeal and focus on practical situations and applications.** Those based on studies or surveys should draw conclusions from the research, analyze the impact on the profession and offer insights or advice that will be useful to readers. Articles that are entirely theoretical or are derived wholly from secondary sources are rarely accepted.

It is recommended that prospective authors read several recent issues of the *Journal of Accountancy* before writing an article.

Readers

Over 40% of the *Journal*'s readers work in industry in positions from staff accountant to chief financial officer. Another 40% of readers are in public practice, in firms ranging in size from a sole practitioner to an international firm of several thousand; some 30,000 of our readers are sole practitioners and a great many others work in small or mid-size firms. The remainder are government personnel, educators or students.

Most accounting issues affect CPAs in both industry and public practice. Therefore, articles should address the needs of both audiences when applicable. Authors should specify which segments of the readership their article addresses and their objectives in writing it. The more the editors know about the author's intent and targeted audience, the easier it is to judge an article's suitability. The larger the audience served, the more likely an article will be accepted.

Subject Matter

Articles in the *Journal* fall into several categories:

Practical. These discuss business problems and offer solutions using actual or hypothetical examples and case studies. See "Making College More Affordable," March'98, page 37. "The Importance of Customer Focus," Apr'97, page 63.

Corporate. These articles explore all aspects of management accounting-for staff accountants to CFOs. See "Communicate Up," Feb'98, page 67. "Surviving Explosive Growth," Dec'97, page 67.

Technical. These articles usually cover new standards or practices that affect all segments of the profession. They explain regulatory actions and their impact. See "Simplifying Earnings Per Share," Aug'97, page 61.

Professional Issues. These articles address issues facing the profession. See "National MAP Survey Results," Aug'97, page 49.

Future. These articles may be based on academic research or fast-moving trends that will have an immediate or very near future impact on the profession. Articles based on academic research should focus on its practical applications. See "Handling the Small Public Audit Client," May'97, page 53. "Are You Ready for the New Accounting," Aug'97, page42.

Length

Feature articles should be a maximum of 2,000 words (8 double-spaced, typed pages). The *Journal* also accepts short, narrowly focused articles for its columns. They should be a maximum of 1,000 words. Such articles are particularly useful when based on the author's own experience.

Style

The first paragraph should say what the article is about and why the reader would be interested in it. Include essential background information on the topic here. Relate the rest of the article to subjects mentioned in the introductory paragraph. If you must include technical jargon or complicated terms in the text, follow them with brief explanations. Weave essential references into the narrative; do not use footnotes or endnotes.

Authors should supply numerical data or a fact to create at least one small graphic to illustrate an important element contained in the article or related to the background or history of the content. See "The ABCs of Supervision," Feb'98, page 72.

Manuscript Requirements

Print, double-spaced, on only one side of plain white paper. Use black ink.

Do **NOT** use any special formatting-such as boldface, underlining or indents-other than that needed to produce a standard document.

The Editorial and Review Processes

Submit all manuscripts on an exclusive basis. If the *Journal* learns that a manuscript has been submitted to any other publication, it will not consider the article.

The *Journal* uses editorial advisers to assist in selecting material for publication. This group of advisers consists of about 55 professionals with broad experience, including those in public accounting firms of varying sizes, CPAs in commerce, industry, and education and those with particular expertise in various specialties.

Manuscripts undergo anonymous reviews. Authors receive acknowledgments before the manuscripts are forwarded to reviewers for evaluations and recommendations. Acceptance is based on practicality, readability, technical soundness, originality and interest to readers. The review process generally takes about eight weeks. All manuscripts receive a careful, judicious review, and the editors make every effort to assist the author in revising and editing a manuscript if, in the opinion of the reviewers, the subject is worth pursuing.

Once an article is accepted, an editor contacts the author to discuss any recommended changes. After revisions, the article is edited to conform to *Journal* style. The author receives a final manuscript for review and final approval. The author cannot rewrite at this time, but can make essential changes or corrections. Authors are given a proposed publication date. Regrettably, the *Journal*'s budget makes no provision for payment of honoraria for published articles. However, as a token of appreciation, authors of feature articles receive a specially bound copy of the magazine containing their article, as well as ten copies of the issue.

Submission Checklist

[ ]Submit article on an exclusive basis
[ ] Send 5 copies
[ ] Place author's name on title page only
[ ] Submit typewritten, double-spaced copy on plain paper with no logos or letterhead

[ ] Send a disc along with the hardcopy
[ ] Write on the disc label:
    1) Author's name
    2) Word processing program used
    3) Name of document
[ ] Do not use special formatting in the text.
[ ] Do not send electronic artwork unless it has already been discussed with a *Journal* editor
[ ] Include data for opening page graphic
[ ] Include examples and/or case study(s).

Editors
To discuss a manuscript or article idea with a *Journal* editor, contact:

Financial Reporting, Accounting, Personal Financial Planning, Tax, Employee Benefits, Not-for-Profit: **Peter Fleming** (201) 938-3286 PFleming@AICPA.org

Auditing, Web site Technology, Professional Standards, Assurance Services, Practice Management: **Richard Koreto** (201) 938-3412 RKoreto@AICPA.org

Marketing, Practice Management, Government, International, Litigation: **John von Brachel** (201) 938-3287 JVonbrachel@AICPA.org

Technology, Management Accounting: **Stanley Zarowin** (201) 938-3289 SZarowin@AICPA.org

Manuscripts or questions about editorial policy should be directed to:

Sarah Cobb, Assistant Editor
Journal of Accountancy
American Institute of CPAs
Harborside Financial Center
201 Plaza Three
Jersey City, NJ 07311-9801
(201) 938-3290
SCobb@AICPA.org
or
Vincent Nolan, Assistant Editor
(201) 938-3540 Vnolan@AICPA.org

Journal of Accounting and Computers

ADDRESS FOR SUBMISSION:

William J. Read, Managing Editor
Journal of Accounting and Computers
Bentley College
Department of Accountancy
175 Forest Street
Waltham, MA 02154-4705
USA
Phone: 781-891-2525
Fax: 781-891-2896
E-Mail: wread@bentley.edu
Web: www.swcollege.com/acct/jac/
Address May Change:

PUBLICATION GUIDELINES:

Manuscript Length: 11-15
Copies Required: Three
Computer Submission: No
Format: N/A
Fees to Review: 0.00 US$

Manuscript Style:
  , Accounting Review

CIRCULATION DATA:

Reader: Academics
Frequency of Issue: Yearly
Copies per Issue: 1,001 - 2,000
Sponsor/Publisher: Bentley College/South-
    Western College Publishing
Subscribe Price: 0.00 US$

REVIEW INFORMATION:

Type of Review: Blind Review
No. of External Reviewers: 2
No. of In House Reviewers: 1
Acceptance Rate: 33-40%
Time to Review: 2 - 3 Months
Reviewers Comments: Yes
Invited Articles: 0-5%
Fees to Publish: 0.00 US$

MANUSCRIPT TOPICS:
Accounting Information Systems; Accounting Theory & Practice; Auditing; Computer & Tech. Integration in Pedagogy; Econometrics; Micro Economics

MANUSCRIPT GUIDELINES/COMMENTS:

Mission Statement
The *South-Western/Bentley Journal of Accounting and Computers* is published as a service to the academic accounting community. Our goal is to continue to provide timely information on the general subject of computers and accounting education. In order to obtain the widest possible dissemination of important ideas, we may publish papers previously presented at conferences, and we may republish versions of papers published in conference proceedings. Also, we may publish invited papers that have not gone through our formal review process, which will he indicated as such.

Call For Papers
The *South-Western/Bentley Journal of Accounting and Computers (SBJAC)* is seeking papers for publication in future volumes. It is the current editorial policy of the *SBJAC* to publish

papers of interest to accounting educators and related to the use of computers in accounting education. Of special interest at this time are the following topics:

1. The impact on accounting education of the use of certain computer applications in accounting practice. Present examples include spreadsheets, database management systems, and expert systems.

2. New and innovative approaches to using the computer in accounting education, e.g., interactive computerized learning technologies.

3. Results of experiments conducted to study the impact of integrating the computer into accounting courses. Examples include student questionnaires and measurements of student achievement. Less formal assessments of the impact of integration are also appropriate.

4. Evaluations of software packages available for use in accounting courses.

5. Studies of logistical issues such as computer laboratories, student ownership of microcomputers, and software licensing.

6. Individual courses and overall curriculum designs as they are related to computers and accounting.

This list is not meant to be all inclusive, but is meant to provide ideas of topics consistent with the current mission of the *SBJAC*.

Refereeing Procedure

Manuscripts are reviewed first by the Managing Editor to establish consistency with the *SBJAC* editorial policy. If the paper meets the editorial policy of the *SBJAC*, it is then blind-reviewed. Authors can, in most cases, expect a 10-12 week turnaround.

Instructions To Authors

All manuscripts should he typed on one side of 8 1/2" x 11" paper and should be double-spaced, except for indented quotations, references, and footnotes. Allow a margin of at least 1" on all sides of each page. Authors should include a cover sheet with the title of the manuscript and the author's name, title, affiliation, and complete mailing address. The title of the paper, but not the author's name, should appear on the **Abstract** page and on the first page of the text. An Abstract, not to exceed 200 words, should he presented on a separate page immediately preceding the text. The Abstract should summarize the paper's contents and/or its focus or purpose. Number all pages, including exhibits, appendices, and references, consecutively.

References to works of other authors or studies should he noted in square brackets in the text of the article and should contain the author's name, year of publication of the work cited, and page numbers where appropriate. For example, [Bloes and Mock, 1988] or [Currie, 1988, 62]. References in the text should provide sufficient information to refer the reader to the References list.

A **Reference List** including only literature cited in the text should accompany the article. This list should appear at the end of the article and list all references in alphabetical order by the last name of the first author. Only the first initial of each author's name is necessary.

Examples: Hirsch, Jr., M. L., and J. G. Louderback, *Cost Accounting: Accumulation, Analysis, and Use,* 3d ed. (Cincinnati: South-Western Publishing Co., 1992).

Greer, D. P., H. R. Stocker, and C. R. Skousen, "Integrating Commercial Microcomputer General Ledger Software into the First College Accounting Course," *Kent/Bentley Journal of Accounting and Computers* , Vol. VII (Fall, 1991): 1-16.

Footnotes should be used for notes to the textual material that are not necessary to the discussion in the text itself. Number footnotes consecutively.

Submission Procedure

Submit one original and two copies to the Managing Editor of the *South-Western/Bentley Journal of Accounting and Computers:*

Professor William J. Read
Managing Editor, *South-Western/Bentley Journal of Accounting and Computers*
Department of Accountancy
Bentley College
175 Forest Street
Waltham, MA 02154-4705

Materials Access Policy

Our purpose is to facilitate an exchange of ideas among those involved in accounting education. Many of our articles concern the development of assignments, software, and other teaching materials. To be included in the *South-Western/Bentley Journal of Accounting and Computers,* an article must discuss teaching material and software (programs or "templates") available to our readers free-of-charge or on a cost-recovery basis. If an article discusses assignments developed using software developed by someone other than the author (e.g., Lotus® 1-2-3®, Pre-Audit, Integrated Accounting on Microcomputers), only the assignments need be available from the article's author. The *South-Western/Bentley Journal of Accounting and Computers* reserves the right to reject articles that promote a product more than they exchange ideas about accounting education.

Reproduction Policy

The *South-Western/Bentley Journal of Accounting and Computers* is copyrighted by South-Western College Publishing in Cincinnati, Ohio, and Bentley College of Waltham, Massachusetts. Permission is granted to reproduce any of the contents of the *South-Western/Bentley Journal of Accounting and Computers* for pedagogical purposes, if the source of the copy and the *South-Western/Bentley Journal of Accounting and Computers* are shown on the reproduction. Written permission from the Managing Editors is required for reproduction to be used for any other purposes. No part of the *South-Western/Bentley Journal of Accounting and Computers* can be reproduced for resale.

Journal of Accounting and Economics

ADDRESS FOR SUBMISSION:

R.Ball, R.L.Watts, J.L. Zimmerman, Eds.
Journal of Accounting and Economics
University of Rochester
William E. Simon Grad. Schl. of Bus. Adm
Rochester, NY 14627
USA
Phone: 716-275-4063
Fax: 716-442-6323
E-Mail: pratt@ssb.rochester.edu
Web:
Address May Change:

CIRCULATION DATA:

Reader: Academics
Frequency of Issue: Quarterly
Copies per Issue: 1,001 - 2,000
Sponsor/Publisher: Elsevier Science
    Publishing Co.
Subscribe Price: 70.00 US$

PUBLICATION GUIDELINES:

Manuscript Length: 20+
Copies Required: Four
Computer Submission: Yes
Format: MS-DOS/PC-DOS OR Macintosh
Fees to Review: 150.00 US$ Subscriber
    180.00 US$ Non-subscriber

Manuscript Style:
    See Manuscript Guidelines

REVIEW INFORMATION:

Type of Review: Blind Review
No. of External Reviewers: 1
No. of In House Reviewers: 0
Acceptance Rate: 11-20%
Time to Review: 1 - 2 Months
Reviewers Comments: Yes
Invited Articles: 0-5%
Fees to Publish: 0.00 US$

MANUSCRIPT TOPICS:

Accounting Information Systems; Accounting Theory & Practice; Auditing; Cost Accounting; Government & Non Profit Accounting; Public Policy Economics; Tax Accounting

MANUSCRIPT GUIDELINES/COMMENTS:

Description

The *Journal of Accounting and Economics* encourages the application of economic theory to the explanation of accounting phenomena. The *Journal of Accounting and Economics* provides a forum for the publication of the highest quality manuscripts which employ economic analyses of accounting problems. Reading the *Journal of Accounting and Economics* provides the most accessible insight into the research that is influencing contemporary accounting scholars and students.

A wide range of methodologies are encouraged and covered:
* the determination of accounting standards;
* government regulation of corporate disclosure;
* the information content and role of accounting numbers in capital markets;
* the role of accounting in financial contracts and in monitoring agency relationships;

- the theory of the accounting firm;
- government regulation of the accounting profession;
- statistical sampling and the loss function in auditing;
- the role of accounting within the firm.

Guide for Authors
1. Papers must be in English.

2. Manuscripts should be submitted in quadruplicate with the appropriate submission fee to the Editorial Assistant. *For complete up-to-date addresses of Editors please check the link to Editorial board at the beginning of these instructions.*

Submission fee is used to encourage quicker response from the referees who are paid a nominal fee if they return the manuscript within three weeks. The submission fee of US$ 150 must accompany all manuscripts submitted by authors who currently subscribe to the Journal of Accounting and Economics and US$ 180 for non-subscribers. The submission fee will be refunded for all accepted manuscripts (unless it was previously waived). There are no page charges. Cheques should be made payable to the *Journal of Accounting and Economics.*

Submission of a paper will be held to imply that it contains original unpublished work and is not being submitted for publication elsewhere. The Editor does not accept responsibility for damage or loss of papers submitted. Upon acceptance of an article, author(s) will be asked to transfer copyright of the article to the publisher. This transfer will ensure the widest possible dissemination of information.

3. Submission of accepted papers as electronic manuscripts, i.e., on disk with accompanying manuscript, is encouraged. Electronic manuscripts have the advantage that there is no need for re-keying of text, thereby avoiding the possibility of introducing errors and resulting in reliable and fast delivery of proofs. The preferred storage medium is a 5.25 or 3.5 inch disk in MS-DOS format, although other systems are welcome, e.g., Macintosh (in this case, save your file in the usual manner; do not use the option 'save in MS-DOS format"). Do not submit your original paper as electronic manuscript but hold on to disk until asked for this by the Editor (in case your paper is accepted without revisions). Do submit the accepted version of your paper as electronic manuscript. Make absolutely sure that the file on the disk and the printout are identical. Please use a new and correctly formatted disk and label this with your name; also specify the software and hardware used as well as the title of the file to be processed. Do not convert the file to plain ASCII. Ensure that the letter 'I' and digit '1', and also the letter 'O' and digit '0' are used properly, and format your article (tabs, indents, etc.) consistently. Characters not available on your word processor (Greek letters mathematical symbols, etc.) should not be left open but indicated by a unique code (e.g. gralpha, alpha, etc., for the Greek letter a) Such codes should be used consistently throughout the entire text; a list of codes used should accompany the electronic manuscript. Do not allow your word processor to introduce word breaks and do not use a justified layout. Please adhere strictly to the general instructions below on style, arrangement and, in particular, the reference style of the journal.

4. Manuscripts should be double spaced, with wide margins, and printed on one side of the paper only. All pages should be numbered consequently. Titles and subtitles should be short. References, tables, and legends for the figures should be printed on separate pages.

5. The first page of the manuscript should contain the following information: (i) the title; (ii) the names. and institutional affiliations. of the authors; (iii) an abstract of not more than 100 words. A footnote on the same sheet should give the name, address, and telephone and fax numbers of the corresponding author [as well as an e-mail address].

6. The first page of the manuscript should also contain at least one classification code according to the Classification System for Journal Articles as used by the *Journal of Economic Literature*; in addition, up to five key words should be supplied.

7. Acknowledgements and information on grants received can be given in a first footnote, which should not be included in the consecutive numbering of footnotes.

8. Footnotes should be kept to a minimum and numbered consecutively throughout the text with superscript Arabic numerals.

9. Displayed formulae should be numbered consecutively throughout the manuscript as (1), (2), etc. against the right-hand margin of the page. In cases where the derivation of formulae has been abbreviated, it is of great help to the referees if the full derivation can be presented on a separate sheet (not to be published).

10. References to publications should be as follows: 'Smith (1992) reported that...' of 'This problem has been studied previously (e.g., Smith et al., 1969.)' The author should make sure that there is a strict one-to-one correspondence between the names and years in the text and those on the list. The list of references should appear at the end of the main text after any appendices, but before tables and legends for figures. It should be double spaced and listed in alphabetical order by author's name. References should appear as follows:

For monographs

Hawawini, G. and I. Swary, 1990, Mergers and acquisitions in the U.S. banking industry: Evidence from the capital markets (North-Holland, Amsterdam).

For contributions to collective works

Brunner, K. and A.H. Meltzer, 1990, Money supply, in: B.M. Friedman and F.H. Hahn, eds., Handbook of monetary economics, Vol, 1 (North-Holland, Amsterdam). 357-396.

For periodicals

Griffiths, W. and G. Judge, 1992, Testing and estimating location vectors when the error covariance matrix is unknown, Journal of Econometrics 54, 121-138.

Note that journal titles should not be abbreviated.

11. Illustrations will be reproduced photographically from originals supplied by the author; they will not be redrawn by the publisher. Please provide all illustrations in quadruplicate one high-contrast original and three photocopies. Care should be taken that lettering and symbols are of a comparable size. The illustrations should not be inserted in the text, and should be marked on the back with figure number, title of paper, and author's name. All graphs and diagrams should be referred to as figures, and should be numbered consecutively in the text in Arabic numerals. Illustration for papers submitted as electronic manuscripts should be in traditional form.

12. Tables should be numbered consecutively in the text in Arabic numerals and printed on separate sheets.

Any manuscript which does not conform to the above instructions may be returned for the necessary revision before publication.

Page proofs will be sent to the corresponding author. Proofs should be corrected carefully; the responsibility for detecting errors lies with the author. Corrections should be restricted to instances in which the proof is at variance with the manuscript. No deviations from the version accepted by the Editors are permissible without the prior and explicit approval by the Editors; these alterations will be charged. Twenty-five reprints of each paper are supplied free of charge to the corresponding author; additional reprints are available at cost if they are ordered when the proof is returned.

Journal of Accounting and Finance Research

ADDRESS FOR SUBMISSION:

Roger Calcote, Editor
Journal of Accounting and Finance
  Research
American Academy of Accounting &
  Finance
220 Oliver Drive
Brookhaven, MS 39601
USA
Phone: 601-833-9741
Fax: 601-823-3666
E-Mail: pfuller@ccaix.jsums.edu
Web:
Address May Change: 1/27/01

PUBLICATION GUIDELINES:

Manuscript Length: 11-15
Copies Required: Three
Computer Submission: No
Format: N/A
Fees to Review: 180.00 US$
    90.00 US$ Attendee AAAFR Meeting

Manuscript Style:
    See Manuscript Guidelines

CIRCULATION DATA:

Reader: Academics
Frequency of Issue: Quarterly
Copies per Issue: Less than 1,000
Sponsor/Publisher: USM Publication and
  Printing Services
Subscribe Price: 135.00 US$

REVIEW INFORMATION:

Type of Review: Blind Review
No. of External Reviewers: 2
No. of In House Reviewers: 2
Acceptance Rate: 21-30%
Time to Review: 2 - 3 Months
Reviewers Comments: Yes
Invited Articles: 0-5%
Fees to Publish: 0.00 US$

MANUSCRIPT TOPICS:

Accounting Information Systems; Accounting Theory & Practice; Auditing; Capital
Budgeting; Cost Accounting; Fiscal Policy; Government & Non Profit Accounting;
International Economics & Trade; International Finance; Portfolio & Security Analysis; Real
Estate; Tax Accounting

MANUSCRIPT GUIDELINES/COMMENTS:

Associate Editor: Philip Fuller, DBA

The *Journal of Accounting And Finance Research* is the official publication of the American
Academy of Accounting and Finance.

Papers published in The Journal were presented at a previous annual meeting of the Academy
and went through a review process. Only papers presented at the Academy's annual meeting
and published in the proceedings of the annual meeting are considered for The Journal.
Unsolicited manuscripts are not accepted.

The Academy's annual meeting is held in New Orleans, Louisiana during the first or second week of December.

Requests for information about the Academy, The Journal or the annual meeting should be sent to American Academy of Accounting and Finance, 220 Oliver Dr., Brookhaven, MS 39601, USA.

Format Instructions
All instructions that follow are mandatory for the final copy of your paper. These instructions are laid out in the format you should use. We are following the style of *Accounting Horizons*, generally.

Title
The title should be in CG Times (Scalable) size 16 font, all capital letters, centered at the top of the first page, and beginning on or near the 1.50" line. Titles of more than one line should be single-spaced.

Authors
The author(s), name(s) and affiliation(s) should be centered and single-spaced, beginning on the second line below the title. Do not use titles such as Dr. or Assistant Professor, etc. Use CG Times (Scalable) size 14 font. The rest of the paper should be in CG Times (Scalable) size 12 font.

Headings
All headings should be in bold type. First-level headings should be centered and set in all caps. Second-level headings should be set flush left with initial caps. Do not use headings other than these two. Separate headings from preceding and succeeding text by one line space.

Abstract
Introduce the paper with an abstract of approximately 150-200 words. Begin in the left column with the first-level heading, "ABSTRACT."

Body
The body of the paper should be single-spaced and should follow the abstract. Use a first-level heading of some type after the abstract and before the first paragraph of the body of the paper to separate the two.

Figures And Tables
Figures and tables should be placed either "in-column" or at the top of the page as close as possible to where they are cited. First-level headings state the table or figure number and may be followed by second-level subheadings. A sample of a full page table is shown at the top of the next page and a sample of an "in-column" table follows.

TABLE I		
Margins		
Column	Left	Right
1	1.00	7.50

Space Between Columns .5

Scalable fonts smaller than CG 12 may be used to fit a table "in-column" provided, in the author's opinion, the data is still legible.

TABLE 2
Checklist for Papers

- Prepare using WordPerfect (any version)
- Submit disk copy on 3.5" disk (final version only)
- Submit four (4) hard copies printed on 300 dot per inch (minimum) laser printer
- Use CG Times (Scalable), size 12 font (or the nearest thing to it available on your laser printer) for the body of the paper
- Title of paper: All caps, bold type, single-spaced, centered across both columns. Use CG Times (Scalable), size 16 font
- Authors: include affiliations. Use CG Times (Scalable), size 14 font
- Headings: Only two allowed; 1st level, all caps, centered, bold; 2nd level, initial caps, flush left, bold
- Scale tables and figures to avoid use of paste, glue, or tape
- Lay-out: two columns, except for title, authors, and tables and figures
- Margins:

	Top	Bottom	Column	Left	Right
	0.875"	0.75"	1	1.00"	4.00"
			2	4.50	7.50

- Headers: Include a blank two-line header on each page
- Page numbers: Do not type in; lightly pencil on back of pages
- Number of pages: Limited to 15
- Submit the final version of your paper by March 1, 1997.

Calling References
Use *Accounting Horizons* style for calling references.

Footnotes
The use of footnotes is strongly discouraged.

Equations

All equations should be placed on a separate line and numbered consecutively, with the equation numbers placed within parentheses and aligned against the right margin.

$$R_1 = f(X_1)$$

References (Bibliography)

Since the bibliography should only include those references cited in the paper, it should be referred to as "REFERENCES", a first-level heading. References should be listed at the end of the paper and follow *Accounting Horizons* style.

Appendices

Appendices should immediately follow the body of the paper, precede the references, and should be referred to as "**APPENDIX**", a first-level heading. If you have more than one appendix, number each consecutively with a second-level heading.

Typing And Printing Instructions

Word Processing Software And Type Size

Papers are to be prepared using WordPerfect (any version through 6.1) and submitted on a 3.5" disk as well as four (4) in laser-printed, hard copy. The preferred type is "CG Times (Scalable) size 12. This document is prepared in that type. If not available on your laser printer, please use the type font that most closely matches this.

Layout And Margins

Except for the title and author(s) information, papers are to be laid out using WordPerfect's Balanced Newspaper Column feature. Set the column margins as follows:

Column	Left	Right
1	1.00	4.00
2	4.50	7.50

All paragraphs should be indented 0.3". Set the top and bottom margins of the paper at 0.875" and 0.75" respectively. Use 'Full Justification' and be sure to turn WordPerfect's hyphenation feature on to obtain reasonable appearing spacing. Do not skip a line between paragraphs

Spacing

Single-space the body of the paper. Double-space before and after all headings. Triple-space after the last authors' name preceding the abstract heading.

Page Numbers

Don't type in page numbers. Keep pages in sequence and lightly pencil in the page number on the back of each page.

Headers

Include a blank two-line header in CG Scale 12 on each page after the title page. Failure to include the blank header will affect pagination and can result in the return of your paper for correction.

Journal of Accounting and Public Policy

ADDRESS FOR SUBMISSION:

Lawrence Gordon & Stephen Loeb, Editors
Journal of Accounting and Public Policy
University of Maryland
Robert H. Smith School of Business
College Park, MD 20742
USA
Phone: 301-314-2255 or 2207
Fax: 301-314-9157
E-Mail: sloeb@rhsmith.umd.edu
Web:
Address May Change:

PUBLICATION GUIDELINES:

Manuscript Length: No Limit
Copies Required: Three
Computer Submission: No
Format: N/A
Fees to Review: 0.00 US$

Manuscript Style:
 Chicago Manual of Style, & Journal
 Instructions

CIRCULATION DATA:

Reader: Academics
Frequency of Issue: Quarterly
Copies per Issue: 5 Times/ Year
Sponsor/Publisher: Elsevier Science
 Publishing Co.
Subscribe Price: 80.00 US$ Individual
 374.00 US$ USA Institution
 390.00 US$ Institution Europe/Japan

REVIEW INFORMATION:

Type of Review: Blind Review
No. of External Reviewers: 2
No. of In House Reviewers: 1
Acceptance Rate: 11-20%
Time to Review: 2 - 3 Months
Reviewers Comments: Yes
Invited Articles: 0-5%
Fees to Publish: 0.00 US$

MANUSCRIPT TOPICS:
Accounting Information Systems; Accounting Theory & Practice; Auditing; Cost Accounting; Econometrics; Fiscal Policy; Micro Economics; Public Policy Economics

MANUSCRIPT GUIDELINES/COMMENTS:

Description. The relationship and mutual effects on each other of accounting and public policy is an increasingly important area of research. *Journal Of Accounting and Public Policy* serves researchers, educators, policymakers, and practitioners in both disciplines by publishing research results and serving as a forum for the exchange of ideas. Preference is given to papers that illuminate, through theoretical or empirical analysis, the effects of accounting on public policy and vice-versa. Also encouraged are creative, interdisciplinary review papers that advance the understanding of the fields and their impact on each other. Subjects treated in this Journal include accounting as it interfaces with economics, public administration, political science, social psychology, sociology, policy science, and law.

Guide For Authors
All manuscripts should be submitted to: Lawrence A. Gordon and Stephen E. Loeb, College of Business and Management, University of Maryland, College Park, MD 20742. Manuscripts

are submitted with the understanding that they are original, unpublished works and are not being submitted elsewhere.

Manuscript. Submit the original and three photocopies of the manuscript, typed double-spaced on 8 1/2 x 11 in. bond paper. On the title page include names and addresses of authors, academic or professional affiliations, and the complete address of the author to whom proofs and reprint requests should be sent.

Also provide a running title of less than 45 characters and spaces, which will appear on alternate pages in the journal. Include an Abstract and a list of Key Words that best code the contents of the article for indexing purposes. The text proper begins on the following page and ends with a citation of acknowledgments, whenever appropriate. References, tabular material, figure captions, and footnotes follow. Tables and figures are numbered in order of their appearance with Arabic numerals, and each should have a brief descriptive title. Footnotes to the text are numbered consecutively with superior Arabic numerals.

Mathematical Notation. Use typewritten letters, numbers, and symbols whenever possible. Identify boldface, script letters, etc. at their first occurrence. Distinguish between one and the letter "l" and between zero and the letter "O" whenever confusion might result.

References. Citation in text is by name(s) of author(s), followed by year of publication in parentheses. For references authored by more than two contributors use first author's name and et al. For multiple citations in the same year use a, b, c after year of publication. The reference list should be typed alphabetically according to the following style:

Journal. Agapos, A.M. and Dunlap, P.R. Feb. 1970. The theory of price determination in government-industry relationships. *Quarterly Journal of Economics* 84(1): 85-99.

Book. Fisher, F. M. 1966. *The Identification Problem in Econometrics*. New York: McGraw-Hill.

Edited Book. Weiss, I. W. 1974. The concentration-profits relationship and antitrust. In Industrial Concentration: *The New Learning (H*. J. Gold Schmidt, H. M. Mann, and J. F. Weston, eds.) Boston: Little Brown, pp. 184-233.

Illustrations. Unmounted, glossy, black and white photographs or India ink drawings on white paper should accompany the original copy of the manuscript. Photocopies are suitable for the other three copies of the manuscript. To facilitate identification and processing, on the back of each figure write the number, first author's name, and indicate which side is the top. Captions appear on a separate page.

Proofs and Reprints. The Corresponding author will receive proofs, which should be corrected and returned within ten days of receipt. The author is responsible for proofreading the manuscript; the publisher is not responsible for any error not marked by the author on proof. Corrections on proof are limited to printer's errors; no substantial author changes are allowed at this stage. Reprints may be ordered prior to publication; consult the price list accompanying proofs.

Copyright. Upon acceptance of an article by the journal, the author(s) will be asked to transfer copyright of the article to the publisher, Elsevier Science Inc. This transfer will ensure the widest possible dissemination of information under the U.S. Copyright law.

Journal of Accounting Case Research

ADDRESS FOR SUBMISSION:

Eldon Gardener, Editor
Journal of Accounting Case Research
University of Lethbridge
Accounting Education Resource Center
4401 University Drive
Lethbridge, Alberta, T1K 3M4
Canada
Phone: 403-329-2726
Fax: 403-329-2038
E-Mail: gardner@uleth.ca
Web:
Address May Change:

PUBLICATION GUIDELINES:

Manuscript Length: Any
Copies Required: Five
Computer Submission: No
Format: N/A
Fees to Review: 0.00 US$

Manuscript Style:
    See Manuscript Guidelines

CIRCULATION DATA:

Reader: Academics
Frequency of Issue: 2 Times/ Year
Copies per Issue: Less than 1,000
Sponsor/Publisher: University
Subscribe Price: 60.00 US$

REVIEW INFORMATION:

Type of Review: Blind Review
No. of External Reviewers: 2
No. of In House Reviewers: 0
Acceptance Rate: 21-30%
Time to Review: 2 - 3 Months
Reviewers Comments: Yes
Invited Articles: 0-5%
Fees to Publish: 0.00 US$ Subscriber
    60.00 US$ Non-Subscriber

MANUSCRIPT TOPICS:

Accounting Information Systems; Accounting Theory & Practice; Auditing; Capital Budgeting; Cost Accounting; Government & Non Profit Accounting; Tax Accounting

MANUSCRIPT GUIDELINES/COMMENTS:

Editorial Policy

The *Journal Of Accounting Case Research* publishes cases on accounting and related topics, and educational manuscripts related to the use of case materials in accounting. Cases and Teaching Notes should be separated, and notes and references should appear at the end of the manuscript double-spaced manuscripts, on one side of the paper only, submitted with a diskette in WordPerfect or Microsoft Word containing all of the case material and teaching notes, are requested.

Cases submitted for review should have a separate title page with names and affiliations of all authors thereon. No names or references to the individuals involved in writing the case should be contained in the manuscript itself.

Cases should have a clear set of issues on which decisions are required, and they should be well written in the English or French language. Any exhibits, tables, graphs or charts should be prepared in camera-ready form on separate pages, preferably in WordPerfect or Microsoft Word compatible form. A detailed teaching note is required, including some indication of courses in accounting for which the case is suitable; classroom format; other possible areas of use for the case; issues for discussion; directions for analysis, and any background material that would be relevant or appropriate for the case.

All cases submitted for review should be available for publication without restriction, unless a sponsoring agency (such as a research funding agency or post-secondary educational institution) also holds a copyright. Under such circumstances, the agency should be willing to allow publication in the *Journal Of Accounting Case Research*, subject to minimal restrictions on use by subscribers.

A forwarding letter that contains either or both of the following, as applicable, should accompany cases submitted for review:

1. The source of the material and the authorization of the provider of the material for publication of the case in the *Journal Of Accounting Case Research* by the Accounting Education Resource Centre.

2. A statement that any other material not provided by a specific source, as in (1), has been obtained from fictional or public domain sources, and that no copyrighted material has been used without permission.

It is the policy of the journal to have a minimum of two blind reviews, by qualified academic and/or professional reviewers, of all materials considered for publication. The Centre provides reviewers with guidelines, and their recommendations are given a careful and thorough consideration in publication decisions. The ultimate decision on publication, however, rests with the Editor and the Management Board of the Centre.

The Accounting Education Resource Centre will hold the copyright on all published cases jointly with the author unless otherwise stated. Publication in other venues will be allowed by the journal if permission is requested in writing and a suitable royalty arrangement (if applicable) is made.

The following note is placed at the bottom of the first page of any case accepted for publication:

This case was prepared by John Doe of the University of Big City, Big City, State, and County as the basis for class discussion rather than to illustrate either effective or ineffective handling of a managerial situation. Distributed by the Accounting Education Resource Centre, The University of Lethbridge, @ 199x. All rights reserved to the author and to the Accounting Education Resource Centre. Permission to use the case in classes of instruction, without restriction is provided to subscribers of the journal unless otherwise stated.

Submission Of Cases

Five copies of cases and articles should be submitted (with teaching notes where applicable) to the Editor. Facsimile copies are not acceptable for publication, but authors may submit a copy in this manner for preliminary consideration by the editor.

Previously published material, or materials under review for publication elsewhere are not acceptable. Materials presented to workshops or in Proceedings are not construed to be previously published.

There is no submission fee for subscribers to *The Journal Of Accounting Case Research*. Non-subscribers are required to pay the annual subscription fee, or demonstrate that it has been paid, prior to review of materials submitted.

For manuscript submissions and case copyright information, contact the Editor.

Journal of Accounting Education

ADDRESS FOR SUBMISSION:

James E. Rebele, Editor
Journal of Accounting Education
Lehigh University
College of Business and Economics
Rauch Business Center
621 Taylor Street
Bethlehem, PA 18015-3117
USA
Phone: 610-758-3682
Fax: 610-758-6429
E-Mail: james.rebele@lehigh.edu
Web:
Address May Change:

PUBLICATION GUIDELINES:

Manuscript Length: None Required
Copies Required: Four
Computer Submission: No
Format: N/A
Fees to Review: 0.00 US$

Manuscript Style:
         See Manuscript Guidelines

CIRCULATION DATA:

Reader: Academics
Frequency of Issue: Quarterly
Copies per Issue: 1,001 - 2,000
Sponsor/Publisher: Elsevier Science
    Publishing Co.
Subscribe Price: 72.00 US$

REVIEW INFORMATION:

Type of Review: Blind Review
No. of External Reviewers: 3
No. of In House Reviewers: 0
Acceptance Rate: 11-20%
Time to Review: 2 - 3 Months
Reviewers Comments: Yes
Invited Articles: 0-5%
Fees to Publish: 0.00 US$

MANUSCRIPT TOPICS:

Above Topics with Educational Focus; Accounting & Tax Policy; Accounting Information Systems; Accounting Theory & Practice; Auditing; Cost Accounting; Government & Non Profit Accounting; Tax Accounting

MANUSCRIPT GUIDELINES/COMMENTS:

All **American submissions** should be sent to the Editor at the above address.
All **Other submissions** should be sent to the International Editor at the address below.
        David Alexander and Jon Simon
        School of Accounting, Business and Finance
        The University of Hull
        Hull HU6 7RX, UK

1. The *Journal of Accounting Education* (JAEd) is a refereed journal dedicated to promoting excellence in teaching and stimulating research in accounting education. The Journal provides

a forum for exchanging ideas, opinions, and research results among accounting educators throughout the world.

2. The JAEd has four sections: a Main Section, and International Perspective Section, a Teaching and Educational Notes Section and a Case Section. Articles in the Main Section present in-depth analyses of the topics discussed. The International Perspectives Section is designed to provide and awareness of the international educational environment including changes and developments in countries and regions around the world. The Teaching and Educational Notes section is designed to further the goal of providing a forum; this section contains short papers with information of interest to readers of the JAEd. The Case Section provides a vehicle for dissemination of material for use in the classroom. The case materials should aid in providing a positive learning experience for both student and professor and should be available for use by our readers.

All manuscripts are sent to an associate editor who selects two reviewers for a blind review. The reviewers use three criteria for evaluating papers: (1) readability, (2) relevance and (3) reliability. The evaluation for readability is two-fold. First, it is necessary to ensure that accounting educators involved in the area discussed in the paper can readily understand the paper. References should not impede the flow of the paper, and unnecessary or obscure jargon should not be used. The details of research design and statistical methods should be in an appendix rather than in the body of the paper. The statistical methodology is necessary for the review, but may not be published with the paper.

Worthy papers are reviewed twice for grammar; once before the reviewers receive it and a second time prior to publication. It is preferred that a paper be examined closely by a grammarian before it is submitted for review. Poor readability can impede the ability of a reviewer to evaluate the contribution of a paper, and may lead to rejection. All papers accepted for publication in the JAEd must have a high level of readability.

The second criterion is relevance. A paper is relevant if it has the potential to influence the process of educating accounting students. A paper that appeals to a broad spectrum of JAEd readers or is unique or innovative has a better probability of influencing the process of educating accounting students, and is more relevant than a paper without these features.

The third criterion is reliability. A paper is reliable if the conclusions of the paper can be reasonably inferred from the arguments. Reliability is not hard to assess when a paper is statistical or involves empirical research with which the reviewer is familiar. Authors can improve the probability of acceptance of a paper by including a section on the limitations of the research techniques.

When a paper relies on verbal analysis, reliability is harder to assess. Reviewers have to depend on their own knowledge of the subject to ensure the arguments are relevant to the question addressed and that the paper is internally consistent.

The heart of a quality journal is the presentation of meaningful content in readable and usable form. The staff of the JAEd is committed to ensuring these high standards.

Manuscript Requirements. Authors should send four copies of their manuscript (and survey instrument, if applicable) for review. There is no review fee. All manuscripts should be typed double-spaced on 8-1/2" x 11" bond paper.

A letter to the Editor must be enclosed requesting review and possible publication; the letter must also state that the manuscript has not been previously published and is not under review at another journal. The letter should include the corresponding author's address, telephone and FAX numbers, and e-mail address, if available (as well as any upcoming address change). This individual will receive all editorial correspondence. Upon acceptance for any publication, the author(s) must complete a Transfer of Copyright Agreement form.

Title Page: The title page should list (1) the article; (2) the authors' names and affiliations at the time the work was conducted; (3) corresponding authors' address, telephone and FAX numbers; and e-mail address (if available); (4) a concise running title; (5) an unnumbered footnote giving a complete mailing address for reprint requests; and (6) any acknowledgements.

Abstract: An abstract should be submitted that does not exceed 150 words in length. This should be typed on a separate page following the title page.

Style and References. Manuscripts should be carefully prepared using the *Publication Manual of The American Psychological Association*, for style. The reference section must be double-spaced and works cited must be listed. Avoid abbreviations of journal titles and incomplete information.

Sample Journal Reference:
Raymond, M.J. (1964). The treatment of addiction by aversion conditioning with apomorphine. *Behaviour Research and Therapy*, 3, 287-290.

Sample Book Reference:
Barlow, D.H., Hayes, S.C., & Nelson, R.O. (1984). *The scientist practitioner: Research and accountability in clinical and educational settings*. New York: Pergamon Press.

Tables and Figures: Do not send glossy prints, photographs or original artwork until acceptance. Copies of all tables and figures should be included with each copy of the manuscript. Upon acceptance of a manuscript for publication, original, camera-ready figures and any photographs must be submitted, unmounted and on glossy paper. Photocopies, blue ink or pencil are not acceptable. Use black India ink, and type figure legends on a separate sheet. Write the article title and figure number lightly in pencil on the back of each.

Page proofs and Offprints: Page proofs of the article will be sent to the corresponding author. These should be carefully proofread. Except for typographical errors, corrections should be minimal, and rewriting the text is not permitted. Corrected page proofs must be returned within 48 hours of receipt. Along with the page proofs, the corresponding author will receive a form for ordering offprints and full copies of the issue in which the article appears. Twenty-five (25) free offprints are provided; orders for additional reprints must be received before printing in order to qualify for lower publication rates. All coauthor reprint requirements should be included on the reprint order form.

Journal of Accounting Literature

ADDRESS FOR SUBMISSION:

Bipin Ajinkya & Stephen K. Asare, Eds.
Journal of Accounting Literature
University of Florida
Accounting Research Center
Gainseville, FL 32611
USA
Phone: 352-392-0155
Fax: 352-392-7962
E-Mail: murphyk@notes.cba.ufl.edu
Web:
Address May Change:

PUBLICATION GUIDELINES:

Manuscript Length: Any
Copies Required: Three
Computer Submission: No
Format: N/A
Fees to Review: 25.00 US$

Manuscript Style:
   No Reply

CIRCULATION DATA:

Reader: Business Persons, Academic
Frequency of Issue: Yearly
Copies per Issue: Less than 1,000
Sponsor/Publisher: Fisher School of
   Accounting, University of Florida
Subscribe Price: 22.00 US$
   32.00 US$ Library

REVIEW INFORMATION:

Type of Review: Editorial Review
No. of External Reviewers: 2
No. of In House Reviewers: No Reply
Acceptance Rate: 21-30%
Time to Review: 2 - 3 Months
Reviewers Comments: Yes
Invited Articles: No Reply
Fees to Publish: 0.00 US$

MANUSCRIPT TOPICS:
Accounting Information Systems; Accounting Research; Accounting Theory & Practice;
Auditing; Cost Accounting; Government & Non Profit Accounting; International Accounting;
Tax Accounting

MANUSCRIPT GUIDELINES/COMMENTS:

Journal of Accounting Research

ADDRESS FOR SUBMISSION:

The Editor
Journal of Accounting Research
University of Chicago
Graduate School of Business
1101 East 58th Street
Chicago, IL 60637
USA
Phone: 773-702-7460
Fax: 773-702-0458
E-Mail: jar@gsb.uchicago.edu
Web: See Manuscript Guidelines
Address May Change:

CIRCULATION DATA:

Reader: Academics
Frequency of Issue: 2 Times/ Year
Copies per Issue: 2,001 - 3,000
Sponsor/Publisher: Institute of Professional
    Accounting /Grad. Sch. of Bus., U. of
    Chicago
Subscribe Price: 75.00 US$ Academician
    90.00 US$ Library/Practitioner
    35.00 US$ Single Issue

PUBLICATION GUIDELINES:

Manuscript Length: Varies with Topic
Copies Required: Four
Computer Submission: No
Format: N/A
Fees to Review: 75.00 US$

Manuscript Style:
    Chicago Manual of Style

REVIEW INFORMATION:

Type of Review: Editorial Review
No. of External Reviewers: Varies
No. of In House Reviewers: Varies
Acceptance Rate: Varies
Time to Review: No Reply
Reviewers Comments: Yes
Invited Articles: 0-5%
Fees to Publish: 0.00 US$

MANUSCRIPT TOPICS:

Accounting Theory & Practice; Auditing; Cost Accounting; Government & Non Profit
Accounting; Monetary Policy; Tax Accounting

MANUSCRIPT GUIDELINES/COMMENTS:

Web Page: http://gsbwww.uchicago.edu/research/journals/jar

1. The JAR accepts for review unpublished, original research in the fields of empirical,
analytic and experimental accounting.

2. A cover or title page should indicate the name, address, phone number, and email address
of the author to receive correspondence and should include an abstract of not more than 100
words. In a letter to the editors, the authors should clearly state the purpose of the paper and
its expected contribution.

3. All material should be typed **double-spaced** including text, footnotes, references and
appendices. Leave at least 1 1/2 inch margins at top, bottom, and sides of each page. If

possible, send the typed original of all material, not a photocopy. If you must submit a photocopy, please be sure all pages are clean and clear. All photocopies should be one-sided. Footnotes are to be typed **double-spaced** and placed together at the end of the manuscript. They should not appear at the bottom of pages within the text.

4. **References**: If references are given in the text or notes, the following form should be used: White [1970, p. 104] states, "...." or (see Green and Black [1975], White [1970; 1974]). Place dates of publication in square brackets, not in parentheses. References are to be typed **double-spaced** and placed at the end of the manuscript. Place references in alphabetical order and do not number them. Give place of publication as well as publisher and date of publication for books cited. Do not put the author's name in all capitals. Include in your references only those works that are cited in the text. And please double check that all references cited in the text appear in the References. (See a recent copy of the Journal for other questions of style in the references.)

5. **Mathematical Expressions**: Mathematical expressions should be indented or centered on the page. If they are numbered, the number should appear in parentheses at the right hand margin of the page.

The same format should be used consistently throughout the paper. Long equations may begin at the left margin and extend into the right margin. Vectors should be underlined to distinguish them from other expressions. Vectors will be set in boldface type. If an underbar is not a vector, please make a note on a separate sheet of paper for the copy editor.

6. **Enumerations**: Enumerations or lists should be displayed in paragraph form. Numbers and letters used to enumerate items should be set in parentheses. An example is given below:

Sample firms met the following criteria:
1. listed on the Compustat data base for the years 1970 to 1980,
2. market value of common equity greater than $200 million, and
3. earnings forecast data available in **value line**.

7. **Tables and figures**: Each table is to be typed on a separate sheet of paper. The information contained in the body of the table may be single spaced; textual material in the table (such as footnotes) should be double spaced. Tables are to be numbered with Arabic (not Roman) numerals. Example: TABLE 1, TABLE 2, etc. (note that TABLE is in capitals). The title of a table is to be typed in capitals and lowercase, not in all capitals. Example: Summary of Data from Period 1. Tables should avoid vertical rules and should have a double rule at the top and a single rule at the bottom, before the notes (if any). Also, **do not** send tables that have been reduced through xerographic process. Instead, send the **large originals(s)**.

8. **Figures** are photographed and reproduced in the Journal from original copy (i.e., they are not typeset). Therefore, it is imperative that camera-ready figures be professionally drawn in black ink on high contrast copy paper. The figures must be of sufficiently high quality to be photographed. Also, the artist must draw the figure axes and any symbols that are part of the figure. The legend should be typed on a separate sheet of paper since it will be typeset. If a

figure is drawn on graph paper, please be sure the paper is lined in blue (which will not reproduce in the photograph) **not** in green, red, or black.

9. The **legends, labels and footnotes** for all figures and tables should be sufficiently complete to make the table or figure self-contained. In other words, the reader should be able to understand the table or figure without reading the text. The following items should appear somewhere in the legend, column labels, row labels, axis labels, or footnotes:

1. Description of the content of the numbers or symbols in the body of the table or the content of the figure. This description should include the dimensions of all numbers, e.g., daily returns.
2. Sample description, including size, period and, if relevant, a subsample description.
3. Definition, in words, of the symbols, equations and terms used in the figure or table.

10. Notes to the copy editor should be submitted on a separate sheet of paper.

Journal of Accounting, Auditing & Finance

ADDRESS FOR SUBMISSION:

Jeffrey Callen, Editor
Journal of Accounting, Auditing & Finance
New York University
Stern School of Business
40 West 4th Street, Suite 312
New York, NY 10012-1118
USA
Phone: 212-998-0059
Fax: 212-998-4001
E-Mail: jcallen@stern.nyu.edu
Web:
Address May Change:

CIRCULATION DATA:

Reader: Academics
Frequency of Issue: Quarterly
Copies per Issue: Less than 1,000
Sponsor/Publisher: Greenwood Publishing
Subscribe Price: 85.00 US$
    160.00 US$ for 2 Year Subscription

PUBLICATION GUIDELINES:

Manuscript Length: 20+
Copies Required: Three
Computer Submission: No
Format: N/A
Fees to Review: 100.00 US$

Manuscript Style:
    See Manuscript Guidelines

REVIEW INFORMATION:

Type of Review: Blind Review
No. of External Reviewers: 1
No. of In House Reviewers: 1
Acceptance Rate: 10%
Time to Review: 2 - 3 Months
Reviewers Comments: Yes
Invited Articles: 0-5%
Fees to Publish: 0.00 US$

MANUSCRIPT TOPICS:

Accounting Information Systems; Accounting Theory & Practice; Auditing; Cost Accounting; Econometrics; Government & Non Profit Accounting; Industrial Organization; International Finance; Micro Economics; Portfolio & Security Analysis; Public Policy Economics; Tax Accounting

MANUSCRIPT GUIDELINES/COMMENTS:

1. Under new editorship, the *Journal Of Accounting, Auditing, And Finance* (JAAF) has a new orientation. High quality, academic refereed articles will be accompanied by non-academic renderings of accepted manuscripts, and published simultaneously. These will be written in less technical language and directed to the practitioner.

2. The Journal will consider papers covering a broad spectrum of topics in finance. These may include, but are not necessarily restricted to, analytical or empirical contributions in areas such as theories of market equilibrium, concepts of "efficient markets", normative or descriptive theories of financial management, and investment decisions under uncertainty.

3. A serious attempt will be made to process manuscripts promptly. Upon acceptance of a paper, the author will be asked to provide a concise, non-academic version, describing the research problem, design, methodology, results and implications for practitioners. A professional editor will be available to assist the author in editing and styling the abbreviated version. As a result, the work will be read by both academic peers and a wide audience of practitioners, the latter typically not having been exposed to research written in technical, academic language. Thus, the condensed version will provide the critical bridge between the academic and professional communities.

4. Three copies of each manuscript should be submitted to: Jeffrey Callen, New York University, Stern School of Business, 40 West 4th Street, Suite 312, New York, NY 10012-1118.

5. Use only 8-1/2" x 11" white bond paper. Do not use "erasable" paper. All manuscript copy, including text, footnotes, charts, quotations, etc., must be typed double-spaced, on one side of the paper only.

6. Sources of material should be numbered in brackets consecutively in the text throughout the article, starting with (1). These references are to be typed on a separate page entitled "References" at the end of the manuscript. Minor changes should be made between the lines of the typescript, not in the margins. That is, typographical errors and slight corrections of the text or footnotes may be written (please print) on the manuscript in pen. If corrections are lengthy or complex, retype the entire manuscript page.

7. Illustrations accompanying manuscripts should be numbered, provided with suitable legends (again, typed double-spaced on 8-1/2 x 11" sheets), and market lightly in pencil on the back, with the name of the author and the title of the article. Illustrations such as original drawings or graphs are to be drawn in black India ink. Typewritten or freehand lettering is not acceptable. All lettering must be done professionally. Do not staple or paper clip illustrations. Put all illustrations between sheets of cardboard before mailing, to prevent folds. Tables and exhibits should be numbered consecutively. Center main headings within the article, type secondary headings flush with the left-hand margin.

8. A strong effort should be made to keep the punctuation simple. Most authors overuse parentheses, italics and quotation marks, which are simply edited out in the publication process.

9. If an article includes any previously copyrighted material (other than short quotation), the publisher must have letters of permission to reprint from the copyright holder and from the author if he or she is not the copyright holder. These letters must be submitted at the same time as the manuscript.

10. The Journal normally publishes articles only if they have not yet appeared or been accepted for publication elsewhere. There is generally no objection, however, to having articles that appear in the Journal reprinted in other publications at a later date, if appropriate permission is requested from the publisher at that time.

11. Authors of accepted papers will be furnished with copies of the issue in which their paper appears.

Journal of Accounting, Ethics & Public Policy

ADDRESS FOR SUBMISSION:

Robert W. McGee, Editor
Journal of Accounting, Ethics & Public
    Policy
Dumont Inst. for Public Policy Research
71 South Orange Avenue, Suite 260
South Orange, NJ 07079
USA
Phone:
Fax:
E-Mail: bob@dumontinst.com
Web:
Address May Change:

PUBLICATION GUIDELINES:

Manuscript Length: 11-25
Copies Required: Three
Computer Submission: No
Format: N/A
Fees to Review: 0.00 US$

Manuscript Style:
    Uniform System of Citation (Harvard
    Blue Book), & Accounting Review
    Style

CIRCULATION DATA:

Reader: Academics
Frequency of Issue: Quarterly
Copies per Issue: Less than 1,000
Sponsor/Publisher: Dumont Institute for
    Public Policy Research
Subscribe Price: 48.00 US$ Individuals
    148.00 US$ Institutes

REVIEW INFORMATION:

Type of Review: Blind Review
No. of External Reviewers: 2
No. of In House Reviewers: 1
Acceptance Rate: 21-30%
Time to Review: 1 Month or Less
Reviewers Comments: Yes
Invited Articles: 11-20%
Fees to Publish: 0.00 US$

MANUSCRIPT TOPICS:
Accounting Ethics; Accounting Theory & Practice; Fiscal Policy; Public Policy Economics;
Tax Accounting

MANUSCRIPT GUIDELINES/COMMENTS:

Desired Length: The preferred length is 11-25 pages, double-spaced. However, we are more interested in quality than quantity, so a shorter or longer length will also be considered.

Blind Review: Yes, after the editor has determined that the paper is suitable for refereeing.

Selection Criteria: The paper must be well written and on a topic included under preferred subject matter.

Approximate Lead Time to Publication After Acceptance: An abstract will be posted on our website and perhaps other places within 30 days after final acceptance. The article will appear in paper form within 1-3 months thereafter.

238

Style Requirements: The cover page should include only the title of the paper and the names, addresses, institutional affiliations and telephone numbers of all authors. Acknowledgments, if any, should also be included here. The first page of the article should include the title and a 100 to 150 word abstract (indented). All references are to be by footnote. There is no reference section at the end of the article. The first time an article is cited, full particulars should be given. For example: Murray N. Sabrin, "Issues in Tax Reform," Northwestern Journal of Taxation, Vol. 14:2 (Fall, 1995), 422-437, at 425. Pages 422-437 represent the place where the article may be found. Page 425 refers to the page where the thought or quote may be found. Shorter citations may be given for subsequent references. For example, Sabrin at 436. Books should be cited as follows: Tibor R. Machan, Accounting Ethics (New York: Basic Books, 1996), 162. To cite items other than articles or books, use your best judgment.

Journal of Bank Cost & Management

ADDRESS FOR SUBMISSION:

Journal Editor
Journal of Bank Cost & Management
Association for Management Information
   in Financial Services (AMI)
7950 E. La Junta Road
Scottsdale, AZ 85255-2798
USA
Phone: 602-515-2160
Fax: 602-515-2101
E-Mail: ami@amifs.org
Web: www.amifs.org
Address May Change:

CIRCULATION DATA:

Reader: Business Persons
Frequency of Issue: 3 Times/ Year
Copies per Issue: Less than 1,000
Sponsor/Publisher: National Association of
   Bank Cost and Management Accounting
Subscribe Price: 90.00 US$
    100.00 US$ International

PUBLICATION GUIDELINES:

Manuscript Length: 16-20
Copies Required: Two
Computer Submission: Yes
Format: Almost any WP
Fees to Review: 0.00 US$

Manuscript Style:
   See Manuscript Guidelines

REVIEW INFORMATION:

Type of Review: Editorial Review
No. of External Reviewers: 1
No. of In House Reviewers: 1
Acceptance Rate: 70%
Time to Review: 3 - 4 Months
Reviewers Comments: No
Invited Articles: 0-5%
Fees to Publish: 0.00 US$

MANUSCRIPT TOPICS:
Accounting Information Systems; Accounting Theory & Practice; Auditing; Cost Accounting

MANUSCRIPT GUIDELINES/COMMENTS:

Call For Papers
The *Journal Of Bank Cost & Management Accounting*, published by the Association for Management Information In Financial Services, seeks articles on issues relevant to management accounting in financial institutions. Articles should be on a subject of interest to practitioners in the field of bank cost and management accounting and should reflect the views of the author. Authors should not hesitate to submit articles that present a minority or unusual view as long as that view is effectively presented. A sample copy of the Journal will be provided to prospective authors upon request.

The Journal is published three times a year and distributed to 700 subscribers worldwide. The Journal generally publishes articles that have not appeared or been accepted for publication elsewhere. Exceptions to this policy may be approved if the author obtains a release from the copyright holder.

Authors of accepted papers will be furnished with six (6) copies of the issue in which their paper appears. Where multiple authors are involved, each author will be given four (4) copies. Complete address and telephone information for each author should be included with each article submitted. The publisher will pay $100 for each published article.

Guidelines For Preparation Of Manuscripts

Format—The entire manuscript, including text, footnotes, charts, and quotations, must be typed, double-spaced on plain 8 1/2" x 11" paper, leaving one-inch margins on all sides. The title of the article and author's name and title should appear on page one of the manuscript. Headings should be used to give structure to the article and to order the text in a logical format. The premise of the article and the conclusion(s) should be clearly stated.

Length—Manuscripts may be of any length in the above format, generally over ten pages. The final determinant of an acceptable length is the subject matter of the article. The Editor reserves the right to edit manuscripts for length.

Style—Punctuation should be kept simple, adding to the readability of the article. Tables and exhibits should be numbered and printed on separate sheets of paper whenever possible; they should be clearly referenced in the body of the manuscript. Footnotes should include the author's name, title of reference, publisher, and date. Unless a direct quote is used, no page or volume numbers are required in the footnotes. References or bibliographies should be typed on a separate page, entitled "References", at the end of the manuscript.

Review and Editing

Submission—Authors are strongly encouraged to submit their manuscripts on computer disk in any major software program format; one clear paper copy of the manuscript must be included with each disk. (Call AMI with any questions about disk format.) Alternatively, two copies (one original, one photocopy) of each manuscript may be submitted to the Editor at the address shown above. If an article includes copyrighted material, (other than short quotations), submissions must be accompanied by a letter of permission to reprint from the copyright holder.

Review/Editing—Articles are screened by the Editor and may be sent out to reviewers for comment in certain cases. Manuscripts are evaluated based on coverage of the subject and whether it will be of interest to readers. Each manuscript is edited for grammar, punctuation, and structure, and may be returned to the author with suggestions for rewriting.

If a manuscript is accepted for publication, a release form will be sent to the author. The signed release form must be returned within 15 days. Published articles become the property of the AMI and may not be reprinted without the written permission of the publisher.

Journal of Business

ADDRESS FOR SUBMISSION:

Douglas W. Diamond, Editor
Journal of Business
University of Chicago
Graduate School of Business
1101 East 58th Street
Chicago, IL 60637
USA
Phone: 773-702-7140
Fax: 773-702-0458
E-Mail: job@gsb.uchicago.edu
Web:
Address May Change:

PUBLICATION GUIDELINES:

Manuscript Length: No Reply
Copies Required: Two
Computer Submission: No
Format: N/A
Fees to Review: 50.00 US$

Manuscript Style:
 See Manuscript Guidelines

CIRCULATION DATA:

Reader: Academics
Frequency of Issue: Quarterly
Copies per Issue: 2,001 - 3,000
Sponsor/Publisher: The University of
 Chicago Press
Subscribe Price: 27.00 US$

REVIEW INFORMATION:

Type of Review: Blind Review
No. of External Reviewers: 1-2
No. of In House Reviewers: 1
Acceptance Rate: 11-20%
Time to Review: 2 - 3 Months
Reviewers Comments: Yes
Invited Articles: 0-5%
Fees to Publish: 0.00 US$

MANUSCRIPT TOPICS:
Accounting Theory & Practice; Econometrics; Industrial Organization; Insurance;
International Economics & Trade; International Finance; Macro Economics; Micro
Economics; Monetary Policy; Portfolio & Security Analysis; Real Estate

MANUSCRIPT GUIDELINES/COMMENTS:

1. **All manuscripts must be double-spaced** (text, references, footnotes, etc.). Allow right and
left-hand margins of at least 1-1/2 inches each.

2. **First Page Of Manuscript**
    A.   Title should be at least 2 inches from the topic edge of the page.
    B.   Allow 1-inch space, and on a separate line type the name(s) of the author(s).
    C.   One inch below this, on a separate line, type author(s) affiliation.
    D.   On a separate sheet, an abstract of not more than 100 words.

3. **References Follow The Text**. They should be typed on a separate page or pages in
alphabetical order by authors' last names. Each line after the first line of each reference should

be indented 1/2 inch. All references must be referred to in the text by author's name and year of publication. Note that journal titles should not be abbreviated. Reference style is as follows:

A.   For periodicals
    Jones, R.Y., and Brown, E.B. 1985. Transactions costs and the stock market. Journal of Business 23 (April): 178-85.
    Smith, J.D. 1960. Economic theory. Journal of Political Economy 67 (May): 126-42.
B.   For a book title
    Donahue, C.L. The Economics of Western Europe. 2 vols. New York: Oxford University Press.
C.   For contributions to collective works
    Smith, J.D. 1942. Predictions in economic theory. In C.E. Lang (ed.), Sociology as a Force. 2d ed. New York: Farrar & Rinehart.

In the text, references should appear as follows: "Smith (1942) showed that..." For multiple references by the same author in the same year, alphabetize by article title, adding a after the first reference date, b after the second, etc. For example:

Jones, C.D. 1971a. Social Trends. Boston: Beacon Press.
Jones, C.D. 1971b. Tax deductions. Finance 7 (December): 218-35.
In the text they are referred to as Jones (1971a), or (Jones 1971a).

4. **Footnotes** (typed paragraph style) should be placed together on typed sheets following the references. They should be numbered in order and correspond with the numbers in the text. In both places, footnote numbers should be shown as superscripts (i.e., slightly above the line). For example:

(Text)...in that study[3] (footnote)
3 Numerous studies have shown that

Footnotes are not necessary if only used to refer to a work cited. In this case, the information should be placed in the text in parenthesis. Example: (see Jones 1956, pp. 8-15). Footnotes are only necessary for further explanation of something within the text. An acknowledgement footnote should be unnumbered and should precede any numbered footnotes.

5. **Tabular Material**
Each table should be on a separate sheet of paper following the footnotes. Each table should be numbered and should be referred to in order in the text.

6. **Illustrations**
Each illustration (figure) should be on a separate sheet of paper and should follow the tabular material. Legends for the illustrations should be typed in order on a sheet of paper that should accompany the illustrations. All illustrations should be referred to in order in the text as figure 1, figure 2, etc.

7. Miscellaneous
Any unusual symbols or abbreviations in the text should be identified in the margin (in pencil). **Please prepare one original typescript (not a carbon) and one clear xerox copy of the manuscript.**

8. Instructions For Preparation Of Figures
Illustrations are expensive; be certain that yours are essential and do not repeat material presented in the text.

9. Cite all illustrations in the text (as Figure X), numbering them in one consecutive series. A circled note in the margin enables the editor or printer to place the figure correctly in the text.

10. Art work submitted with the manuscript ordinarily should be 8-1/2 by 11 inches or smaller. Plan line drawings for reduction of 50% or more; this will minimize flows. Remember that not only the overall dimensions but also the thickness of individual lines, spaces, and letters will be reduced proportionally.

Note: India ink drawings are obsolete. Nearly all figures now are computer drawn.

Journal of Business Finance & Accounting (JFBA)

ADDRESS FOR SUBMISSION:

Richard J. Briston, Managing Editor
Journal of Business Finance & Accounting
(JFBA)
University of Hull
School of Accounting, Business & Finance
Hull, England, HU6 7RX
U.K.
Phone: 01 482 466374
Fax: 01 482 466377
E-Mail: r.j.briston@accfin.hull.ac.uk
Web: www.blackwellpublishers.co.uk
Address May Change:

CIRCULATION DATA:

Reader: Academics
Frequency of Issue: 10 Times/ Year
Copies per Issue: 1,001 - 2,000
Sponsor/Publisher: Basil Blackwell Ltd.
Subscribe Price: 206.00 US$
    612.00 US$ Library

PUBLICATION GUIDELINES:

Manuscript Length: 11-30
Copies Required: Three
Computer Submission: No
Format: N/A
Fees to Review: 75.00 US$
    37.50 US$ Personal Subscribers

Manuscript Style:
    See Manuscript Guidelines

REVIEW INFORMATION:

Type of Review: Blind Review
No. of External Reviewers: 2
No. of In House Reviewers: 1
Acceptance Rate: 11-20%
Time to Review: 3 - 4 Months
Reviewers Comments: Yes
Invited Articles: 0
Fees to Publish: 0.00 US$

MANUSCRIPT TOPICS:
Accounting Theory & Practice; Auditing; Capital Market Studies; Cost Accounting;
Econometrics; International Finance; Portfolio & Security Analysis

MANUSCRIPT GUIDELINES/COMMENTS:

Length Of Manuscript: 11-20 pages, but occasionally both longer and shorter are accepted -
shorter papers as "Notes".

1. All manuscripts should be submitted to: The Editors, *Journal Of Business Finance &
Accounting*. Manuscripts are considered on the understanding that they are original,
unpublished works not concurrently under consideration for publication elsewhere. The
receipt of manuscripts will be acknowledged, but the editors and publishers can accept no
responsibility for any loss or non-return of manuscripts. Suitable manuscripts will be given
anonymous review, following which a copy of any review report will be supplied together
with the editors' decision. As regards papers accepted for publication, the author(s) will be
asked to transfer copyright to the publishers. Authors are requested to follow JBFA's
manuscript and style requirements closely, to minimize later delay or redrafting: a fuller

leaflet of "Information for Contributors" is available from the editorial office on request. In particular, authors should draft their papers and footnotes etc. to avoid identifying themselves directly or indirectly, to help ensure a fair review.

2. **Submission Fee**. A submission fee is required for each manuscript submitted to JBFA (other than Replies or Rejoinders), including rewritten and resubmitted manuscripts which had previously been rejected with advice that a rewritten paper could be reconsidered, subject to a further review assessment. However, in all cases the required submission fees are reduced by one-half if the designated author can confirm being a paid-up current subscriber to JBFA. The rates of submission fees may alter with inflation: the latest rates are printed on the inside front cover of the current issue of the journal. Submission fees should accompany the relevant manuscript, in the form of a cheque or draft made payable to the University of Hull or JBFA. If only the half-rate fee is sent, a cover note should give definite confirmation that the author is currently a paid-up subscriber.

3. **Manuscript Requirements**. Submit three photocopies of the manuscript (together with any submission fee), typed double-spaced (preferably on international-size A4 paper). On the title page include the names, titles and institutional affiliations of all the author(s), and also the complete address of the designated author to whom decisions, proofs and reprint request should be sent. Also provide a running title of fewer than 50 characters and spaces, which will appear on alternate pages in the journal. If the paper is to include any acknowledgements these should be typed as a footnote on the title page. The second page should repeat the full title of the paper, (but not the author(s)' names) and contain the Abstract of the paper, not exceeding 100 words for full-length papers, or 60 words for shorter Notes, Comments, Replies or Rejoinders. The third page may repeat the full title of the paper (but not the author(s)' names) and here the text proper begins. The main text should be followed by any appendices, by any footnotes (which should be kept to the essential minimum, identified in the text by superscript numerals and listed together at the end, not separately at the bottom of each page), and by the list of source references (see below). Tables and figures should be numbered in order of their appearance with Arabic numerals, and each should have a concise descriptive title (and source, where relevant).

4. B. Citation in the text is by name(s) of author(s), followed by year of publication (and page numbers where relevant) in parentheses. For references authored by more than two contributors use the first author's name and 'et al.'. For multiple citations in the same year use a, b, c, immediately following the year of publication. The source reference list should be typed in alphabetical order, and in accord with the following examples of style.

Amey, L.R. (1979a), Budget Planning and Control Systems (Pitman, 1979).

_____ (1979b), "Budget Planning: A Dynamic Reformulation", Accounting and Business Research (Winter 1979), pp. 17-24.

Lee, T.A. (1981), "Cash Flow Accounting and Corporate Financial Reporting" in Essays in British Accounting Research, M. Bronwich and A. Hopwood, eds. (Pitman, 1981), pp. 63-78.

246

Peasnell, K. V., L.C.L. Skerratt and P.A. Taylor (1979), "An Arbitrage Rationale for Tests of Mutual Fund Performance", Journal of Business Finance & Accounting (Autumn 1979), pp. 373-400.

5. **Mathematical And Statistical Material**. Mathematical notation should be used only when its rigor and precision are essential to comprehension, and authors should explain in narrative format the principal operations performed. Preferably detailed mathematical proofs and statistical support should be relegated to appendices. Any equations used should be numbered sequentially in parentheses positioned flush with the right-hand margin. Whilst the journal does not wish to publish unnecessary mathematical or statistical detail, or specimen questionnaires, supplementary information of these kinds may be of assistance to the editors and reviewers in assessing papers, and authors are invited to submit such supporting evidence as separate documents clearly marked as being for information rather than publication.

6. **Illustrations**. All graphs, charts, etc. submitted with papers must be referred to in the text, and be fully legible and clearly related to scales on the axes. If illustrations are numerous, a proportion may have to be deleted unless the author is able to supply artwork of camera-ready quality or to reimburse the journal for the cost of artwork.

7. **Proofs, Offprints And Prizes**. The designated author will receive proofs, which should be corrected and returned within ten days of receipt. This author is responsible for proofreading the manuscript: the editors/publishers are not responsible for any error not marked by the author on the proofs. Corrections to proofs are limited to rectifying errors: no substantial author's changes can be allowed at this stage unless agreement to pay full costs if communicated with the return of proofs. Similarly, offprints in excess of the twenty-five free copies automatically supplied to the designated author (for sharing among any co-authors) must be ordered at the time of the return of proofs, in accord with the instructions and price list accompanying the proofs. Following publication, papers (other than papers authored by members of the Board) will be eligible for consideration of merit by the Board of Editors for the award of the Paish Prize in honour of Professor F.W. Paish (for papers in Business Finance) or the Baxter Prize in honour of Professor W.T. Baxter (for papers in Accounting and Control). The prizes may be awarded annually and are currently of the value of ú100 each.

8. **Comments And Replies**. The journal welcomes non-trivial Comments on papers previously published in JBFA. To avoid publishing Comments based on misunderstanding, and to obtain Replies quickly so that they can be published simultaneously with the Comments, it is required that draft Comments should be sent to the original authors for their reactions, prior to any formal submission to the editors for publication.

Journal of Business, Industry and Economics

ADDRESS FOR SUBMISSION:

Keith Atkinson, Editor
Journal of Business, Industry and
    Economics
Delta State University
Box 3222
Cleveland, MS 38733
USA
Phone: 662-846-4217
Fax: 662-846-4215
E-Mail: katkinsn@dsu.deltast.edu
Web:
Address May Change:

PUBLICATION GUIDELINES:

Manuscript Length: 6-10
Copies Required: Three
Computer Submission: Yes
Format: No Reply
Fees to Review: 50.00 US$

Manuscript Style:
    See Manuscript Guidelines

CIRCULATION DATA:

Reader: Academics
Frequency of Issue: 2 Times/Year
Copies per Issue: Less than 1,000
Sponsor/Publisher: Delta State University
Subscribe Price: 0.00 US$

REVIEW INFORMATION:

Type of Review: Blind Review
No. of External Reviewers: 2
No. of In House Reviewers: No Reply
Acceptance Rate: 70%
Time to Review: 2 - 3 Months
Reviewers Comments: Yes
Invited Articles: 0-5%
Fees to Publish: 0.00 US$

MANUSCRIPT TOPICS:

Accounting Information Systems; Accounting Theory & Practice; Auditing; Cost Accounting; Government & Non Profit Accounting; Tax Accounting

MANUSCRIPT GUIDELINES/COMMENTS:

Journal of Construction Accounting & Taxation

ADDRESS FOR SUBMISSION:

Tony Powell, Managing Editor
Journal of Construction Accounting &
    Taxation
Warren, Gorham & Lamont/RIA Group
395 Hudson Street, 4th Floor
New York, NY 10014
USA
Phone: 212-367-6374
Fax: 212-367-6718
E-Mail: tpowell@riag.com
Web: http://wgLcorpfinance.com
Address May Change:

CIRCULATION DATA:

Reader: Business Persons, Academic
Frequency of Issue: Bi-Monthly
Copies per Issue: 3,001 - 4,000
Sponsor/Publisher: RIA Group
Subscribe Price: 190.00 US$

PUBLICATION GUIDELINES:

Manuscript Length: Any
Copies Required: Two
Computer Submission: Yes
Format: MS Wd or WdPerfect
Fees to Review: 0.00 US$

Manuscript Style:
    Chicago Manual of Style

REVIEW INFORMATION:

Type of Review: Editorial Review
No. of External Reviewers: 2
No. of In House Reviewers: 2
Acceptance Rate: 50%
Time to Review: 2 - 3 Months
Reviewers Comments: No
Invited Articles: 31-50%
Fees to Publish: 0.00 US$

MANUSCRIPT TOPICS:

Accounting Information Systems; Accounting Theory & Practice; Auditing; Benchmarking;
Construction Accounting & Taxation; Cost Accounting; Insurance; International Finance;
Legal Issues; Management Theory; Project Management; Risk; Tax Accounting

MANUSCRIPT GUIDELINES/COMMENTS:

Name of Co-Editor:	John Corcoran
Web:	http://www.pencormazur.com
Fax#:	(602) 9496-9516

Name of Co-Editor:	John Metz
Web:	http://www.sikich.com
Fax#:	(630) 264-4080

Publication Address:	Journal of Construction Accounting and Taxation
	Warren, Gorham & Lamont / RIA Group
	395 Hudson Street, 4th Floor, New York, NY 10014

Profile

The *Journal of Construction Accounting & Taxation*'s readers are primarily CPA's in public practice who specialize in construction industry accounting. Readers also include CFO's, controllers, attorneys, surety underwriters, contractors and anyone else involved in the financial aspects of the construction industry.

Articles and columns cover topics such as alternative dispute resolution, alternative minimum tax, alternative tax issues for small contractors, analytical review of contracts, auditing, benchmarking techniques, bidding and estimating, bonding, budgeting, capital budgeting, case studies, CFO/controller issues, change orders, choice of accounting method, claims, completed contract method (completion criteria), compliance, contract claims (accounting and financial reporting issues), cost controls, cost management, costing, design/build, downsizing equipment costing, equipment leasing, estate planning, estimating, federal income tax for large contractors, financing, fraud detection, homebuilders (audit and tax issues), information technology (computers, software, accounting systems, etc.) internal auditing, insurance options, job reporting, key controls, limited partnerships, local tax issues, managing cash flow, minimizing tax liability, percentage-of-completion method (measuring progress, pitfalls) productivity, real estate development taxation, revenue recognition, risk management, sales and use taxes, scheduling, Special Issue (and Special Sections in an issue), state and local taxes (excise taxes, gross receipts, payroll taxes, property taxes, unitary taxation, use taxes) surety (choosing a surety, working with surety), transfer of ownership, valuation, value engineering, and more!

General Information for Authors

1. We welcome the submission of articles offering practical information and ideas on construction accounting and taxation. Manuscripts for publication, and correspondence relating to them, should be sent to Tony Powell, Managing Editor.

2. While the utmost care will be given to all manuscripts submitted, we cannot accept responsibility for unsolicited manuscripts. Articles accepted for publication are subjected to editorial revision.

3. Articles must include a brief author bio and an Executive Summary. It is strongly suggested that articles end with a Conclusions paragraph.

4. Because the journal is produced through a desktop publishing system, articles must be submitted on diskette (WordPerfect or Word), along with a hard copy. Articles should be double-spaced with liberal margins.

5. Within your article, use many headings and subheadings to break up and emphasize your points. Type all headings flush with the left-hand margin; underline all main headings, but not secondary headings.

6. Illustrations and graphs (exhibits) accompanying manuscripts are to be produced in black laser-printed form. Typewritten or freehand lettering is not accepted. All lettering must be

typeset. Do not staple or paperclip illustrations. Put all illustrations between sheets of cardboard before mailing, to prevent folding.

7. Place references, endnotes, etc., at the end of the article, separate from the text. Endnote and reference citations should generally follow the *Chicago Manual of Style*. This material must also be typed and double-spaced.

8. End notes (which are used in lieu of footnotes) start with "1" and continue consecutively until the end of the article. Endnotes should begin with a paragraph indent.

9. If you are reprinting in your article any previously copyrighted material other than a short quotation—for example, graphs—the publisher must have letters of permission to reprint from the copyright holder and from the author if he or she is not the copyright holder. These letters must be submitted at the same time as the manuscript.

10. Except in rare cases, the *Journal of Construction, Accounting and Taxation* only publishes articles if they have not yet appeared or been accepted for publication elsewhere. There is generally no objection, however, to having articles that appear in the Journal reprinted in other publications at a later date, if appropriate permission is requested from us at that time.

Journal of Corporate Accounting and Finance

ADDRESS FOR SUBMISSION:

Edward J. Stone
Journal of Corporate Accounting and
    Finance
John Wiley & Sons, Inc.
605 Third Avenue
New York, NY 10158-0012
USA
Phone: 212-850-6197
Fax: 212-850-6866
E-Mail: scho@wiley.com
Web:
Address May Change:

PUBLICATION GUIDELINES:

Manuscript Length: 16-20
Copies Required: Two
Computer Submission: Yes
Format: Wd. 6.0, WdPer., Others
Fees to Review: 0.00 US$

Manuscript Style:
    See Manuscript Guidelines

CIRCULATION DATA:

Reader: Business Persons
Frequency of Issue: Quarterly
Copies per Issue: No Reply
Sponsor/Publisher: John Wiley & Sons, Inc.
Subscribe Price: 288.00 US$
    312.00 US$ Outside of North America

REVIEW INFORMATION:

Type of Review: Blind Review
No. of External Reviewers: 1
No. of In House Reviewers: 1
Acceptance Rate: 40%
Time to Review: 1 Month or Less
Reviewers Comments: No
Invited Articles: 11-20%
Fees to Publish: 0.00 US$

MANUSCRIPT TOPICS:
Accounting Theory & Practice; Auditing; Cost Accounting

MANUSCRIPT GUIDELINES/COMMENTS:

The *Journal of Corporate Accounting and Finance* is directed to corporate accounting and financial executives and outside auditors and accountants working with corporations.

Articles should address this readership and be informative, analytical, and practical, but not highly technical. We seek material that will offer our readership new insights into, and new approaches to, corporate finance and accounting issues.

Manuscripts are considered for publication with the understanding that they represent original material, and are offered exclusively and without fee to The *Journal Of Corporate Accounting And Finance.*

Articles must not have been published previously and may not simultaneously be submitted elsewhere.

An **original** and **two copies** of the manuscript must be submitted. Any accompanying artwork or exhibits must be submitted as black and white originals suitable for reproduction.

Articles should range from **3,700-7,500 words** (15-30 pages), double-spaced on one side only of 8 1/2" x 11" heavy-duty white bond paper.

Margins should be set to allow for **55 characters per line**. A 1 1/2" margin should be left at the top and bottom of each manuscript page.

Try to use as **few footnotes** as possible. If they are indispensable to the subject, they should appear **double-spaced on a separate page** at the end of the article.

Send **photocopies of the original source of lengthy quotations**. This enables us to confirm the absolute accuracy of the quotation.

Please seek **clarity, brevity, and pertinence**. Titles of articles should be short and clear. All accepted manuscripts are subject to editing.

A **brief** -50 words or less- **biographical sketch** of the author should accompany the article. The sketch should name the author's position, company or other professional organization, and field of expertise.

A 100-to-125-word **summary of the article** should also be provided.

All unsolicited manuscripts must be accompanied by a self-addressed, stamped envelope. Otherwise, they cannot be returned to the author.

Address articles to the Editor at John Wiley & Sons, Inc.

Journal of Corporate Taxation

ADDRESS FOR SUBMISSION:

Eugene M. Krader, Managing Editor
Journal of Corporate Taxation
RIA Group
395 Hudson Street
New York, NY 10014
USA
Phone: 212-971-5194
Fax: 212-971-5025
E-Mail: ekrader@riag.com
Web:
Address May Change:

PUBLICATION GUIDELINES:

Manuscript Length: 20+
Copies Required: Two
Computer Submission: Yes
Format: N/A
Fees to Review: 0.00 US$

Manuscript Style:
    Chicago Manual of Style

CIRCULATION DATA:

Reader: , Lawyers & Accountants
Frequency of Issue: Quarterly
Copies per Issue: 4,001 - 5,000
Sponsor/Publisher: RIA Group
Subscribe Price: 130.00 US$

REVIEW INFORMATION:

Type of Review: Editorial Review
No. of External Reviewers: 1
No. of In House Reviewers: 1
Acceptance Rate: 21-30%
Time to Review: 2 - 3 Months
Reviewers Comments: Yes
Invited Articles: 21-30%
Fees to Publish: 0.00 US$

MANUSCRIPT TOPICS:

Accounting Information Systems; Accounting Theory & Practice; Auditing; Corporate Taxation; Cost Accounting; Tax Accounting

MANUSCRIPT GUIDELINES/COMMENTS:

Journal of Cost Analysis & Management

ADDRESS FOR SUBMISSION:

Dr. William F. Bowlin, Editor
Journal of Cost Analysis & Management
University of Northern Iowa
Department of Accounting
Cedar Falls, IA 50614-0127
USA
Phone: 319-273-7101
Fax: 319-273-2922
E-Mail: bud.bowlin@uni.edu
Web:
Address May Change:

PUBLICATION GUIDELINES:

Manuscript Length: 16-20
Copies Required: Five
Computer Submission: Upon Acceptance
Format: N/A
Fees to Review: 0.00 US$

Manuscript Style:
      See Manuscript Guidelines

CIRCULATION DATA:

Reader: , Cost Analylists
Frequency of Issue: 2 Times/Year
Copies per Issue: 2,001 - 3,000
Sponsor/Publisher: Society of Cost
   Estimating and Analysis
Subscribe Price: No Reply

REVIEW INFORMATION:

Type of Review: Blind Review
No. of External Reviewers: 2
No. of In House Reviewers: 1
Acceptance Rate: 21-30%
Time to Review: 2 - 3 Months
Reviewers Comments: Yes
Invited Articles: 0-5%
Fees to Publish: 0.00 US$

MANUSCRIPT TOPICS:

Cost Accounting; Cost Analysis; Cost Estimate; Econometrics; Economic Development;
Production/ Operations

MANUSCRIPT GUIDELINES/COMMENTS:

Editors: W.F. Bowlin, University of Northern Iowa

    and   J. Kantor, University of Windsor
           Faculty of Business Administration
           University of Windsor, Windsor, Ontario N9B 3P4
           Tel: 519-253-4232 ext. 3142, E-mail: kantor@uwinsor.ca

Statement of Editorial Policy

The *Journal of Cost Analysis & Management is* published by the Society of Cost Estimating
and Analysis- It is a refereed journal dedicated to promoting excellence in cost estimating,
cost analysis, and cost management. Its objective is to improve the theory arid practice of cost
estimating, analysis and management by promoting high quality applied and theoretical

research. The Journal. provides a forum for exchanging ideas, opinions, and research results among `cost' educators and practitioners around the world.

The Journal seeks to publish research that is interesting, stimulating, and intellectually rigorous. Papers involving a variety of topics, settings and research methods are solicited. The methodology used in papers submitted for publication may be analytical or empirical. Manuscripts related to a broad range of cost topics for any sector of the economy—manufacturing, service, retail, government, anal not-for-profit—are desired. New theories, topical areas, and research methods are encouraged. Areas of interest include, but are not limited to, industrial engineering, economics, health care, operations/production management, construction management, business administration, and cost (managerial) accounting.

Manuscripts should be sent to either of the Editors who will initiate the review process. The review will use three criteria for evaluating papers: (1) readability; (2) relevance; and (3) reliability.

All papers accepted for publication in JCA&M must have a high level of readability. Poor readability can impede the ability of a reviewer to evaluate the contribution of a paper and may lead to rejection. It is necessary to ensure the paper can be readily understood by individuals involved in the area discussed in the paper. References should not impede the flow of the paper and unnecessary of obscure jargon should not be used. The details of the statistical methodology should be in an appendix rather than in the body of the paper if they are not central to the focus of the manuscript.

The second criterion is relevance. A paper is relevant if it has the potential to influence cost estimating, analysis, or management. A paper that appeals to a broad spectrum of readers or is unique or innovative has a better possibility of influencing costing practice and theory development and therefore, is more relevant than a paper without these features.

The third criterion is reliability. A paper is reliable if the conclusions of the paper can be reasonably inferred from the arguments. Reliability is not bard to assess when a paper is statistical or involves empirical research with which the reviewer is familiar. Authors can improve the probability of acceptance of a paper by including a section on the limitations of the research techniques.

When a paper relies on verbal analysis, reliability is harder to assess. Reviewers have to depend on their own knowledge of the subject to ensure the arguments are relevant to the question addressed and that the paper is internally consistent.

In summary, for a manuscript to be acceptable for publication, the research question should be of interest to the intended readership, the research should be well-designed and well-executed, and the material should be presented effectively and efficiently,

Submission Requirements
Authors should send five copies of their manuscript (and survey instrument, if applicable) for review. There is no review fee.

A letter to the Editor must be enclosed requesting review and possible publication.

The letter must also state that the manuscript has not been previously published and is not under review for another journal. The letter should include the corresponding author's address, telephone and FAX numbers, and E-mail address, if available (as well as any upcoming address change). This individual will receive all editorial correspondence.

Format
1. All manuscripts should be typed on one side of 8 ½ x 11 good quality paper anal be double-spaced, except for indented quotations.
2. Manuscripts should be as concise as the subject and research methods permit.
3. Margins should be at least one inch from top, bottom and sides to facilitate editing and duplication.
4. To assure anonymous review, authors should not identify themselves directly or indirectly in their papers. Single authors should not use the editorial "we."
5, A cover page should include the title of the paper, the author's name, title and affiliation, entail address, any acknowledgments, and a footnote indicating whether the author would be willing to share the data (see later paragraph in this statement).
6. All pages, including tables, appendices and references, should be serially numbered.
7. Headings should be arranged so that major headings are centered, bold and capitalize. Second level headings should be flush left, bold and both upper and lowercase. Third level headings should be flush left, bold, italic and both upper and lowercase. Fourth level headings should be paragraph indent, bold and lower case. Headings and subheadings should not be numbered. For example:

A CENTERED, BOLD, ALL CAPITALIZED, FIRST LEVEL HEADING

A Flush Left, Bold, Upper and Lower Case, Second Level Heading

A .*Flush Left Bold, Italic, Upper and Lower Case, Third Level Heading*

A paragraph indent, bald, lower case, fourth level leading. Team starts....

Abstract
An abstract of 100 to 150 words should be presented on a separate page immediately preceding the text of the manuscript. The abstract page should contain the title of the manuscript but should not identify the author(s). Abstracts should contain a concise statement of the purpose of the manuscript, the primary method or approaches used, and the main results or conclusions. .

Footnotes
Textual footnotes should be used only for extensions and useful excursions whose inclusion in the body of the manuscript might disrupt the continuity. Footnotes should be double-spaced, numbered consecutively throughout the manuscript with superscript Arabic numerals, and placed at the end of the text.

Tables and Figures

Authors should note the following general requirements:

1. Each table and figure (graphic) should appear on a separate page and should be placed at the end of the text. Each should bear an Arabic number and a complete title indicating the exact contents of the table or figure.
2. A reference to each table or figure should be made in the text.
3. The author should indicate by marginal notation where each table or figure should be inserted in the text, e.g., (Insert table X here).
4. Tables or figures should be reasonably interpreted without reference to the text.
5. Source lines and notes should be included as necessary.
6. When information is not available, use "NA" capitalized with no slash between.
7. Figures must be prepared in a form suitable for printing.

Mathematical Notation

Mathematical notation should be employed only where its rigor and precision are necessary, and in such circumstances authors should explain in the narrative format the principal operations performed. Notations should be avoided in footnotes. Unusual symbols, particularly if handwritten, should be identified in the margin when they first appear. Displayed material should clearly indicate the alignment, superscripts and subscripts. Equations should be numbered in parentheses flush with the right-hand margin.

Questionnaires and Experimental Instruments

Manuscripts reporting on field surveys or experiments should include questionnaires, cases, interview plans or other instruments used in the study.

Documentation

Citations: Work cited should use the: "author-date system" keyed to a list of *works in the* reference list (see below). Authors should make an effort to include the relevant page numbers in the cited works.

1. In the text, works are cited as follows: author's last name and date, without comma, in parentheses: for example, (Jones 1987); with two authors: (Jones and Freeman, 1973); with more than two: (Jones et al, 1985); with more than one source cited together (Jones 1987; Freeman 1986); with two or more works by one author: (Jones 1985 1987).
2. Unless confusion would result, do not use "p." or "pp." Before page numbers: for example, (Jones 1987,115).
3. When the reference list contains more than one work of an author published in the same year, the suffix a, b, etc., follows the date in the text citation: for example, (Jones 1987a) or (Jones 1987a; Freeman 1985b).
4. If an author's name is mentioned in the text, it need not be repeated in the citation; for example, "Jones (1987, 115) says..."
5. Citations to institutional works should use acronyms or short titles where practicable: for example, (GAO 1966); (AICPA Cohen Commission Report 1977). Where brief, the full title of an institutional work might be shown in a citation: for example, (ICAEW *The Corporate Report* 1975). 6. If the manuscript refers to statutes, legal treatises or court cases, citations acceptable in law reviews should be used.

258

Reference List: Every manuscript must include a list of references containing only those works cited. Each entry should contain all data necessary for unambiguous identification.

1. Arrange citations in alphabetical order according to surname of the first author or the name of the institution responsible for the citation.

2. Use authors' initials instead of proper names.

3. In listing more than one name in references (Rayburn, L., and B. Harrelson,...) there should always be a comma before "and."

4. Dates of publication should be placed immediately after authors' names.

5. Titles of journals should not be abbreviated.

6. Multiple works by the same author(s) should be listed in chronological order of publication. Two or more works by the same author(s) in the same year are distinguished by letters after the date.

Sample entries are as follows:

American Accounting Association, Committee on the Future, Content, and Scope of Accounting Education (The Bedford Committee). 1986. Future accounting education: Preparing for the expanding profession. *Issues in Accounting Education* (Spring): 168-195.

Ajzen, l:. 1987. Attitudes, traits, and actions: Dispostional prediction of behavior in personality and social psychology. In *Advances in Experimental Social* Psychology edited by L. Berkovitz, New York, NY: Academic Press.

Grizzle, J.E., C.F. Starmer, axed G:G. Koch, 1969. Analysis of categorical data by linear models. *Biometrics* 25: 489-504.

Notes: Notes are not to be used for documentation. As noted in a previous paragraph, textural notes should be used only for extensions and useful excursions of information that, if included in the body of the text, might disrupt its continuity.

Policy on Data Availability
Authors are encouraged to male their data available for use by others in extending or replicating results reported in their articles. Authors of articles which report data dependent results should footnote the status of data availability and, when pertinent, this should be accompanied by information on how the data nay be obtained.

Text Preparation on Disk
An electronic version on disk should be sent with the final accepted version of the paper to the Editor. The hard copy and electronic files must match exactly. All word processing packages are acceptable.

Page Proofs and Offprints
Page proofs of the article will be sent to the corresponding author. these should be carefully proofread. Except for typographical errors, corrections should be minimal, and rewriting of text is not permitted. Corrected page proofs must be returned with 48 hours of receipt.

Journal of Cost Management

ADDRESS FOR SUBMISSION:

Tony Powell, Managing Editor
Journal of Cost Management
Warren, Gorham & Lamont/ RIA Group
395 Hudson Street
New York, NY 10014
USA
Phone: 212-367-6374
Fax: 212-367-6718
E-Mail: tonypowell@riag.com
Web:
Address May Change:

PUBLICATION GUIDELINES:

Manuscript Length: 16-20
Copies Required: Three
Computer Submission: Yes
Format: MS Word
Fees to Review: 0.00 US$

Manuscript Style:
    Chicago Manual of Style

CIRCULATION DATA:

Reader: Business Persons
Frequency of Issue: Bi-Monthly
Copies per Issue: 5,001 - 10,000
Sponsor/Publisher: RIA Group
Subscribe Price: 195.00 US$

REVIEW INFORMATION:

Type of Review: Blind Review
No. of External Reviewers: 1
No. of In House Reviewers: 1
Acceptance Rate: 21-30%
Time to Review: 2 - 3 Months
Reviewers Comments: Yes
Invited Articles: 6-10%
Fees to Publish: 0.00 US$

MANUSCRIPT TOPICS:
Accounting Information Systems; Cost Accounting

MANUSCRIPT GUIDELINES/COMMENTS:

Manuscript Preparation
We welcome the submission of articles on any topic related to cost management. Case studies are also welcome. The article should be written with an eye toward aiding the reader in improving the financial and non-financial performance of his or her business using cost management techniques. For editorial inquiries, contact

Lawrence S. Maisel, Editor-in-Chief
Principal
Nextera/SIGMA Consulting Group
530 Willowbrook Office Park, Fairport, NY 14445
Tel. (716) 383-4100 Fax (914) 381-2750
e-mail: LSM33@AOL.COM

Manuscripts for publication, and correspondence relating to them, should be sent to Tony Powell, Managing Editor.

- While the utmost care will be given to all manuscripts submitted, we cannot accept responsibility for unsolicited manuscripts. Articles accepted for publication are subject to editorial revision.

- Articles must include a brief author bio and an Executive Summary. It is strongly suggested that articles end with a Conclusions paragraph.

- Articles must be submitted on diskette (WordPerfect 5.1 preferable), along with a hard copy. Articles should be double-spaced with liberal margins. Length should be 20 to 25 pages.

- Within your article, use many headings and subheadings to break up and emphasize your points. Type all headings flush with the left-hand margin. End notes are used, not footnotes.

- Illustrations and graphs (exhibits) accompanying manuscripts should be supplied in black laser-printed form. Typewritten or freehand lettering is not acceptable. All lettering must be typeset. Do not staple or paper clip illustrations. Put all illustrations between sheets of cardboard before mailing, to prevent folds.

- If you are reprinting in your article any previously copyrighted material, the publisher must have letters of permission to reprint from the copyright holder. These letters must be submitted together with the manuscript.

- Except in rare cases, *The Journal of Cost Management* only publishes articles if they have not yet appeared or been accepted for publication elsewhere. There is generally no objection, however, to having articles that appear in this publication reprinted in other publications at a later date if appropriate permission is requested from us at that time.

Style

- Contributors are writing for an audience with varying degrees of knowledge. Therefore, when addressing sophisticated or complex issues, the writing should be sufficiently clear and simple to be useful to nonexperts. Assume that some readers will *not* have specific knowledge of the particular topic being discusses. All readers, whether expert or not, do need guidance on relatively complex questions and, at times, on the more basic ones.

- Each article requires a strong organizational structure. Be sure to state the main point(s) of the article at the outset rather than at the end. Avoid unnecessary modifiers and qualifying phrases. Always choose the simplest word that is accurate.

- Illustrate the concepts presented in the article with narrative or dollars-and-cents examples, step-by-step checklists, sidebars, and charts. These devices help readers apply the advice and make it easier for them to grasp the concepts.

- Headings should be as short, while still guiding the reader through the discussion.

- Use sidebars to break up the text and enhance your article. Sidebars can highlight additional information; explain a concept further; offer tips, suggestions, and cautions; compare advantages disadvantages; and present checklists. Sidebars can also contain information that is useful to the reader but does not fit into the organizational structure of your article.

Journal of Deferred Compensation: Non-Qualified Plans & Exec. Compensation

ADDRESS FOR SUBMISSION:

Bruce J. McNeil, Editor-In-Chief
Journal of Deferred Compensation: Non-
    Qualified Plans & Exec. Compensation
Dorsey and Whitney, LLP
Pillsbury Center South
220 South Sixth Street
Minneapolis, MN 55402-1498
USA
Phone: 612-340-5640
Fax: 612-340-7800
E-Mail: mcneil.bruce@dorseylaw.com
Web:
Address May Change:

PUBLICATION GUIDELINES:

Manuscript Length: 21-25
Copies Required: Two
Computer Submission: No
Format: N/A
Fees to Review: 0.00 US$

Manuscript Style:
    See Manuscript Guidelines

CIRCULATION DATA:

Reader: Business Persons
Frequency of Issue: Quarterly
Copies per Issue: 1,001 - 2,000
Sponsor/Publisher: Panel Publishers, a
    division of Aspen Publishers, Inc.
Subscribe Price: 164.00 US$

REVIEW INFORMATION:

Type of Review: Editorial Review
No. of External Reviewers: 2
No. of In House Reviewers: No Reply
Acceptance Rate: 65%
Time to Review: 1 Month or Less
Reviewers Comments: Yes
Invited Articles: 21-30%
Fees to Publish: 0.00 US$

MANUSCRIPT TOPICS:
Employee Benefits; Government & Non Profit Accounting; Insurance; Tax Accounting

MANUSCRIPT GUIDELINES/COMMENTS:

Journal of Deferred Compensation (JDC) is devoted to providing practical information and ideas to professionals who deal with the tax, legal, and business planning aspects of nonqualified plans and executive compensation.

JDC emphasizes quality and clarity of exposition. Reviewers consider the following criteria in assessing submissions: value of the information to the journal's audience, substantive contribution to the broadly defined field of nonqualified plans and executive compensation, and overall quality of manuscript. The decision to publish a given manuscript is made by the Editor-in-Chief, relying on the recommendations of the reviewers.

Submission of a manuscript clearly implies commitment to publish in the journal. Papers previously published or under review by other journals are unacceptable. Articles adapted from book-length works-in-progress will be considered under acceptable copyright arrangements.

Manuscript Specifications

Manuscripts submitted for publication should not exceed 40 typewritten pages; the publisher encourages submission of shorter papers. All textual material notes and references must be double-spaced in a full-size non-proportional typeface (e.g., 12 pt. Courier), on one side only a 8 ½ x 11" good quality paper, with 1 ½" margins all around. All pages must be numbered. Notes and references must be placed separately, double-spaced, as endnotes.

Within the article, use short subheadings for organization and emphasis. Include a cover sheet with title, author's address and affiliations, mailing address, and phone and fax numbers.

Artwork, including tables, charts and graphs, must be of camera-ready quality. Each should be on a separate page placed at the end of the text, with proper placement indicated within text (e.g., "Insert Table 2 here")

Three high-quality copies of the manuscript should be submitted to the Editor-in-Chief. Include a biographical statement of 50 words or less.

Acceptance

Once an article has been formally accepted, the author must submit the article to the publisher in two formats: three high-quality manuscript copies and a WordPerfect 5.1 or ASCII computer file on 3 ½" floppy diskette labeled with the file type and name, software version, article title, and author's name. No other software is acceptable.

The publisher retains copyright and articles are subject to editorial revision. There is no payment for articles: authors receive five copies of the issue in which the article is published. Manuscripts not accepted for publication are not returned. Authors should keep a copy of any submission for their files.

Manuscript submissions and inquiries should be directed to:

For business and production matters, contact

Bruce J. McNeil, Editor-in-Chief
Journal of Deferred Compensation
Pillsbury Center South
220 South Sixth Street
Minneapolis, Minnesota 55402-1498
Tel: (612) 340-5640
Fax: (612) 340-7800
mcneil.bruce@dorseylaw.com

Panel Publishers, Inc.
36 West 44th Street
New York, NY 10036
212-354-4545

Journal of International Accounting Auditing & Taxation

ADDRESS FOR SUBMISSION:

Kathleen E. Sinning, Editor
Journal of International Accounting
    Auditing & Taxation
Western Michigan University
3182 Haworth College of Business
Kalamazoo, MI 49008-3899
USA
Phone: 616-387-5259
Fax: 616-387-5710
E-Mail: kathleen.sinning@wmich.edu
Web:
Address May Change:

PUBLICATION GUIDELINES:

Manuscript Length: 21-25
Copies Required: Three
Computer Submission: No
Format: N/A
Fees to Review: 25.00 US$

Manuscript Style:
    See Manuscript Guidelines

CIRCULATION DATA:

Reader: Business Persons, Academics
Frequency of Issue: 2 Times/ Year
Copies per Issue: Less than 1,000
Sponsor/Publisher: Elsevier Science
    Publishing Co
Subscribe Price: 85.00 US$ Individual
    242.00 US$ Institution

REVIEW INFORMATION:

Type of Review: Blind Review
No. of External Reviewers: 2
No. of In House Reviewers: 0
Acceptance Rate: 21-30%
Time to Review: 2 - 3 Months
Reviewers Comments: Yes
Invited Articles: 0-5%
Fees to Publish: 0.00 US$

MANUSCRIPT TOPICS:
Accounting Information Systems; Accounting Theory & Practice; Auditing; Cost Accounting; Government & Non Profit Accounting; International Accounting; Tax Accounting

MANUSCRIPT GUIDELINES/COMMENTS:

Philosophy of the Journal
The *Journal Of International Accounting, Auditing, And Taxation* publishes articles that deal with all areas of international accounting, including auditing, taxation and management advisory services. The journal's goal is to bridge the gap between academic researchers and practitioners by publishing readable papers with a practical emphasis that are relevant to the development of the field of accounting.

Critiques of current practices and the measurement and reporting of their effects on business decisions, general purpose solutions to problems through tax models, essays on world affairs which affect accounting practice, and applied research findings of interest to both academics and practitioners are within the scope of the journal.

Manuscript Guidelines and Editorial Policy

1. Manuscripts should be typewritten and double-spaced on 8 1/2" by 11" white paper. To help process accepted papers, a word processing program that is able to create an IBM compatible ASCII file should be used.

2. A separate title page must be included which indicates the author's name, address, affiliation, telephone number, e-mail address, and any acknowledgments. This information should not appear on any other page.

3. A separate abstract page should include the title of the manuscript, an abstract that does not exceed 200 words, and key words for referencing. The abstract should include a statement of the purpose of the manuscript, the methods used, and the major results, conclusions, and recommendations.

4. Topical headings should be in caps and centered. Subheadings should be flush with the left margin. Only the not be numbered. All pages should be numbered in the upper right hand corner except the title page first letter of each word in the subheading should be capitalized. Headings and subheadings should, abstract page, and page one of the manuscript.

5. Tables, figures and exhibits should appear on separate pages. Each should be numbered with Arabic numerals and have an appropriate title. The tables and exhibits should be included in the manuscript after the Reference page. Indicate in the text where the tables should be located by noting:
[Table 1 About Here]

6. Explanatory notes should be limited but when necessary, should appear on a separate page titled Notes. The Notes page should be placed before the Reference page.

7. References should be cited in the text by including in parentheses the last names of the authors, date of publication, and page number(s), if appropriate. The References page should include only works actually cited in the text and should list the cited works in alphabetical order. The following format should be used for references:

O'Connor, W.F. 1992. A comparative analysis of the major areas of tax controversy in developed countries. Journal of International Accounting Auditing and Taxation 1: 61-79.

Schweikart, J., S. Gray and C. Roberts (eds). 1994. International Accounting - Case Approach. New York, NY: McGraw-Hill.

8. Manuscripts currently under review by other publications or manuscripts that have been published should not be submitted. A statement to that effect should be included in the cover letter accompanying the submission.

9. Submit three (3) copies of the manuscript and research instrument and a check made payable to JIAAT for the $25 non-refundable submission fee to Kathleen E. Sinning, Editor (See Address for Submission).

Journal of International Taxation

ADDRESS FOR SUBMISSION:

Robert Gallagher, Managing Editor
Journal of International Taxation
Warren, Gorham & Lamont/RIA Group
395 Hudson Street
New York, NY 10014
USA
Phone: 212-807-2193
Fax: 212-337-4183
E-Mail: rgallagher@riag.com
Web: www.riatax.com/journals
Address May Change:

CIRCULATION DATA:

Reader: , International Tax Accountants
Frequency of Issue: Monthly
Copies per Issue: 2,001 - 3,000
Sponsor/Publisher: N/A
Subscribe Price: 290.00 US$
  380.00 US$ Overseas

PUBLICATION GUIDELINES:

Manuscript Length: 21-25
Copies Required: One
Computer Submission: Yes
Format: Word, WordPerfect
Fees to Review: 0.00 US$

Manuscript Style:
  See Manuscript Guidelines

REVIEW INFORMATION:

Type of Review: Editorial Review
No. of External Reviewers: 0
No. of In House Reviewers: 1
Acceptance Rate: 50% +
Time to Review: 1 Month or Less
Reviewers Comments: No
Invited Articles: 50% +
Fees to Publish: 0.00 US$

MANUSCRIPT TOPICS:

Economic Development; Fiscal Policy; International Economics & Trade; International Finance; Tax Accounting; U.S./Foreign Tax Provisions

MANUSCRIPT GUIDELINES/COMMENTS:

1. We welcome the submission of articles offering practical information and ideas on tax planning for U.S. entities and individuals engaging in international transactions and foreign entities and individuals engaging in U.S. transactions. Articles should focus on matters of importance to practitioners and provide practical information on tax, legal, and business aspects affecting such taxpayers and transactions. Manuscripts for publication, and correspondence relating to them, should be sent to the Managing Editor.

2. All articles will be reviewed for acceptance by our Editor-in-Chief, or the Journal's Board of Advisors.

3. Articles should be submitted in one hardcopy version (typed, double-spaced, 81/2" x 11") and one electronic version, either via e-mail or diskette, preferably WordPerfect. Length should be 15-35 double-spaced typed pages.

4. Within the article, please use some headings and subheadings to break up and emphasize your points. Type all headings flush with the left-hand margin, all capital letters for main headings but not secondary headings.

It is not necessary to use codes for different fonts, justification, line spacing, margin changes, tab settings, etc., as these will be deleted in the editorial process.

5. Footnotes and reference citations should generally follow the examples shown below.

1   Wyndelts and Fowler, "Avoiding Allocations to Goodwill Under the Asset-Acquisition Rules," 71 JTAX 392 (December 1989).

2   Bush Bros and Co., 87 TC 424 (1982), aff'd 670 F.2d 819 (CA-6, 1984), cert. den.

3   Morgenstern, 56 TC 44 (1971).

4   Rev. Rul. 75-223, 1975-1 CB 109; Rev. Rul. 89-121, 1999-47 IRB 25.

5   Hodel v. Va. Surface Mining and Reclamation Ass'n, 483 F. Supp. 425 (DC Ala., 1980).

6   H.R. 1313, 97th Cong., 1st Sess. § 11601 (1981).

7   H. Rep't No. 99-313, 99th Cong., 2d Sess. 719 (1987).

8   Temp. Reg. 1.132-5T(e).

9   GCM 38481, 3/5/81.

10 TD 8115, 12/16/86.

6. If you are reprinting in your article any previously copyrighted material other than short quotations, the publisher must have letters of permission to reprint from the copyright holder and from the author if he is not the copyright holder. These letters must be submitted at the same time as the manuscript.

7. Articles and columns published in *The Journal of International Taxation* will be copyrighted by the Publisher, which retains all reproduction, translation, and distribution rights in any media, including electronic reproduction, Except in rare instances, *The Journal of International Taxation* not yet appeared or been accepted for publication elsewhere. There is generally no objection to having articles that appear in *The Journal of International Taxation* reprinted in other publications at a later date if appropriate permission is requested from us at that time.

Journal of Libertarian Studies

ADDRESS FOR SUBMISSION:

Hans-Hermann Hoppe, Editor
Journal of Libertarian Studies
Mises Institute
518 West Magnolia Avenue
Auburn, AL 36832-4528
USA
Phone: 702-845-3227
Fax: 702-369-9469
E-Mail: hoppeh@nevada.edu
Web:
Address May Change:

PUBLICATION GUIDELINES:

Manuscript Length: 16-25
Copies Required: Three
Computer Submission: Yes
Format: No Reply
Fees to Review: 0.00 US$

Manuscript Style:
      Chicago Manual of Style

CIRCULATION DATA:

Reader: Academics, Educated Laymen,
   Professionals
Frequency of Issue: Quarterly
Copies per Issue: 1,001 - 2,000
Sponsor/Publisher: Ludwig von Mises
   Institute, Auburn, AL
Subscribe Price: 29.00 US$

REVIEW INFORMATION:

Type of Review: Blind Review
No. of External Reviewers: 2
No. of In House Reviewers: 2
Acceptance Rate: 6-10%
Time to Review: 1 - 2 Months
Reviewers Comments: Yes if reviewers
   agree
Invited Articles: 0-5%
Fees to Publish: 0.00 US$

MANUSCRIPT TOPICS:

Economic History; Fiscal Policy; Government & Non Profit Accounting; Industrial
Organization; Insurance; International Economics & Trade; International Finance; Macro
Economics; Micro Economics; Monetary Policy; Philosophical Issues

MANUSCRIPT GUIDELINES/COMMENTS:

The *Journal Of Libertarian Studies* will publish scholarly work in philosophy, political
science, economics, history, law, sociology, geography, anthropology, education and biology,
as it pertains to libertarianism. Whether or not the scholar is personally a libertarian will not
be a criterion for acceptance of a manuscript; rather, the criterion will be whether an article
will advance the discipline of libertarianism, regardless of the personal beliefs of the author.

Journal of Management Accounting Research

ADDRESS FOR SUBMISSION:

Anthony A. Atkinson, Editor
Journal of Management Accounting
   Research
University of Waterloo
School of Accountancy
, N2L 3G1
Canada
Phone: 519-888-4567 ext. 6510
Fax: 519-888-7562
E-Mail: aatkinson@uwaterloo.ca
Web:
Address May Change: 12/31/00

PUBLICATION GUIDELINES:

Manuscript Length: 16-20
Copies Required: Three
Computer Submission: No
Format: N/A
Fees to Review: 50.00 US$

Manuscript Style:
   Chicago Manual of Style

CIRCULATION DATA:

Reader: Academics
Frequency of Issue: Yearly
Copies per Issue: No Reply
Sponsor/Publisher: American Accounting
   Association/ Management Accounting
   Section
Subscribe Price: No Reply

REVIEW INFORMATION:

Type of Review: Blind Review
No. of External Reviewers: 2
No. of In House Reviewers: 0
Acceptance Rate: 0-5%
Time to Review: 2 - 3 Months
Reviewers Comments: Yes
Invited Articles: 0-5%
Fees to Publish: 0.00 US$

MANUSCRIPT TOPICS:
Cost Accounting; Management Accounting

MANUSCRIPT GUIDELINES/COMMENTS:

Editorial Policy
The Management Accounting Section of the American Accounting Association publishes the Journal of Management Accounting Research (JMAR). Its objective is to contribute to improving the theory and practice of management accounting by promoting high-quality applied and theoretical research. The primary audience for this publication is the membership of the Management Accounting Section of the American Accounting Association and other individuals interested in management accounting.

"Management Accounting" for purposes of this publication is to be broadly conceived. We will publish papers involving a variety of topics, settings, and research methods. The research methods used in papers submitted for publication may be analytical or empirical. We invite manuscripts related to internal reporting and decision making, the interface between internal and external reporting, profit and not-for-profit organizations, service and manufacturing organizations and domestic, foreign and multi-national organizations. New theories, topical areas, and research methods are encouraged.

As a publication of the American Accounting Association, the high standards applicable to the journals of the Association will be maintained. For a manuscript to be acceptable for publication, the research question should be of interest to the intended readership, the research should be well designed and well executed, and the material should be presented effectively and efficiently.

Review Process
Each paper submitted to JMAR is subject to the following review procedures:

1. The Editor will review the paper for general suitability for this publication.
2. For those papers that are judged suitable, a detailed blind review by two reviewers takes place.
3. Using the recommendations of the reviewers, the Editor will decide whether the particular paper should be accepted as is, revised, or rejected for publication.

The process described above is a general process. In any particular case, deviations may occur from the steps described.

Submission of Manuscripts
Authors should note the following guidelines for submitting manuscripts:

1. Manuscripts currently under consideration by another journal or other publisher should not be submitted. The author must state that the work is not submitted or published elsewhere.
2. Where firm- or organization-specific data released by a firm or organization are used in a manuscript, a signed release allowing identification of any person(s) or organization(s) in the manuscript must accompany the manuscript.
3. Four copies should be submitted together with a check for $50 in U.S. funds made payable to the American Accounting Association. Submissions should be sent to Anthony A. Atkinson, School of Accountancy, University of Waterloo, Waterloo, Ontario N2L 361 CANADA. The submission fee is non-refundable.
4. The author should retain a copy of the paper.
5. In the case of manuscripts reporting on field surveys or experiments, 4 copies of the instrument (questionnaire, case, interview plan, or the like), must be submitted.
6. Revisions must be submitted within 12 months from request, otherwise they will be considered new submissions.

Manuscripts not conforming to these guidelines will be returned to the author.

Comments
The journal does not have a regular section for Comments. Authors who wish to comment on articles previously published in JMAR should first communicate directly with the author(s) of the original article to eliminate any misunderstandings or misconceptions. If substantive issues still remain after the written exchange of views with the author(s), the Commentator may submit to JMAR the residue of the proposed Comment. Four copies of the correspondence

between the Commentator and the author(s) of the original article should be submitted to the Editor together with four copies of the comment manuscript. All other editorial norms also apply to proposed Comments.

Manuscript Preparation and Style

The *Journal of Management Accounting Research's* manuscript preparation guidelines follow (with a slight modification) documentation 2 of the *Chicago Manual of Style* (14th ed.; University of Chicago Press). Another helpful guide to usage and style is *The Elements of Style,* by William Strunk, Jr., and E. B. White (Macmillan). Spelling follows *Webster's International Dictionary.*

Format

1. Manuscripts should be typed on one side of 8 1/2 x 11" good quality paper and be double-spaced, except for indented quotations.

2. Manuscripts should be as concise as the subject and research method permit, generally not to exceed 7,000 words.

3. Margins should be at least one inch from top, bottom, and sides to facilitate editing and duplication.

4. To assure anonymous review, authors should not identify themselves directly or indirectly in their papers. Single authors should not use the editorial "we."

5. A cover page should include the title of the paper, the author's name, title and affiliation, any acknowledgments, and a footnote indicating whether the author would be willing to share the data (see last paragraph in this statement).

6. All pages, including tables, appendices and references, should be serially numbered.

7. Spell out numbers from one to ten, except when used in tables and lists, and when used with mathematical, statistical, scientific or technical units and quantities, such as distances, weights and measures. For example: *three days; 3 kilometers; 30 years.* All other numbers are expressed numerically.

8. In nontechnical text use the word *percent;* in technical text the symbol % is used. (See. the *Chicago Manual* for discussion of the correct usage.)

9.   a. Use a hyphen (-) to join unit modifiers or to clarify usage. For example: a well-presented analysis; re-form. See *Webster's* for correct usage.

   b. En dash (-) is used between words indicating a duration, such as hourly time or months or years. No space on either side.

   c. Em dash (-) is used to indicate an abrupt change in thought, or where a period is too strong and a comma is too weak. No space on either side.

10. The following will be Roman in all cases: i.e., e.g., ibid., et al., op. cit.

11. Initials: A. B. Smith (space between); States, etc.,. U.S., U.K. (no space between).

12. When using "Big 6" or "Big 8," use Arabic figures (don't spell out).

13. Ellipsis should be used not periods, example ... not.

14. Use "SAS No. #" not "SAS #"

15. Use only one space after periods, colons, exclamation points, question marks, quotation marks -any punctuation that separates two sentences.

16.   a. Use real quotation marks-never inch marks: use " and N' not " and."

   b. Use real apostrophes, not the foot marks: use not

17. Punctuation used with quote marks:

18. a.Commas and periods are always placed inside the quotation marks.

b.Colons and semicolons go outside the quotation marks.

c.Question marks and exclamation points go in or out, depending on whether they belong to the material inside the quote. If they belong to the quoted material, they go inside the quote marks, and vice versa.

19. Punctuation and parentheses: Sentence punctuation goes after the closing parentheses if what is inside the parentheses is part of the sentence (as is this phrase). This also applies to commas, semicolons and colons. If what is inside the parentheses is an entire statement of its own, the ending punctuation should also be inside the parentheses.

20. Headings should be arranged so those major headings are centered, bold and capitalized. Second level headings should be flush left, bold and both upper and lowercase. Third level headings should be flush left, bold, italic and both upper and lower case. Fourth level headings should be paragraph indent, bold and lower case. Headings and subheadings should not be numbered. For example:

A CENTERED, BOLD, ALL CAPITALIZED, FIRST LEVEL HEADING

A Flush Left, Bold, Upper and Lower Case, Second Level Heading

A Flush Left, Bold, Italic, Upper crud Lower Case, Third Level Heading

A paragraph indent, bold, lower case, fourth level heading. Text starts....

Abstract
An abstract of no more than 150 words should be presented on a separate page immediately preceding the text. The abstract should be nonmathematical and include a readable summary of the research question, method and the significance of the findings and contribution. The title, but not the author's name or other identification designations, should appear on the abstract page.

Tables and Figures
The author should note the following general requirements:

1.Each table and figure (graphic) should appear on a separate page and should be placed at the end of the text. Each should bear an Arabic number and a complete title indicating the exact contents of the table or figure.

2.A reference to each table or figure should be made in the text.

3.The author should indicate by marginal notation where each table or figure should be inserted in the text, e.g., (Insert Table X here).

4.Tables or figures should be reasonably interpreted without reference to the text.

5.Source lines and notes should be included as necessary.

6.When information is not available, use "NA" capitalized with no slash between.

7.Figures must be prepared in a form suitable for printing.

Mathematical notation should be employed only where its rigor and precision are necessary, and in such circumstances authors should explain in the narrative format the principal operations performed. Notation should be avoided in footnotes. Unusual symbols, particularly if hand-written, should be identified in the margin when they first appear. Displayed material should clearly indicate the alignment, superscripts and subscripts. Equations should be numbered in parentheses flush with the right-hand margin.

Documentation

Citations: Work cited should use the "author-date system" keyed to a list of works in the reference list (see below). Authors should make an effort to include the relevant page numbers in the cited works.

1. In the text, works are cited as follows: author's last name and date, without comma, In parentheses: for example, (Jones 1987); with two authors: (Jones and Freeman 1973); with more than two: (Jones et al. 1985); with more than one source cited together (Jones 1987; Freeman 1986); with two or more works by one author: (Jones 1985, 1987)

2. Unless confusion would result, do not use "p." or "pp." before page numbers:for example, (Jones 1987,115).

3.When the reference list contains more than one work of an author published in the same year, the suffix a, b, etc. follows the date in the text citation: for example, (Jones 1987x) or (Jones 1987x; Freeman 1985b).

4. If an author's name Is mentioned in the text, It need not be repeated in the citation; for example, "Jones (1987, 115) says ....

5.Citations to institutional works should use acronyms or short titles where practicable: for example, (AAA ASOBAT 1966); (AICPA *Cohen Commission Report* 1977). Where brief, the full title of an institutional work might be shown in a citation: for example, (ICAEW *The Corporate Report* 1975).

6.If the manuscript refers to statutes, legal treatises, or court cases, citations acceptable in law reviews should be used.

Reference List: Every manuscript must include a list of references containing only those works cited. Each entry should contain all data necessary for unambiguous identification. With the author-date system, use the following format recommended by the *Chicago Manual:*

1.Arrange citations in alphabetical order according to surname of the first author or the name of the institution responsible for the citation.
2.Use author's initials instead of proper names.
3.In listing more than one name in references (Rayburn, L., and B. Harrelson) there should always be a comma before "and."
4.Dates of publication should be placed immediately after authors' names.
5.Titles of journals should not be abbreviated.
6.Multiple works by the same author(s) should be listed in chronological order of publication. Two or more works by the same author(s) in the same year are distinguished by letters after the date.

275

Sample entries are as follows:

American Accounting Association, Committee on Concepts and Standards for External Financial Reports. 1977. *Statement on Accounting Theory and Theory Acceptance.* Sarasota, *FL:* AAA.

Banker, R., G. Potter, and R. Schroeder. 1992. An empirical study of manufacturing overhead cost drivers. Working paper, University of Minnesota.

Berliner, C., and J. A. Brimson, eds. 1988. *Cost Management for Today's Advanced Manufacturing: The CAM-1 Conceptual Design.* Boston, MA: Harvard Business School Press.

Cooper, R. 1987a. The two-stage procedure in cost accounting: Part one. *Journal of Cost Management* (Summer): 43-51.

_____, 1987b. The two-stage procedure in cost accounting: Part two. *Journal of Cost Management* (Fall): 39-45

Einhorn, H. J., and R. Hogarth. 1981. Behavioral decision theory: Processes of judgment and choice. *Journal of Accounting Research* 19 (1): 1-31.

Horngren, C. T. 1962. Choosing accounting practices for reporting to management. *N.A.A. Bulletin* 19 (September): 3-15.

Kaplan, R. S. 1985. Accounting lag: The obsolescence of cost accounting systems. In *The Uneasy Alliance: Managing the Productivity-Technology Dilemma,* edited by K. Clark, R. Hayes, and C. Lorenz, 195-226. Boston, MA: Harvard Business School Press.

Takeuchi, H., and J. A. Queich. 1983. Quality is more than making a good product. *Harvard Business Review* 61:139-145.

Footnotes: Footnotes are not used for documentation. Textual footnotes should be used only for extensions and useful excursions of information that if included in the body of the text might disrupt its continuity. Footnotes should be consecutively numbered throughout the manuscript with superscript Arabic numerals. Footnote text should be double-spaced and placed at the end of the article.

Policy on Reproductions

The objective of JMAR is to promote wide dissemination of the results of theoretical and applied research and other scholarly inquiries into the broad field of managementaccounting.

Permission is hereby granted to reproduce any of the contents of JMAR for use in courses of instruction, so long as the source and American Accounting Association copyright are indicated in any such reproductions.

Written application must be made to the Editor for permission to reproduce any of the contents of JMAR for use in other than courses of Instruction - e.g., inclusion in books of readings or in other publications Intended for general distribution. In consideration for the grant of permission by JMAR in such instances, the applicant must notify the author(s) in writing of the Intended use to be made of each reproduction. Normally, JMAR will not assess a charge for the waiver of copyright.

Except where otherwise noted in articles, the copyright interest has been transferred to the American Accounting Association. Where the author(s) has (have) not transferred the copyright to the Association, applicants must seek permission to reproduce (for all purposes) directly from the author(s).

Policy on Data Availability
The following policy, adopted by the Executive Committee of the AAA in April 1989, is applicable to all manuscripts submitted to *JMAR:*

...authors are encouraged to make their data available for use by others ....
Authors of articles that report data dependent results should footnote the
status of data availability and, when pertinent, this should be accompanied
by information on how the data may be obtained.

Journal of Public Budgeting, Accounting & Financial Management

ADDRESS FOR SUBMISSION:

Dr. Khi V. Thai, Editor
Journal of Public Budgeting, Accounting &
   Financial Management
Florida Atlantic University
University Tower
221 S.E. Second Avenue
Fort Lauderdale, FL 33301
USA
Phone: 954-762-7635
Fax: 954-762-5693
E-Mail: thai@fau.edu
Web:
Address May Change:

PUBLICATION GUIDELINES:

Manuscript Length: 20+
Copies Required: Three
Computer Submission: No
Format: N/A
Fees to Review: 0.00 US$

Manuscript Style:
   American Psychological Association

CIRCULATION DATA:

Reader: Academics
Frequency of Issue: Quarterly
Copies per Issue: Less than 1,000
Sponsor/Publisher: Academic Press, Inc./
   Florida Atlantic University
Subscribe Price: 275.00 US$ Library

REVIEW INFORMATION:

Type of Review: Blind Review
No. of External Reviewers: 3
No. of In House Reviewers: 0
Acceptance Rate: 6-10%
Time to Review: 2 - 3 Months
Reviewers Comments: Yes
Invited Articles: 21-30%
Fees to Publish: 0.00 US$

MANUSCRIPT TOPICS:

Fiscal Policy; Government & Non Profit Accounting; International Finance; Monetary Policy;
Public Budgeting; Public Policy Economics; Tax Accounting

MANUSCRIPT GUIDELINES/COMMENTS:

Editorial Policy

Published four times a year, *Public Budgeting and Financial Management* is a refereed
journal, which aims at advancement and dissemination of research in the field of public
budgeting and financial management. The journal concentrates on the development of theories
and concepts so that the field's boundaries can be established. The cognate areas constituting
the focus of this publication are disciplines that concern how a budget is prepared, decided
and implemented.

278

Practitioners and scholars are encouraged to submit manuscripts to the journal. Papers—whether empirical, field study, or conceptual—should help to serve the need for more active communication and greater exchange of thought, research and practical experiences among scholars and practitioners throughout the world. Appropriate topics for papers include various aspects of public budgeting and financial management such as (a) governmental accounting and financial reporting; (b) politics of budgeting, budgetary process and techniques; public financial management including cash management, risk management, debt management; (d) tax and expenditure policies, and (e) other issues related to governmental accounting, budgeting, financial management and fiscal policies.

Priority will be given to papers having carefully developed methods, insightful conceptual development, and practical and analytical solutions to government financial management problems. Interdisciplinary approaches are welcome.

Directions For Submission
1. Three (3) copies of the manuscript must be submitted to the Editor.

2. A cover letter must accompany each submission indicating the name, address, telephone number, and fax number of the corresponding author.

3. Only original papers will be accepted, and copyright of published papers will be vested in the publisher. The general format of the manuscript should be as follows: title of article, names of author, abstract, and text discussion.

4. The abstract should not have more than 100 words. Whenever possible, the text discussion should be divided into such major sections as **introduction, methods, results, discussion, acknowledgments, and references**. Manuscripts should be submitted typed, double-spaced, on one side only. The entire typing area on the title page should be four and one-half inches wide by five and one-half inches long. The major headings should be separated from the text by two lines of space above and one line of space below. Each heading should be in capital letters, centered, and in bold. Secondary headings, if any, should be flush with the left margin, in bold characters, and have the first letter of all main words capitalized. Leave two lines of space above and one line of space below secondary headings. All manuscripts should be left- and right-hand margin justified.

Acknowledgments of collaboration, sources of research funds, and address changes for an author should be listed in a separate section at the end of the paper after the section on References.
Explanatory Footnotes should be kept to a minimum and be numbered consecutively throughout the text and aggregated in sequence under the heading **notes**, at the end of the text but before **references**.
References should be in the APA manuscript style of citation, and aggregated in the alphabetical order at the end of the manuscript under the heading, **References**.

5. For detailed guidelines, please contact the editorial office at the above address.

Journal of Real Estate Taxation

ADDRESS FOR SUBMISSION:

Catherine Graff, Editor
Journal of Real Estate Taxation
RIA Group
395 Hudson Street
New York, NY 10014
USA
Phone: 212-807-2194
Fax: 212-337-4207
E-Mail: c.graff@riag.com
Web:
Address May Change:

PUBLICATION GUIDELINES:

Manuscript Length: 20+
Copies Required: Three
Computer Submission: Yes
Format: N/A
Fees to Review: 0.00 US$

Manuscript Style:
    Chicago Manual of Style

CIRCULATION DATA:

Reader: , Lawyers & Accountants
Frequency of Issue: Quarterly
Copies per Issue: 4,001 - 5,000
Sponsor/Publisher: RIA Group
Subscribe Price: 130.00 US$

REVIEW INFORMATION:

Type of Review: N/A
No. of External Reviewers: 1
No. of In House Reviewers: 1
Acceptance Rate: 21-30%
Time to Review: 2 - 3 Months
Reviewers Comments: Yes
Invited Articles: 31-50%
Fees to Publish: 0.00 US$

MANUSCRIPT TOPICS:
Federal Taxation of Real Estate; Real Estate

MANUSCRIPT GUIDELINES/COMMENTS:

Journal of State Taxation

ADDRESS FOR SUBMISSION:

James T. Collins, Editor-in-Chief
Journal of State Taxation
University of Wisconsin-Milwaukee
School of Business Administration
3210 North Maryland Avenue
Milwaukee, WI 53211
USA
Phone: 414-229-6642
Fax: 414-229-2265
E-Mail:
Web:
Address May Change:

PUBLICATION GUIDELINES:

Manuscript Length: 15-40
Copies Required: Three
Computer Submission: Yes with 3 hard
  copies
Format: MS Word 6.0, WdPerfect, DOS
Fees to Review: 0.00 US$

Manuscript Style:
  Chicago Manual of Style

CIRCULATION DATA:

Reader: Academics, Business Persons,
  CPA, Attorney, Gov't
Frequency of Issue: Quarterly
Copies per Issue: 1,001 - 2,000
Sponsor/Publisher: Panel Publishing
  Company
Subscribe Price: 185.00 US$

REVIEW INFORMATION:

Type of Review: Editorial Review
No. of External Reviewers: 1
No. of In House Reviewers: 1
Acceptance Rate: 50%
Time to Review: 1 - 2 Months
Reviewers Comments: No
Invited Articles: 6-10%
Fees to Publish: 0.00 US$

MANUSCRIPT TOPICS:
State and Local Taxation; Tax Accounting

MANUSCRIPT GUIDELINES/COMMENTS:

The *Journal of State Taxation* is devoted to articles that contribute to professional practice and provide timely analysis, creative strategies, and workable solutions to state tax problems. Articles should address tax strategies and tax legislation in a timely, up-to-date manner.

The Journal emphasizes quality and clarity of exposition. Reviewers will consider the following criteria in assessing potential contributions: the value of the information to the Journal's audience, the substantive contribution to the broadly defined field of state taxation, and the overall quality of the manuscript. The decision to publish a given manuscript is made by the Editor-in-Chief.

Submission of a manuscript implies a commitment to publish in the Journal. Previously published papers and papers under review by another journal are not acceptable. Articles for prior publication adapted from book-length works in progress will be considered, with attention given to the necessary copyright arrangements.

Manuscript Specifications. Manuscripts should not exceed 40 typewritten pages; the publisher also encourages the submission of shorter articles. All material should be double spaced, on one side only of 8 1/2" x 11" good-quality paper, with 1 1/2" margins left, right, top, and bottom. References should be double spaced and placed at the end of the text, on a separate page headed "References." Notes may be left embedded in the text, but they should be printed as double-spaced endnotes rather than footnotes. Improperly prepared manuscript will be returned to the author for prepreparation.

Within the article, use headings and subheadings to break up text and emphasize points; type them flush left. Number all pages of text. Contributors should attach a cover sheet giving title, author affiliation, current mailing address, fax number, and phone number. To ensure anonymity in the review of manuscripts, the first page of the text should show only the title of the manuscript at the top of the page. Each table or figure should be positioned on a separate page at the end of the article; point of insertion should be indicated at the proper place in text (e.g., "Table 2 about here").

Tables should be in whatever program the article was written in, preferably Microsoft Word. Graphs or charts must be submitted as separate files in either Microsoft Word or Microsoft Excel and in black and white only. Embedded graphs or charts that have been prepared in another software program cause significant problems, as the editor and compositor cannot access them in order to key in editorial changes. Authors who cannot use Word or Excel should do one of the following: (a) supply a laser copy of black-and-white artwork (note, however, that color copies cannot be scanned, and that changes cannot be made on laser copies); (b) submit a copy of the graph as well as the data points that were used to create it (the compositor cannot recreate the graphs without these data); (c) submit as PowerPoint documents (these must be saved as .GIF files).

Routing and Handling Submissions. Three high-quality copies of the manuscript should be submitted to the Editor-in-Chief (at address indicated below). An abstract of 125 to 150 words and a biographical statement of no more than 50 words written in the third person, each one on a separate page, should accompany the manuscript.

Acceptance. Once an article has been formally accepted by the Editor-in-Chief, the author must submit the article to the publisher in two formats: three high-quality manuscript copies should accompany a disk, preferably in MS Word 6.0 (WordPerfect DOS or Windows files are also acceptable). Each disk must be labeled with software program and version, file name, author name, article title, and journal title.

The copyright will be retained by the publisher. Articles are subject to editorial revision. There is no payment for articles; authors receive ten copies of the issue in which their article is published.

Manuscripts not accepted for publication will not be returned. Authors are advised to keep the original copies of their manuscripts for their files.

282

Manuscripts submitted for publication and inquiries about the suitability of a manuscript should be addressed to James T. Collins, Editor-in-Chief.

For business and production matters, contact the Managing Editor:

Joel L. Bromberg
Panel Publishers, Inc.
1185 Avenue of the Americas, 37th Floor
New York, NY 10036
(212) 597-0200 ext. 373
jbromnberg@ aspenpubl.com

Journal of Taxation

ADDRESS FOR SUBMISSION:

Joseph I. Kraf, Editor
Journal of Taxation
RIA Group
395 Hudson Street
New York, NY 10014
USA
Phone: 212-337-2195
Fax: 212-337-4186
E-Mail: jtaxn@riag.com
Web:
Address May Change:

PUBLICATION GUIDELINES:

Manuscript Length: 16 - 25
Copies Required: One
Computer Submission: Required
Format: WordPerfect
Fees to Review: 0.00 US$

Manuscript Style:
    See Manuscript Guidelines

CIRCULATION DATA:

Reader: , Tax Accountants, Tax Attorneys
Frequency of Issue: Monthly
Copies per Issue: 10,001 - 25,000
Sponsor/Publisher: RIA Group
Subscribe Price: 215.00 US$

REVIEW INFORMATION:

Type of Review: Editorial Review
No. of External Reviewers: 1
No. of In House Reviewers: 1
Acceptance Rate: 45%
Time to Review: 1 Month or Less
Reviewers Comments: No
Invited Articles: 50% +
Fees to Publish: 0.00 US$

MANUSCRIPT TOPICS:

Federal Taxation; Generation-Skipping Transfer Tax; Gift, Income, or Estate Taxation; State and Local Taxation; Tax Accounting

MANUSCRIPT GUIDELINES/COMMENTS:

Articles are written by sophisticated tax professionals (lawyers and accountants) for their colleagues, and should have a practical orientation.

Exclusive submission required.

Journal of the American Taxation Association

ADDRESS FOR SUBMISSION:

Frances Ayres, Editor
Journal of the American Taxation
   Association
University of Oklahoma
Michael F. Price College of Business
School of Accounting
Norman, OK 73019-4004
USA
Phone: 405-325-5768
Fax: 405-325-7348
E-Mail: fayres@ou.ed
Web:
Address May Change:

PUBLICATION GUIDELINES:

Manuscript Length: Under 35
Copies Required: Three
Computer Submission: No
Format: N/A
Fees to Review: 25.00 US$

Manuscript Style:
    See Manuscript Guidelines

CIRCULATION DATA:

Reader: Academics
Frequency of Issue: 2 Times/ Year
Copies per Issue: 1,001 - 2,000
Sponsor/Publisher: American Taxation
   Association
Subscribe Price: 10.00 US$
    85.00 US$ Member/AAA & ATA
    40.00 US$ 2 Years/Library, Inst.

REVIEW INFORMATION:

Type of Review: Blind Review
No. of External Reviewers: 2
No. of In House Reviewers: 0
Acceptance Rate: 11-20%
Time to Review: 2 - 3 Months
Reviewers Comments: Yes
Invited Articles: 0-5%
Fees to Publish: 0.00 US$

MANUSCRIPT TOPICS:
Fiscal Policy; Tax Accounting; Taxation

MANUSCRIPT GUIDELINES/COMMENTS:

Editorial Policy
JATA solicits unpublished manuscripts not currently under consideration by another journal or publisher. Papers presented in connection with a formal program (regional or national) of the American Taxation Association, American Accounting Association, or similar organizations or societies may be submitted provided the manuscript does not appear in whole or in part (other than a brief abstract) in the proceedings of the event. Reference to its presentation should be made on the manuscript's title page at the time of submission. Transmittal letters should include a statement that the manuscript or a similar one has not been published and is not, nor will be, under consideration for publication elsewhere while being reviewed by JATA. In addition, the authors must notify the Editor and include an explanation if any of the results contained in the submitted research have been, or will be, reported in another publication.

JATA is a research publication of the American Taxation Association. As such, one of its responsibilities is the dissemination of a wide variety of tax knowledge to its readership. To fulfill this responsibility, the journal accepts several types of articles. These articles include, but are not limited to, legal research, quantitative research, theoretical research, and descriptive pieces dealing with tax topics of general interest to its readership. Manuscripts pertaining to education research that disseminate information related to the teaching of taxation also are solicited. Educational studies should contain evidence that they have been classroom tested, that students have profited from the experience, and all other relevant research information. In addition, the Editor invites the submission of comments concerning articles which appear in current or past editions of the journal.

All manuscripts received by JATA are acknowledged and then sent to two reviewers for evaluation. When the two reviewers are inconclusive about publication or rejection of a manuscript, one or more additional reviewers may be selected form members of the Editorial Board or Ad Hoc Reviewers. It is hoped that the entire review process can be completed and the manuscript returned to the author within eight weeks. Acceptances are conditioned on the fact that the author will make all necessary changes to reflect revisions in the tax law that occur between the date of acceptance and the date of publication.

INSTRUCTIONS FOR SUBMISSION OF MANUSCRIPTS
Quantity And Format
Authors must submit three copies of each manuscript and should retain one copy for their files. When the research is reporting the results of field surveys or experiments, three copies of the instrument (e.g., questionnaire or case) also should be submitted. All manuscripts should be typed on one side of 8-1/2" x 11" paper and contain margins of at least one inch to facilitate editing and duplicating. Except for indented quotations, footnotes, and references, the manuscript should be double-spaced. Manuscript length should not exceed 35 double spaced pages.

The author's name and other identifying information should appear on the title page but not on any other part of the manuscript. The title page should contain the manuscript title, the author's name, professional title, affiliation, and acknowledgements. These items should be typed exactly as they are to appear in print. An abstract page must follow the title page and show the title of the paper plus a summary of the research questions, methodology, and principal findings. Abstract length is limited to 150 words. The manuscript title also should appear on the first page of the text.

When not in lists, numbers from one through ten should be spelled out, except where decimals are used. All other numbers should be written numerically.

Additional references regarding style and usage may be made to articles published in previous issues of JATA (or to *A Manual of Style*; Chicago: The University of Chicago Press).

Tables And Figures
Each table and figure should appear on a separate page of the manuscript and contain its own number. The table and figure should have a title and an Arabic number reference. The text

should contain clear notation where each table or figure is to be inserted in the text. Four lines should be skipped before and after the notation.

Literature Citations

Footnotes are not used for literature citations. Instead, citations are by the author's name and year of publication in the body of the text, shown in square brackets. For example, references to several sources should be shown as follows: [Anderson, 1985, p. 358; Limberg and Jones, 1988, pp. 61-62]. Citations to institutional works should employ acronyms where possible, for example, [CBO, 1981]. A reference to a work with more than two authors should list only the first name followed by et al., e.g. [Streuling et al., 1987]. The suffix a, b, etc. should follow the year when the Reference list contains more than one work published by an author in a year. Citations to tax treatises, tax services, public laws, and committee reports, etc. should follow the same form, e.g., [U.S. Congress, 1986; U.S. IRS, 1988].

Reference to a single regulation, government promulgation, or court case should be made in the form illustrated below. Generally, references to multiple works of the same type (e.g., two revenue rulings) or multiple works of different types (e.g., a revenue ruling and a court case) should be made through the use of a footnote unless they are of a brief nature which does not disrupt the flow of the text.

The form of tax citations often encountered is presented below.

[I.R.C. § 1248(a)].   [43 TC 1654 (1975)].
[Treas. Reg. § 1.1248-3(a)(4)].   [TC Memo 1943-496 (1943)].
[Rev. Rul. 82-1, 1982-1 CB 417].   [370 F. Supp. 69 (DC-Tx., 1974)].
[Rev. Proc. 82-1, 1982-1 CB 751].   [656 F. 2d 659 (Ct. Cl., 1981)].
[LTR 8108047 (11/26/80)].   [411 F. 2d 1275 (CA-6, 1975)].
[388 U.S. 1492 (1980)].

Other footnote references should follow the style used in previous issues of JATA (or suggested in *A Uniform System of Citation* published by The Harvard Law Review Association, Gannett House, Cambridge, MA 02138).

Textual footnotes should be provided for extensions to the discussion but only when inclusion in the body of the manuscript might disrupt its continuity. They should be in a separate section at the end of the manuscript. Such footnotes should be kept to a minimum and numbered consecutively throughout the manuscript.

Reference List

Manuscripts must include a list of References following the text and containing only those works actually cited. Entries should be in alphabetical order according to the surname of the first author or the name of the institution under whose auspices the work was published. Initials (rather than proper names) should be used. Multiple works by the same author should be listed in chronological order. The reference list should exclude regulations, I.R.S. promulgations (e.g., revenue rulings and revenue procedures), and court cases. Examples of references are as follows:

287

Dawson, J. P., P. M. Neupert, and C. P. Stickney. 1980. Restating financial statements for alternative GAAPs: Is it worth the effort? Financial Analysts Journal (November-December): 38-46.

Dworin, L. 1985. On estimating corporate tax liabilities from financial statements. Tax Notes (December 2): 965-971.

Feldstein, M., L. Dicks-Mireaux, and J. Poterba. 1983. The effective tax rate and the pretax rate of return. Journal of Public Economics (July): 129-58.

_____. 1986. The use of effective tax rates in tax policy. National Tax Journal (September): 285-292.

_____, J. B. Shoven, and J. Whalley. 1978. General equilibrium analysis of U.S. taxation policy. 1978 Compendium of Tax Research U.S. Treasury. Washington, D.C.: U.S. Government Printing Office: 23-58.

Gambola, M. J. and J. E. Ketz. 1983. A note on cash flow and classification patterns of financial ratios. The Accounting Review (January): 105- 114.

Healy, P. 1985. The impact of bonus schemes on the selection of accounting principles.Journal of Accounting and Economics (April): 85-107.

Kern, B. B. and M. H. Morris. 1992. Taxes and firm size: The effect of tax legislation during the 1980s. The Journal of the American Taxation Association 14 (Spring): 80-96.

Malitz, I. B. and M. S. Long. 1986. The investment-financing nexus: Some empirical evidence, The Revolution in Corporate Finance J. M. Stern and D. H. Chew, Jr., eds. New York: Basil Blackwell. 112-18.

Omer, T. C., K. Molloy, and D. Ziebart. 1991. Measurement of effective corporate tax rates using financial statement data. The Journal of The American Taxation Association 13 (Spring): 57-72.

Scholes, M. S. and M. A. Wolfson. 1992. Taxes and Business Strategy A Planning Approach. Englewood Cliffs, New Jersey: Prentice Hall.

Shaw, W. H. 1987. Safe harbor or muddy waters. The Accounting Review (April): 385-400.

Shevlin, T. and S. Porter. 1992. The corporate tax comeback in 1987 some further evidence. The Journal of the American Taxation Association 14 (Spring): 58-79.

Spooner, G. M. 1986. Effective tax rates from financial statements. National Tax Journal (September): 293-306.

Stickney, C. P., R. L. Weil, and M. A. Wolfson. 1983. Income taxes and tax-transfer leases: General Electric's accounting for a Molotov cocktail. The Accounting Review (April): 439-459.

U.S. General Accounting Office. 1990. Tax Policy--1987 Company Effective Tax Rates Higher Than in Prior Years GGD-90-69 (May). Washington D.C.: U.S. Government Printing Office.

Weber, R. P. 1985. Allocation of consolidation taxes--fiction in financial statements. The Journal of The American Taxation Association 7 (Fall): 44-51.

Wheeler, J. E. 1988. An academic look at transfer pricing in a global economy. Tax Notes (July 4): 87-96.

Wilkie, P. J. 1988. Corporate average effective tax rates and inferences about relative tax preferences. The Journal of the American Taxation Association 10 (Fall): 75-88.

_____. 1992. Empirical evidence of implicit taxes in the corporate sector. The Journal of the American Taxation Association 14 (Spring): 97-116.

288

_____ and S. T. Limberg. 1990. The relationship between firm size and effective tax rate: A reconciliation of Zimmerman [1983] and Porcano [1986]. The Journal of the American Taxation Association 11 (Spring): 76-92.

Witte, John F. 1985. The Politics and Development of the Federal Income Tax. Madison Wisconsin: The University of Wisconsin Press.

Zmijewski, M. and R. Hagerman. 1981. An income strategy approach to the positive theory of accounting standard setting/choice. Journal of Accounting and Economics (August): 129-149.

Leader's Edge (Michigan CPA)

ADDRESS FOR SUBMISSION:

Marla Janess, Editor
Leader's Edge (Michigan CPA)
Michigan Association of CPAs
PO Box 5068
5840 Corporate Drive, Suite 200
Troy, MI 48007-5068
USA
Phone: 248-267-3700
Fax: 248-267-3737
E-Mail: macpa@michcpa.org
Web: www.michcpa.org
Address May Change:

PUBLICATION GUIDELINES:

Manuscript Length: 1-2
Copies Required: One
Computer Submission: Yes
Format: N/A
Fees to Review: 0.00 US$

Manuscript Style:
    American Psychological Association

CIRCULATION DATA:

Reader: Business Persons, CPAs,
    Academics, Finance Professionals
Frequency of Issue: Monthly
Copies per Issue: 16,000
Sponsor/Publisher: Michigan Association of
    Certified Public Accountants
Subscribe Price: 20.00 US$

REVIEW INFORMATION:

Type of Review: Editorial Review
No. of External Reviewers: 1
No. of In House Reviewers: 3
Acceptance Rate: 0-5%
Time to Review: 2 - 3 Months
Reviewers Comments: No
Invited Articles: 0-5% CPA Authored
Fees to Publish: 0.00 US$

MANUSCRIPT TOPICS:
Accounting Information Systems; Accounting Theory & Practice; Agribusiness; Auditing; Automobile Dealers & Suppliers; Construction Accounting & Taxation; Ethics; Financial Institutions; Financial Management; Government & Non Profit Accounting; Health Care Administration; International Economics & Trade; International Finance; Legal Issues; Multi-Disciplinary Practice; Small Business Entrepreneurship; Tax Accounting

MANUSCRIPT GUIDELINES/COMMENTS:

Types Of Manuscripts Sought
We publish original articles of interest to practitioners, those in business and in educational fields. Submitted articles should offer help in resolving questions that arise in practice, advice in implementing published standards and guidelines, insight to problems, with, preferably workable solutions, or report on the status of developing issues. Our articles should be of broad interest, although some could relate to specific industries or techniques. Articles should be of immediate interest and timely to the profession.

Manuscript Preparation

- Articles should be typed and double-spaced, ranging in length from one to two pages, and submitted electronically.

- Short biographies of each author should be submitted with the article. Authors should include their educational background, employment, professional associations and other relevant information.

- Authors should also submit a photo with their articles. Black-and-white photos are preferred, however color photos will be acceptable. Do not submit Polaroids. If you do not wish to have your photo in the newsletter, please make a note of that when sending in the article.

- Due to space constraints, it may not always be possible to run your article in the next issue. Please indicate if the content of your article may soon be outdated.

- Include both a headline and byline with your article.

Content

- Development of all articles should consider the questions who, what, when, where, why and how.

- Specific examples, case histories and quote should be an essential part of any article. Whenever possible, please illustrate your points with examples from your personal experience. Facts and figures are invaluable to the reader. Use them liberally.

- Write your article in the active voice using strong verbs. For example, "This situation demands your attention," rather than "Your attention is needed."

- Keep your copy relaxed; this isn't a scholarly magazine. Second person "you" in addressing members is acceptable. Avoid using the fist person "I."

- *Leader's Edge* does not use footnotes. Give attribution to your source within the copy of your article. For example, state, "According to a recent study by...," or "The Wall Street Journal reports..."

- Check your copy carefully before submitting. Have you duplicated any information? Are you repeating a word or phrase frequently throughout the article? Are your paragraphs or sentences too lengthy?

Review

- All articles are reviewed by the MACPA Editorial Board and, if appropriate, by the Column Editor in which the article would appear.

Graphics

- Charts and photographs can help emphasize and clarify points you believe should be made in the articles. Graphics should be done as neatly as possible with a description of what the graphic illustrates.

- Unless a specific request is made, graphics and photos will not be returned to the author(s).

Editing

- The MACPA staff edits all manuscripts accepted for both content and style.

- Standards for style are set by the MACPA staff to follow professional publishing practices.

Management Accounting Quarterly

ADDRESS FOR SUBMISSION:

Kathy Williams, Editor
Management Accounting Quarterly
10 Paragon Drive
Montvale, NJ 07645
USA
Phone: 201-573-9000 ext 271
Fax: 201-573-0639
E-Mail: kwilliams@imanet.org
Web:
Address May Change:

CIRCULATION DATA:

Reader: Business Persons, Academics
Frequency of Issue: Quarterly
Copies per Issue: More than 25,000
Sponsor/Publisher: Institute of Management
  Accountants (IMA)
Subscribe Price: Undecided

PUBLICATION GUIDELINES:

Manuscript Length: 21-25
Copies Required: Four
Computer Submission: Yes
Format: MS Word
Fees to Review: 0.00 US$

Manuscript Style:
  Chicago Manual of Style

REVIEW INFORMATION:

Type of Review: Blind Review
No. of External Reviewers: 3+
No. of In House Reviewers: 2
Acceptance Rate: 11-20%
Time to Review: 4 - 6 Months
Reviewers Comments: Yes
Invited Articles: 11-20%
Fees to Publish: 0.00 US$

MANUSCRIPT TOPICS:

Accounting Education; Accounting Information Systems; Accounting Theory & Practice;
Cost Accounting; Economic Development; Government & Non Profit Accounting;
International Economics & Trade

MANUSCRIPT GUIDELINES/COMMENTS:

Applied research pertaining to all areas of cost/management accounting written with a
managerial perspective; also accounting education topics.

Management Accounting Research

ADDRESS FOR SUBMISSION:

Editorial Office
Management Accounting Research
Block A2
Westbrook Centre
Milton Road
Cambridge, CB4 1YG
UK
Phone: 44 161 275 4020
Fax: 44 161 275 4023
E-Mail: r.scapens@man.ac.uk
Web:
Address May Change:

PUBLICATION GUIDELINES:

Manuscript Length: 26-30
Copies Required: Four
Computer Submission: No
Format: N/A
Fees to Review: 0.00 US$

Manuscript Style:
See Manuscript Guidelines

CIRCULATION DATA:

Reader: Academics
Frequency of Issue: Quarterly
Copies per Issue: Less than 1,000
Sponsor/Publisher: Chartered Institute of
Management Accountants/Academic
Press
Subscribe Price: 165.00 Pounds Insitution
75.00 Pounds Personal
140.00 US$ Personal

REVIEW INFORMATION:

Type of Review: Blind Review
No. of External Reviewers: 2
No. of In House Reviewers: 1
Acceptance Rate: 21-30%
Time to Review: 4 - 6 Months
Reviewers Comments: Yes
Invited Articles: 0-5%
Fees to Publish: 0.00 US$

MANUSCRIPT TOPICS:
Accounting Information Systems; Cost Accounting; Management Accounting

MANUSCRIPT GUIDELINES/COMMENTS:

Submission of manuscripts
Four copies of any manuscripts for consideration should be sent to the Editorial Office.

Principle authors are responsible for ensuring that co-authors agree to the inclusion of their names before submission of a manuscript.

Acceptance criteria
Submission of a paper to the Journal automatically implies that the manuscript is not concurrently under consideration for publication elsewhere. All papers submitted will normally only be published subject to double blind review. In the interests of a fair review, authors should try and avoid the use of anything which would make their identity obvious. Referees are asked to comment upon the originality, authority, comprehensiveness, contribution, interest and usefulness of a submitted paper. All papers are also subjected to

294

editorial review which, whilst covering style and quality of communication, may also cover academic and scholarly content. The editors make every effort to give a decision on manuscripts within 12 weeks of receipt.

Preparation of manuscripts
Articles should be typed double-spaced throughout the text on A4 (212 x 297 mm) paper; with a margin of about 3 cm all round.

Table and Figure legends should be typed separately and placed at the end of the manuscript. Two photocopies of each should accompany the manuscript.

All pages should be numbered serially.

The title page should include the article title, authors' names and affiliations, the name and address of the person to whom proofs are to be sent, a running head of not more than 50 characters and any acknowledgements.

Articles should be arranged as follows:
(i) An abstract of about 150 words along with 3-6 key words
(ii) Main text in the sections, Introduction, Materials and Methods, Results, and Discussion (best presented as separate sections but may be combined).
(iii) References

Key words
Three to six key words or short phrases should be provided to assist indexers in cross-indexing the paper.

Illustrations
All illustrations must be cited in the text and in sequence. If line drawings are submitted they should be in black ink and drawn to approximately 1.5 to 2 times their required size for publication.

All authors wishing to use illustrations already published must first obtain the permission of author and publisher and/or copyright holders and give precise reference to the original work.

Tables
Tables should be numbered in series and must be cited in the text in sequence. Headings should be provided but otherwise the data should be self-explanatory.

References
In the text references should include the author's name, the year of publication, and the relevant page numbers if required; e.g. (Innes and Mitchell, 1990, p.6). For more than two authors, the reference should be abbreviated as follows: (Rickwood et al., 1990, p.37). Multiple references to works by the same author(s) in a single year should be distinguished in the text (and in the bibliography) by a, b, c, etc. following the year of publication.

The manuscript should include a bibliography containing only those references cited in the text and arranged in alphabetical order according to the surname of the first author. Full bibliographical details are required in the following style:

Examples
1. Bromwich, M., 1977. The use of present valuation models in published accounting reports, *The Accounting Review*, July, 587-596.
2. Broadbent, J., 1992. Change in organizations: a case study of the use of accounting information in the NHS, British Accounting Review, 24, 343-367.
3. Belkaoui, A., 1985. *Accounting Theory*, 2nd edition, San Diego, Harcourt Brace Jovanovich.

Footnotes
Footnotes should be numbered sequentially in the text and appear on a separate sheet at the end of the paper.

Proofs
Authors are expected to correct proofs quickly and not to make revisions on proofs; revisions made on proofs may be charged for. No payments are made to authors.

Copyright/offprints
Authors submitting a manuscript do so on the understanding that if it is accepted for publication, copyright in the article in all forms and media, shall be assigned exclusively to the publisher. The Copyright Transfer Agreement, which may be copied from the pages following the Instructions to Authors or found on the journal home page [on website], should be signed by the appropriate person(s) and should accompany the original submission of a manuscript to this journal. The transfer of copyright does not take effect until the manuscript is accepted for publication. The written consent of the publisher must be obtained if any article is to be published elsewhere in the same form, in any language. It is the policy of the publisher that authors need not obtain permission in the following cases only: (1) to use their original figures or tables in their future work; (2) to make copies of their papers for use in their classroom teaching; and (3) to include their papers as part of their dissertation.

In consideration for the assignment of copyright, 25 offprints of each paper will be supplied. Further offprints may be ordered at extra cost; the offprint order form will be sent with the proofs.

Manuscripts On Disk
When supplying the final version of your article please include, where possible, a disk of your manuscript prepared on PC-compatible or Apple Macintosh computers, along with the **hard copy print out**. Standard 5 ¼" or 3 ½" size disks and most word processing packages are acceptable, although any version of WordPerfect or Microsoft Word are preferred.

Please follow these guidelines carefully
Include and ASCII version on the disk, together with the word-processed version if possible.

- Ensure that the files are not saved as read-only.
- Manuscripts prepared on disks must be accompanied by four hard copies, including all figures, printed with double spacing, and which may be used if setting from the disk proved impractical.
- Ensure the final version of the hard copy and the file on disk are the same. It is the authors' responsibility to ensure complete compatibility. If there are differences the hard copy will be used.
- The directives for preparing the paper in the style of the Journal as set out in the Instructions to Authors must be followed, i.e.: ensure the document is in the following order: Title; Authors; Addresses; Acknowledgements; Abstract; Key words; Introduction; Materials and Methods; Results; Discussion; References; Appendices; Figure legends; Tables; Footnotes.
- The operating system and the word processing software used to produce the article should be noted on the disk (i.e. DOS/Word Perfect), as well as all file names. If UNIX, method of extraction should also be noted.
- The disk/tape should be labeled with the journal reference number (if known), author name(s), hardware and software used to generate the disk file.
- Do not include copyright material, e.g. word processing software or operating system files, on the disk because this can create difficulties with Customs clearance.
- Package floppy disks in such a way as to avoid damage in the post.

Additional points to note
- Use two carriage returns to end headings and paragraphs.
- Type text without end of line hyphenation, except for compound words.
- Do not use lower case "l" for "1" or "O" for "0". (The have different typesetting values.)
- Footnotes, tables and figure captions should be saved in a separate file from the main text of the manuscript. However, please ensure clear hard copies are supplied as they will almost certainly be typeset from the hard copy.
- Be consistent with punctuation and only insert a single space between words and after punctuation.
- Please include a list of any special characters you have had to use, e.g. Greek, maths.

Illustrations submitted on disk
Author's illustrations should also, where possible, be supplied as both hard copy and electronic files. Figures drawn using Aldus Freehand (Apple Macintosh) and saved as Encapsulated PostScript files (EPS) are preferred and should be supplied on a separate disk.

Editor-in-Chief
R. W. Scapens, University of Manchester, School of Accounting and Finance, Crawford House, Manchester M13 9PL, UK. Tel. 44-161-2754020, Fax 44-161-2754023. Email: r.scapens@man.ac.uk

Management Science

ADDRESS FOR SUBMISSION:

Hau L. Lee, Editor-in-Chief
Management Science
Stanford University
Department of Industrial Engineering
  and Engineering Management
Stanford, CA 94305-4024
USA
Phone: 415-723-0514
Fax: 415-725-8799
E-Mail: haulee@leland.stanford.edu
Web:
Address May Change:

PUBLICATION GUIDELINES:

Manuscript Length: 32
Copies Required: Four
Computer Submission: No
Format: N/A
Fees to Review: 0.00 US$

Manuscript Style:
  See Manuscript Guidelines

CIRCULATION DATA:

Reader: Academics
Frequency of Issue: Monthly
Copies per Issue: 5,001 - 10,000
Sponsor/Publisher: INFORMS
Subscribe Price: 130.00 US$ Individual
    298.00 US$ Library/Corporate
    55.00 US$ Member

REVIEW INFORMATION:

Type of Review: Editorial Review
No. of External Reviewers: 3
No. of In House Reviewers: 0
Acceptance Rate: 11-20%
Time to Review: 4 - 6 Months
Reviewers Comments: Yes
Invited Articles: 0-5%
Fees to Publish: 0.00 US$

MANUSCRIPT TOPICS:

Accounting Information Systems; Accounting Theory & Practice; Auditing; Cost Accounting; Government & Non Profit Accounting

MANUSCRIPT GUIDELINES/COMMENTS:

1. *Management Science* seeks to publish articles that identify, extend, or unify scientific knowledge pertaining to management. Articles must be readable, well-organized, and exhibit good writing style. Other important criteria are originality and significant contribution including the capacity to provide generalizations within the framework of application-oriented methods.

2. As much as possible, papers suitable for *Management Science* should be readable by those comfortable with undergraduate mathematics. We accept the use of graduate level mathematics only if it is essential for understanding. All articles and notes, if judged potentially suitable for *Management Science*, will be refereed by at least two competent readers.

298

3. Of special interest is the **methodological** approach to the implementation of real applications of *Management Science*, without losing sight of behavioral and economic realities. Papers should reflect the mutuality of interest of managers and management scientists in the total exercise of the management function. Authors seeking up-to-date information about specific Departmental Editorial Objectives should send their request to: Professor Hau L. Lee, Stanford University, Department of Industrial Engineering and Engineering Management, Stanford, CA 94305-4024.

4. The submission of a paper to *Management Science* for refereeing means that the author certifies the manuscript is not copyrighted; nor has it been accepted for publication (or published) by any refereed journal; nor is it being refereed elsewhere, at the same time. If the paper (or any version of it) has appeared, or will appear, in a non-refereed publication, the details of such publication must be made known to the editor at the time of submission so that the suitability of the paper for *Management Science* can be assessed. *Management Science* requires that at least one of the authors of each accepted article sign a Copyright Transfer Agreement form. For further information write: Professor Hau L. Lee (address above).

5. *Management Science* seeks to publish significant articles that identify extend, or unify scientific knowledge pertaining to management. Submissions from all countries are welcome. TIMS is an international society of management scientists and encourages world-wide contributions.

6. Articles must be readable, well-organized and of good writing style. Additional criteria for publication are **originality and significant contribution** which provide generalizations and permit applications of *Management Science* methodology (model-building and algorithm construction.) All articles and notes, if judged potentially suitable for Management Science will be refereed by at least two competent readers. The editors will secure additional refereeing when warranted.

7. Original theory, which is not dependent on substantial mathematical content, should be submitted to *Management Science*. Theory contributions requiring a high degree of mathematical abstraction should not be submitted to *Management Science*, but should instead be directed to the joint publication of TIMS and ORSA, *Mathematics of Operations Research*.

8. Articles are expected to provide models and algorithms of well-defined structure. Descriptions of important applications of *Management Science* which do not detail the modeling structure of the system should not be submitted to *Management Science*. They should instead by directed to *Interfaces*, another joint publication of TIMS and ORSA, which publishes nonmathematical descriptions of *Management Science*.

9. In general, the mathematical methodology must be at the most accessible level of abstractness appropriate to the problem which is being discussed. As much as possible, papers suitable for *Management Science* should be readable by those comfortable with undergraduate mathematics. However, while we insist upon eliminating the unnecessary use of graduate level mathematics, if it is essential for understanding, we accept its use. State-of-the-art surveys are suitable when such reporting is warranted. Of special interest is the **methodological** approach to the implementation of real applications of *Management Science*.

Attention should be focused on the problems of developing and converting management theory into practice without losing sight of behavioral and economic realities. Papers should reflect the mutuality of interest of managers and management scientists in the total exercise of the management function.

10. Questions such as the following are significant in evaluating papers submitted for publication:
1. Does the paper make original and substantive contribution to the literature of *Management Science*?
2. Is the paper similar in whole or in part to a paper or papers published in any journal but especially in *Management Science*?
3. Is the title concise descriptive and explicit?
4. Does the abstract properly summarize the important content of the paper? Is it readable and usable by managers?
5. Is the paper clear precise logical error-free and in keeping with page length requirements (see Instructions to Authors)?
6. Is adequate credit given to other contributors in the field; are references complete?
7. Are there revisions which will make the paper more acceptable? Is the paper more suitable for another journal?

11. *Management Science* also publishes brief articles requiring refereeing which are designated as Notes at the suggestions of the authors editors or referees. Letters and brief comments published as Communications are un-refereed. A yearly index is published. Precis appear in *Management Science* to advise readers about papers that are available from authors upon request.

12. The submission of a paper to *Management Science* for refereeing means that the author certifies the manuscript is not copyrighted; nor has it been accepted for publication (or published) by any refereed journal; nor is it being refereed elsewhere at the same time. If the paper (or any version of it) has appeared or will appear in a non-refereed publication the details of such publication must be made known to the editor at the time of submission so that the suitability of the paper for *Management Science* can be assessed.

13. Figures must be drafted in India ink on white paper in a form suitable for reduction. Lettering should be professional or uniform size and large enough to be legible when the figure is reduced to final size of 1/4 page. Special attention should be given to line weights; that is the lines of the lettering should be the same thickness as the lines of the figure. Typewritten lettering on figures is not acceptable. Figures should be designated by Arabic numerals and the captions should be typed double-spaced on a separate sheet rather than lettered on the figures themselves.

14. Manuscripts which do not conform to this format, if accepted, are subject to considerable delay pending revisions since it is not possible to have them typeset until suitable copy and art have been furnished.

15. **Submission of a paper to *Management Science* for refereeing means that the author(s) certifies that the manuscript has not been published previously nor currently submitted for publication elsewhere.**

16. Manuscripts, tentatively accepted for publication, must be accompanied by a Copyright Transfer Agreement signed by at least one of the authors (who agrees to inform the others, if any), or, in the case of "work made for hire", by the employer. The form of copyright transfer will be sent by the TIMS business office to the responsible author who must return it signed, to the Technical Editors, TIMS, 146 Westminster Street, Providence, Rhode Island 02903. Papers will not be finally accepted, nor will they begin editorial processing until the release is received. This written transfer of copyright, which previously was assumed to be implicit in the act of submitting a manuscript, is necessary under the 1978 United States of America copyright law.

17. Important: The length of papers submitted for publication in *Management Science* should be determined by author requirements. However, our objective is to insure that as many worthy papers as possible will appear in each issue. Consequently, our publication policy is to use not more pages than necessary to communicate fully the purposes, methods and applications of well-written papers that make a contribution to *Management Science* .

18. All Departments of this Journal are refereeing typewritten manuscripts of up to 32 double-spaced manuscript pages (including figures references and tables).

19. Papers exceeding 16 Journal pages (including charts, tables and figures) can be submitted as extensions of present knowledge. (Assuming 250 words per double-spaced typewritten page, 32 manuscript pages produce 16 Journal pages. Each figure constitutes about 1/4 of a Journal page.) Such papers must be accompanied by an abridged version that will satisfy the 16 Journal page constraint. The unabridged paper will be refereed. If accepted in a form exceeding 16 Journal pages, then the abridged version will be reviewed, and approved for its readability and accurate representation of the author's ideas. The satisfactory abridged version will be published. Copies of the full-length, refereed, nonabridged version will be available upon request, at cost, from: Business Office, INFORMS, 901 Elkridge Landing Road, Suite 400, Linthicum, MD, 21090-2909.

20. Manuscripts intended for publication may be sent to the appropriate Departmental Editor or to the Editor-in-Chief for the assignment. The Departmental Editor will see to it that manuscripts accepted for refereeing will be sent to at least two referees. Every effort will be made to complete refereeing in a reasonable interval. Length of time that papers requiring revision are with the author(s) is regularly published as a footnote to accepted articles.

21. All manuscripts submitted for consideration should be typed on 8-1/2" by 11" paper and should be double-spaced throughout, including references, footnotes, and abstract. We request four copies of the paper for the reviewing process. All manuscripts should be preceded by a nonmathematical abstract (as understandable to managers as possible) of not more than 500 words. Papers may be submitted in any language, but English and French are the official language of the Institute.

22. Mathematical notation should be selected so as to simplify the typesetting process. Authors should attempt to make mathematical expressions in the body of the text as simple as possible. Greek letters and unusual symbols (if handwritten rather than typed) should be labeled whenever they first appear in the manuscript, as should letter symbols "oh" and "el" (as distinguished from the numbers "zero" and "one"). Some useful alternatives to expensive notation are:

Expensive notations

$$e^{\dfrac{-x^2 + y^2}{a}}, \quad \dfrac{7}{8}, \quad \dfrac{a+b}{c}, \quad \cos \dfrac{\dfrac{1}{x}}{\sqrt{a + \dfrac{b}{x}}}$$

Alternatives

$$\exp((-x^2 + y^2)/a) \quad 7/8, \quad (a+b)/c, \quad \dfrac{\cos(1/x)}{\sqrt{a + b/x}}$$

24. Displayed material should clearly indicate the alignment that is desired. If the equations are numbered, the numbers should be given in parentheses, flush with the right margin of the page.

25. Footnotes should be numbered consecutively and typed, double-spaced, in a separate list at the end of the paper. In text, footnotes are indicated by superscript numbers alone. Footnote numbers should never be attached to mathematical symbols. Material that normally would appear as a footnote should be placed in the body of the text when it will not impair readability.

26. All references are to be listed alphabetically by author at the end of the paper and should be double-spaced. Reference callouts in the body of the text should be indicated by the year of publication in parentheses, e.g. (1960).

27. References appear in the following style:

WINDAL, PIERRE M. AND DOYLE L. WEISS, "An Interactive GLS Procedure for Estimating the Parameters of Models with Autocorrelated Errors Using Data Aggregated Over Time", J. Business, 53 (October 1980), 415-424.

28. **Submissions** Please submit four copies of each manuscript to the appropriate Departmental Editor or to the Editor-in-Chief. Departmental Editors are listed below. The Statement of Objectives for each department has been published in *Management Science*, and the issue is identified by the date following each department title.

29. **Departmental Editors**:

ACCOUNTING
Professor Bala Balachandran
Northwestern University

Kellogg Graduate School of Management
Evanston, IL 60208
847-491-2678   Fax: 847-467-1202
jpp667@nwu.edu

BUSINESS STRATEGY
Professor Rebecca Henderson
Massachusetts Institute of Technology
Sloan School of Management, E52-543
Cambridge, MA 02142
617-253-6618   Fax: 617-674-2402
rhenders@mit.edu

DECISION ANALYSIS
Professor James E. Smith
Duke University
Fuqua School of Business
Durham, NC 27708-0120
919-660-7770   Fax: 919-684-2818
james.e.smith@duke.edu

DECISION ANALYSIS
Professor Dr. Martin Weber
Universitat Mannheim
Lehrstuhl fur Finanzwirtschaft, insb.
Mannheim - Germany 68131
49-621-292-5450   Fax: 49-621-292-1168
weber@bank.bwl.uni-mannheim.de

FINANCE
Professor Phelim P. Boyle
University of Waterloo
School of Accountancy
Waterloo, Ontario, Canada N2L 3G1
519-885-1211   Fax: 519-888-7562
pboyle@uwaterloo.ca

INFORMATION SYSTEMS
Professor Chris F. Kemerer
University of Pittsburgh
278A Mervis Hall
Pittsburgh, PA 15260
412-648-1572   Fax: 412-624-2983
ckemerer@katz.business.pitt.edu

INTERDISCIPLINARY MANAGEMENT RESEARCH AND APPLICATIONS
Professor Abraham Seidmann

University of Rochester
W.E. Simon School of Business Administration
Rochester, NY 14627
716-275-5694   Fax: 716-273-1140
seidmannav@ssb.rochester.edu

MANUFACTURING, DISTRIBUTION AND SERVICE OPERATIONS
Professor Awl Federgruen
Columbia University
Graduate School of Business
New York, NY 10027
212-854-4106   Fax: 212-864-4857
afedergr@research.gsb.columbia.edu

MANUFACTURING, DISTRIBUTION AND SERVICE OPERATIONS
Professor Luk Van Wassenhove
INSEAD
Technology Management Area Boulevard de
Fontainebleau Cedex, France F77305
(1) 60 72 4326 Fax: (1) 60 72 42 42
wassenhove@insead.fr

MANUFACTURING, DISTRIBUTION AND SERVICE OPERATIONS
Professor Wallace Hopp
Northwestern University
Dept. of Industrial Engineering and Management
Evanston, IL 60208-3119
847-491-3669   Fax: 847-491-8005
hopp@nwu.edu

MARKETING
Professor Dipak Jain
Northwestern University
J. L. Kellogg Graduate School of Management
Evanston, IL 60208-2001
847-491-2840   Fax: 847-467-2747
d-jain@nwu.edu

MATHEMATICAL PROGRAMMING AND NETWORKS
Professor Thomas M. Liebling
Ecole Polytechnique Federale de Lausanne
Department of Mathematiques
Ecublens, Lausanne 1015,
41 21 693 2503   Fax: 41 21 693 22 20
thomas.liebling@epfl.ch

ORGANIZATIONAL PERFORMANCE, STRATEGY, AND DESIGN
Professor Linda Argote
Carnegie Mellon University
Graduate School of Industrial Administration
Pittsburgh, PA 15213
412-268-3683   Fax: 412-268-7064
argote@cmu.edu

PUBLIC SECTOR APPLICATIONS
Professor Bruce Golden
The University of Maryland
College of Business and Management
College Park, MD 20742
301-405-2232   Fax301-314-9157
bgolden@umdacc.umd.edu

PUBLIC SECTOR APPLICATIONS
Professor Jonathan P. Caulkins
Carnegie Mellon University
H. John Heinz III School of Public Policy
Pittsburgh, PA 15213-3890
412-268-5064   Fax: 212-268-7036
caulkins@andrew.cmu.edu

R&D/INNOVATION AND ENTREPRENEURSHIP
Professor Ralph Katz
Northeastern University
College of Business Administration
Boston, MA 02115
617-373-4724   Fax: 617-373-2491
rkatz@cba.neu.edu

STOCHASTIC MODELS AND SIMULATION
Professor Paul Wasserman
Columbia University
Graduate School of Business,
New York, NY 10027-6902
212-854-4102   Fax: 212-316-9180
pg20@columbia.edu

SUPPLY CHAIN MANAGEMENT
Professor Christopher Tang
UCLA
Anderson School of Management
Los Angeles, CA 90095
310-825-4203   Fax: 310-206-3337
ctang@anderson.ucla.edu

30. STATEMENT OF DEPARTMENTAL OBJECTIVES

Accounting

This department solicits and processes for publication papers reporting the results of high quality research that make original and significant contributions to the analysis, design development, and use of accounting systems.

Accounting Systems contributions may deal with the general area of accounting systems and the economics/ management sciences of accounting: the analysis, design and development of complex accounting choices, contracting, incentives and of communications, information processing and decision making within them. Illustrative topic areas may include financial and behavioral systems, information resource management, decision support activities, balanced scorecard and performance measures, planning and control, man-machine systems, information economics, accounting system implementation, and so on.

Accounting contributions may deal with the general areas of financial, managerial and tax accounting, as well as auditing, accounting for nonprofit organizations, social, national and environmental accounting and other related areas. Analytic or empirical investigations are welcome, as are those that rely on an economic or a behavioral paradigm. Editorial policies concern only the quality of the manuscript and its interest to the management science community.

The department encourages the submission of papers dealing with research and applications of management science in the accounting systems and accounting areas. Papers may be either theoretical or applied, but none will be published that are not both innovative and important to the development of the area. Applied research is innovative when existing models and methods of underlying disciplines are applied to a real-world situation in a creative manner, particularly when positive results are obtained in a previously "unexplored" area. Good applied research should be sensitive to the availability of empirical data, measurement and computational requirements and/or implementation issues in actual organizations.

The Department also solicits survey papers on important topic areas, provided they contribute a synthesis of the state-of-the-art in research, as well as a tutorial discussion of the subject.

To be accepted for review manuscripts should strive to meet these Departmental Objectives; they must also conform to the requirements and standards of *Management Science*. (See Editorial Policies and Instruction to Authors for further detail). Manuscripts should be submitted directly to the Departmental Editor for consideration.

Business Strategy

In the past two or three decades, research on business strategy has coalesced into a recognizable applied field. We define business strategy research to include: Theory and data on choices of actions, and plans for implementation that have long-term consequences for the firm; the study of factors which cause some firms to succeed and others to fail; and the study of how firms manage resources that are imperfectly tradeable and hence tied to the firm. All three definitions create paradigms which spawn distinct types of studies. We are eager to publish the best studies of all these types in the new Business Strategy Department of *Management Science*.

The Department will have two prejudices which reflect the traditional orientation of the journal and distinguish it from other outlets for strategy research.

First, because we believe that disciplines discipline thinking, we especially welcome business strategy papers firmly rooted in the soil of a social science. Discipline-based research might find roots in Economics (e.g. industrial organization, economics of the firm); operations (quality and delivery-time control, information technology); political science (e.g., political economy of inter- or intrafirm influence); psychology (e.g. individual and group judgments by general managers): and sociology (e.g., social networks, organizational ecology). Some of these topics overlap with the scope of the Organizational Performance Strategy and Design Department. Please consult their statement of Editorial Objectives (March 1990). or contact one or both Departmental Editors if you are unsure which Department would be more suitable for a particular submission.

Second, we encourage theorizing and empirical work closely tied to theory. We value simplicity in construction and execution of empirical work. For example we think testing a single hypothesis powerfully, and broadly, can be more valuable than testing many hypotheses simultaneously with idiosyncratic data or methods. Experimental tests are welcome, if they are carefully designed using principles established by experimenters in psychology or economics (or if they violate these principles defensibly). Case studies will be published if they show promise of replicability and achieve a particularly high standard of quality, reflecting both methodological sophistication and unique insight.

We are likely to publish articles about familiar topics, including:
- Diversification
- Economies of scale and scope
- Models of competition
- The influence of compensation and incentive systems
- The influence of top management teams
- Managerial cognition and strategic choice
- Implementation of strategies
- Corporate governance
- Acquisition and divestment
- Corporate restructuring
- Joint ventures and strategic alliances
- Introduction of new products.

(Of course, we are most eager to consider articles about topics which are *not* on this list, if they break new ground.)

Writing counts. Authors should write crisply and communicate well. Limit cumbersome notation and unfamiliar jargon. Use appendices for certain proofs technical asides, and details of data sources or computation. Ideally, tables and figures should make a sharp point with little help from the text. Write a fresh abstract summarizing the paper and enticing the reader rather than simply copying part of the paper. Be pithy; *Management Science* rarely publishes long papers.

We will strive to provide quick turnaround on papers and thoughtful constructive criticism. Some papers will be returned immediately if they are judged to be unsuitable.

Decision Analysis
The Decision Analysis Department publishes articles that create, extend, or unify scientific knowledge pertaining to decision analysis and decision making. We seek papers that describe concepts and techniques for modeling decisions as well as behaviorally oriented papers that explain or evaluate decisions or judgments. Papers may develop new theory or methodology, address problems of implementation, present empirical studies of choice behavior or decision modeling, synthesize existing ideas, or describe innovative applications. In all cases, the papers must be based on sound decision-theoretic and/or psychological principles and reasoning.

Decision settings may consist of any combination of certainty or uncertainty; competitive or non-competitive situations; individuals, groups, or markets; and applications may include personal decisions as well as decisions of firms or governments. Due to the interdisciplinary nature of the field, papers may draw upon work in a wide variety of disciplines, including management science, operations research, economics, probability and statistics, mathematics, engineering, psychology, sociology, philosophy, and political science. Moreover, the editors are open to interdisciplinary articles that use decision-theoretic principles and procedures to study decision making in areas such as marketing, finance, operations, accounting, decision support systems, medicine, and public policy. If, however, a paper fits clearly within the interests of another department of *Management Science* and its contribution is not primarily related to decision analysis or decision making, then the paper should be submitted to this other department rather than the Decision Analysis department.

The department currently has two departmental editors to cover the breadth of the field. In general, papers that are theoretically or methodologically oriented should be sent to Jim Smith. Papers that are behaviorally or descriptively oriented should be sent to Martin Weber. Papers that incorporate both elements may be sent to either editor at the author's choice; the departmental editors may however forward papers to each other if they feel the other is better suited to handle the paper. If the departmental editor finds the paper to be appropriate for consideration by the Decision Analysis department, the publication decision will be based upon its quality according to criteria that include originality, importance and significance for decision-analysis practice and/or theory, potential managerial significance, and clarity of writing style.

Finance
The Finance Department of *Management Science* seeks papers on topics that deal with the finance area broadly defined. We are looking for creative work that is innovative, significant and technically correct. Authors should clearly explain the importance of the results to a general audience. The technical level should not be too advanced; for example the

mathematical level should not stray beyond that of a good undergraduate degree in mathematics.

We welcome papers from across the field of paradigms in the finance field and encourage applications to a broad range of problems in the area. We are interested in both in the creation of new theoretical models as well as methodological extensions of existing theory. The department particularly encourages articles that lead to fresh new insights. The department is also interested in papers which conduct rigorous test of existing theories as well as empirical/ quantitative studies. In particular the department welcomes submissions of papers in the area of computational finance.

Authors of empirical and quantitative papers should provide or make available enough information and data so that the results are reproducible. The paper should be written in a clear and concise manner. The author should explain the importance of the results to the non-specialist. It is our aim to provide both a speedy turnaround and constructive referees' reports.

Information Systems
The IS department at *Management Science* seeks high quality, rigorous papers that examine Information Systems in the context of the role of management in organizations. The department seeks to publish papers that will have a significant impact on research and practice. Note that all papers must address how their results should impact managerial practice.

High quality research can be done in a variety of ways, including mathematical analyses, computer simulations, laboratory experiments, field data, rigorous argument, or review of the literature. Regardless of the methodology used, it must be sufficiently rigorous that the uncommitted reader can assign high credibility to the result.

The department will support a wide variety of research topics, and it is expected that these specific topics will change over time, as the technology underlying research in this area is undergoing constant and rapid change itself. Typically, however, research will find itself focusing on research problems of either a technical, organizational, or economic nature.

Authors are reminded that their manuscripts must adhere to the *Management Science* guidelines for length. See the instructions for authors in any recent issue, or at the INFORMS publications WWW site http://www.informs.org/pubs/pubshome/html. Authors should submit five copies of their papers to the departmental editor, who will forward them to an appropriate Associate Editor.

Interdisciplinary Management Research and Applications
The multidisciplinary and interfunctional nature of the Management Science profession has been recognized since its inception. Recently, there has been increased recognition by executives for the need to implement such interdisciplinary team approaches for solving complex problems that may have a multitude of societal, political, and business dimensions. This department tries to meet the growing need for research on major management problems

that incorporate several functional perspectives, and that deal with new and nontraditional areas. Other problems and issues that will be considered include:

- business forecasting;
- compensation policies;
- electronic commerce;
- environmental policies;
- financial information systems;
- international corporate strategies
- management of quality improvement programs;
- organizational controls;
- product life-cycle management from marketing, design and manufacturing perspectives;
- project management;
- yield and revenue management; and
- other studies and applications which involve several disciplinary or cross-functional issues.

We actively solicit the submissions of original and imaginative manuscripts that are expected to be of significant interest to the Journal's readership. In particular, we are looking for manuscripts that analyze actual applications, that consolidate several functional areas of management in novel and innovative ways, and build upon several research disciplines in an original manner. Special efforts will be made by the departmental editor to provide the authors with referee reports within four months.

Manuscripts might be practice oriented or theoretical. Practice-oriented submissions should deal with real applications, not with proposed or unimplemented designs. They should provide a critical examination of the methodology and of the general value and impact of the reported application. Theoretical submissions should be problem driven, rather than motivated by hypothetical scenarios. They should exhibit scientific rigor and original analytical or conceptual frameworks that provide new and substantial managerial insights.

Submitted papers should have several attributes. First, papers should display clear evidence of synergism across several functional areas; they should not be narrowly focused. To help the departmental editor evaluate a submission, please motivate the reasons for your submission to this particular department in your cover letter. Identify the major disciplines upon which you have drawn in your paper, and explain the unique features of it. This information will be used to help select the associate editor and referees who will further evaluate your contributions. Second, authors should write manuscripts that are clear and accessible to the largest segment of the Journal readership. The use of appendices is recommended for in-depth exposition of various technical details.

Finally, given the particular nature of this department, potential contributors are strongly encouraged to communicate directly with the editor-in-chief or with the departmental editor prior to formally submitting manuscripts. This communication might verify the potential match between the paper's and the department's objectives.

Manufacturing, Distribution and Service Operations

This department encourages the publication of manuscripts which increase scientific knowledge of operations management in manufacturing, distribution and service. Papers dealing with production and/or delivery of goods and services are appropriate.

The department seeks papers that develop or use management science models and methods for problems and issues arising in the management of manufacturing, distribution and service operations. Of particular interest are papers that deal with strategic concerns such as the choice and impact of new production or information technology, and papers that may provide insight or simple models for guiding manufacturing or service policy. The department encourages papers that examine the planning and coordination of activities and resources within a manufacturing, distribution or service operation, as well as papers that consider the design, location and layout of these operations. Papers that consider the measurement of productivity, flexibility, quality or costs in some operational setting are especially welcome.

All manuscripts submitted for review will be expected to display both scientific rigor and managerial relevance. Simple analytical models will be expected to yield insight into their real world counterparts. Papers concerned with complex algorithms will be expected to address the issues of computability and implementation. Papers that extend established models need to provide significant improvements to or generalizations of the existing models and results. Papers which describe an application or system implementation will be expected to be of some general interest and have some transferable value. The design and analysis of heuristics is encouraged; however, heuristics must be analytically-based and scientifically tested (e.g., the use of analytically derived lower bounds and/or carefully controlled simulation tests).

Authors may submit their papers to any one of the three Departmental Editors.

Marketing

The Marketing Department of *Managerial Science* is interested in scientific papers which use theory, methodology, and/or measurement to address relevant marketing problems. We seek out and publish papers that make significant contributions to the development of marketing science. We suggest the following flexible guidelines:

Marketing Theory. The science of marketing is fortunate now to have 30 or more years of solid empirical evidence with respect to marketing phenomena. Recently, we have seen an explosion of research using this empirical base to derive a set of mathematical marketing theory. We encourage more theoretical papers. Such papers will be judged on relevance and creativity, as well as technical merit. The development of the theory should be supported by relevant empirical evidence. (Citations to published works are sufficient.) Furthermore, the implications of the theory should be relevant, that is, they either enable a manager to better perform his task or enable the scientist to better understand marketing phenomena. (Try to interpret all results intuitively and investigate the sensitivity of your results to changes in assumptions.)

Interface Between Marketing and Other Disciplines. One of the many strengths of *Management Science* is its interdisciplinary base. Research work that explicitly addresses issues related to the integration of the marketing management function with other functions such as R&D and operations management is particularly encouraged. Such submissions will be reviewed by experts in the relevant areas. We encourage authors to demonstrate the additional and unique insights gained from such analyses.

Methodology. Methodology papers can include decision-making models, forecasting methods or measurement techniques which are relevant primarily to marketing, but could also be of interest to other disciplines.

Decision-making models should use marketing theory and empirical evidence to provide management a usable tool for solving relevant problems. These papers will be judged on relevance, usability, and effectiveness. We encourage authors to demonstrate empirically the feasibility of their models' inputs and the usefulness of their models' outputs.

Forecasting methods can include econometrics, time-series analyses, subjective probability-based methods, as well as innovative approaches to combining them. Papers submitted should demonstrate their contribution to marketing by focusing on marketing phenomena and comparing the new method with relevant state-of-the-art marketing models. We also encourage tests of the methodology and holdout samples, predictions to new situations, predictions forward in time, etc.

Measurement techniques can include preference measurements, perceptual mapping, psychometrics, scaling procedures, etc. Measurement techniques that are employed at the individual level and then aggregated to obtain managerially relevant statistics are particularly encouraged. We also encourage explicit recognition of measurement errors and new solutions as to how they should be addressed. Papers will be judged on reliability, validity, and their managerial implications.

Behavioral Science. We encourage marketing papers which use or test theories of consumer behavior such as moods, judgements, emotional responses, and decision making. we also encourage papers addressing behavioral issues related to marketing managers' moves and responses in the context of competitive signaling, consumer dynamics, and environmental changes. Such papers should provide substantive evidence based on which new marketing theories can be developed and marketing methodologies further improved. Such papers should discuss and demonstrate relevance to marketing problems. Papers which integrate quantitative methods with behavioral theories are strongly encouraged.

Applications. We learn through experience. If *Management Science* in marketing is to be relevant, it must be applicable. We encourage papers which a apply theories, models, or methodologies which have been previously published. Such papers should include a discussion of the problem, the analyses to address the problem and an interpretation of the impact of the analyses. We view such papers as cumulative empirical experience adding to the base of marketing science. We are interested, particularly, in papers providing in-depth analyses and describing implementations of management science-based approaches in industries that have not traditionally received much attention, such as the leisure and entertainment industries.

Other. All other papers will be considered on a case-by-case basis. Our main criterion of publication is that the paper make an original and substantial contribution to the marketing literature. The paper should be written with a sufficient degree of conciseness and clarity so that it is accessible to management practitioners. For example, use active voice, write abstracts as a "report in miniature," write introductions so they can be read by all readers, highlight implications, make use of technical appendices, use clear notation, define variables unambiguously, avoid unnecessary jargon and algebra, etc.

Mathematical Programming & Networks

Papers sought by this department are those which promise noticeable improvements in managerial applications based on mathematical programming and networks. Genuine contributions to theory, algorithmic design and evaluation, modeling, and user practice are welcome. Papers whose utilitarian potential is largely speculative, however, should be directed to other journals.

We are especially interested in:

- computational studies or theoretical analyses that illuminate the *relative effectiveness* of algorithms for problems of realistic size and complexity
- contributions to the *model design process* in which real problems are confronted with available mathematical programming and artwork techniques
- well-documented *applications* teaching lessons of transferable value about the use of these techniques in supporting managerial decision making
- methodological *proposals* for the use of mathematical programming and network techniques as a source of insights and as a problem-solving tool
- expository *survey articles* that help bring important branches of the field into better focus through unifying principles or selective emphasis.

Prospective authors are advised that clarity is regarded as a virtue second only to substance. In each paper, the abstract and the introduction should spell out its contribution in nontechnical terms, without unnecessary formalisms and with clear reference to the practical problems that motivated the research.

Organizational Performance, Strategy and Design

The department encourages the publication of papers applying the analytical frameworks of the management sciences to individual, group, organizational and interorganizational behavior. A major emphasis is on papers concerned with understanding and improving organizational performance, strategy and design.

We take a broad approach to organizational performance. Examples of performance dimensions include organizational survival, productivity, quality, timeliness, profitability, flexibility, responsiveness, the development of organizational competence, employee development, and contributions to a larger system. In addition to papers that examine performance at the organizational level of analysis, we are also interested in papers focusing on the performance of the groups and departments that comprise organizations and of the networks in which organizations are embedded. Papers need not explicitly measure a performance dimension but they should have implications for organizational performance, strategy, and design.

We view organizational strategy as the means through which an organization attains its performance goals. Organizational design involves the prescription of the organization's structures and processes in order to improve its performance and survival prospects.

We wish to publish innovative papers from different disciplines, including anthropology, cognitive sciences, economics, information systems, organizational behavior, political science, psychology and sociology. Both theoretical and empirical papers are welcome. We are open to a variety of methods, including archival analyses, surveys, field studies, laboratory studies, simulations, case studies and mathematical modeling.

The editors and reviewers have three overarching questions in mind as they review research submitted to the department. First, is the research interesting and important? Second, has the paper demonstrated what it says it has? Evaluating and ruling out alternative explanations for the paper's findings will strengthen the analysis and increase confidence in the findings. Third, does the paper advance our understanding of organizational performance, strategy, and design? Papers for which the answers to these questions are judged to be yes by the editors and reviewers will be published in the journal. We want to publish the best and the most innovative papers on organizational performance, strategy, and design.

Public Sector Applications

The Public Sector Applications Department of *Management Science* seeks high-quality, well-written papers that emphasize innovative and state-of-the-art uses of management science methods in modeling and solving important decision problems encountered in the public sector. In particular, one key goal of the Department is to publish papers that describe high-impact modeling efforts. Another goal is to publish informative and comprehensive survey articles, especially those that discuss promising opportunities for future research. We take a broad view of the field and will consider papers that describe applications in such diverse areas as the environment, natural resource management (including fisheries management, forestry, wildlife management, and water resources management), energy, health care, housing, defense education, public safety, transportation, recreation, regulatory policy, regional planning, and taxation.

We are seeking to publish papers that make a significant contribution to the scholarly literature on the application of management science methods to the public sector. We envisage that most papers will strive to inform management scientists, as well as government decision makers, about interesting new ways of formulating, analyzing, and solving public sector problems. We also encourage submissions that develop new and original theories and concepts and papers that describe unusual and atypical modeling efforts.

Prospective authors should bear in mind that the departmental editors and associate editors are committed to the timely review and publication of interesting applications of management science in the public sector.

R&D/Innovation And Entrepreneurship

The management of innovative and entrepreneurial activities has become a topic of growing concern and interest within most technology-based organizations, especially in light of today's highly competitive international arena. Within the R&D/Innovation and Entrepreneurship Department, we are looking for original manuscripts that will advance our understanding of the many wide-ranging issues and problems associated with the management of research and technology. Such advancement could come from careful empirical investigations, from clear theoretical conceptualizations or models, from novel syntheses or comprehensive reviews of existing studies, or from well-argued case studies.

Our emphasis is on furthering our understanding of the management process particularly as it relates to the research, development, and engineering tasks necessary to carry out effective innovation. Manuscripts should have a clear problem focus. They should seek to extend our knowledge and perspective of important management problem areas or certain management tools and techniques. Authors submitting their work should articulate what is already known and should try to ground their study within existing streams of research theories and empirical findings. It is through the submission of interesting work that both builds on past results and stimulates future developments that we hope to establish a more coherent, cumulative, and relevant body of knowledge and understanding.

We invite all papers dealing with issues related to the management of innovation and technological activities. Because of the interdisciplinary nature of our focus, we encourage authors from a variety of disciplines to contribute to our department. Illustrative examples of relevant topics are:

- The effective utilization and management of technical professionals
- Project management including project selection. evaluation, and resource utilization
- Organizational structures and designs for enhancing innovation and entrepreneurial efforts
- Managing technological changes and discontinuities
- Managing communications and information flows
- Managing product and process innovations
- Enhancing the commercialization of new technologies
- Managing relationships and interfaces across organizational and functional areas
- Organizing and managing for faster decision-making and product development cycles
- Measuring and improving productivity and quality within R&D
- Managing the locus of innovation among R&D, manufacturing, suppliers, and customers
- Managing global technologies and multicorporate R&D centers
- Technology planning and forecasting
- Technology transfer including the diffusion and adoption of innovation and technological know-how
- Economics of R&D
- Venture capital management and new venture strategies
- Managing corporate and global alliances and joint ventures
- Patents, licensing, and intellectual property rights
- Integrating technology with strategic planning

- Public policy, government regulations, and R&D
- Management systems and rewards for innovation and entrepreneurship

Papers submitted to this department should be well written and based on sound methodological research and concepts. Both empirical and conceptual papers are welcome. Authors should keep in mind the managerial focus of our journal and should address the usefulness of their papers.

Stochastic Models and Simulation

The Applied Stochastic Models Department and the Simulation Department were recently combined into a new department of Stochastic Models and Simulation. The commonality of techniques and applications between the two areas makes the merger natural: simulation is an important tool in the study of stochastic systems, and stochastic process theory underlies much of simulation research and practice. The new Department hopes to bring together the best of the two topics and to feature new directions for both.

The Department seeks papers that contribute to the modeling, analysis, or simulation of stochastic systems through advances in methodology or application. A paper in the area may contribute through theoretical development, through algorithmic advances, or through innovative modeling and applications. Survey articles on topics of broad or growing interest are also welcome. The Department attaches particular importance to scientific rigor and to clarity of exposition.

There are currently many other outlets for publication of work on stochastic models and simulation. Compared with more specialized journals, the Department seeks papers that emphasize issues of broad interest over purely technical contributions. The mathematical level of the work should be appropriate to the contribution but excessive formalism is discouraged. Deferring necessary technical material to appendices can help make research papers accessible to a wider audience.

The Department welcomes papers in such areas as inventory and production, service operations, statistical and computational issues in simulation, telecommunications, variance reductions techniques, and all aspects of the application of probability to management science. The Department is particularly eager to attract papers in novel areas of theory and application of stochastic modeling and simulation, such as financial engineering and risk management, public health and health care operations, environmental and catastrophic risks, extremal events and insurance, new approaches to simulation efficiency, Markov chain Monte Carlo, and quasi-Monte Carlo methods.

Supply Chain Management

To compete successfully in the global market, companies need to manage the effectiveness and efficiency of the operations that manufacture and distribute their products or services to their customers. Supply chain management deals with the management of materials, information and financial flows in a network consisting of suppliers, manufacturers, distributors, retailers, and customers. Many industries have found it challenging to manage these flows efficiently and effectively.

316

There are three types of flows in a supply chain that require careful planning and coordination. Material flows involve both physical product flows from suppliers to customers through the chain as well as the reverse flows via product returns, servicing, recycling, and disposal. Information flows involve order transmission and delivery status. Financial flows involve credit terms payment schedules, and consignment and title ownership arrangements. These flows cut across companies and sometimes ownership arrangements. These flows cut across companies and sometimes even industries.

The Department of Supply Chain Management processes papers that focus on the coordination and integration of the flows in a supply chain consisting of multiple sites and organizations with multiple independent decision makers. (For papers that do not quite fit the above description, the author(s) should submit their papers to the Department of Manufacturing, Distribution and Service Operations.) The papers to be processed by the Department of Supply Chain Management can be:

- theoretical work motivated by real life problems and situations
- applications based on real cases
- conceptual work that provides a framework to analyze problems in industry
- empirical studies based on real data
- surveys of existing literature and industrial practice

Examples of topics include: product and process designs for supply chain management; structuring supply chains for mass customization; third party logistics; outsourcing and contract manufacturing; supplier contracting; incentive and performance measures; global supply chain management; quick response and cycle time reduction; multiproduct and multilocation production and inventory coordination; consolidation, warehousing, scheduling and coordination of transportation and production flows; and industry-wide supply chain integration.

All paper submissions should comply with the Editorial Policy and the Instructions for Authors located on the front inside cover of any issue of *Management Science*. Please submit four copies of the paper to the Departmental Editor of Supply Chain Management at the address printed above.

EDITORIAL STATEMENT

Management Science is a scholarly journal published to scientifically address the problems, interests and concerns of organizational decision-makers. Through publication of relevant theory and innovative applications, we serve the needs of both academicians and practitioners. In addition to articles from traditional fields such as operations research, mathematics, statistics, industrial engineering, psychology, sociology and political science, we publish cross-functional, multidisciplinary research to reflect the diversity of the management science profession. We also publish relevant articles and seek to stimulate research in emerging domains, such as those created by globalization of the economy, changes in public policy, and improvements in technology.

SUBMISSIONS

The following are requirements for a manuscript submitted to *Management Science*:

- papers are not more than 32 pages including figures and tables, printed on 8 1/2" X 11" paper;
- 12-point font, and one-inch margins on all four sides;
- double-spaced throughout, including abstract, references, and footnotes;
- a nonmathematical abstract (as understandable to readers as possible) of not more than 200 words;
- four copies for the reviewing process; and
- a list of five potential referees on a separate sheet of paper with several lines describing why they would be | good reviewers, area of expertise, title, full mailing addresses, phones, fax, and e-mail. The suggested referees should not have a conflict of interest with the author(s). A person has a conflict of interest with (a) his/her major professor or a student for whom the person served as a major professor, (b) people working at the same institution, (c) coauthors on work completed or in progress _during the last four years.
- when a paper is accepted for publication, we must have a hard copy of the final version plus a disk in either Word, WordPerfect, or Tex.

Please submit manuscripts to the appropriate Departmental Editor or to the Editor-in-Chief. Departmental Editors are listed on the journal masthead.

Managerial Auditing Journal

ADDRESS FOR SUBMISSION:

Gerald Vinten, Editor
Managerial Auditing Journal
Southampton Business School
East Park Terrace
Southampton, SO14 0RH
UK
Phone: 44 (0) 1703-319318
Fax: 44 (0) 1703-337438
E-Mail: gerald.vinten@solent.ac.uk
Web: www.mcb.co.uk
Address May Change:

CIRCULATION DATA:

Reader: Business Persons, Academics
Frequency of Issue: 9 Times/Year
Copies per Issue: No Reply
Sponsor/Publisher: MCB University Press
    Limited-UK
Subscribe Price: 2499.00 US$ USA
    3249.00 AUS$ Australasian
    6599.00 Euro + $629.90 VAT Rest of
    World

PUBLICATION GUIDELINES:

Manuscript Length: 26-30
Copies Required: Two
Computer Submission: Yes Email
Format: See Manuscript Guidelines
Fees to Review: 0.00 US$

Manuscript Style:
    See Manuscript Guidelines

REVIEW INFORMATION:

Type of Review: Blind Review
No. of External Reviewers: 2
No. of In House Reviewers: 1
Acceptance Rate: 80%
Time to Review: 1 - 2 Months
Reviewers Comments: Yes
Invited Articles: 6-10%
Fees to Publish: 0.00 US$

MANUSCRIPT TOPICS:
Accounting Information Systems; Accounting Theory & Practice; Auditing; Business Ethics; Computer Security; Cost Accounting; Government & Non Profit Accounting; Industrial Organization; Internal Auditing; Management

MANUSCRIPT GUIDELINES/COMMENTS:

About The Journal
Articles submitted to the journal should be original contributions and should not be under consideration for any other publication at the same time. Submissions should be sent to:

The Editor
Professor Gerald Vinten, Deputy Dean, Southampton Business School, East Park Terrace, Southampton, SO14 ORH.

Editorial Objectives
Managerial Auditing Journal uniquely addresses the changing function of the auditor; with particular reference to the managerial aspects of the role and the positive impact the professional can have on company policy and development.

Auditors, once employed for the express purpose of checking the accounts for fraudulent practice, have now developed a more supportive role, guiding and maintaining continual improvement. This new approach is reflected in MAJ, which takes its readers beyond traditional conventions and looks at the ways in which contemporary auditors are improving both managerial and organizational performance.

MAJ presents a wide range of material with an emphasis on practical examples from expert practitioners, making it relevant to a broad readership. Its concentration on modern practice creates a useful forum for the development of new thinking and practice within the profession.

Unique Attributes
The journal provides: a forum for those within a broad managerial as well as professional interest in audit to explore current practices, ideas and experience; a framework of explanation and guidance on developments and research; and perspectives on professional and career development. Papers accepted for publication are double blind-refereed to ensure academic rigor and integrity.

- Key Journal Audiences
- Academics and researchers
- Auditors
- Finance directors
- General managers
- Internal and external auditors
- Management consultants

Coverage
The journal's wide coverage includes:
- Career issues
- Communicating the results of audits
- Corporate Governance
- Environmental auditing
- Ethical considerations
- Information Technology
- Internal and External Auditing
- Internal Control
- Management theory and auditing practice
- Operational Audit Areas
- Performance Measurement
- People and assets auditing
- Social auditing processes

The Reviewing Process
Each paper submitted is subject to the following review procedures:
1. It is reviewed by the editor for general suitability for this publication.

2. If it is judged suitable two reviewers are selected and a double blind review process takes place.

3 Based on the recommendations of the reviewers, the editor then decides whether the particular article should be accepted as it is, revised or rejected.

The process described above is a general one. The editor, however, may, in some circumstances, vary this process.

Article Features And Formats Required Of Authors

There are a number of specific requirements with regard to article features and formats, which authors should note carefully:

1. Word length

Articles should be between 3,000 and 8,000 words in length. Longer articles, and monographs by negotiation.

2. Title

A title of not more than eight words in length should be provided.

3. Autobiographical note

A brief autobiographical note should be supplied including full name, appointment, name of organization and e-mail address.

4. Word processing

Please submit to the Editor two copies of the manuscript in double line spacing with wide margins.

5. Headings and sub-headings

These should be short and to-the-point, appearing approximately every 750 words. Headings should be typed in capitals and underlined; sub-headings should be typed in upper and lower case and underlined. Headings should not be numbered.

6. References

References to other publications should be in Harvard style. They should contain full bibliographical details and journal titles should not be abbreviated. For multiple citations in the same year use a, b, c immediately following the year of publication. References should be shown as follows:

Within the text - author's last name followed by a comma and year of publication all in round brackets, e g. (Fox, 1994).

At the end of the article a reference list in alphabetical order as follows:
   (a) For books:
   surname, initials, year of publication, title, publisher, place of publication, e.g. Casson, M. (1979), Alternatives to the Multinational Enterprise, Macmillan, London.
   (b) For chapter in edited in book:
   surname, initials, year, title, editor's surname, initials, title, publisher, place, pages, e.g.

Bessley, M. and Wilson, P. (1984), "Public policy and small firms in Britain", in Levicki, C. (Ed.), Small Business Theory and Policy, Croom Helm, London, pp. 111-26.
(c) For articles:
surname, initials, year, title, journal, volume, number, pages, e.g.
Fox, S. (1994), "Empowerment as a catalyst for change: an example from the food industry", Supply Chain Management, Vol. 2 No. 3, pp. 29-33.

If there is more than one author list surnames followed by initials. All authors should be shown. Electronic sources should include the URL of the electronic site at which they may be found.

Notes/Endnotes should be used only if absolutely necessary. They should be identified in the text by consecutive numbers enclosed in square brackets and listed at the end of the article.

7. Figures, charts, diagrams
Use of figures, charts and diagrams should be kept to a minimum and information conveyed in such a manner should instead be described in text form. Essential figures, charts and diagrams should be referred to as figures and numbered consecutively using arabic numerals. Each figure should have a brief title and labelled axes. Diagrams should be kept as simple as possible and avoid unnecessary capitalization and shading In the text, the position of the figure should be shown by typing on a separate line the words "take in Figure 1".

8. Tables
Use of tables should be kept to a minimum. Where essential, these should be typed on a separate sheet of paper and numbered consecutively and independently of any figures included in the article. Each table should have a number in roman numerals, a brief title, and vertical and horizontal headings. In the text, the position of the table should be shown by typing on a separate line the words "take in Table 1". Tables should not repeat data available elsewhere in the paper.

9. Photos, illustrations
Half-tone illustrations should be restricted in number to the minimum necessary. Good glossy bromide prints should accompany the manuscripts but not be attached to manuscript pages. Illustrations unsuitable for reproduction, e.g. computer-screen capture, will not be used. Any computer programs should be supplied as clear and sharp print outs on plain paper. They will be reproduced photographically to avoid errors.

10. Emphasis
Words to be emphasized should be limited in number and italicized. Capital letters should be used only at the start of sentences or in the case of proper names.

11. Abstracts
Authors must supply an abstract of 100-150 words when submitting an article. It should be an abbreviated, accurate representation of the content of the article. Major results, conclusions and/or recommendations should be given, followed by supporting details of method, scope or purpose. It should contain sufficient information to enable readers to decide whether they should obtain and read the entire article.

12. Keywords

Six keywords should be included which encapsulate the principal subjects covered by the article. Minor facets of an article should not be keyworded. These keywords will be used by readers to select the material they wish to read and should therefore be truly representative of the article's main content.

Preparation For Publication

13. Final submission of the article

Once accepted by the Editor for publication, the final version of the article should be submitted in manuscript accompanied by an email file attachment or 3.5" disk of the same version of the article marked with: disk format; author name(s); title of article; journal title; file name. This will be considered to be the definitive version of the article and the author should ensure that it is complete, grammatically correct and without spelling or typographical errors.

In preparing the disk, please use one of the following formats:

* for text prepared on a PC - AMI Pro, FrameMaker, Office Writer, Professional write, RTF, Word or WordPerfect;
* for text prepared on a Macintosh system - FrameMaker, MacWrite, MS Works, Nisus 3, RTF, Word, WordPerfect WriteNow or ASCII
* for graphics, figures, charts and diagrams, please use one of the following formats:

File type	Programs	File extension
Windows Metafile	Most Windows programs	wmf
WordPerfect Graphic	All WordPerfect software	.wpg
Adobe Illustrator	Adobe Illustrator	.ai
	Corel Draw	
	Macromedia Freehand	
Harvard Graphics	Harvard Graphics	.cgm
PIC	Lotus graphics	.pic
Computer/Graphics		
Metafile	Lotus Freelance	.cgm
DXF	Autocad	.dxf
	Many CAD programs	
GEM	Ventura Publisher	.gem
Macintosh PICT	Most Macintosh Drawing	

Only vector type drawings are acceptable, as bitmap files (extension .bmp, .pcx or .gif) print poorly. If graphical representations are not available on disk, black ink line drawings suitable for photographic reproduction and of dimensions appropriate for reproduction on a journal page should be supplied with the article.

If you require technical assistance in respect of submitting an article please consult the relevant section of MCB's World Wide Web Literati Club on http://www.mcb.co.uk/literati/nethome.htm or contact Mike Massey at MCB, e-mail: mmassey@mcb.co.uk

14. Journal Article Record Form
Each article should be accompanied by a completed and signed Journal Article Record Form. This form is available from the Editor or can be downloaded from MCB's World Wide Web Literati Club on http://www.mcb.co.uk/literati/nethome.htm

Managerial Auditing Journal is published by MCB University Press, 60/62 Toller Lane, Bradford, West Yorkshire BD8 9BY, UK. Tel: +44 1274 777700, Fax: +44 1274 785200 or 785201.

324

Massachusetts CPA Review Online

ADDRESS FOR SUBMISSION:

Cheryl McCloud, Communications Director
Massachusetts CPA Review Online
MA Soc. of Certified Public Accountants
105 Chauncy Street, 10th Floor
Boston, MA 02111
USA
Phone: 617-556-4000
Fax: 617-556-4126
E-Mail: cmccloud@mscpaonline.org
Web:
Address May Change:

PUBLICATION GUIDELINES:

Manuscript Length: 6-10
Copies Required: Two
Computer Submission: Yes
Format: MAC/PC, Text WP or ASCII
Fees to Review: 0.00 US$

Manuscript Style:
See Manuscript Guidelines

CIRCULATION DATA:

Reader: Business Persons
Frequency of Issue: Quarterly on disk
Copies per Issue: 5,001 - 10,000
Sponsor/Publisher: Massachusetts Society
of Certified Public Accountants
Subscribe Price: 20.00 US$

REVIEW INFORMATION:

Type of Review: Blind Review
No. of External Reviewers: 0
No. of In House Reviewers: 2
Acceptance Rate: No Reply
Time to Review: 2 - 3 Months
Reviewers Comments: No
Invited Articles: No Reply
Fees to Publish: 0.00 US$

MANUSCRIPT TOPICS:
Accounting Information Systems; Accounting Theory & Practice; Auditing; Cost Accounting; Economic Development; Fiscal Policy; Government & Non Profit Accounting; Industrial Organization; Insurance; International Finance; Tax Accounting

MANUSCRIPT GUIDELINES/COMMENTS:

1. The editors often receive inquiries from CPAs and other who would like to write articles for the *CPA Review*, but aren't sure what we need or how to get started. Here are some hints and guidelines for authors on what the *CPA Review* editors are seeking.

2. Pertinent and interesting articles are the lifeblood of any magazine. Relevant articles are essential to the continuing quality of the *CPA Review*. We will always have a need for practical and suitable articles of interest to Massachusetts' professional accountants, financial executives, and educators.

3. The editors specifically consider the following questions in reviewing articles for publication in the Review.
    Is the topic suitable and of interest to our Massachusetts and New England readers?

Does the article contribute new ideas or insights?
Is the article concise and does the author cover the subject in sufficient depth?

4. The types of manuscripts that we are most likely to publish fall into three categories:

1. articles that help solve practice problems or that advance "leading edge" management accounting techniques,
2. penetrating analysis of important developments in taxation, education, computers, management advisory services, business, accounting and auditing, and
3. insightful, pertinent opinion, interviews, letters, and short articles with a how-to-do-it or local Massachusetts slant. Highly theoretical papers are less desirable than practical, relevant articles primarily based on examples drawn from your experience.

5. The Review has had a generally favorable reaction to its series of interviews and roundtable discussions with prominent educators, business leaders, and political figures. We will continue to publish such articles from time to time.

6. A succinctly written article covering a suitable topic in depth will probably be published. The author's professional writing ability is a less important consideration.

7. Each issue of the *CPA Review* is dedicated to a specific theme. This does not necessarily mean that the entire magazine is devoted to a particular topic. The editors will consider creative and apposite articles at any time regardless of our current editorial plans. If you want to write about a topic that does not exactly fit into our editorial calendar and guidelines, please let us know. Our objective is to cover a variety of topics in every issue that will appeal to most of our readers. If the topic excites you, it probably is of interest to others. The timing of your submission is, however, important. We encourage you to write to or call a *CPA Review* editor about your ideas and suggestions for future articles.

8. Often, a brief and specific outline of a proposed manuscript can serve as a prompt means of obtaining a reaction to your ideas. Of course, the final acceptance of an article for publication can only be made after reading the completed manuscript.

9. The editors believe that attractive illustrations enhance the treatment and presentation of published. Although they are not mandatory, effective graphs and photographs of appropriate size are a definite plus.

10. You may also with to review the last few issues of the *CPA Review* for an indication of writing styles, formats, and subjects used by our authors in the past.

11. Not every article warrants feature treatment in the Review. We will consider letters and shorter articles for use in departments (such as CPA Focus and Feedback and State Taxation) or in the *CPA Newsletter* of the Massachusetts Society of Certified Public Accountants. "Sidebar" stories to major articles in the Review are always welcome. (A sidebar story might present in a brief format a case history, a practical example, or a human-interest angle related to the feature article.)

12. There are, in short, numerous writing opportunities for prospective authors in the *CPA Review*. The editors are eager to assist anyone who would like to write for the magazine. We need you! The greater the number of quality manuscripts that we have to choose from the better we can achieve the primary goal of the *CPA Review*: to furnish useful, practical, and interesting information to our readers that will help them in their professional careers.

13. Clarity of thought and economy of words are two precious characteristics of well-written articles. Feature article treatment requires that the discussion of the topic be comprehensive. The *CPA Review* editors prefer:
1.   feature articles of 1,500 words,
2.   supplementary stories and sidebars of about 500 words, and
3.   letters to the editor of less than 750 words

Such brevity of expression might be difficult for some writers. The editors suggest that authors use the following style conventions and formats to help attain the appropriate level of topic coverage and article length:

* Write mostly in the active voice.
* Use relatively short sentences and paragraphs for most of the article. Keep it simple; make it forceful.
* Avoid the use of extensive checklists, footnotes, and tabulations.
* Review your manuscript for consistency of expression and format. (Eliminate any inconsistent or redundant material.)
* Don't overuse arcane jargon or technical lingo.

14. By adhering to the following minor "rules", you will make life less complicated for the CPA Review editors responsible for reviewing your manuscript:

* Include a cover page indicating the suggested article title, the author's name, address, and telephone number, and the date.
* Type your manuscript with double spacing and with generous margins. (Eight to ten typed pages, double spaced is about the maximum length for a feature article.)
* Submit three copies of the manuscript to facilitate the editorial and review process.
* Identify all borrowed or quoted material and identify sources in footnotes or references.
* Send readable charts, tables, and other informative graphics. (Rough drawings are acceptable, but camera-ready artwork is a real help.) Label all artwork submitted.
* Use brief titles and section subheadings.

15. Usually, two or three editors and staff members read each manuscript for editorial consideration and technical content. We attempt to complete the review process and notify authors regarding acceptance within 45 days.

16. There you have it - a few guidelines and suggestions for having your article published in the *CPA Review*. We wish you success. Our *CPA Review* readers and we look forward to reading your article.

Multinational Business Review

ADDRESS FOR SUBMISSION:

Suk-Hi Kim, Editor
Multinational Business Review
University of Detroit Mercy
College of Business Administration
PO Box 19900
4001 W. McNichols Road
Detroit, MI 48221-0900
USA
Phone: 313-993-1264
Fax: 313-993-1673/1052
E-Mail: kimsuk@mich.com
Web: www.mich.com/~kimsuk/
Address May Change:

PUBLICATION GUIDELINES:

Manuscript Length: 16-20
Copies Required: Three
Computer Submission: Yes
Format: N/A
Fees to Review: 40.00 US$
        20.00 US$ Journal Subscribers

Manuscript Style:
, Journal of International Business
Studies

CIRCULATION DATA:

Reader: Business Persons, Academics
Frequency of Issue: 2 Times/Year
Copies per Issue: Less than 1,000
Sponsor/Publisher: University of Detroit
    Mercy
Subscribe Price: 30.00 US$ Individual
        60.00 US$ Institution
        15.00 US$ Student

REVIEW INFORMATION:

Type of Review: Blind Review
No. of External Reviewers: 1
No. of In House Reviewers: 1
Acceptance Rate: 35%
Time to Review: 2 - 3 Months
Reviewers Comments: Yes
Invited Articles: 0-5%
Fees to Publish: 0.00 US$

MANUSCRIPT TOPICS:

Accounting Information Systems; Auditing; International Accounting; International Economics & Trade; International Finance; Portfolio & Security Analysis; Regional Economics; Tax Accounting

MANUSCRIPT GUIDELINES/COMMENTS:

Subscribers outside the U.S. add $10 for postage.

Multinational Business Review (MBR) is published twice annually by the College of Business Administration at the University of Detroit Mercy. The journal welcomes application-oriented articles dealing with international aspects of accounting, finance, management, and marketing. The editors are interested in publishing studies on thought-provoking topics for business executives and academicians. Each article is blind refereed. Reviewers will judge submissions particularly on conceptual clarity and practicability. Authors are requested to submit three copies of the paper and follow the *Manuscript Preparation and Style Guide for Authors of the Journal of International Business Studies*. Each submission should be accompanied with a fee of $20 for MBR's subscribers or $40 for non-subscribers which will be applied to a one year subscription to the journal. Writers should also include an abstract of 80 to 120 words which present the principle points of the article. Authors will receive confirmation when their articles are received. Editorial decisions will be sent to authors no more than 90 days later. Send manuscripts to the Editor.

National Accounting Journal (The)

ADDRESS FOR SUBMISSION:

W. Terry Dancer, Editor
National Accounting Journal (The)
Arkansas State University
905 Rosemond Avenue
Jonesboro, AR 72401
USA
Phone: 870-935-1579
Fax: 870-932-1459
E-Mail: dancer@cherokee.astate.edu
Web:
Address May Change:

PUBLICATION GUIDELINES:

Manuscript Length: 16-20
Copies Required: Three
Computer Submission: No
Format: N/A
Fees to Review: 50.00 US$

Manuscript Style:
, Accounting Review Style

CIRCULATION DATA:

Reader: Academics
Frequency of Issue: 2 Times/ Year
Copies per Issue: Less than 1,000
Sponsor/Publisher: World Wide Publishing
Subscribe Price: 100.00 US$

REVIEW INFORMATION:

Type of Review: Blind Review
No. of External Reviewers: 2
No. of In House Reviewers: 1
Acceptance Rate: 21-30%
Time to Review: 1 - 2 Months
Reviewers Comments: No
Invited Articles: 0-5%
Fees to Publish: 25.00 US$ Per Page

MANUSCRIPT TOPICS:

Accounting Education; Accounting Information Systems; Accounting Theory & Practice; Auditing; Cost Accounting; Government & Non Profit Accounting; Tax Accounting

MANUSCRIPT GUIDELINES/COMMENTS:

Statement of Policy

The *National Accounting Journal* (NAJ) is a refereed Accounting journal dedicated to the promotion of excellence in Accounting Education and the advancement of Accounting knowledge. The Journal provides a forum for the exchange of ideas, concepts, theories, and research results among college and university level educators. The journal will publish items ranging from brief educational notes to full length manuscripts. The intended readership of this journal is accounting academicians and accounting practitioners.

Manuscripts are subject to blind review. Reviewers will assess the professional quality with which the manuscript was prepared and evaluate the appropriateness for inclusion of the manuscript in the journal.

Manuscripts submitted to IJBD are expected to be free from grammatical and spelling errors. Authors are expected to have their manuscript examined by a grammarian before submitting a paper for review.

Manuscript Requirements

Three copies of each item submitted for review should be sent to: Dr. W. Terry Dancer, Editor, The National Accounting Journal, 905 Rosemond Avenue, Jonesboro, Ar., 72401. During the 1999-2000 year, the review fee for completed manuscripts will be $50.00, and the review fee for brief educational notes (three pages or less) will be $25.00. If a paper is accepted for publication, authors will be assessed a $25.00 per page publication fee.

The initial review process will require about six weeks. The focus on this initial review will be on the content of the item being reviewed. The format of your original submission is far less important than the content of the paper submitted. Authors of accepted papers will be given specific instructions for the appropriate format of the item to be published.

A letter of transmittal must accompany each paper submitted for review. The letter of transmittal should include the authors complete mailing address, affiliation, telephone number, fax number,, and E-mail address if available. Author names should be mentioned only on the title page.

Authors of accepted items will be required to submit a disk containing a file with the final version of the item keyboarded in Word perfect or Word and a hard copy of their final version. The Times New Roman 12pt font should be used exclusively, except where a special font is necessary. The table function should be used for all tables. Citations should be made in square brackets using the authors' last name, date, and where necessary, page number and a shortened form of the title. *The Accounting Review* should be referred to as an example of the correct style for citations.

By submitting a manuscript, the authors agree to transfer the right to the publisher to reproduce and distribute the item published. Authors may expect all items received by NAJ to be reviewed in a timely and efficient manner.

Subscription requests from libraries and individuals should be sent to the address noted above. The subscription rate for 1999-2001 is $100.00 per year.

National Public Accountant

ADDRESS FOR SUBMISSION:

Daniell T. Griffin, Editor
National Public Accountant
Director of Marketing & Communications
National Society of Accountants
1010 North Fairfax Street
Alexandria, VA 22314
USA
Phone: 703-549-6400
Fax: 703-549-2984
E-Mail: nsa@wizard.net
Web: www.nsacct.org
Address May Change:

PUBLICATION GUIDELINES:

Manuscript Length: 2,000 Wds. Max
Copies Required: Three
Computer Submission: Yes
Format: See Guidelines
Fees to Review: 0.00 US$

Manuscript Style:
See Manuscript Guidelines

CIRCULATION DATA:

Reader: Business Persons
Frequency of Issue: Monthly
Copies per Issue: 10,001 - 25,000
Sponsor/Publisher: National Society of
   Accountants
Subscribe Price: 20.00 US$

REVIEW INFORMATION:

Type of Review: Editorial Review
No. of External Reviewers: 1
No. of In House Reviewers: 2
Acceptance Rate: 50%
Time to Review: 2 - 3 Months
Reviewers Comments: No
Invited Articles: 6-10%
Fees to Publish: 0.00 US$

MANUSCRIPT TOPICS:

Accounting Information Systems; Accounting Theory & Practice; Auditing; Cost Accounting; Government & Non Profit Accounting; Industrial Organization; Insurance; Portfolio & Security Analysis; Real Estate; Tax Accounting

MANUSCRIPT GUIDELINES/COMMENTS:

The *National Public Accountant is* published monthly by the National Society of Accountants. A refereed professional journal, it reaches over 20,000 readers, including accountants in public practice, government officials, lawyers, bankers, college and university professors and students, management consultants and data processing personnel.

Specifications

Send three copies of manuscripts, typed, double-spaced, with 1" margins on all sides. Include any tables, charts, graphs, illustrations and pictures. Avoid overuse of passive voice and of the verb "to be."

You also need to send us the article on computer disk (either Macintosh or IBM-compatible) including the text, tables, charts and graphs, as applicable. Graphics should be in black and white or grayscale. The file should be in either WordPerfect or ASCII format, and the disk should be high density. *It is very important that we receive a disk with each submission. Your bio must be included on the disk with the article (either in a separate file, or at the bottom of the article). Hard copy of bios will not be retyped Also, we will be happy to run a photo* if *you wish to send one.* [Materials may be e-mailed to nsamrkt@wizard.net]

Average length of feature articles is from six to ten typed, double-spaced pages, or approximately 2,000 words. **Caution: Exceeding the word limit may cause an otherwise good article to be rejected.** Please check with the editor if you have a longer paper and wish to run a series.

Subjects
Articles should be practical and written for the independent practicing accountant and businessperson. Avoid using the term "CPA"; use "accountant" instead.

We invite you to submit manuscripts on such subjects as accounting, business management, taxation, financial and estate planning, computers, liability or other topics of interest to independent practitioners and their small business clients. Avoid topics which pertain only to CPAs, or functions which are performed only by CPAs.

Procedure
Upon receipt, manuscripts are sent to the NSA Editorial Review Board for consideration. The review process takes a *minimum of two months.* The author will be notified of the Board's decision. If accepted, the article is scheduled for publication. Rejected articles are not returned. Upon publication, the author receives three complimentary copies of NPA. NPA reserves the right to reschedule articles or drop them from publication at any time for any reason.

For more information, contact: *Kimberlee Lippencott, Editor 1010 N.* Fairfax St. Alexandria, VA 22314-1574 phone 703-549-6400, fax 703-549-2984, e-mail nsamrkt@lwizard.net

NPA works two months ahead of press time. For example, on January 1, March issue materials are due. On February 1, April materials are due. In certain situations, the editor will allow late materials, provided there is still space available. The advertising schedule is different and questions should be directed to the Communications & Marketing department. *Advertising Contact.* Jody Crisp-Felski, Marketing Assistant 703-549-6400, ext. 1326. Fax 703-549-2984.

Special Topics Issues
In June of each year, NPA is dedicated almost exclusively to technology and software topics.

The September issue of each year is dedicated to practice management, building a client base, and dealing with office/staff issues and problems.

Our December issue focuses on federal tax and tax law changes. This issue provides our sought-after Tax Organizer for members.

Client Report

Every other issue of NPA contains our Client Report, providing members' clients simple, easy-to-understand updates and information. The Report is camera-ready, provides a space for members to insert a business card, and is easily reproduced by a copier machine or professional printer.

Requested Topics

The Editorial Review Board is currently seeking articles of a practical, how-to nature on the topics of oil, gasoline, forestry, fishing, farming, racing, border states accounting (Canada and Mexico), manufacturing, restaurants, gambling, scholarship, divorce, estate planning, non-profits, quality assurance review, Section 263A: (how it is conducted; how it is handled), state accountancy boards, how to prepare web sites, sexual harassment, racism, and gender bias.

Visit NSA's web site at www. nsacct.org

National Tax Journal

ADDRESS FOR SUBMISSION:

Douglas Holtz-Eakin, Editor
National Tax Journal
Syracuse University
426 Eggers Hall
Syracuse, NY 13244-1020
USA
Phone: 315-443-9464
Fax: 315-443-1081
E-Mail: ntj@maxwell.syr.edu
Web:
Address May Change:

PUBLICATION GUIDELINES:

Manuscript Length: Any
Copies Required: Four
Computer Submission: Yes
Format: All but Leading Edge
Fees to Review: 0.00 US$

Manuscript Style:
     Chicago Manual of Style

CIRCULATION DATA:

Reader: Business Persons, Academics, &
    Tax Practioners/Policymakers
Frequency of Issue: Quarterly
Copies per Issue: 3,001 - 4,000
Sponsor/Publisher: National Tax
    Association
Subscribe Price: 60.00 US$
    65.00 US$ Foreign

REVIEW INFORMATION:

Type of Review: Blind Review
No. of External Reviewers: 3
No. of In House Reviewers: 1
Acceptance Rate: 11-20%
Time to Review: 4 - 6 Months
Reviewers Comments: Yes
Invited Articles: 31-50%
Fees to Publish: 0.00 US$

MANUSCRIPT TOPICS:
Econometrics; Fiscal Policy; Government & Non Profit Accounting; Public Policy
Economics; Real Estate; Regional Economics; Tax Accounting

MANUSCRIPT GUIDELINES/COMMENTS:

This is a refereed journal that is designed to be read by academics, tax administrators,
businesspersons, lawyers and accountants interested in government finance.

New Accountant

ADDRESS FOR SUBMISSION:

Editor
New Accountant
3525 West Peterson
Chicago, Il 60659
USA
Phone: 773-866-9900
Fax: 773-866-9907
E-Mail:
Web:
Address May Change:

CIRCULATION DATA:

Reader: Academics
Frequency of Issue: 7 Times/Year
Copies per Issue: More than 25,000
Sponsor/Publisher: Profit Oriented Corp.
Subscribe Price: 21.00 US$ Student
  85.00 US$ Library

PUBLICATION GUIDELINES:

Manuscript Length: 6-10
Copies Required: One
Computer Submission: Yes
Format: Microsoft Word 6.0
Fees to Review: 0.00 US$

Manuscript Style:
  No Reply

REVIEW INFORMATION:

Type of Review: Blind Review
No. of External Reviewers: 0
No. of In House Reviewers: 2
Acceptance Rate: 21-30%
Time to Review: 1 Month or Less
Reviewers Comments: No
Invited Articles: 6-10%
Fees to Publish: 0.00 US$

MANUSCRIPT TOPICS:

Accounting Information Systems; Auditing; Capital Budgeting; Government & Non Profit
Accounting; Insurance; International Finance

MANUSCRIPT GUIDELINES/COMMENTS:

Articles for *New Accountant* must appeal to students.

Ohio CPA Journal (The)

ADDRESS FOR SUBMISSION:

Erin Lasch, Managing Editor
Ohio CPA Journal (The)
535 Metro Place South
PO Box 1810
Dublin, OH 43017-7810
USA
Phone: 614-764-2727
Fax: 614-764-5880
E-Mail: elasch@ohio-cpa.com
Web:
Address May Change:

PUBLICATION GUIDELINES:

Manuscript Length: 2,000-3,000 Words
Copies Required: Four
Computer Submission: Yes with hard copy
Format: 3 1/2 Diskette
Fees to Review: 0.00 US$

Manuscript Style:
    See Manuscript Guidelines

CIRCULATION DATA:

Reader: Business Persons
Frequency of Issue: Quarterly
Copies per Issue: 1,001 - 2,000
Sponsor/Publisher: Ohio Society of CPAs
Subscribe Price: 20.00 US$

REVIEW INFORMATION:

Type of Review: Blind Review
No. of External Reviewers: 2
No. of In House Reviewers: 2
Acceptance Rate: 11-20%
Time to Review: 2 - 3 Months
Reviewers Comments: Yes
Invited Articles: 0-5%
Fees to Publish: 0.00 US$

MANUSCRIPT TOPICS:

Accounting Information Systems; Accounting Theory & Practice; Auditing; Capital Budgeting; Cost Accounting; Econometrics; Economic History; General Business; Government & Non Profit Accounting; Insurance; International Economics & Trade; International Finance; Portfolio & Security Analysis; Public Policy Economics; Real Estate; Small Business Entrepreneurship; Tax Accounting

MANUSCRIPT GUIDELINES/COMMENTS:

Statement Of Purpose
The purpose of *The Ohio CPA,* journal is to provide information that is useful to members in providing services to employers and/or clients.

Articles and columns submitted for the Journal undergo a review and are accepted on a first and exclusive basis.

Articles
Topics Articles published in *The Ohio CPA,* journal, beginning with the April-June 1999 issue, will follow themes. The editorial calendar provides a listing of tentative themes and

submission dates. The Journal welcomes papers on the topics listed in the editorial calendar. We do encourage articles that are relevant to the CPA in Ohio.

Article length
An appropriate length for articles is 2,000-3,000 words. Some topics may need more or less space, depending on the scope of the topic.

Format
Authors should submit a copy to the managing editor via mail, fax or e-mail. Tables, charts, graphs, etc. are encouraged and should be formatted one to a page, at the end of the paper; they can be submitted in any format, as long as they are legible (they will be typeset by the Journal. In addition, please submit a 3 ½ inch computer diskette containing an electronic version of your article.

Style
The article should be written in a dear, concise manner. Write it as if the reader were a CPA who happens not to be an expert on the topic you are covering. Define any abbreviations and acronyms that are not commonplace. Provide detail where needed, and keep in mind that the article should leave the reader with a clear understanding of the topic discussed. Practical, relevant examples of issues discussed are strongly encouraged.

Department Columns
Topics The columns will continue to carry timely, newsy and topical information. Our current list of department columns includes:
- Administration of a Professional Practice
- Accounting & Auditing Update
- Assurance Services
- Computers and Technology
- Corporate Resource and Risk Management
- Federal Tax Issues
- Governmental Services
- Personal Financial Planning
- Quality Control & Peer Review
- Recent Publications
- State & Local Tax Issues
- AICPA Vision Project

Column Length
Desired length is no more than 1,300 words. Send one double-spaced hard copy to the, *Journal's* editor and managing editor at the address below.

Submit your articles columns to the Managing Editor at the address listed above or

the Editor, Peter D. Woodlock, CPA, Editor, The Ohio CPA Journal, Youngstown State University, 410 Wick Avenue, Youngstown, OH 44555-3084, Tel. 330-742-1873, Fax. 330-742-1459

Accounting and Auditing Update
J. Gregory Bushon, CPA, Wright State University, Dept. of Accountancy, Dayton, OH 45435

Administration of a Professional Practice
Gary S. Shamis, CPA, Saltz, Shamis & Goldfarb, CPA's, 31105 Bainbridge Road, Cleveland, OH 44139

Computers and Technology
Gregory H. Toman, CPA, Kentner Sellers CPA's, 801 Falls Creek Drive, Dayton, OH 45377

Federal Tax Topics
Michael Droppleman, CPA, FirstMerit Bank, N.A., 121 South Main Street, Suite 200, Akron, OH 44308

Governmental Services
Mark S. Weatherman, CPA, Clark, Schaefer, Hackett & Company, 2525 N. Limestone Street, Suite 103, Springfield , OH 45503

Personal Finance Planning
Angelo A. DiMarzio, CPA, S.G. Donahue & Co., Inc. 105 East Fourth Street, Suite 800, Cincinnati, OH 45202

Quality Control
Joseph R. Weaver, CPA, Weaver & Evans CPA's, 2375 East Main Street, Columbus, OH 43209-2421

Recent Publications
Thomas R. Pressly, CPA, Indiana University of Pennsylvania, Department of Accounting, Eberly College of Business, Indiana, PA 15705-1087

State and Local Tax Issues
W. Paul Wickham, CPA, Pricewaterhouse Coopers LLP, BP America Building, 200 Public Square, 27th Floor, Cleveland, OH 44114-2301

Corporate Resource and Risk Management
Peter Woodlock, CPA, Department of Accounting & Finance, Williamson College of Business Administration, Youngstown State University, Youngstown, OH 44555

Oil, Gas & Energy Quarterly

ADDRESS FOR SUBMISSION:

Larry Crumbley, Editor
Oil, Gas & Energy Quarterly
Louisiana State University
Department of Accounting
3106A CEBA Building
Baton Rouge, LA 70803
USA
Phone: 225-388-6231
Fax: 225-388-6201
E-Mail: dcrumbl@unix1.sncc.lsu.edu
Web:
Address May Change:

PUBLICATION GUIDELINES:

Manuscript Length: 11 - 20
Copies Required: Two
Computer Submission: Yes
Format: Wordstar or WordPerfect
Fees to Review: 0.00 US$

Manuscript Style:
See Manuscript Guidelines

CIRCULATION DATA:

Reader: Business Persons
Frequency of Issue: Quarterly
Copies per Issue: 4,001 - 5,000
Sponsor/Publisher: Profit Oriented Corp.
Subscribe Price: 120.00 US$

REVIEW INFORMATION:

Type of Review: Blind Review
No. of External Reviewers: 2
No. of In House Reviewers: 1
Acceptance Rate: 21-30%
Time to Review: 2 - 3 Months
Reviewers Comments: No
Invited Articles: 11-20%
Fees to Publish: 0.00 US$

MANUSCRIPT TOPICS:
Finance & Investments; Natural Resources; Oil and Gas; Tax Accounting; Taxation

MANUSCRIPT GUIDELINES/COMMENTS:

1. Chapter title should be in all capital letters and centered. Author's name should be centered and have initial caps. ("Initial caps" indicates that the first letter in each significant word is capped and the rest is in lower case.) First level headings—flush left, initial caps; second level headings—centered, initial caps; third level headings—flush left, initial caps and underscored; fourth level headings—beginning of paragraph; it ends with a period and is underscored to distinguish it from text.

[See next page for examples of heading format.]

2. Examples of Heading Format:

Determining a Distributive Share of Property in Oil and Gas Finance

John. J. Johnson

Property Values

Taxable Income From the Property

Gross Income
In general. The tax was enacted as part of an overall.

3. Indent paragraphs five spaces. Use abbreviations sparingly. Acceptable illustrations; original artwork, glossy black-and-white photographs, ink drawings, printed forms and materials. (Photocopies, unless very clear and legible, are usually not acceptable.)

4. References first appearing in the text should be written out, followed by a short form in parentheses. Later they should appear in the shortened form.
For examples:

"Internal Revenue Service (Service)"; subsequently, Service."

"Internal Revenue Code (Code) Section XXX"; subsequently, "Code Section XXX."

"Statement of Financial Accounting Standards (SFAS) No. 39"; subsequently, "SFAS No. 39."

5. Footnotes may be at the end of the article or at the bottom of the page. Abbreviate wherever possible. Examples:

I.R.C. XXX
Treas. Reg. 1.415-1 (b) (but: Temporary Treas. Reg.)
Ltr. Rul. (but: Private Ltr. Rul.)

6. Abbreviate names of months and states.

7. Case names are listed without underscores, unless they are incomplete or their citations do not immediately follow.

Some common abbreviations in cases:
9th Cir.
Fed. Reg.
2d cir., 3d Cir.

8. Examples of references to periodical titles in footnotes:

Jones, "The Effect of the Tax Reform Act of 1978 on Limited partnerships," 37 Harv. L Rev. 565, 570-573 (1980).

Blatz & Weirich, "Texas Oil and Gas Taxation," 31 Oild & Gas Tax Q. 249 (Sept. 1979).

9. Example of references to books in footnotes:

Burke & Bohway, Income Taxation of Natural Resources 1206 (1983).

10. Examples of footnotes in general:

1. Brown v. Green, 654 F. Supp. 309, 314-325 (E.D. Cal. 1968), rev'd 437 F. 2d 594 (9th Cir. 1969).
    2. Id. at 202
    3. 15 U.S.C. 104(b).
    4. See note 1 supra.

Operations Research

ADDRESS FOR SUBMISSION:

Lawrence M. Wein, Editor
Operations Research
MIT
Sloan School of Mangement
E53-343
30 Wadworth Street
Cambridge, MA 02142-1347
USA
Phone: 617-253-6697
Fax: 617-258-7579
E-Mail: lwein@mit.edu
Web: op.pubs.informs.org
Address May Change:

PUBLICATION GUIDELINES:

Manuscript Length: Any
Copies Required: Four
Computer Submission: No
Format: N/A
Fees to Review: 0.00 US$

Manuscript Style:
    Chicago Manual of Style

CIRCULATION DATA:

Reader: Academics
Frequency of Issue: Bi-Monthly
Copies per Issue: 10,001 - 25,000
Sponsor/Publisher: Institute for Operations
   Research and Management Science
   (INFORMS)
Subscribe Price: 0.00 US$

REVIEW INFORMATION:

Type of Review: Editorial Review
No. of External Reviewers: 3
No. of In House Reviewers: 1
Acceptance Rate: 21-30%
Time to Review: 4 - 6 Months
Reviewers Comments: Yes
Invited Articles: 0-5%
Fees to Publish: 0.00 US$

MANUSCRIPT TOPICS:

Computer and Decision Technology; Cost Accounting; Decision Analysis; Environment,
Energy and Natural Resources; Manufacturing Service & Supply Chain Operations; Military;
Optimization; OR Chronicle; Policy Modeling; Simulation; Stochastic Models;
Telecommunications; Transportation/ Physical Distribution

MANUSCRIPT GUIDELINES/COMMENTS:

The mission of *Operations Research* is to serve the entire *Operations Research* (OR)
community, including practitioners, researchers, educators, and students. Operations
Research, as the flagship journal of our profession, strives to publish results that are truly
insightful. Each issue of *Operations Research* attempts to provide a balance of well written
articles that span the wide array of creative activities in OR. Thus, the major criteria for
acceptance of a paper in *Operations Research* are that the paper is important to more than a
small subset of the OR community, contains important insights, and makes a substantial
contribution to the field that will stand the test of time.

General Considerations

To submit a paper to *Operations Research,* the author should send the Area Editor the entire manuscript package for review. This includes the Statement of Contribution, Copyright Transfer Agreement, a cover letter, and four copies of the manuscript. This submission can either be in hardcopy format (or in electronic form. The author must check with the appropriate Area Editor as to what electronic forms are acceptable.

Papers not in the fields covered by the Area Editors should be sent to the Editor.

Papers should not be sent to the Associate Editors.

Submission of a manuscript is a representation that the paper has neither been published nor submitted for publication elsewhere, and that, if the work is officially sponsored, it has been released for open publication.

Manuscripts will not be returned to an author unless specifically requested, or unless reviewers have provided annotations that will be of use to the author.

The text should be arranged as follows: title page, abstract, introduction, main sections, appendix, acknowledgment, and references. Appendices and an acknowledgment are optional. If a paper is accepted for publication, the Editor may request (or require) that supporting appendix material is placed online at the *Operations Research* web site. Authors should consider this either during the initial submission phase or during the final revisions of the paper and may wish to design their papers accordingly.

Personal Web Sites. Upon acceptance of a paper to *Operations Research,* the author must remove all copies of the paper from any web sites. The copyright belongs to INFORMS and placement of the paper on a web site is a violation of the copyright transfer agreement.

Observe the following points in preparing manuscripts. Papers not conforming closely to these instructions may be returned to their authors for appropriate revisions or may be delayed in the review process.

1. Statement of Contribution. A statement of contribution is required for each submitted paper. The form is available at the *Operations Research* web site. The purpose of this statement is to aid area editors and reviewers in determining if the paper a) is appropriate for the Journal and b) meets its stated objectives. Once a paper is accepted for publication, this statement will serve as the basis for the news story for the "In This Issue" column.

2. Readability. The abstract and the introduction of every paper must be free of unnecessary jargon and clearly readable by any INFORMS member. These sections should be written in an expository style that will be comprehensible to readers who are not technical experts in the subject matter.

3. Title Page. Each paper should have a title page that contains the authors' names and addresses. The usual acknowledgments should be placed in a separate section at the back of the manuscript.

4. Abstract. Preface each article with a self-contained, one paragraph abstract that summarizes the problem and the principal results and conclusions. It should not contain formulas, references or abbreviations, nor exceed 200 words.

5. Introduction. The introduction must clearly state the problem, the results to be found in the paper and their significance to the OR community. It should not contain equations or mathematical notation. Section numbering and headings begins here.

6. Main Sections. The main sections of the paper must be readable, the level of the mathematics and/or the terminology appropriate to the topic, and the material logically presented.

7. Style. The message of the paper will be enhanced if it is presented in active, forceful, and concise prose. Good writing is a craft at least as difficult as doing operations research. While the Editor and staff will correct minor lapses from good style in the manuscript, they cannot undertake wholesale revisions of poorly written papers. There is no set limit to the number of pages for a paper; however, conciseness and clarity of presentation are important publication criteria.

8. Spacing and Format. Double space manuscripts throughout, including the abstract, subsidiary matter (list of captions, for example), and references. In general, keep figures and tables to a minimum.

Each page of the manuscript should be numbered. Indent the first line of each paragraph.

9. Footnotes. *Operations Research* does not use footnotes; incorporate subsidiary material that would otherwise appear in footnotes in the main text, possibly in parentheses or brackets, or place it in a Notes section at the end of the text, before the Acknowledgment and References. Designate notes by using superscript numerals placed in serial order throughout the text.

10. Acknowledgment. Place acknowledgments of presentation, support and assistance in a final section that precedes the References, not on the title page.

11. References. List only those references that are cited in the text. References in the text should be cited by the author's surname and the year of publication-for example, Flood (1962).

If the reference has two or three authors, cite all of the authors' surnames and the year of publication—Flood, Smith and Jones (1982). If the reference has more than three authors, cite the first author's surname followed by et al. and the year of publication-Brown et al. (1985).

If there is more than one reference by the same author with the same year of publication, the first citation appearing in the text would read Flood (1962a), the second citation would read Flood (1962b), etc.

Do not use parentheses or brackets for dates when the citation is already enclosed within parentheses.

At the end of the paper list references alphabetically by the last name of the first author. Do not number the reference list. Double-space this final section.

For journal references, give the author, year of publication, title, journal name, volume, and pages for example:

FLOOD, M. M. 1962. New Operations Research Potentials. Opns. Res. 10, 423-436.

For book references, give the author, year of publication, title, publisher, city, state, and pages-for example:

MORSE, P. M., AND G. E. KIMBALL. 1951. Methods of Operations Research. John Wiley, New York, 44-65.

For references to working papers or dissertations cite the author, title, type of document, department, university, and location, for example:

ROSENWEIN, M. 1986. Design and Application of Solution Methodologies to Optimize Problems in Transportation Logistics. Ph.D. Dissertation. Department of Decision Sciences, University of Pennsylvania, Philadelphia.

12. Mathematical Expressions. Within the text, use the solidus whenever possible in preference to built-up fractions, e.g., $a/(1 - b)$ exponentials in the form $\exp(\ )$; avoid subscripts or superscripts on subscripts or superscripts; and, in general, minimize unusual typographical requirements. For displayed equations, use built-up fractions. Avoid lengthy equations that will take several lines to typeset (possibly by defining terms of the equations in separate displays).

Make subscripts and superscripts large and clear, and shown in a clearly inferior or superior position. The letter 1 and the numeral 1 and the letter O and the numeral 0, which are identical on most keyboards, should be identified. Symbols and Greek letters should be identified clearly. On their first occurrence, label unusual or ambiguous symbols by marginal notes. The difference between upper and lower case letters should be clear.

Display only those mathematical expressions that must be numbered for later reference or that need to be emphasized. Number displayed equations consecutively throughout the paper; do not number equations by section numbers. Appendix equations can be labeled A1, A2, etc. The numbers should be placed in parentheses to the right of the equation.

13. Tables. Tables should be numbered with Arabic numerals, have a title, and be referred to sequentially in the text. Column headings should be brief and not use abbreviations. Do not use vertical rules. The use of footnotes is encouraged; designate these by lower case letters. The submission of original tables suitable for reproduction is not necessary; all tables will be typeset for consistency. Each table should be on a separate sheet and not interleaved in the text.

14. Figures. Figures should be professionally drawn or laser printed and suitable for photographic reproduction. All figures must be in black and white. Color figures will be printed in black and white and do not scan properly. The author is responsible for the quality of the final form of the figure(s). Figures are scanned and corrections on page proofs are costly.

Do not clutter the figure with information that makes it difficult to read. To avoid an undesirable moiré effect when scanned, figures should be shaded with a coarse pattern rather than a fine screen. Line weights should be consistent and at least .25 points after reduction. Lettering in the body of the figure should be proportional to the graphic and be typed.

Most figures will be reduced to approximately 3 '/4 " in width. For optimal quality, please submit final figures close to that size. All details on the figures should be checked carefully because correction on proofs necessitates reshooting.

Each figure must be cited and will be placed in the order mentioned in the text. Each figure must have a caption and a number (Arabic). Do not place the caption on the original of the figure. Place captions on a separate sheet. Do not differentiate between illustrations and figures.

15. Subject Classification Scheme for the OR/MS Index. Determine the appropriate subject classifications (up to 3) and accompanying descriptive phrases for all work submitted. Choose from one to three subject categories for each manuscript. For every category chosen, write a short phrase that puts the paper in context. (The phrase can be a concise rendering of the title, or it may specify some aspect of the paper that is important but not apparent in the title.) The length of each phrase, including spaces and punctuation, should not exceed 60 characters. This information will be printed on the title page of every article, technical note, and letter that is published. The list of subject keywords can be found at the **Operations Research** web site.

Subject categories and phrases must either appear on the title page of the manuscript (this is the preferred method), or authors may use the bottom half of the Copyright Transfer Agreement.

16. Reprints. *Operations Research* does not have paper charges, nor does it supply free reprints. Authors of accepted articles may order reprints at reasonable rates at the time they submit their corrected galley proofs. Reprints of individual articles are not available from INFORMS.

Managing Editor: Joan E. Wingo
MIT Sloan School of Management
30 Wadsworth Street, E53-336
Cambridge, MA 02142-1347
617-253-6653 (phone); 617-258-7579 (fax)
jwingo@mit.edu

348

OR CHRONICLE
Frederic H. Murphy, Fox School of Business and Management, Temple University, Philadelphia PA 19122
V5256E@vm.temple.edu
(215) 204-8189 (phone); 215) 204-8029 (fax)

POLICY MODELING AND PUBLIC SECTOR OR
Edward H. Kaplan, Professor of Management Sciences and Public Health,
Yale School of Management, Box 208200, New Haven, Connecticut 06520-8200
edward.kaplan@yale.edu
203-432-6031 (phone); 203-432-9995 (fax)

SIMULATION
Michael C. Fu, The Robert H. Smith School of Business, Van Munching Hall, University of Maryland, College Park, MD 20742-1815
mfu@rhsmith.umd. edu http://www.mbs.umd.edu/DIT/faculty/fu.htm
301-405-2241 (phone); 707-897-3774 (fax)

STOCHASTIC MODELS
David D. Yao, Department of Endustrial Engineering and OR, Columbia University
New York, NY 10027-6699
yao @ieor.columbia.edu
212-854-2934 (phone); 212-854-8103 (fax)

TELECOMMUNICATIONS
Robert B. Cooper, Department of Computer Science and Engineering, Florida Atlantic University, Box 3091, Boca Raton, FL 33431-0991
bob @cse.fau.edu
http://www.cse.fau.edu/-bob/
561-297-3673 (phone); 561-297-2800 (fax)

TRANSPORTATION
Paolo Toth, DEIS, University di Bologna, Viale Risorgimento 2, 1-40136 Bologna, Italy
ptoth@deis.unibo.it
+39 051 2093028 (phone); +39 051 2093073(fax)

Pacific Accounting Review

ADDRESS FOR SUBMISSION:

Steven Cahan, Editor
Pacific Accounting Review
Massey University
Faculty of Business Studies
Department of Accountancy
Private Bag 11222
Palmerston North,
New Zealand
Phone: 64 6 350 6106
Fax: 64 6 350 5617
E-Mail: s.f.cahan@massey.ac.nz
Web:
Address May Change:

PUBLICATION GUIDELINES:

Manuscript Length: 15-30
Copies Required: Four
Computer Submission: Yes
Format: ASCII or Word
Fees to Review: 0.00 US$

Manuscript Style:
    No Reply

CIRCULATION DATA:

Reader: Academics
Frequency of Issue: 2 Times/ Year
Copies per Issue: Less than 1,000
Sponsor/Publisher: University
Subscribe Price: 15.00 US$

REVIEW INFORMATION:

Type of Review: Blind Review
No. of External Reviewers: 2
No. of In House Reviewers: 0
Acceptance Rate: 20-25%
Time to Review: 2 - 3 Months
Reviewers Comments: Yes
Invited Articles: 6-10%
Fees to Publish: 0.00 US$

MANUSCRIPT TOPICS:
Accounting Information Systems; Accounting Theory & Practice; Auditing; Cost Accounting; Finance; Government & Non Profit Accounting; Tax Accounting

MANUSCRIPT GUIDELINES/COMMENTS:

Pennsylvania Journal of Business and Economics

ADDRESS FOR SUBMISSION:

Kevin Roth & Carole Anderson, Co-Editors
Pennsylvania Journal of Business and
   Economics
Clarion University of Pennsylvania
Clarion, PA 16214-1232
USA
Phone: 814-393-2055
Fax: 814-393-1910
E-Mail: kroth@clarion.edu
Web:
Address May Change:

PUBLICATION GUIDELINES:

Manuscript Length: 6-10
Copies Required: One
Computer Submission: Yes if accepted
Format: WdPerfect 8, Corel, Word
Fees to Review: 0.00 US$

Manuscript Style:
   American Psychological Association

CIRCULATION DATA:

Reader: Academics
Frequency of Issue: 2 Times/Year
Copies per Issue: Less than 1,000
Sponsor/Publisher: Association of
   Pennsylvania University Business and
   Economic Faculties
Subscribe Price: No Reply

REVIEW INFORMATION:

Type of Review: Blind Review
No. of External Reviewers: 2
No. of In House Reviewers: 1
Acceptance Rate: 50%
Time to Review: 2 - 3 Months
Reviewers Comments: Yes
Invited Articles: 0-5%
Fees to Publish: 0.00 US$

MANUSCRIPT TOPICS:
Accounting Theory & Practice; Auditing; Cost Accounting; Econometrics; Finance; Industrial
Organization; Insurance

MANUSCRIPT GUIDELINES/COMMENTS:

The APUBEF Journal is a refereed journal aimed at publishing the papers of faculty from the
business and economics disciplines within the State System of Higher Education Universities
in Pennsylvania, or from business and economics faculty at comparable institutions from
within Pennsylvania and from surrounding states. While theoretical works are encouraged,
most published papers are empirical or pedagogical in nature.

Manuscript Style
1. Papers **must** be submitted on a 3.5" micro-computer disk using Corel, WordPerfect 8.0, or
Word for DOS. Printer setup should be HP Laserjet 4. A high-quality hard copy of the paper
must accompany your disk.

2. Use 10 point New Times Roman font for the body of the paper and all headings including
the heading for **references**. Use 1" margins all around.

3. Single space the text. Double space between paragraphs and indent the first line five spaces using the tab key. Use full justification.

4. Spell-check before sending the paper and correct all grammatical errors. Also, edit the paper to address the comments and suggestions of the reviewers and editor.

Specific Requirements

1. Start the manuscript with the full title, centered in capitals, bolt print. Following a space, each author and university should be identified, one author per line. No titles (Dr., Mr., Mrs. etc.) are to be used, nor should rank be indicated. Please, no fancy type-styles other than ones specified.

2. After the last author's name and affiliation, double space, center and type the heading **abstract**, bold and all caps. All papers **must** have an abstract of no more than 150 words, which provides a brief synopsis of the paper.

3. The next heading is **introduction**, bold and all caps. Double-space before and after. All major headings MUST follow this format. Secondary headings MUST be in bold print, left justified, first letter capitalized then lower case, with a space above and below each heading.

4. Mathematical expressions and notations should be used judiciously and all symbols should be identified.

5. Tables should be arranged sequentially in the order in which the tables are first mentioned in the text and placed at the end of the manuscript. Type the word Table and its arabic numeral flush left at the top of the table, double space, then type the table title flush left above the table. The explanatory notes to a table such as probability tables, explanations of acronyms, etc. should appear below the table. Use the same 10 point New Times Roman font as used in the text and the tab function to construct the tables. If a "camera-ready" table is to be used, send the original and not a reduced copy for incorporation in the journal.

6. Figures (such as graphs, drawings, photographs, and charts) must be consecutively numbered in arabic numerals, with their captions in the order they appear in the text. All illustrations must be camera-ready; photographs must be of professional quality, and drawings must be prepared in ink. Illustrations should be identified on the back in light pencil with the name of the author and the figure number.

7. Footnotes and end notes are permitted, but not encouraged. In most cases, the material they contain can be incorporated in the text. If footnotes are used, use the automatic footnote function (control F7) and specify a New Times Roman 10 point font for their text. End notes should be in the same 10 point Prestige Elite font as the text and placed after the references.

References

1. When citing references in the text please use parenthesis, author's named, comma and date of publication, i.e., (Wilson, 1996). For up to three authors, cite each and use the "&" for "and", i.e., (Dawes, Dowling & Peterson, 1992). For more than three authors, use the surname of the first author followed by "et al." comma and the year, i.e., (Cravens et al., 1988).

Multiple reference citations in a parentheses should be arranged alphabetically and a semi-colon used to separate them, i.e., (Cravens et al., 1988; Dawes, Dowling & Peterson, 1992; Wilson, 1996). Text citations must correspond accurately to the references in the reference list.

2. References should be listed alphabetically at the end of the manuscript. References with the same authors in the same order are arranged according to the year of publication, the earliest first.

3. An American Psychological Association format is used for the references.

For a journal article:
Buzzell, R. D., Gale, B. T., & Sultan, R.G.M. (1975). Market share - a key to profitability. Harvard Business Review. 75-1. 97-106.

For a proceedings article:
Gronroos, C. (1983). Innovative marketing strategies and organization structures for service firms. Emerging Perspectives on Services Marketing. Berry, L.L., Shostack G.L., & Upah, G.D. eds. Chicago, IL: American Marketing Association. 9-21.

For a book:
Czepiel, J.A. (1992). Competitive Marketing Strategy. (258-263) Englewood Cliffs, NJ: Prentice-Hall.

For more information and examples please refer to the *Publication Manual Of The American Psychological Association*.

Personal Financial Planning

ADDRESS FOR SUBMISSION:

Elizabeth McLeod, Managing Editor
Personal Financial Planning
Warren, Gorham, & Lamont/RIA Group
395 Hudson Street
New York, NY 10014
USA
Phone: 212-337-4276
Fax: 212-337-4207
E-Mail: emcleod@riag.com
Web:
Address May Change:

CIRCULATION DATA:

Reader: Business Persons
Frequency of Issue: Bi-Monthly
Copies per Issue: 2,001 - 3,000
Sponsor/Publisher: RIA Group
Subscribe Price: 135.00 US$

PUBLICATION GUIDELINES:

Manuscript Length: 11-15
Copies Required: Two
Computer Submission: Yes
Format: 3.5 disk, Ms Word 97
Fees to Review: 0.00 US$

Manuscript Style:
    See Manuscript Guidelines

REVIEW INFORMATION:

Type of Review: Editorial Review
No. of External Reviewers: 2
No. of In House Reviewers: 3
Acceptance Rate: 21-30%
Time to Review: 1 Month or Less
Reviewers Comments: No
Invited Articles: 31-50%
Fees to Publish: 0.00 US$

MANUSCRIPT TOPICS:
Economic Development; Insurance; International Economics & Trade; International Finance; Investments; Portfolio & Security Analysis; Retirement Planning

MANUSCRIPT GUIDELINES/COMMENTS:

Personal Financial Planning welcomes articles directed at the financial planning professional. To facilitate manuscript preparation, processing, and editing, please keep the following guidelines in mind:

1. Articles should address subjects that will help the planner better manage his or her practice or aid in the planning and evaluation of investments and other financial strategies for the benefit of the client. Acceptable topics include, but are not limited to: insurance, taxation, retirement planning, real estate, savings and time deposits, futures, stocks and bonds, estate planning, marketing the practice, legal liability, due diligence, practice profitability and management, and planner/client relations. Articles should not promote individual companies.

2. As a general rule, PFP will not publish articles that have been published elsewhere. However, authors may choose to expand on their own ideas or on issues raised in other articles, books, or speeches for an original article in PFP.

3. Manuscripts should be typed double-spaced on one side of 8-1/2" x 11" paper. Manuscripts typed on floppy discs are also welcome. Articles should be a minimum of 10 manuscript pages or at least 2,500 words.

4. To enhance readability, include brief subheads throughout the manuscript. Also, paragraphs should be kept short but no shorter than two sentences. Graphs, charts, tables and sidebars are encouraged. In addition, authors may want to use descriptive case histories to illustrate or emphasize specific points, ideas, or recommendations. All manuscript should be written in the third person.

5. Authors should include brief biographical material.

6. Please address all query letters or manuscripts to the Managing Editor.

7. PFP editors will respond to all unsolicited manuscripts within approximately 4 weeks. Please be advised that we cannot accept responsibility for their return. Also, please note that all manuscripts accepted for publication are subject to editorial revision. We look forward to hearing from you.

Practical Accountant

ADDRESS FOR SUBMISSION:

Howard W. Wolosky, Executive Editor
Practical Accountant
Faulkner & Gray
11 Penn Plaza, 17th Floor
New York, NY 10001
USA
Phone: 212-631-1447
Fax: 212-629-7885
E-Mail:
   howard_wolosky@faulknergray.com
Web:
Address May Change:

PUBLICATION GUIDELINES:

Manuscript Length: 12
Copies Required: Five
Computer Submission: Yes
Format: Word
Fees to Review: 0.00 US$

Manuscript Style:
   See Manuscript Guidelines

CIRCULATION DATA:

Reader: , Accountants in Public Service
Frequency of Issue: Monthly
Copies per Issue: 40,000
Sponsor/Publisher: Profit Oriented Corp.
Subscribe Price: 65.00 US$

REVIEW INFORMATION:

Type of Review: Editorial Review
No. of External Reviewers: No Reply
No. of In House Reviewers: 3+
Acceptance Rate: 6-10%
Time to Review: 1 Month
Reviewers Comments: No
Invited Articles: Under 10%
Fees to Publish: 0.00 US$

MANUSCRIPT TOPICS:

Accounting Information Systems; Accounting Theory & Practice; Auditing; Government &
Non Profit Accounting; Tax Accounting

MANUSCRIPT GUIDELINES/COMMENTS:

General Approach

Articles that are accepted for publication in *The Practical Accountant* deal with the practical
aspects, significance and application of subjects that are of general interest to accountants in
public practice. When appropriate, articles should point out any new business opportunities
and differentiate between the different applications for large, regional or small practices.
Particularly helpful to our readers are tips, examples, worksheets, diagrams, charts, survey
results and step-by-step procedures. Articles should identify any potential pitfalls and
opportunities in the area. Quotes from practicing accountants or representatives of relevant
organizations on the subject should be included since our readers are particularly interested in
what recognized experts think, especially when there is a conflict of opinion.

356

Articles should be interpretative and not just paraphrase statutes, regulations, FASBs, etc. They should be written in the active voice in a conversational manner with short sentences and paragraphs. Lengthy discussions of historical background should be avoided. When citing a case, the author should cite both to RIA and CCH (e.g, Smith, 85-1 USTC 9174, 67 AFTR2d 1219 (CA-6, 1984)). No references to the IRB or CB are necessary when citing to IRS pronouncements (e.g., Rev. Ruls.), the number of the ruling is sufficient.

Potential authors may call Howard W. Wolosky (212-631-1447) to discuss whether the proposed subject matter is appropriate for the editorial needs of *The Practical Accountant*.

Submission Procedure
Feature articles should generally be 3,000 words (approximately 12 double-spaced typed pages). The most important consideration is how the topic is treated, not length of the article. If possible, place footnotes at the end of the article. Include a brief biographical sketch that indicates advanced degrees, firm affiliation, title, professional certifications and any other information that is relevant.

Please submit five copies of the article and a computer disk (3 1/2", if possible) containing the article and identify the software program used (preferably Word). If the article is based on a single case, ruling, accounting standard or similar published material, please also include a copy of the material with the submitted manuscript, if possible. We normally review submitted manuscripts within six weeks of receipt. The cover letter should state that the article has not been submitted to any other publication.

Acceptance of an article cannot guarantee publication as editorial needs can change based on sudden and unexpected developments and page restrictions. We cannot compensate authors for writing articles. Our authors view their articles as contributions to the professional literature and as providing professional recognition to themselves and their firms. We send each author 20 complementary copies of the issue in which the article appears. Additional copies or reprints of just the article are available for a fee.

Submissions should be sent to Howard W. Wolosky, Executive Editor.

Practical Tax Strategies (Taxation for Accountants/Taxation for Lawyers)

ADDRESS FOR SUBMISSION:

Bob Scharin, Editor
Practical Tax Strategies (Taxation for
   Accountants/Taxation for Lawyers)
RIA Group
395 Hudson Street
New York, NY 10014
USA
Phone: 212-807-2966
Fax: 212-337-4207
E-Mail: bscharin@riag.com
Web:
Address May Change:

PUBLICATION GUIDELINES:

Manuscript Length: 21-25
Copies Required: Two
Computer Submission: Yes
Format: MS Word preferred/PC compatible
Fees to Review: 0.00 US$

Manuscript Style:
   See Manuscript Guidelines

CIRCULATION DATA:

Reader: Business Persons, Tax accountants
   & attorneys
Frequency of Issue: Monthly
Copies per Issue: 5,001 - 10,000
Sponsor/Publisher: Warren Gorham &
   Lamont/RIA Group
Subscribe Price: 145.00 US$

REVIEW INFORMATION:

Type of Review: Editorial Review
No. of External Reviewers: 1
No. of In House Reviewers: 1
Acceptance Rate: 21-30%
Time to Review: 2 - 3 Months
Reviewers Comments: No
Invited Articles: 50% +
Fees to Publish: 0.00 US$

MANUSCRIPT TOPICS:
Tax Accounting; Taxation

MANUSCRIPT GUIDELINES/COMMENTS:

Articles intended for publication in *Practical Tax Strategies* should concentrate on practical information and tax planning ideas. They should be written for the general practitioner, not the tax professional. Articles should not discuss theoretical matters or how the law should or could be changed.

To be considered for publication, an article must be submitted to us on an exclusive basis. All manuscripts accepted for review are circulated to an editorial board. Once approved for publication in the print and electronic versions of *Practical Tax Strategies*, each article is subject to editorial revision. Authors receive galley proofs prior to publication and any corrections must be returned to us by the date indicated. There is generally no objection to having an article that appears in *Practical Tax Strategies* reprinted in another publication at a later date, provided appropriate permission is requested from us and attribution given.

Manuscripts should be submitted on diskette and paper. Diskettes should be IBM-compatible. Although we use Word, we can convert from most word processing programs. The hard copy should be on 8 1/2" and 11" white paper, double-spaced with wide margins. Text should run between 18 and 25 pages. Endnotes rather than footnotes should be used, and they should be restricted to citations (without textual explanations). When possible, illustrative examples and forms should be included.

Any editorial questions should be addressed to Bob D. Scharin at (212) 807-2966 (phone) or (212) 337-4207 (FAX).

Research in Accounting Regulation

ADDRESS FOR SUBMISSION:

Gary John Previts, Editor
Research in Accounting Regulation
Case Western University
Weatherhead School of Management
625 Enterprise Hall
Cleveland, OH 44106-7235
USA
Phone: 216-368-2074
Fax: 216-368-4776
E-Mail: gjp@po.cwru.edu
Web: draco.cwru.edu/dept/rar
Address May Change:

PUBLICATION GUIDELINES:

Manuscript Length: 11-15
Copies Required: Three
Computer Submission: Yes
Format: Word 7.0
Fees to Review: 0.00 US$

Manuscript Style:
, See Website

CIRCULATION DATA:

Reader: Business Persons, Academics
Frequency of Issue: Yearly
Copies per Issue: Less than 1,000
Sponsor/Publisher: JAI Press, Inc.
Subscribe Price: 65.00 US$

REVIEW INFORMATION:

Type of Review: Blind Review
No. of External Reviewers: 2
No. of In House Reviewers: No Reply
Acceptance Rate: 25-30%
Time to Review: 3 - 6 Months
Reviewers Comments: Yes
Invited Articles: 15%
Fees to Publish: 0.00 US$

MANUSCRIPT TOPICS:
Accounting Theory & Practice; Auditing; Cost Accounting; Government & Non Profit
Accounting; Public Policy Accounting; Tax Accounting

MANUSCRIPT GUIDELINES/COMMENTS:

We are seeking manuscripts which address regulatory policy relevant to accountancy issues
including research based upon:

(1) self regulatory activities
(2) case law and litigation
(3) government regulation
(4) the economics of regulation, including modeling

The editors encourage submission of original empirical, behavioral or applied research
manuscripts that consider strategic and policy implications for regulation, regulatory model
and markets. Material must be presented using format and language which facilitates

communication to those who address policy issues. Methodological elaboration and technique should be supplied in appendices.

Manuscripts are blind refereed by the manuscript review panel with consultation of the editors.

Submission Information

Volume 14 (2000) initial submissions are due not later than October 1, 1999. Manuscripts are considered up to the deadline. Three printed copies are required with an abstract included. Author(s) identity should be confined to the manuscript cover sheet. A copyright responsibility statement and copyright release by the author(s) is required before publication. Footnotes, citations, and textnotes should conform to the style used in American Accounting Association journals.

Upon acceptance, authors must submit a final, edited version on 3.5 inch Word 7.0 diskette in ASCII file format per RinAR Submission Requirements.

Submit manuscripts to: Gary John Previts, Editor
Telnet: gjp@po.cwru.edu

Manuscript And File Format Requirements

Manuscripts must be submitted both printed and on a 3.5-inch Word 7.0 diskette in ASCII file format. We suggest you print your papers in Courier 10-pitch with 1" margins to facilitate electronic processing. Please do not format your documents with indents, centered titles, justification, etc. (use "block left" format only) and avoid proportional typefaces such as Times Roman. Write the Editor to obtain a complete copy of "RinAR Submission Requirements".

Research on Accounting Ethics

ADDRESS FOR SUBMISSION:

Bill N. Schwartz, Managing Editor
Research on Accounting Ethics
Virginia Commonwealth University
School of Business
Department of Accounting
1015 Floyd Avenue
Richmond, VA 23284-4000
USA
Phone: 804-828-7194
Fax: 804-828-8884
E-Mail: bnschwar@vcu.edu
Web:
Address May Change:

PUBLICATION GUIDELINES:

Manuscript Length: No Reply
Copies Required: Five
Computer Submission: No
Format: N/A
Fees to Review: 40.00 US$

Manuscript Style:
See Manuscript Guidelines

CIRCULATION DATA:

Reader: Academics
Frequency of Issue: Yearly
Copies per Issue: No Reply
Sponsor/Publisher: JAI Press, Inc.
Subscribe Price: 78.50 US$

REVIEW INFORMATION:

Type of Review: Blind Review
No. of External Reviewers: 3
No. of In House Reviewers: 0
Acceptance Rate: 21-30%
Time to Review: 1 - 2 Months
Reviewers Comments: Yes
Invited Articles: 0-5%
Fees to Publish: 0.00 US$

MANUSCRIPT TOPICS:
Accounting Ethics; Accounting Theory & Practice

MANUSCRIPT GUIDELINES/COMMENTS:

Call for Papers. . .

Research on Accounting Ethics seeks thoughtful and well-developed empirical or non-empirical manuscripts on a variety of current topics in accounting ethics, broadly defined. It examines all aspects of ethics and ethics-related issues in accounting including, for example, accountability, financial reporting, organizational control, gender issues, quality concerns, professionals codes, organization and culture, judgment and decision-making litigation and regulation and social responsibility. Acceptable research methods for empirical work include action research, archival analysis, field based studies, financial statement analysis, laboratory experiments, mathematical modeling, psychometrics and surveys.

362

Non-empirical manuscripts should be academically rigorous. They can be theoretical syntheses, conceptual models, position papers, discussions of methodology, comprehensive literature reviews grounded in theory, or historical discussions with implications for current and future efforts. Reasonable assumptions and logical development are essential. Most manuscripts should discuss implications for research.

For empirical reports sound research design and execution are critical. Articles should have well articulated and strong theoretical foundations. In this regard, establishing a link to the non-accounting literature is desirable. Replications and extensions of previously published works are encouraged. As a means for establishing an open dialogue, responses to, or comments on, articles published previously are welcomed.

Submission Information
Five copies are required. Submission Fee is $40.00. Manuscripts should include a cover page which indicates the author's name and address and a separate lead page with an abstract not exceeding 250 words. The author's name and address should not appear on the abstract. In order to assure an anonymous review, authors should not identify themselves directly or indirectly. Reference to unpublished working papers and dissertations should be avoided. Submit manuscripts to: Bill N. Schwartz, School of Business, Virginia Commonwealth University, 1015 Floyd Avenue, Richmond, VA 232844000. Cases: Three copies of Cases and Proposed Teaching Notes should be sent directly to Dean Mintz, School of Business and Public Administration, California State University-San Bernardino, San Bernardino, CA 92407-2397.

Call for Reviewers . . .
Individuals interested in being a member of the editorial review board should contact Professor Schwartz by e-mail at bschwartz@busnet.bus.vcu.edu and explain their interests.

Review of Accounting Information Systems

ADDRESS FOR SUBMISSION:

Ronald C. Clute, Editor
Review of Accounting Information Systems
Western Academic Press
P.O. Box 620760
Littleton, CO 80162
USA
Phone: 303-904-4750
Fax: 303-978-0413
E-Mail: cluter@wapress.com
Web: www.wapress.com
Address May Change:

CIRCULATION DATA:

Reader: Business Persons, Consultants &
CPAs
Frequency of Issue: Quarterly
Copies per Issue: Less than 1,000
Sponsor/Publisher: Western Academic
Press, Inc.
Subscribe Price: 45.00 US$
225.00 US$ Library

PUBLICATION GUIDELINES:

Manuscript Length: 1-20
Copies Required: Three
Computer Submission: Yes
Format: MS Word for Windows
Fees to Review: 0.00 US$

Manuscript Style:
See Manuscript Guidelines

REVIEW INFORMATION:

Type of Review: Blind Review
No. of External Reviewers: 2
No. of In House Reviewers: 1
Acceptance Rate: 40%
Time to Review: 1 Month or Less
Reviewers Comments: Yes
Invited Articles: 0-5%
Fees to Publish: 20.00 US$ Per Page

MANUSCRIPT TOPICS:

Accounting Information Systems; Business Information Systems; Computer Information
Systems

MANUSCRIPT GUIDELINES/COMMENTS:

The Review welcomes articles in all areas of Accounting Information Systems. Both
theoretical and applied manuscripts will be considered for publication. Theoretical
manuscripts must provide a clear link to important and interesting accounting systems
applications. Prospective authors should observe the following editorial requirements:

1. Generally, the format of submitted manuscripts is not important provided that it is double-
spaced and margins are adequate to facilitate editing and duplication. However, the first page
(tear off page) should contain the title and author's name, institution, and e-mail address. The
second page should contain the title, abstract, and so on without naming the author.
Manuscripts must conform to the Review's style guidelines only after acceptance. A copy of
the style guidelines may be found inside the rear cover of the Review or on our home page at
www.wapress.com.

2. Mathematical and statistical notations that are not absolutely essential to the substance of a manuscript should be relegated to an appendix or deleted.

3. The reviewing process generally takes between two and four weeks to complete depending upon the time of year.

4. All manuscripts submitted to the Review are blind refereed by at least two independent reviewers.

5. Manuscripts to be considered for publication should be submitted in triplicate to Western Academic Press, Attn: RAIS, PO Box 620760, Littleton, Colorado 80162, USA.

6. The final version of accepted manuscripts must be submitted in hard copy form and on an IBM compatible 3.5" diskette using Microsoft Word processing.

7. The Review imposes page fees on all accepted manuscripts. These fees are necessary to offset the very substantial cost of putting a manuscript into print. The page fee is $20.00 per author's single-spaced page (with one inch margins) and is due only if the manuscript is accepted for publication. There is no manuscript submission fee.

Review of Accounting Studies

ADDRESS FOR SUBMISSION:

Stefan Reichelstein, Editor
Review of Accounting Studies
University of California-Berkeley
Haas School of Business
Berkeley, CA 94720-1900
USA
Phone: 510-642-2669
Fax: 510-643-1412
E-Mail: rast@haas.berkeley.edu
Web: www.haas.berkeley.edu/rast
Address May Change:

PUBLICATION GUIDELINES:

Manuscript Length: 26-30
Copies Required: Four
Computer Submission: No
Format: N/A
Fees to Review: 100.00 US$

Manuscript Style:
    See Manuscript Guidelines

CIRCULATION DATA:

Reader: Academics
Frequency of Issue: Quarterly
Copies per Issue: No Reply
Sponsor/Publisher: Kluwer Academic
    Publishers
Subscribe Price: No Reply

REVIEW INFORMATION:

Type of Review: Blind Review
No. of External Reviewers: 2
No. of In House Reviewers: 0
Acceptance Rate: 6-10%
Time to Review: 2 - 3 Months
Reviewers Comments: Yes
Invited Articles: No Reply
Fees to Publish: 0.00 US$

MANUSCRIPT TOPICS:
Accounting Theory & Practice

MANUSCRIPT GUIDELINES/COMMENTS:

Aims and Scope
Review of Accounting Studies provides an outlet for significant academic research in accounting including theoretical, empirical, and experimental work. The journal is committed to the principle that distinctive scholarship is rigorous. While the editors encourage all forms of research, it must contribute to the discipline of accounting. Theoretical models need not speak directly to current practice, but accounting information must surface in a major way. Similarly, empirical analysis and experimental tests should relate principally to accounting issues.

Editorial Policy
The *Review of Accounting Studies* is committed to the principle of prompt turnaround on the manuscripts it receives. A new submission will generally not require more than three months with the journal. For the majority of manuscripts the journal will make an accept-reject decision on the first round. Authors will be provided the opportunity to revise accepted

manuscripts in order to accommodate reviewer and editor comments; however, discretion over such manuscripts resides principally with the author(s). An editorial revise and resubmit decision is reserved for new submissions which are not acceptable in their current version, but for which the editor sees a clear path of changes which would make the manuscript publishable.

A major advantage of our decentralized editorship is that expertise can be applied at the editor level across a broad array of research subjects. New submissions are assigned to an editor familiar with the research topic. This editor then selects reviewers for the manuscript and upon receiving the reviewer's comments, the editor communicates directly with the author(s). Back to Index

New submissions should be sent to Stefan Reichelstein, Managing Editor.

Authors should enclose four copies of the manuscript and a $100 submission fee payable to the *Review of Accounting Studies.*

Authors wishing to pay the submission fee by money transfer may do so by transferring the funds to Wells Fargo Bank Account Number 0047 469721, at Routing Number 121000248.

Manuscript Preparation
Final versions of accepted manuscripts (including notes, references, tables, and legends) should be typed double-spaced on 8.5" x 11" (22cm x 29cm) white paper with 1" (2.5 cm) margins on all sides. Sections should appear in the following order: title page, abstract, text appendices, acknowledgements, notes, references, tables figure legends, and figures. Comments or replies to previously published articles should also follow this format with the exception of abstracts, which are not required.

We encourage electronic delivery of accepted papers. It is important that hard copy of the *accepted* paper (along with separate, original figures in camera-ready form) should accompany the electronic version. The hard copy must match the electronic version, and any changes made to the hard copy must be incorporated into the electronic version. Label one 3.5 inch floppy disk with the operating system and word processing program (e.g., DOS/WordPerfect) along with the authors' names, manuscript title, and name of journal to which the paper has been accepted.

Title Page. The title page should include the article title, authors' names and permanent affiliations, and the name, current address, telephone number, and e-mail address of the person to whom the page proofs and reprints should be sent.

Abstract. The following page should also include an abstract of not more than 100 words and double-spaced.

Text. The text of the article should begin on a new page. The introduction should have no heading or number. Subsequent headings (including appendices) should be designated by arabic numerals (1, 2, etc.) and subsection headings should be numbered 1.1, 1.2, etc. Figures, tables, and displayed equations should be numbered consecutively throughout the text 1, 2, etc.). Equation numbers should appear flush right in parentheses.

Appendices. Appendices should appear as a separate section after the text.

Acknowledgements. Acknowledgements should appear as a separate section after the text or appendices and before any notes.

Notes. Notes should be numbered consecutively and designated by superscripts ([1], [2], etc.) in the text. All notes should be typed double-spaced beginning on a separate page following the text or acknowledgements, and before the references.

References. References in the text should follow the author-date format (e.g., Brown (1986), Jones (1978a, 1978b), Smith and Johnson (1983)). References should be typed double-spaced beginning on a separate page following the notes, according to the following samples (journal and book titles may be underlined rather than italicized). References with up to three authors should include the names of each author, references with four or more authors should cite the first author and add "et al." It is the responsibility of the authors to verify all references.

Sample References

Becker, Gordon, Morris DeGroot, and Jacob Marschak. (1964). "Measuring Utility by a Single-Response Sequential Method." *Behavioral Science* 9, 226-232.

Schoemaker, Paul. (1980). Experiments of Decisions Under Risk: The Expected Utility Hypothesis. Boston: Kluwer-Hijhoff Publishing.

Smith, V. Kerry. (1986). "A Conceptual Overview of the Foundations of Benefit-Cost Analysis." In Judith Bentkover, Vincent Covello, and Jeryl Mumpower (eds.), Benefits Assessment: The State of the Art. Dordrech: D. Reidel Publishing Co.

Tables. Tables should be numbered and titled, and typed double-spaced, each on a separate sheet, following the references. Notes to tables should be designated by superscripted letters ([a], [b], etc.) within each table and typed double-spaced on the same page as the table. Use descriptive labels rather than computer acronyms, and explain all abbreviations. When tables are typed on oversized paper, please submit both the original and a reduced copy.

Figures. Figure legends should be numbered and typed double-spaced on a separate sheet following the tables. Figures for accepted manuscripts should be submitted in camera-ready form, i.e., clear glossy prints or drawn in India ink on drafting paper or high quality white paper. Lettering in figures should be large enough to be legible after half-size reduction. Authors should submit one 5" x 7" (13cm x 18cm) original and two photocopies of each figure, with authors' names, manuscript title, and figure number on the back of each original and copy (use gummed labels if necessary to avoid damaging originals). Figures should be enclosed in a separate envelope backed by cardboard and without staples or paper clips.

Review of Derivatives Research

ADDRESS FOR SUBMISSION:

Melissa Parsons
Review of Derivatives Research
Journal Editorial Office
Kluwer Academic Publishers
101 Phillip Drive
Norwell, MA 02061
USA
Phone: 781-871-6300
Fax: 781-871-6528
E-Mail: melissa.parsons@wkap.com
Web: www.kluwer.com
Address May Change:

PUBLICATION GUIDELINES:

Manuscript Length: No Reply
Copies Required: Four
Computer Submission: Yes only if accepted
Format: WdPerfect, MS Word, ASCII
Fees to Review: 50.00 US$

Manuscript Style:
    See Manuscript Guidelines

CIRCULATION DATA:

Reader: Business Persons
Frequency of Issue: Quarterly
Copies per Issue: No Reply
Sponsor/Publisher: Kluwer Academic
    Publishers
Subscribe Price: 230.00 US$ Institution
    66.00 US$ Individual

REVIEW INFORMATION:

Type of Review: Blind Review
No. of External Reviewers: No Reply
No. of In House Reviewers: No Reply
Acceptance Rate: 21-30%
Time to Review: 4 - 6 Months
Reviewers Comments: Yes
Invited Articles: 0-5%
Fees to Publish: 0.00 US$

MANUSCRIPT TOPICS:
Insurance; International Economics & Trade; Portfolio & Security Analysis; Tax Accounting

MANUSCRIPT GUIDELINES/COMMENTS:

Aims and Scope
The proliferation of derivative assets during the past two decades is unprecedented. With this growth in derivatives comes the need for financial institutions, institutional investors, and corporations to use sophisticated quantitative techniques to take full advantage of the spectrum of these new financial instruments. Academic research has significantly contributed to our understanding of derivative assets and markets. The growth of derivative asset markets has been accompanied by a commensurate growth in the volume of scientific research.

The rapid growth of derivatives research combined with the current absence of a *rigorous* research journal catering to the area of derivatives, and the long lead-times in the existing academic journals, underlines the need for *Review of Derivatives Research,* which provides an international forum for researchers involved in the general areas of derivative assets. The Review publishes high quality articles dealing with the pricing and hedging of derivative assets on any underlying asset (commodity, interest rate, currency, equity, real estate, traded or non-traded, etc.).

Specific topics include but are not limited to: econometric analyses of derivative markets (efficiency, anomalies, performance, etc.), analysis of swap markets, market microstructure and volatility issues, regulatory and taxation issues, credit risk, new areas of applications such as corporate finance (capital budgeting, debt innovations), international trade (tariffs and quotas), banking and insurance (embedded options, asset-liability management, risk-sharing issues and the design of optimal derivative securities, risk management, management and control, valuation and analysis of the options embedded in capital projects, valuation and hedging of exotic options, new areas for further development (i.e. natural resources, environmental economics).

Address for Contributors
In an attempt to speed publication of accepted articles, the *Review* has a double-blind refereeing process. The *Review* has a goal of publication within six months after acceptance. Finally, a section of the journal is available for rapid publication on 'hot' issues in the market, small technical pieces, and timely essays related to pending legislation and policy.

Prospective authors are encouraged to submit manuscripts for consideration for publication in forthcoming issues of the *Review of Derivatives Research*. Four copies of the manuscript, together with a check for $75.00 should be sent to the above address.

Manuscript Preparation
Final versions of accepted manuscripts (including notes, references, tables, and legends) should be typed double-spaced on 8.5" x 11" (22 cm x 29 cm) white paper with 1" (2.5 cm) margins on all sides. Sections should appear in the following order: title page, abstract, text, notes, references, tables, figure legends, and figure. Comments or replies to previously published articles should also follow this format with the exception of abstracts, which are not required.

Title Page. The title page should include the title, authors' names and permanent affiliations, and the name, current address, and telephone number of the person to whom page proofs and reprints should be sent.

Abstract. The following page should include an abstract of not more than 100 words and a list of two to six keywords. Also include JEL subject category number.

Text. The text of the article should begin on a new page. The introduction should have no heading or number. Subsequent headings (including appendices) should be designated by arabic numerals (1,2, etc.), and subsection headings should be numbered 1.1, 1.2, etc. Figures, tables, and displayed equations should be numbered consecutively throughout the text (1, 2, etc.). Equation numbers should appear flush left in parentheses and running variables for equations (e.g. $i = 1, \ldots, n$) flush right in parentheses.

Notes. References in the text should follow the author-date format (e.g. Brown (1986), Jones (1978a, 1978b), Smith and Johnson (1983)). References should be typed double-spaced beginning on a separate page following the notes, according to the following samples (journal and book titles may be underlined rather than italicized). References with up to three authors should include the names of each author, references with four or more authors should cite the first author and add "et al." It is the responsibility of the authors to verify all references.

Sample References

Becker, Gordon, Morris DeGroot, and Jacob Marschak. (1964). "Measuring Utility by a Single-Response Sequential Method," *Behavioral Science* 9, 226-232.

Schoemaker, Paul. (1980). *Experiments on Decisions Under Risk: The Expected Utility Hypothesis.* Boston: Kluwer-Nijhoff Publishing.

Smith, V. Kerry. (1986). "A Conceptual Overview of the Foundations of Benefit-Cost Analysis." In Judith Bentkover, Vincent Covello, and Beryl Mumpower (eds.), *Benefits Assessment: The State of the Art.* Dordrecht: D. Reidel Publishing Co.

Tables. Tables should be titled and typed double-spaced, each on a separate sheet, following the references. Notes to tables should be designated by superscripted letters (a, b, etc.) within each table and typed double-spaced on the same page as the table. Use descriptive labels rather than computer acronyms, and explain all abbreviations. When tables are typed on oversized paper, please submit both the original and a reduced copy.

Figures. Figures for accepted manuscripts should be submitted in camera-ready form, i.e. clear glossy prints or drawn in India ink on drafting paper or high quality white paper. Lettering in figures should be large enough to be legible after half-size reduction. Authors should submit one 5" x 7" (13 cm x 18 cm) original and two photocopies of each figure, with authors' names, manuscript title, and figure number on the back of each original and copy (use gummed labels if necessary to avoid damaging originals). Figures should be enclosed in a separate envelope backed by cardboard and without staples or paper clips. Figure legends should be typed double-spaced on a separate sheet following the tables.

Page Proofs and Reprints
Corrected page proofs must be returned within three days of receipt, and alterations other than corrections may be charged to the authors. Authors will receive 50 free reprints, and may order additional copies when returning the corrected proofs.

Electronic Delivery of Accepted Papers
Please send only the electronic version (of ACCEPTED paper) via one of the methods listed below. Note, in the event of minor discrepancies between the electronic version and hard copy, the electronic file will be used as the final version.

Kluwer can accept almost any word processing format (e.g. WordPerfect, Microsoft Word, etc.) as well as ASCII (text only) files. Also, we accept FrameMaker documents as "text only" files. Note, it is also helpful to supply both the source and the ASCII files of a paper. Please submit PostScript files for figures as well as separate, original figures in camera-ready form. A PostScript figure file should be named after its figure number, e.g., figl.eps or circlel.eps.

Via electronic mail

1. 1.Please e-mail electronic version to KAPfiles @ wkap.com
2. Recommended formats for sending files via e-mail:
   - Binary files - uuencode or binhex
   - Compressing files - compress, pkzip, or gzip
   - Collecting files - tar
3. The e-mail message should include the author's last name, the name of the journal to which the paper has been accepted, and the type of file (e.g., LATEX or ASCII).Via anonymous FTP

ftp: ftp.wkap.com
cd: /incoming/production

Send e-mail to KAPfiles@wkap.com to inform Kluwer electronic version is at this FTP site.

Via disk

1. Label a 3.5 inch floppy disk with the operating system and word processing program along with the authors' names, manuscript title, and name of journal to which the paper has been accepted.
2. Mail Disk to
   Kluwer Academic Publisher
   Desktop Department
   101 Philip Drive
   Assinippi Park
   Norwell, MA 02061

Any questions about the above procedures please send e-mail to: dthelp @ wkap.com

Southwest Business and Economics Journal

ADDRESS FOR SUBMISSION:

V. Sivarama Krishnan, Editor
Southwest Business and Economics Journal
Cameron University
School of Business
Business Research Center
2800 W. Gore Boulevard
Lawton, OK 73505
USA
Phone: 580-581-2805
Fax: 580-581-5523
E-Mail: sivarama@cameron.edu
Web:
Address May Change:

PUBLICATION GUIDELINES:

Manuscript Length: 11-15
Copies Required: Three
Computer Submission: Yes
Format: WordPerfect 6.0
Fees to Review: 0.00 US$

Manuscript Style:
    Chicago Manual of Style

CIRCULATION DATA:

Reader: Academics, Business Persons
Frequency of Issue: Yearly
Copies per Issue: 600
Sponsor/Publisher: University
Subscribe Price: 10.00 US$
    15.00 US$ Organization/Library

REVIEW INFORMATION:

Type of Review: Blind Review
No. of External Reviewers: 1
No. of In House Reviewers: 1
Acceptance Rate: 30-35%
Time to Review: 3 - 4 Months
Reviewers Comments: Yes
Invited Articles: 0-30%
Fees to Publish: 0.00 US$

MANUSCRIPT TOPICS:
Accounting Information Systems; Accounting Theory & Practice; Auditing; Cost Accounting; Insurance; Real Estate; Tax Accounting

MANUSCRIPT GUIDELINES/COMMENTS:

The *Southwest Business and Economics Journal* provides a bridge of communication between the business community and the academia. Articles related to all business areas and regional economic development are welcome. The journal has two sections: the first consists of refereed articles from the academic community and an occasional invited article from business practitioners, and the second has abstracts of the business and economic information presented in the Cameron Business Forums. The journal is published once a year.

The target audience includes both academics and the business and professional community.

The *Southwest Business and Economics Journal* is published once a year by the Business Research Center, School of Graduate and Professional Studies, Cameron University, Lawton. OK.

Articles on applied business and economics topics related to all areas of business are invited from faculty and from business professionals.

1. All submitted work must be original work that is not under submission to another journal or under consideration for publication in another form.

2. Authors must submit three double-spaced typewritten copies of their paper.

3. The cover page shall contain the title of the paper, author's name, and affiliation. This page will be removed when the paper is sent to a referee. The first page of text should contain the title but not the name of the author.

4. A separate abstract of not more than 100 words should be included.

5. Each table and figure should be on a separate page at the end of the paper, with proper instructions about their placement in the paper.

6. Footnotes must be consecutively numbered and typed on a separate page and double-spaced.

7. Cite references in the text, placing the publication date in parentheses, e.g., "Banz (1981) was the first...

8. *Southwest Business and Economics Journal* will hold exclusive rights after acceptance.

9. Authors are advised to mention their office and residence telephone numbers and convenient times for contact.

10. Papers should be submitted to the Editor.

We accept computer submissions on 3 ½ " disk formatted in WordPerfect 6.0.

Spectrum

ADDRESS FOR SUBMISSION:

Darryl R. Matthews, Sr., Editor
Spectrum
7249 A Hanover Parkway
Greenbelt, MD 20770
USA
Phone: 301-474-6222
Fax: 301-474-3114
E-Mail: darryl.matthews@compuserve.com
Web:
Address May Change:

PUBLICATION GUIDELINES:

Manuscript Length: 6-10
Copies Required: Four
Computer Submission: No
Format: N/A
Fees to Review: 0.00 US$

Manuscript Style:
    See Manuscript Guidelines

CIRCULATION DATA:

Reader: Business Persons, Academic
Frequency of Issue: 2 Times/Year
Copies per Issue: 3,001 - 4,000
Sponsor/Publisher: Professional Assn.
Subscribe Price: 20.00 US$

REVIEW INFORMATION:

Type of Review: Blind Review
No. of External Reviewers: 2
No. of In House Reviewers: 1
Acceptance Rate: 21-30%
Time to Review: 2 - 3 Months
Reviewers Comments: Yes
Invited Articles: 21-30%
Fees to Publish: 0.00 US$

MANUSCRIPT TOPICS:
Accounting Information Systems; Accounting Theory & Practice; Accounting Topics;
Auditing; Cost Accounting; Econometrics; Fiscal Policy; Micro Economics

MANUSCRIPT GUIDELINES/COMMENTS:

Spectrum is a journal of referred research and original articles published by the National Association of Black Accountants Inc. You are invited to submit manuscripts on financial accounting, managerial accounting, accounting information systems, taxation, governmental and not-for-profit accounting, accounting history, accounting education, auditing, international accounting, behavioral issues in accounting, gender issues in accounting, minority issues in accounting, public interest accounting and ethical issues in accounting.

Manuscripts, double-spaced, can vary in length from five to twenty pages. The paper should be submitted in quadruplicate on 8-1/2" by 11" paper and on a 3-1/2" diskette in WordPerfect 6.0. All manuscripts submitted should include a cover page, an abstract, and references of only those cited. All pages except the cover page should be numbered. The cover page should present the name, title, affiliation and telephone number of each author and acknowledgements, if any. Authors should be identified only on the cover page. The abstract, on the following page should be less than 150 words and should state the purpose of the study, primary methods used, and the main conclusions. Footnotes should not include literature citations, but citations should appear as follows in brackets: [author name, year] or if the citation is a direct quote: [author name, year, p. XXX]; for example [Damtew and Mapp, 1990]. Endnotes should be used only to provide explanations that would other wise disrupt the continuity of the paper.

References should be listed on a separate page at the end of the manuscript and headed "References." Examples of reference style follow:

Booker, Q., "Accounting for Debt and Equity Securities Investments Under SFAS 115, "Spectrum" (Spring/Summer 1994): 36-44. Fiske, S., and S. Taylor, Social Cognition, New York Random House, 1984.

Prather, J. and Rueschoff, N., An analysis of International Accounting Research in U.S. Academic Accounting Journals, 1980 through 1993, "Accounting Horizons (March 1996): 1-17.

Stewart, J., and B. Birkett, "Universal Availability of Professional Education Through Accounting Student Organizations: A Case Study, "Working paper, National Association of Black Accountants Annual Conference, Atlanta, Georgia, July 1993.

References should contain no abbreviations.

Each table and figure should appear on a separate page, sequentially numbered, and descriptively titled. In the text of the manuscript, the author(s) should indicate where each table/figure should be placed. if questionnaires, cases, interviews or other instruments are used, they should be included at the end of the manuscript as an exhibit or appendix.

If you are interested in submitting a manuscript for consideration for publication in *Spectrum*, or would like further information about manuscript style, please contact Darryl R. Matthews, Sr., Editor.

State Tax Notes Magazine

ADDRESS FOR SUBMISSION:

Carol Douglas, Editor
State Tax Notes Magazine
Tax Analysts
6830 N. Fairfax Drive
Arlington, VA 22213
USA
Phone: 703-533-4451
Fax: 703-533-4484
E-Mail: cdouglas@tax.org
Web:
Address May Change:

CIRCULATION DATA:

Reader: Business Persons, Academic, Gov't
Frequency of Issue: Weekly
Copies per Issue: 1,001 - 2,000
Sponsor/Publisher: Tax Analysts
Subscribe Price: 999.00 US$

PUBLICATION GUIDELINES:

Manuscript Length: Up to 30
Copies Required: One
Computer Submission: Yes
Format: MS Word
Fees to Review: 0.00 US$

Manuscript Style:
    No Reply

REVIEW INFORMATION:

Type of Review: Editorial Review
No. of External Reviewers: 0
No. of In House Reviewers: 1
Acceptance Rate: 50 %
Time to Review: 1 Month or Less
Reviewers Comments: No
Invited Articles: 21-30%
Fees to Publish: 0.00 US$

MANUSCRIPT TOPICS:
Fiscal Policy; State and Local Taxation; Tax Accounting

MANUSCRIPT GUIDELINES/COMMENTS:

Use above submission address or Email: statenotes@tax.org

Strategic Finance Magazine

ADDRESS FOR SUBMISSION:

Kathy Willliams, Ediltor
Strategic Finance Magazine
10 Paragon Drive
Montvale, NJ 07645
USA
Phone: 201-573-9000 ext 271
Fax: 201-573-0639
E-Mail: kwilliams@imanet.org
Web: www.strategicfinancemag.com
Address May Change:

PUBLICATION GUIDELINES:

Manuscript Length: 11-15
Copies Required: Four
Computer Submission: Yes
Format: MS Word
Fees to Review: 0.00 US$

Manuscript Style:
    Chicago Manual of Style

CIRCULATION DATA:

Reader: Business Persons
Frequency of Issue: Monthly
Copies per Issue: More than 25,000
Sponsor/Publisher: Institute of Management
    Accountants
Subscribe Price: 140.00 US$
    70.00 US$ Nonprofit Organizations

REVIEW INFORMATION:

Type of Review: Blind Review
No. of External Reviewers: 3
No. of In House Reviewers: 2
Acceptance Rate: 11-20%
Time to Review: 2-6 Months
Reviewers Comments: Yes
Invited Articles: 31-50%
Fees to Publish: 0.00 US$

MANUSCRIPT TOPICS:

Accounting Information Systems; Auditing; Corporate Finance; Cost Accounting; Fiscal Policy; Industrial Organization; Insurance; International Economics & Trade; International Finance; Monetary Policy; Portfolio & Security Analysis; Tax Accounting

MANUSCRIPT GUIDELINES/COMMENTS:

What Should You Write About?

Strategic Finance and *Management Accounting Quarterly* publish only original material that contributes to the profession of management accounting and financial management.

We recommend that you study several issues of our magazines before you write and submit your manuscript. The best advice is to write only about the topics you know best and with which you've had experience.

Preparing Your Manuscript

Your manuscript should be submitted on plain white 8 ½" x 11" paper in a printed format, either typed or generated by a PC. Leave sufficient margins on all sides (one inch is recommended). The text should be double-spaced.

Write the title of your manuscript and the names of author(s) on a cover page. Do not put an author's name on anything but the cover page because all manuscripts are reviewed "blind." If there is more than one author, list the authors' names in the order you want them to appear in print. Number each page at the bottom.

Length of Manuscript. Most manuscripts we publish are approximately 10-15 typewritten double-spaced pages. Ideal length is about 1,500 to 2,000 words for *Strategic Finance*. Manuscripts for *Management Accounting Quarterly* can be longer.

Abstract. Please provide an abstract or summary of your article on a separate sheet of paper. The editors use this abstract to summarize and introduce your article in the table of contents.

Tables and Figures. Your manuscript will be strengthened if you can illustrate your points. Graphic illustrations should be kept simple and in proportion to the manuscript's length. There should be a specific reference in the text to each table or figure in your manuscript, and put each table or figure on a separate sheet of paper.

Bio and Footnotes. Please include brief biographies of all authors with your manuscript, and make sure they contain a phone number and/or e-mail address for each author. Where necessary, footnotes should be on a separate page at the end of the manuscript. In references cited, please include author's full name, title of publication, name of publisher, date of publication, and page numbers where applicable.

Submitting Your Manuscript
Send four copies of your manuscript when submitting it for publication, as this step will help speed up the manuscript review process.

Your manuscript must be accompanied by an official transmittal form, which you can obtain from your chapter's manuscript director or by contacting the Publications staff. Manuscripts without this form will be returned to the author.

The criteria for acceptable manuscripts for chapter competition purposes are:
1. IMA is given exclusive publication rights.
2. Manuscripts must be accompanied by an Authorization to Publish form signed by all authors.
3. Manuscripts must not have been previously published.
4. They must be submitted in English through the chapter in completed form for publication.
5. If authored by a nonmember, they must be accompanied by author's mailing address.
6. They must not be a poem, outline, abstract, thesis, school term/research paper, unedited speech, or previously accepted manuscript.
7. Manuscript topics should reflect "leadership strategies in accounting, finance, and information management."
8. The content of the manuscript must be timely.

The Review Process
All manuscripts submitted through the IMA chapter competition are reviewed in a two-stage process to determine if they are appropriate for publication. An acceptable manuscript

submitted on time earns a maximum number of points based on chapter size. (See *Chapter Competition for Trophies and Awards* booklet.)

Each manuscript is assigned a control number when the Publications staff receives it. The author is notified of this control number via a postcard, so when you want to know the status of your manuscript, please refer to this number when you contact the staff.

Technical Review. Each manuscript undergoes a blind review by three independent reviewers who have expertise in specific areas. All references to the author are deleted from the original and copies. Members of the manuscript appraisal committee base their evaluations on the following seven major criteria:

1. Is the topic of the manuscript relevant for our readers?
2. How well was the topic covered? Was it a thorough analysis and description of the topic? Were any assertions made that were not supported by the evidence and data supplied?
3. Is the manuscript original and not a rehash of what has been published previously?
4. Is it practical? Can our readers use the information to benefit their companies and careers?
5. Is it technically correct and sound?
6. Is the topic timely? Does the manuscript reflect the latest pronouncements and research? Does it represent a new development or innovation of which our members should be aware?
7. Is the material presented clearly and concisely?

When these manuscript appraisal forms are returned to the editorial department after review, the three grades are then averaged to determine the overall grade assigned to the manuscript. Reviewers are asked to recommend that the manuscript be published, revised, or rejected and to provide reasons for their recommendations. We also ask them for suggestions on how the technical content of the manuscript can be improved. (Recommendations made by the technical review committee to either publish or reject the manuscript will not influence the number of points that the chapter received after the initial acceptance.) Based on the review committee's comments and further evaluation by the editorial staff of the magazine, manuscripts will either be considered for publication or rejected.

Publication
If your manuscript is selected for publication, you will be notified within eight weeks after the review process is complete. Within eight months you will be notified regarding the date of the issue in which your article is scheduled to appear. If your manuscript has been saved on a floppy disk, please send us the disk in ASCII or Microsoft Word format.

An editor on the staff will edit your manuscript and send you the edited copy, a computer-generated clean copy, and a copyright permission form. Please review the editing, make any changes on the printed proof, sign the copyright form, and return all material within five days of receipt. During the editing process, an editor or editorial assistant will contact you to discuss tables or figures to illustrate the article or any other matters pertaining to the content.

Complimentary Copies. After the article is published, you will be sent 10 copies for your personal use. You can order additional copies or reprints by contacting the IMA Publications staff.

Return of Your Manuscript. If your manuscript is rejected, we'll let you know as soon as the decision is made. If you would like your manuscript returned to you, please include a self-addressed stamped envelope in your package. Remember to keep a copy of your article for your own records. The Publications Department cannot be responsible for retaining rejected manuscripts.

Awards

The IMA member authors of the top manuscripts submitted through the competition, determined by the grade average and published in the last year, are presented Certificates of Merit for their outstanding contributions to accounting literature. IMA member authors of the top three manuscripts, as determined by an editorial advisory committee, will be presented Lybrand Gold, Silver, and Bronze Medals, respectively.

Tips For Effective Writing

Publications staff editors carefully edit every manuscript scheduled for publication. They follow a number of general principles in the editing process. Here are some suggestions for effective writing:

- Write punchy lead paragraphs that will "grab" readers and pull them into the article.
- Avoid long introductions. Get right to the point. Tell the reader exactly what you plan to do.
- Avoid jargon and acronyms. Readers don't like to go back and check their meaning.
- Don't pad your manuscript. It will be obvious to the editor and to the reader-if the editor lets the material stand.
- Avoid long, complex sentences. Break a complex thought into two or more sentences.
- Don't assume that the reader knows as much as you do. Carefully explain or define a term that isn't commonly used or was coined at your company.
- Use the active voice, not passive. Instead of writing "it was accomplished in 10 days," say "We finished the project in 10 days."
- Write a conclusion that sums up your major points and makes a statement on why the article is of importance to the reader.

Suggested Topics For Strategic Finance Authors

1. Treasury
2. Cash Management & Banking Relations
3. Corporate Development and Strategic Planning
4. Financing
5. Investor Relations
6. International Finance/IASC
7. Insurance (especially operational liability)
8. Financial Risk Analysis and Management (risks and opportunities)

9. Employee Benefits
10. Retirement Plans and Pension Administration
11. Leasing
12. Investment Management and the Equity Market (I PO)
13. Management Information Systems
14. Other Technology Issues
15. Real Estate (such as valuation of private and public corporate enterprises)
16. SEC and FASB Regulatory Issues and other governmental regulations
17. Financial Reporting
18. Mergers & Acquisitions & Restructuring
19. Controllership
20. Budgeting & Planning
21. Capital Budgeting
22. Cost Accounting
23. ABM/Target Costing/Theory of Constraints
24. Corporate Taxes
25. Enterprise Resource Planning
26. Performance Measurement and Evaluation
27. Ethics
28. Intellectual Capital
29. R&D and New Product Development
30. Life-Cycle Product Analysis
31. Joint Ventures
32. Management of Human Resources/Employee Training and Education/Behavior
33. Communications and Presentation Skills
34. Internal Auditing
35. Awareness of External Auditing
36. Liquidation and Bankruptcy
37. Economical/Competitive Environment
38. Current Asset Utilization (A/R, Inventory Management)
39. Business Law
40. Bargaining Unit Negotiation
41. Outsourcing
42. Purchasing
43. Quantitative Analysis (statistics)
44. Industrial Engineering (factory floor optimization)

Tax Adviser

ADDRESS FOR SUBMISSION:

Nicholas J. Fiore, Editor
Tax Adviser
Tax Adviser
American Insitute of CPAs
Harborside Financial Center
102 Plaza III
Jersey City, NJ 07311-3881
USA
Phone: 201-938-3444
Fax: 201-521-5447
E-Mail:
Web:
Address May Change:

PUBLICATION GUIDELINES:

Manuscript Length: 12-20
Copies Required: Two
Computer Submission: Yes
Format: Microsoft Word
Fees to Review: 0.00 US$

Manuscript Style:
      See Manuscript Guidelines

CIRCULATION DATA:

Reader: , Tax Practitioners
Frequency of Issue: Monthly
Copies per Issue: 28,000
Sponsor/Publisher: American Institute of
   CPAs
Subscribe Price: 98.00 US$

REVIEW INFORMATION:

Type of Review: Blind Review
No. of External Reviewers: 2
No. of In House Reviewers: 0
Acceptance Rate: 50%
Time to Review: 1 Month or Less
Reviewers Comments: Yes
Invited Articles: 50% +
Fees to Publish: 0.00 US$

MANUSCRIPT TOPICS:
Tax Accounting; Taxation

MANUSCRIPT GUIDELINES/COMMENTS:

The Tax Adviser consists of 64 pages and covers a wide range of tax information. As an editorial objective, *The Tax Adviser* deals with both technical and policy aspects of taxation—providing practical, administrative, and technical commentary through articles and regular departments. Thus, the material has a broad range of appeal—satisfying the needs of anyone who must keep informed on Federal tax matters. Qualified articles will be accepted from CPAs, lawyers, tax executives, and professors.

It is assumed that your article has been submitted exclusively to *The Tax Adviser*; articles are not considered on any other basis. It is our practice to send the article to at least two of our Editorial Advisers for their opinion on publishing the article, technical advice and constructive comments. The reviewers are expected to submit their decision within one month.

Regrettably, our budget does not provide for compensating authors of articles. However, as a token of our appreciation, an author will receive five copies of the issue containing his article. Also, 50 reprints of the article itself will be made available on request.

It would greatly facilitate the processing of your article if you would observe the guidelines listed below for preparing your manuscript. Of course, if it is not convenient for you to do so, we will still welcome your material.

Title And Author: On a top sheet, give the title of the article, your name and professional affiliation.

Typing: All articles should be typed on one side of 8-1/2" x 11" white paper, double-spaced, with a left hand margin of about two inches.

Copies: If practical, send us **two copies** for submission to reviewing Editorial Adviser.

Footnotes: Type all footnotes double-spaced and appropriately numbered on separate (the last) pages of the manuscript. also, see "Citations" on page 3.

Length Of Manuscript: Normally, an article should run at least 12-20 pages -- which will equal approximately 4-7 pages in the magazine. A shorter one can be published in a regular department of the magazine (e.g., Tax Clinic).

Citations: Preferably, citations should be confined to footnotes. In any event, give only the "handle" (case name, etc.) in the text. (For example, if the Schlude decision is frequently referred to in the article, state: "In Schlude1 , the Supreme Court..."). In citations, exclude "Commissioner", "U.S.", or the district director's name; they are unnecessary.

Suggestions For Preparation Of Tax Articles

It is the objective of *The Tax Adviser* to provide a high quality periodical. To accomplish this objective, we hope to publish material that will make an important contribution to tax literature. In general, subjects will be treated in depth rather than by survey or summary approach.

As an aid to the preparation of material for *The Tax Adviser*, the following suggestions are offered. Undoubtedly, some of the suggestions will be inappropriate for some subjects. Follow them only if you deem them appropriate and helpful.

1. Avoid the "cut and paste" approach to the preparation of articles, since such material really adds little to tax literature.

2. To the extent that the subject involves novel concepts (e.g., "tax preferences"), the article should be prepared on the premise that the readers are students rather than experts. Accordingly, new terms that will be used frequently should be fully explained at the outset.

3. The article should be analytical and interpretive, not merely a rearrangement or rewording of the statute, regulations, committee reports, etc. Thus, statutory or regulatory arrangement or language should not be slavishly followed or quoted.

4. Note and comment on unintended benefits or hardships, ambiguities and practical problems of compliance and administration.

5. Explanation of prior law or regulations should be included only to the extent it facilitates understanding of new legislation or regulations. In addition, the history of a concept, as exemplified through court decisions, should generally be extremely limited.

6. Exemplify as imaginatively as possible. If warranted, modify examples in regulations or committee reports. If examples in regulations or committee reports seem inconsistent with the Code, criticize them. Consider giving examples of what the statute or regulations

1. clearly includes,
2. clearly excludes and
3. ambiguously includes or excludes.

A brief example may be worth a thousand words of explanation.

7. Tax planning opportunities in text or through comprehensive examples should be covered where appropriate.

General Writing Hints

These writing hints are based on several articles, notably one by Jerome K. Pescow, CPA. We hope you find them helpful. However, do not feel obliged to follow those which you feel are incompatible with your personality, writing style and habits, and the article you are writing.

Outline first: A good working outline will insure a well-organized article, if nothing else.

Use subheadings: Many subheadings will naturally flow from the outline. If thoughts are kept within the boundaries of a subheading, your article will be easier to read.

Watch quotes: Ask yourself: Is that quotation necessary and is all of it relevant? An article loaded with quotations may look more like a "scissors and paste job" than an original writing.

Polish later: First get your thoughts on paper; then work over the wording.

Opening "blues": If you have difficulty writing a satisfactory opening at the beginning, do it last.

Write as you speak: Avoid stilted or pompous words and phrases that you would not use in your speech. Consider dictating your first draft.

Write for your audience: You can write on the premise that the readers of *The Tax Adviser* are familiar with most tax terms. However, you should define or explain any term whose exact meaning is essential to a better understanding of your article. Furthermore, if an article is devoted to a narrow phase of a tax subject, it is a good practice to include a general discussion of the subject as background. Such background material may be included near the beginning of the article, or as a footnote.

Simple to complex: Starting with the complex will leave your readers mystified, a feeling that they may never shake. Flashback explanations are more appropriate to mystery novels than tax essays.

Exclude digressions from the text: True, digressions can be noteworthy; if so, use them as footnotes. When included in the text, digressions can be disconcerting at best and confusing at worst.

Use examples, exhibits, etc.: Use examples and/or exhibits whenever possible. They should make the narrative clearer.

Listing technique: Where series of topics or subjects are referred to consecutively, list them vertically rather than horizontally.

Subjects For Major Articles
General suggestions:
This section is devoted to providing guidelines for the selection of specific subjects for articles. That is, by outlining several broad categories of articles, it may stimulate you or others in your firm to select a topic of interest. Note that certain articles are cited from *The Tax Adviser* to exemplify each approach.

1. Significant recent developments in a given area.
This type of article separates fact from opinion. That is, the ruling or court decision is digested and set in regular type. Then the author's comments (tax planning hints, critiques, etc.) follow in clearly distinguishable type.

See Abbin and Carlson, "Significant Recent Developments in Estate Planning" (September and November 1988).

2. In-depth treatment of a narrow point.
No subject is too narrow to be a subject for a tax article -- assuming that it requires (without padding) at least 12 manuscript pages.

See Robinson and Mark, "The 90-Day Letter Quandary" (December 1988); and Schnee, "Ordinary Loss and Surrender of Stock" (August 1988).

3. Estate planning articles.
Because tax practitioners are, in general, not very sophisticated in estate planning, there is a great latitude for selection of subjects in this area. That is, the subject matter -- but not the treatment -- could be less sophisticated.

4. Analysis of current development(s).
An example of this type of article would be an analysis of a significant Supreme Court case.

See Fortin and Dennis-Escoffier, "The Pritchett Reversal" (March 1989); and Schnee and Roberts, "The Arkansas Best Decision" (November 1988).

5. Community property articles.
Despite the fact that affluent taxpayers are migrating to and from community property states in increasing numbers and the population of such states has been growing disproportionately, the national tax periodicals seem to provide insufficient coverage of community property. Therefore, this tax area should provide a fertile source of specific subjects for articles that will interest a number of common-law (as well as community property) state practitioners.

See Seago, "The income tax consequences of community property divisions at divorce" (July 1982).

6. Several articles covering one aspect of a broad area.
This approach has been taken with respect to consolidated returns and ERISA, and could be applied to other areas, such as subpart F.

See Erickson, "Passive Activity Dispositions" (May 1989); and Bandy and Kramer, "Planning with the Passive Activity Loss Limitation Regulations" (November 1988).

7. Trade or business profiles.
Articles dealing with everyday or special tax problems of a trade or business, such as a bank or insurance company.

See Stara, "Taxation of the Franchisee and Franchisor" (January 1989); and Duer, Horvitz and Coberly, "Captive Insurance Companies" (March 1988).

8. Tax policy.
This type of article should deal with matters of tax policy on essentially a technical, rather than purely political, basis.

See Raby, "The Role of Disclosure in Tax Return Preparation" (March 1989); and Schindler, "Intercorporate Transfer Pricing" (May 1988).

9. Subjects requiring current coverage.
Subjects that have been covered extensively in the not-too-recent past may still be worthy of coverage because of accounting, economic or other reasons.

See Olsen and Kuchinos, "The New 'Passive Foreign Investment Company' Rules" (December 1988).

10. Proposed or recently adopted regulations.

Although TTA may publish the AICPA Tax Division's comments on proposed regulations, we seldom publish commentary by an individual on proposed regulations. Articles on adopted regulations are always welcomed.

See Willens, Mason and Choate, "The Final Sec. 355 Regulations" (April 1989).

11. Problems, pitfalls and planning opportunities.

This type of article would deal with the problems, etc., concerning a given tax subject on the basis that the reader is already familiar (or can become familiar) with the general rules. That is, technical explanations would be limited to that relevant to the problem, etc., at issue.

See Kauter and Stefanis, "Sec. 4980A: Excess Retirement Distributions and Accumulations" (march 1989); Nordhauser, Nordhauser and Slattery, "Taxable or Tax-Exempt Bonds?" (December 1988); and Strauss and Bush, "Fiscal-Year Nonconformity" (April 1988).

12. Checklists.

For example, see Kessler, "Post-mortem planning checklist" (July 1982). Note that often these are estate planning articles and are quasi-tax in character.

13. New laws.

Of course, new laws provide a fertile source of articles. TTA's experience with recent legislation shows that quality rather than time is of the essence to the publication of articles on new laws. Since the tax services can come out quicker with surveys of new laws, no real purpose is served by stressing time in publishing articles in TTA.

See McConnell, "Highlighting the Tax Reform Act of 1986 for individuals" (October 1986); Willens "The corporate provisions of the Tax Reform Act of 1986" (October 1986); and Green, "Highlights of the Deficit Reduction Act of 1984" (September 1984).

Listed below are some general subjects for articles suggested by *The Tax Adviser*'s Editorial Advisers and staff.

- AMT issues.
- Accounting periods and methods.
- Bonds and exempt obligations.
- Capital gains.
- Citizens living abroad.
- Compensation techniques.
- Compliance and penalties.
- Computers in tax practice.
- Consolidated return planning.
- Corporate mergers and acquisitions.
- Current developments in depreciation.
- Deductions and credits.

- Earnings and profits problems.
- Employee benefits.
- Employee stock options.
- Estate planning strategies.
- Family tax issues (divorce, community property, etc.)
- Foreign corporations and nonresident aliens doing business in the United States.
- Foreign income and taxpayers.
- Imputed interest.
- Inventory.
- Life insurance in estate planning.
- Life insurance issues.
- PHC issues.
- Partnership issues.
- Passive loss planning.
- Payroll taxes: acquisitions and mergers.
- Pensions.
- Planning for Sec. 531 (accumulated earnings tax).
- Post-mortem checklist.
- Pre-publication costs (expenses accrued by authors, what's deductible...).
- Real estate ownership.
- Related party transactions -- accruals and sales.
- S corporations.
- Stock redemption agreements.
- Tax effect on the individual stockholder caught in the middle of a takeover, buyout, etc.
- Tax planning involving spreadsheet analysis.
- Tax practice management.
- Taxation of financial institutions.
- Taxation of life insurance companies.
- Unincorporated profit-sharing plans (Keoghs).

Tax Lawyer (The)

ADDRESS FOR SUBMISSION:

Gersham Goldstein, Editor-In-Chief
Tax Lawyer (The)
American Bar Association
740 15th Street, N.W.
Washington, DC 20005
USA
Phone: 202-662-8681
Fax: 202-662-8682
E-Mail: dunna@staff.abanet.org
Web: www.abanet.org
Address May Change:

PUBLICATION GUIDELINES:

Manuscript Length: 30+
Copies Required: Three
Computer Submission: Yes
Format: MsWd for Windows, ASCII, or
   Word
Fees to Review: 0.00 US$

Manuscript Style:
   Uniform System of Citation (Harvard
   Blue Book)

CIRCULATION DATA:

Reader: Academics, Lawyers, Accountants,
   Gov't Officials
Frequency of Issue: Quarterly
Copies per Issue: 22,000
Sponsor/Publisher: American Bar
   Association
Subscribe Price: 83.00 US$

REVIEW INFORMATION:

Type of Review: Editorial Review
No. of External Reviewers: 3+
No. of In House Reviewers: 1
Acceptance Rate: 6-10%
Time to Review: 1 - 2 Months
Reviewers Comments: Yes
Invited Articles: 21-30%
Fees to Publish: 0.00 US$

MANUSCRIPT TOPICS:
Domestic Tax Issues; International Tax; Tax Accounting

MANUSCRIPT GUIDELINES/COMMENTS:

Tax Management Real Estate

ADDRESS FOR SUBMISSION:

Donald B. Reynolds, Jr., Editor
Tax Management Real Estate
Silverstein and Mullens, P.L.L.C
1776 K Street, N.W., Suite 800
Washington, DC 20006
USA
Phone: 202-452-7958
Fax: 202-452-7989
E-Mail: dbr@silvmul.com
Web:
Address May Change:

CIRCULATION DATA:

Reader: Business Persons
Frequency of Issue: Monthly
Copies per Issue: 1,001 - 2,000
Sponsor/Publisher: Tax Management, Inc.
Subscribe Price: 262.00 US$

PUBLICATION GUIDELINES:

Manuscript Length: 20+
Copies Required: One
Computer Submission: Yes
Format: 1.44 MB
Fees to Review: 0.00 US$

Manuscript Style:
    See Manuscript Guidelines

REVIEW INFORMATION:

Type of Review: Editorial Review
No. of External Reviewers: 1
No. of In House Reviewers: 1
Acceptance Rate: 50%
Time to Review: 1 Month or Less
Reviewers Comments: Yes
Invited Articles: 50% +
Fees to Publish: 0.00 US$

MANUSCRIPT TOPICS:
Real Estate; Tax Accounting; Taxation

MANUSCRIPT GUIDELINES/COMMENTS:

1. Law journal quality original articles fully cited as to authorities used.

2. Short notes, reviews, letters welcomed.

3. Submission of MS with computer diskette and hard copy appreciated.

4. *Uniform System Of Citation* (14th Edition)

Information For Authors
The coverage and scope of the *Tax Management Real Estate Journal* is broad because of the numerous issues that arise in the taxation of real estate transactions. In addition to "typical" real estate subjects, it also includes such matters as partnerships and Subchapter S, tax shelters, low-income housing, tax-exempt bonds, real estate financing, installment sales, FIRPTA, tax-free exchanges of property, and transactional aspects of real estate. The Journal

strives to publish original articles of law journal quality, adequately researched and with the requisite citations of authorities, which will be of use to tax professional involved in real estate transactions and sophisticated real estate investors.

Each monthly issue usually contains one or two principal articles of a length of from six to fifteen printed pages. Since one typeset page holds four to five double spaced manuscript pages, this means the typical article can vary from twenty-five to sixty typewritten pages. Longer articles are sometimes divided in two and printed in successive issues. The publisher's deadline is the last Wednesday of each month, so articles are needed as early in the month as possible in order that they may be fully reviewed and, if appropriate, discussed with the author by phone. Naturally, the sooner the manuscript is made available the better, since occasionally it is necessary to return one to the author for revision. The editor also welcomes shorter articles, commentaries and opinions, and reviews of books and real estate software.

Please include a two or three sentence **biography** that can be used as a non-numbered footnote on the first page and a one or two paragraph **abstract** that will precede the main body of the text. The abstract should state the subject and purpose of the article and major conclusions and recommendations.

Manuscripts should be typed double-spaced with a table of contents to assist in their review (and with footnotes at the end if the author's word processor has that capability). If possible, please include a 3-1/2" HD diskette containing the article, marked to show the file name(s) and the name of the WP software. No fee is paid for contributions submitted to the Journal, but incidental expenses, such as Federal Express, will be reimbursed on request. Ten extra copies of issues containing their published articles are routinely provided to authors with larger quantities being made available by advance arrangements.

Advisory board presentations. Twice a year (usually on the third Thursdays of December and June at 5:30 p.m. in the Waldorf Astoria Hotel) the Tax Management Real Estate Advisory Board meets in New York City for the presentation of three papers on real estate taxation. Papers presented at Advisory Board meetings are duplicated and mailed to board members about the first of the month during which the meeting is held. Authors are encouraged to make any revisions they wish subsequent to the board meeting and prior to publication. Such revised manuscripts are needed by the end of the month in which the meeting was held. The speakers are reimbursed for hotel, meal and travel expenses.

Sponsorship: Tax Management, Inc., Bureau of National Affairs, Washington, DC

Tax Notes

ADDRESS FOR SUBMISSION:

Christopher Bergin, Editor
Tax Notes
6830 North Fairfax Drive
Arlington, VA 22213
USA
Phone: 703-533-4468
Fax: 703-533-4440
E-Mail: cbergin@tax.org
Web: www.tax.org
Address May Change:

CIRCULATION DATA:

Reader: Academics, Lawyers, Acountants,
   Policy Experts, Lawmakers
Frequency of Issue: Weekly
Copies per Issue: 2,001 - 3,000--plus
   electronic
Sponsor/Publisher: Tax Analysts
Subscribe Price: 1849.00 US$
   462.00 US$ Special Professor Rate

PUBLICATION GUIDELINES:

Manuscript Length: Any
Copies Required: One
Computer Submission: Yes
Format: Any
Fees to Review: 0.00 US$

Manuscript Style:
   See Manuscript Guidelines

REVIEW INFORMATION:

Type of Review: Editorial Review
No. of External Reviewers: 0
No. of In House Reviewers: 3
Acceptance Rate: 50 %
Time to Review: 1 Month or Less
Reviewers Comments: No
Invited Articles: 0-5%
Fees to Publish: 0.00 US$

MANUSCRIPT TOPICS:

Accounting Information Systems; Federal Taxation; Fiscal Policy; Tax Accounting

MANUSCRIPT GUIDELINES/COMMENTS:

We have a very fast turn around, so we are informal. Most submitters are aware of our style
and we edit from there; those that are not can get instructions from the editors.

Taxes - The Tax Magazine

ADDRESS FOR SUBMISSION:

Kurt Diefenbach, Editor
Taxes - The Tax Magazine
CCH, Incorporated
2700 Lake Cook Road
Riverwoods, IL 60015
USA
Phone: 847-267-2415
Fax: 847-267-2519
E-Mail: taxes@cch.com
Web:
Address May Change:

PUBLICATION GUIDELINES:

Manuscript Length: Any, 11-20 average
Copies Required: Two
Computer Submission: Yes
Format: 1 disk or E-Mail Attachment
Fees to Review: 0.00 US$

Manuscript Style:
, CCH, Incorporated Federal Tax Pub.

CIRCULATION DATA:

Reader: Business Persons
Frequency of Issue: Monthly
Copies per Issue: 10,001 - 25,000
Sponsor/Publisher: Profit Oriented
  Corporation
Subscribe Price: 195.00 US$

REVIEW INFORMATION:

Type of Review: Editorial Review
No. of External Reviewers: 0
No. of In House Reviewers: 1
Acceptance Rate: 21-30%
Time to Review: 1 - 2 Months
Reviewers Comments: No Reply
Invited Articles: 11-20%
Fees to Publish: 0.00 US$

MANUSCRIPT TOPICS:
Federal Taxation; State and Local Taxation; Tax Accounting; Taxation

MANUSCRIPT GUIDELINES/COMMENTS:

We include the 12-15 manuscripts that we publish in our annual University of Chicago's Federal Tax Conference issue. Without these manuscripts, the invited articles would be 5% or less.

1. We publish articles relating to business laws and public responsibility, computers and data processing, economics and banking, and finance and investments if they relate to accounting and taxation - our main topics.

2. We have no hard-and-fast rules on articles submitted to *Taxes*. However, we prefer a typed, double-spaced manuscript. The footnotes should also be double-spaced and positioned at the bottom of the pages on which they appear in the text. We also like to work with the original copy, as opposed to a manuscript that is a reproduction. Most of our articles run from approximately 6,500 words.

3. We prefer articles dealing with subjects that are timely and of national interest. In particular, we prefer analysis of new laws, cases, rulings, regulations, and areas of tax controversy in which the author presents his or her opinion concerning the validity, significance, and/or impact of the question in point, along with fresh ideas or tax planning strategies.

4. We do not pay for articles contributed. We provide authors with 10 copies of the magazine. Usually we schedule articles for publication two to five months in advance.

Tennessee CPA Journal

ADDRESS FOR SUBMISSION:

Joyce Friedman, Senior Editor
Tennessee CPA Journal
201 Powell Place
P.O. Box 187
Brentwood, TN 37024-0187
USA
Phone: 615-377-3825
Fax: 615-377-3904
E-Mail: jfriedman@tncpa.org
Web:
Address May Change:

PUBLICATION GUIDELINES:

Manuscript Length: 1-10
Copies Required: Three
Computer Submission: Yes
Format: Microsoft Word
Fees to Review: 0.00 US$

Manuscript Style:
    See Manuscript Guidelines

CIRCULATION DATA:

Reader: , Tennessee Certified Public
    Accountants
Frequency of Issue: 10 Times/ Year
Copies per Issue: 5,001 - 10,000
Sponsor/Publisher: Professional Association
Subscribe Price: No Reply

REVIEW INFORMATION:

Type of Review: Blind Review
No. of External Reviewers: 3
No. of In House Reviewers: 2
Acceptance Rate: 50%
Time to Review: 2 - 3 Months
Reviewers Comments: Yes
Invited Articles: 11-20%
Fees to Publish: 0.00 US$

MANUSCRIPT TOPICS:

Accounting Information Systems; Accounting Theory & Practice; Auditing; Economic Development; Estate Taxation & Manning; Government & Non Profit Accounting; International Economics & Trade; International Finance; Real Estate; Tax Accounting

MANUSCRIPT GUIDELINES/COMMENTS:

Content

Articles should be on issues relevant to CPAs practicing in Tennessee. Our audience is primarily accountants in public practice, although approximately 40 percent of our members also serve industry, government, and education. Articles related to specific industries are acceptable.

Articles should be of a practical nature, offer guidance in complex situations, methods to improve practice, or help resolve questions arising in practice. We accept some articles which are based on questionnaires. References to specific statistical tests should be included in the footnotes. Our readers are primarily interested in the results of the questionnaire and conclusions which may properly be drawn from the results.

Factual accuracy is the responsibility of the author. Facts should be thoroughly checked before the manuscript is submitted.

Self-Study Questions

Authors should include two one-sentence True/False questions taken from the subject matter of each article submitted to *The Tennessee CPA Journal*. These questions will be used for possible inclusion in the CPE Self-Study Exam which accompanies each issue of *The Tennessee CPA Journal*. (See sample self-study exam attached.)

Format

Manuscripts should be typed on 8 1/2" x 11" paper, double-spaced. Paragraphs should be indented three spaces. Quotations of more than three lines, footnotes, and references should be single-spaced and indented. Please allow one-inch margins to facilitate editing.

The names(s) of the author(s) should not be on the manuscript itself. Numbers from one through nine should be spelled out, except where decimals are used or where the numbers are in tabular form. Numbers above ten should be written numerically. The manuscript should be written in third person and in non-sexist language. Articles by one author should not employ the editorial "we."

We recommend *The Elements Of Style* by William Strunk, Jr., and E. B. White (published in paperback by Macmillan Publishing Co., Inc.) as a guide to style and usage.

Biography Of Author(s)

Names, title, education, employers, and brief biographical information (e.g. professional memberships) should be on a separate cover page which includes the title of the manuscript. Also, please include complete address and business telephone number.

Length

We accept manuscripts which will run from one to three pages of our publication (950 to 2,000 words).

Headings

Major headings should be centered. Subheadings should be flush left with the margin.

Tables And Figures

Each table or figure should be placed on a separate page and have a number and a title. Each table or figure must be referred to in the text. Indicate by a double row of dashes and an insert note where the table or figure should appear in the text:

Insert Figure 1 here

Footnotes
Textual footnotes should be used for definitions and explanations which might disrupt the reading continuity if placed in the body of the manuscript. Numerous footnotes and citations do not necessarily make for a better article and are not an indication of thorough research.

Reference List
When the manuscript cites other literature, a list of references must be included at the end of the text. References must be complete bibliography references, including page or paragraph numbers. Arrange entries alphabetically by surname of the first author. Works without authors should also be listed alphabetically. Multiple works by the same author(s) are listed in publication date order. Samples of entries are:

American Institute of Certified Public Accountants. Report of the Study on Establishment of Accounting Principles, *Establishing Accounting Principles* (1972).
Sprouse, R T., Accounting for What-You-May-Call-Its," *Journal of Accountancy* (August 1966), pp. 45-54.

Literature Citations
To cite sources of references, use square brackets in the body of the text to enclose the author's name and page number, if appropriate. If two references were published in one year, use a, b, c to indicate which work listed in the reference list is referred to, e.g. [Armstrong, 1977]; [Sprouse and Moonitz, 1962, p. 2]; [Hendricksen, 1973a]. Citations to professional publications should employ acronyms where practical e.g., [APB Opinion No. 30]; (SFAS No 95]. If an author's name is mentioned in the text, it should not be repeated in the citation, e.g., "Armstrong [1977, p. 40] says . . ."

If a reference has three or more authors, list only the last name of the first author followed by "et al."

References to statutes, legal treatises or court cases should use citations acceptable in law reviews.

Submission of Manuscripts
Three copies of each manuscript should be submitted. TSCPA does not require copyright assignment or transfer from authors; however, TSCPA requests first publication rights. A Publication Release Form is required to be filled out by all authors upon submission.

Manuscripts should be sent to Assistant Editor Scott Guptill at the Tennessee Society of CPA's, Box 187, Brentwood, TN 37024-0187

Each person submitting manuscripts will receive a letter of acknowledgement.

Web Site Publication
TSCPA is currently building its web site at www.tncpa.org. Published authors will be encouraged to participate in on-line discussions on our web site as well as provide an abridged version of their article for publication on our web site.

Review Process

Manuscripts are peer reviewed. This blind refereed process takes one to two months. Authors will be notified concerning acceptance, recommended revision, or rejection of their manuscripts. Manuscripts will not be returned.

Manuscripts on Disk

We also encourage the submission of manuscripts on disk using Macintosh Microsoft Word or Windows versions Microsoft Word 5.X or earlier or WordPerfect 5.0 or earlier. Only one hard copy need be submitted with the diskette.

Today's CPA

ADDRESS FOR SUBMISSION:

Jim Desimone, Editor
Today's CPA
14860 Montfort Drive, Suite 150
Dallas, TX 75240
USA
Phone: 972-687-8512
Fax: 972-687-8646
E-Mail: jdesimone@tscpa.net
Web:
Address May Change:

CIRCULATION DATA:

Reader: Business Persons
Frequency of Issue: Bi-Monthly
Copies per Issue: More than 25,000
Sponsor/Publisher: Texas Society of
   Certified Public Accountants
Subscribe Price: 28.00 US$

PUBLICATION GUIDELINES:

Manuscript Length: 6-10
Copies Required: Five
Computer Submission: Yes
Format: WordPerfect
Fees to Review: 0.00 US$

Manuscript Style:
   See Manuscript Guidelines

REVIEW INFORMATION:

Type of Review: Blind Review
No. of External Reviewers: 2
No. of In House Reviewers: 2
Acceptance Rate: No Reply
Time to Review: 2 - 3 Months
Reviewers Comments: No
Invited Articles: 31-50%
Fees to Publish: 0.00 US$

MANUSCRIPT TOPICS:

Accounting Information Systems; Accounting Theory & Practice; Auditing; Capital Budgeting; Cost Accounting; Econometrics; Economic Development; Economic History; Fiscal Policy; Government & Non Profit Accounting; Industrial Organization; Insurance; International Economics & Trade; International Finance; Macro Economics; Micro Economics; Portfolio & Security Analysis; Public Policy Economics; Real Estate; Tax Accounting

MANUSCRIPT GUIDELINES/COMMENTS:

Today's CPA is a refereed, bimonthly magazine of the Texas Society of Certified Public Accountants. It serves as the primary vehicle for conveying information to more than 31,000 CPAs statewide—the largest number of in-state CPAs participating in state accounting societies. This award-winning publication features articles and columns that focus on issues, trends and developments affecting CPAs, their employers, clients and employees. Always striving to keep CPAs abreast of the latest developments in all facets of business, *Today's CPA* endeavors to develop editorial content that challenges our readers while communicating items of importance.

Getting Published Getting your manuscript published in *Today's CPA* can be a relatively easy task if you keep the following in mind. First, a query letter should be sent—or telephone call made—to the Technical Editor. Your query letter should outline ideas under consideration for inclusion in your manuscript.

Second, it would be helpful if you sent a brief synopsis/abstract to the technical editor to aid in identifying your manuscript's focus. The synopsis/abstract should state the article's purpose; research conducted, if appropriate; and conclusions or results.

Third, five high quality copies of your manuscript should be sent to the technical editor. *Today's CPA* does retain the right of first publication-please let us determine acceptance before sending the manuscript to other publications.

Fourth, since the magazine is refereed, manuscripts are reviewed by two or more accounting professionals upon receipt to better determine appropriateness, technical accuracy and readability. We try to acknowledge manuscripts fairly soon after receiving them. The review process takes approximately six to eight weeks. At that time, you will be notified of the results.

Fifth, if your manuscript is accepted by the review panel, you may be asked to make modifications. In addition, you should keep in mind that the editorial staff may refine your article to conform with journalistic style. Titles and subtitles also may be rewritten to correspond with design elements chosen especially for your composition. There is no need to worry about the final look of your article--*Today's CPA* takes pride in using a number of Texas' talented designers, illustrators and photographers.

What To Write. Writing about what you know will enable you to create an article that is both more effective and more interesting to readers. More effective because you care about your subject. More interesting because it interests you. Your article can't lose when it:
- relates to Texas or Southwest business, economy and legislation;
- discusses emerging professional or business issues and trends;
- examines the latest in computer technology:
- ties in with current events;
- covers topics of general interest as well as in-depth technical subjects; or
- serves as a contribution to an established column in *Today's CPA*.

For sample magazine copies, send your request to: Editor; *Today's CPA*; Texas Society of Certified Public Accountants; 1421 W. Mockingbird Lane, Suite 100; Dallas, TX 75247-4957.

Preferred Style When typing your manuscript, use five-inch columns and double-spaced lines. The rule of thumb is to have no more than 20 of such lines per letter-size page. Try to keep your article to 14 pages (equivalent to four pages of text in the magazine), including exhibits, tables, graphs, charts and footnotes. Double-double space between subheads/sub-titles. Indent each new paragraph three spaces.

- Exhibits can entice a reader to take a closer look at an article. Be sure to provide clean, easy-to-read copies of such items.
- Lend extra credibility to your authorship of the article. Include information about yourself--and your co-authors--such as full name, professional designations, occupational title, place of employment, contributions to other publications and special assignments.

- Do not punctuate acronyms. For example, TSCPA, AICPA, MBA, GAAP or IRS do not have periods. Exceptions to the rule are acronyms with lowercase letters, such as Ph.D. and Ch.FC. In addition, do not put an apostrophe in an acronym's plural form unless it is possessive. For example: Two CPAs are going to the seminar. The CPA's license is important. Also, articles (e.g., an, a, the) typically are not used before acronyms. However, "the IRS" is one exception.

- When using the names of elected governmental officials, be sure to include their party affiliation as well as city and/or state. Examples of preferred style are Texas Gov. Ann Richards (D-Austin), United States President George Bush (R-TX).

- Rule of thumb regarding the use of commas and semi-colons--when in doubt, leave it out. In addition, preferred style is not to include a final series comma unless the sentence structure is complex.

- When using bullets for emphasis, sentence fragments and those following colons should begin with a lowercase letter and be punctuated as part of a sentence. Complete sentences should begin with a capital letter and be punctuated as complete sentences.

- "More than" is preferred to "over."

- All references to the Uniform CPA Examination should be capitalized.

- Use "who," not "which" or "that," to refer to people. Use "which" to set off a parenthetical clause, setting the clause off with commas. Use "that" to introduce a clause essential to a sentence.

- Never use a hyphen when the compound includes the word "very" or an adverb ending in -ly, such as a "very good time" or "an easily remembered rule."

- Write numbers under 10 in word form; for 10 or more, use arabic numerals. The exceptions to the rule are percentages, which are always arabic numerals, and street addresses.

- When working with manuscripts, the editorial staff of *Today's CPA* uses WordPerfect 5.0 software for word processing. Copy is then down-loaded onto Ventura Desktop Publishing for Layout. Although it is not required, providing your manuscript on either a WordPerfect or ASCII diskette—in addition to the five high-quality copies—will save valuable production time.

Troy State University Business and Economic Review

ADDRESS FOR SUBMISSION:

Janet Kervin, Editor
Troy State University Business and
   Economic Review
Troy State University
102 Bibb Graves Hall
Troy, AL 36082
USA
Phone: 334-670-3524
Fax: 334-670-3636
E-Mail:
Web:
Address May Change:

PUBLICATION GUIDELINES:

Manuscript Length: 21-25
Copies Required: Three
Computer Submission: Yes
Format: MS Word
Fees to Review: 0.00 US$

Manuscript Style:
   American Psychological Association

CIRCULATION DATA:

Reader: Academics, Business Persons,
   Public Policy Influencers
Frequency of Issue: 2 Times/Year
Copies per Issue: 5,001 - 10,000
Sponsor/Publisher: University
Subscribe Price: 0.00 US$

REVIEW INFORMATION:

Type of Review: Blind Review
No. of External Reviewers: 2
No. of In House Reviewers: 1
Acceptance Rate: No Reply
Time to Review: 2-6 months
Reviewers Comments: Yes
Invited Articles: 6-10%
Fees to Publish: 0.00 US$

MANUSCRIPT TOPICS:
Accounting Information Systems; Accounting Research; Accounting Theory & Practice;
Auditing; Cost Accounting; Tax Accounting

MANUSCRIPT GUIDELINES/COMMENTS:

The *TSU Business and Economic Review* is a practically oriented journal which publishes high quality, applied research topics related to all business disciplines.

Manuscripts with highly statistical analyses and/or strong theoretical orientations are discouraged. Manuscripts should be written to appeal to individuals in business and professional positions, public administrators, business consultants and business educators. Simple statistical analyses, tables, graphs, and illustrations are encouraged. Manuscripts should not be an endorsement of a particular product or service.

Submissions should not exceed 25 typed, double-spaced pages (one-inch margins). A brief biographical sketch of each author and a black-and-white glossy photograph of each author are requested. (Photographs should be of head and shoulders only—males in coat and tie, please.)

The title page should include the title, the name(s) of the author(s) and address, phone number and e-mail address of each author. The first page of the manuscript should include the title but no author name(s). Submit three copies to the editor and include the manuscript on diskette in MS Word or WordPerfect. Only one copy should include the title page described above.

The manuscript should not be submitted to (or published in) other publications while being considered by the *TSU Business and Economic Review*.

White Paper (The)

ADDRESS FOR SUBMISSION:

Dick Carozza, Editor
White Paper (The)
Assn. of Certified Fraud Examiners
The Gregor Building
716 West Avenue
Austin, TX 78701
USA
Phone: 800-245-3321
Fax: 512-478-9297
E-Mail: dick@cfenet.com or katie@cfenet.
Web: www.cfenet.com
Address May Change:

PUBLICATION GUIDELINES:

Manuscript Length: 11-15
Copies Required: Three
Computer Submission: Yes
Format: Ms Wd, WdPerfect, Mac
Fees to Review: 0.00 US$

Manuscript Style:
   Associated Press Stylebook

CIRCULATION DATA:

Reader: Business Persons
Frequency of Issue: Bi-Monthly
Copies per Issue: 10,001 - 25,000
Sponsor/Publisher: Assn. of Certified Fraud
   Examiners
Subscribe Price: 36.00 US$ USA
   56.00 US$ All other countries

REVIEW INFORMATION:

Type of Review: Blind Review
No. of External Reviewers: 2
No. of In House Reviewers: 3+
Acceptance Rate: 11-20%
Time to Review: 2 - 3 Months
Reviewers Comments: No
Invited Articles: 0-5%
Fees to Publish: 0.00 US$

MANUSCRIPT TOPICS:
Auditing; Fraud & White-collar Crime

MANUSCRIPT GUIDELINES/COMMENTS:

Purpose
The White Paper is a 60-page, four-color magazine published bi-monthly by the Association of Certified Fraud Examiners as a service to its Members and others interested in the deterrence and detection of fraud and white-collar crime. Articles published in *The White Paper* cover a variety of topics related to white-collar crime, including forensic accounting; fraud investigation techniques; white-collar crime statutes, legislation and regulatory issues; computer and management information systems abuse; industry-specific concerns such as insurance, health care, and financial institution fraud; and case studies of actual incidents of fraud and embezzlement accompanied by the practical fraud examination methods used in the resolution of the cases.

Audience
Articles published in *The White Paper* are directed at a wide range of professionals with an interest in white-collar crime, including internal auditors, forensic accountants, loss prevention

professionals, investigators, law enforcement officials, financial officers, and academicians. The primary audience is Certified Fraud Examiners (CFE) who has been granted the professional designation by the Association of Certified Fraud Examiners.

Queries
The editors encourage potential authors to submit completed manuscripts; however, query letters, outlines, or summaries will be accepted for consideration.

Style
Articles for *The White Paper* should be written in a clear, straightforward style. Though some academic papers are accepted, *The White Paper* is not an academic journal; scholarly formats and styles should be avoided. **Readers want articles and columns containing practical principles they can apply immediately in their positions and careers**.

Authors should use short sentences and paragraphs, similar to the style of most magazines and newspapers. It is strongly suggested that articles lead off with interesting case examples of the frauds discussed. The remainder of the article then can be devoted to how that type of fraud is investigated and resolved.

Successful articles contain strong examples, anecdotes, current facts and figures, and sound approaches to solving problems in the detection and deterrence of white-collar crime. Major points should be supported and adequately analyzed. Articles rejected by *The White Paper* reviewers are often overly broad; inappropriate in tone; written for the wrong audience; too short; inadequately supported or researched; or deal with topics, approaches, or techniques that are elementary to experienced fraud examiners.

Commercialism
Submitted manuscripts should not be linked to proprietary products or procedures unless the article is an excerpt from a book. Specific commercial services, products, or organizations should not be written about unless they are necessary to the article, such as a review of fraud examination software or a publication.

Manuscript Preparation
When submitting a manuscript that has been approved for publication, the author(s) should provide a full name, academic or professional title, academic degrees, professional credentials, complete address (including e-mail), and telephone and fax numbers.

Manuscripts should be submitted on plain white paper (8-1/2 inches x 11 inches), double-spaced with one-inch margins. Space only once between sentences. Manuscripts should range from five to 12 pages in length, or from 1,500 to 4,000 words. Graphs, charts, and tables should be provided when appropriate, and may constitute additional pages.

Footnotes should be designated numerically in the text, and should be placed on a separate page at the end of the manuscript. Footnotes should follow this format:

Books
Full name(s) of author(s), title of book, publisher, city of publisher, year published, page(s) of reference.

Articles
Full name(s) of author(s), title of article, title of periodical, issue date, volume and number, page(s) of article.

Authors should suggest titles for their manuscripts and provide a brief abstract. In most cases, titles will be reworded by the editors to fit style and space constraints.

Graphics
Computer-generated tables, charts, and graphs should be used where possible to help emphasize and clarify points in the article, and to provide graphic interest. Reproduced or hand-drawn exhibits may be acceptable. Artwork need not be camera-ready. The information in exhibits should be kept as simple and readable as possible.

Tables, charts, and graphs should be cited in the text. Authors should refer to them as exhibits, and number them consecutively. The exhibit should include a brief title as well. For example, "Exhibit 1: ABC Co. Statement of Income."

Submission Format
Manuscripts can be submitted on a double-sided, double-density PC disk or e-mailed to dick@cfenet.com or katie@cfenet.com. The text must be saved in Microsoft Word 5.0 or higher or in a text format. Two copies (double-spaced) of a manuscript should be submitted. To ensure an anonymous and impartial review, author(s) name(s), affiliations, biographies, and other identifying information should be deleted from one of the copies, to the extent possible.

Review Process
Manuscripts submitted to *The White Paper* are reviewed by the editors and members of a peer board. Reviewers consider each manuscript on the basis of technical accuracy, usefulness to readers, and timeliness. Authors should allow approximately four to eight weeks for the review process.

If reviewers believe a manuscript is not appropriate for *The White Paper*, the author(s) will be notified by letter, telephone, or e-mail. If reviewers believe additional clarification or information is needed before a manuscript can be evaluated, the author(s) will be asked to make changes before a final decision is made.

If a manuscript is accepted, the author(s) will be notified by letter, telephone, or e-mail. The editors and author(s) then will work closely on preparing the manuscript for publication. A final version of the article will be sent to the author(s) before it is sent to press.

Author Compensation

The White Paper does not pay authors for providing manuscripts. Authors receive five complimentary copies of the issue in which their articles appear. Reprints are available on a custom basis only.

Publication Scheduling

The White Paper operates on a two- to four-month lead schedule. That is, the staff begins planning an issue approximately four months before the publication date. When combined with the time needed for editing and review, six or more months may elapse from the time a manuscript is received until it is published.

Other factors affecting the publication date are the existing backlog of manuscripts already accepted, the subject matter of the manuscript (an article on a similar topic may have appeared recently), or an issue's theme.

Copyright

The Association of Certified Fraud Examiners assumes sole copyright of any article published in *The White Paper*. *The White Paper* follows a policy of exclusive publication. Articles published elsewhere generally are not accepted. Permission of the publisher is required before an article can be copied or reproduced. Requests for reprinting an article must be directed in writing to the publisher or editor. (See attached Author's Agreement.)

AUTHOR'S AGREEMENT

Title of Article:

Author (s):

Publication: *The White Paper*

The Association of Certified Fraud Examiners (hereinafter "ACFE"), 716 West Avenue, Austin, TX 78701, and the undersigned_____
(hereinafter "author(s)"), of_____
in *The White Paper*, a publication of ACFE, hereby agree as follows:

(a) The author(s) specifically warrants to ACFE that the above-named article is an original work created by the author(s) and that it does not infringe on the rights of others, including copyrights, and that all source material has been attributed.

(b) The author(s) specifically warrants that they have obtained permission and copyright releases for materials quoted, adapted, or otherwise included in the article.

(c) The author(s) specifically grants ACFE the right to print the article in any edition of *The White Paper* magazine selected by ACFE. The author(s) warrants that the article has not been and will not be printed in any other publications prior to its publication in The White Paper. The author(s) reserve the right to withdraw the article if it becomes outdated before publication.

(d) The author(s) specifically grants to ACFE the right to publish the article in *The White Paper* and the non-exclusive right to reprint the article in any other ACFE publication, including promotional pieces.

(e) ACFE recognizes that the author may grant reprint permission to other publications. The author(s) specifically agrees that if the article is reprinted either individually or as part of any

408

other publication, credit will be given to "*The White Paper* (month/year), a publication of the Association of Certified Fraud Examiners, Austin, TX, © 19XX as the source of first publication. The author(s) agree to notify ACFE of all reprints.

(f) The author(s) and ACFE agree that the only consideration for the rights granted to ACFE is the publication of the article by ACFE in *The White Paper*. The author(s) and ACFE agree that all expenses involved in production, publication, and promotion of the article (i.e. fax, express delivery, phone, research, etc.) will be borne by the party incurring the expense.

(g) In the event the above article is not published by ACFE or is withdrawn by the author(s) before publication, this agreement becomes null and void.

_____

_____

_____   _____
Author(s)   Date

_____   _____
ACFE   Date

Econometrics

Journal Name	Type Review	No. Ext. Rev.	Accept. Rate	Page
Corporate Finance Review	Editorial	2	21-30%	137
CPA Journal	Blind	3+	21-30%	141
Critical Perspectives on Accounting	Blind	3	6-10%	143
International Journal of Accounting	Blind	2	30%	172
International Tax and Public Finance	Blind	3	11-20%	191
Journal of Accountancy	Blind	3+	11-20%	206
Journal of Accounting and Finance Research	Blind	2	21-30%	217
Journal of Business	Blind	1-2	11-20%	241
Journal of International Taxation	Editorial	0	50% +	267
Journal of Libertarian Studies	Blind	2	6-10%	269
Leader's Edge (Michigan CPA)	Editorial	1	0-5%	289
Management Accounting Quarterly	Blind	3+	11-20%	292
Multinational Business Review	Blind	1	35%	327
Ohio CPA Journal (The)	Blind	2	11-20%	336
Personal Financial Planning	Editorial	2	21-30%	353
Review of Derivatives Research	Blind		21-30%	368
Strategic Finance Magazine	Blind	3	11-20%	377
Tennessee CPA Journal	Blind	3	50%	395
Today's CPA	Blind	2		399

International Finance

Journal Name	Type Review	No. Ext. Rev.	Accept. Rate	Page
Academy of Accounting and Financial Studies Journal	Blind	2	11-20%	3
Accounting and Business (Certified Accountant)	Blind		21-30%	7
Accounting Research Journal	N/A	2	21-30%	47
Advances in International Accounting	Blind	2	50%	73
Asia-Pacific Financial Markets	Editorial	1-2	40%	95
British Accounting Review (The)	Blind	2	21-30%	114
CA Magazine	Editorial	1	6-10%	117
CMA Management Magazine	Blind	1	21-30%	127
Commentaries on the Law of Accounting & Finance	Blind	2	50%	129
Corporate Finance Review	Editorial	2	21-30%	137
Critical Perspectives on Accounting	Blind	3	6-10%	143
International Journal of Accounting	Blind	2	30%	172
International Tax Journal	Blind	2	50%	195
Journal of Accountancy	Blind	3+	11-20%	206
Journal of Accounting and Finance Research	Blind	2	21-30%	217
Journal of Accounting, Auditing & Finance	Blind	1	10%	234
Journal of Business	Blind	1-2	11-20%	241
Journal of Business Finance & Accounting (JFBA)	Blind	2	11-20%	244
Journal of Construction Accounting & Taxation	Editorial	2	50%	248
Journal of International Taxation	Editorial	0	50% +	267
Journal of Libertarian Studies	Blind	2	6-10%	269
Journal of Public Budgeting, Accounting & Financial Management	Blind	3	6-10%	277

Journal Name	Type Review	No. Ext. Rev.	Accept. Rate	Page
Leader's Edge (Michigan CPA)	Editorial	1	0-5%	289
Massachusetts CPA Review Online	Blind	0		324
Multinational Business Review	Blind	1	35%	327
New Accountant	Blind	0	21-30%	335
Ohio CPA Journal (The)	Blind	2	11-20%	336
Personal Financial Planning	Editorial	2	21-30%	353
Strategic Finance Magazine	Blind	3	11-20%	377
Tennessee CPA Journal	Blind	3	50%	395
Today's CPA	Blind	2		399
Macro Economics				
Construction Management and Economics	Blind	4	50%	130
Corporate Finance Review	Editorial	2	21-30%	137
Critical Perspectives on Accounting	Blind	3	6-10%	143
International Journal of Accounting	Blind	2	30%	172
Journal of Business	Blind	1-2	11-20%	241
Journal of Libertarian Studies	Blind	2	6-10%	269
Today's CPA	Blind	2		399
Micro Economics				
Behavioral Research in Accounting	Blind	2	11-20%	107
Chartered Accountants' Journal of New Zealand	Editorial	2	50%	124
Construction Management and Economics	Blind	4	50%	130
Corporate Finance Review	Editorial	2	21-30%	137
Critical Perspectives on Accounting	Blind	3	6-10%	143
European Accounting Review	Blind	2	11-20%	147
International Journal of Accounting	Blind	2	30%	172
Journal of Accountancy	Blind	3+	11-20%	206
Journal of Accounting and Computers	Blind	2	33-40%	210
Journal of Accounting and Public Policy	Blind	2	11-20%	221
Journal of Accounting, Auditing & Finance	Blind	1	10%	234
Journal of Business	Blind	1-2	11-20%	241
Journal of Libertarian Studies	Blind	2	6-10%	269
Spectrum	Blind	2	21-30%	374
Today's CPA	Blind	2		399
Monetary Policy				
CMA Management Magazine	Blind	1	21-30%	127
Corporate Finance Review	Editorial	2	21-30%	137
Journal of Accounting Research	Editorial	Varies	Varies	231
Journal of Business	Blind	1-2	11-20%	241
Journal of Libertarian Studies	Blind	2	6-10%	269
Journal of Public Budgeting, Accounting & Financial Management	Blind	3	6-10%	277
Strategic Finance Magazine	Blind	3	11-20%	377